D1187993

THE PEOPLING OF BRITAIN

The Peopling of Britain

The Shaping of a Human Landscape

The Linacre Lectures 1999

Edited by
PAUL SLACK
and
RYK WARD

OXFORD
UNIVERSITY PRESS

Great Clarendon Street, Oxford OX2 6DP

Oxford University Press is a department of the University of Oxford.
It furthers the University's objective of excellence in research, scholarship,
and education by publishing worldwide in

Oxford New York

Auckland Bangkok Buenos Aires Cape Town Chennai
Dar es Salaam Delhi Hong Kong Istanbul Karachi Kolkata
Kuala Lumpur Madrid Melbourne Mexico City Mumbai Nairobi
São Paulo Shanghai Singapore Taipei Tokyo Toronto

with associated companies in Berlin

Oxford is a registered trade mark of Oxford University Press
in the UK and in certain other countries

Published in the United States
By Oxford University Press Inc., New York

First published 2002

British Library Cataloguing in Publication Data
Data available

Library of Congress Cataloging in Publication Data
The poepling of Britain : the shaping of a human landscape / edited by Paul Slack
and Ryk Ward.
p. cm. — (The Linacre lectures ; 1999)
Includes bibliographical references and index.
1. Human geography—Great Britain. 2. Land settlement patterns—Great Britain.
3. Great Britain—History. I. Slack, Paul. II. Ward, Ryk. III. Linacre lecture ; 1999.
GF551 .P46 2002 304.2'0941—dc21 2001046487

ISBN 0-19-829759-9

1 3 5 7 9 10 8 6 4 2

Typeset by Best-set Typesetter Ltd., Hong Kong
Biddles Ltd., Guildford & Kings Lynn

ACKNOWLEDGEMENTS

The theme of this ninth series of Linacre Lectures was suggested by my co-editor, Professor Ryk Ward, Fellow of Linacre, to whom I am grateful for stimulus and help in the midst of many other calls upon his time. The College owes thanks also to the Marc Fitch Fund for a grant towards some of the costs of preparing the lectures for publication. Jane Edwards, the College Secretary, once again undertook all the practical arrangements with her customary cheerful efficiency.

P.A.S.
Oxford

CONTENTS

CONTRIBUTORS

Barry Cunliffe, Professor of European Archaeology, University of Oxford.

Clive Gamble, Professor of Archaeology, University of Southampton.

Heinrich Härke, Reader in Archaeology, University of Reading.

John Langton, Lecturer in Human Geography, University of Oxford.

Paul Mellars, Professor of Prehistory and Human Evolution, University of Cambridge.

Martin Millett, Laurence Professor of Classical Archaeology, University of Cambridge.

Ceri Peach, Professor of Social Geography, University of Oxford.

Lord Renfrew of Kaimsthorn, Disney Professor of Archaeology, University of Cambridge.

Andrew Sherratt, Reader in European Archaeology, University of Oxford.

Paul Slack, Principal, Linacre College, and Professor of Early Modern Social History, University of Oxford.

Richard Smith, Reader in Historical Demography, University of Cambridge, and Director, Cambridge Group for the History of Population and Social Structure.

Ryk Ward, Professor of Biological Anthropology, University of Oxford.

Alasdair Whittle, Professor of Archaeology, University of Wales, Cardiff.

Sir Tony Wrigley, past President of the British Academy, and formerly Master of Corpus Christi College and Professor of Economic History, University of Cambridge.

LIST OF FIGURES

LIST OF TABLES

Introduction

Paul Slack and Ryk Ward

FROM the beginnings of human settlement the small marginal fringe of western Europe that eventually became the British Isles has represented a final frontier for successive waves of colonists—each bringing its own set of cultural adaptations and its own ethos into the landscape. Over time both landscape and culture have matured from raw frontier to settled centre, moulded by the advent of agriculture, towns, and industry, and by streams of migration both within Britain and from outside. The chapters in this book, together with some of the comments which followed their original delivery as lectures, trace the various phases of that process, showing how much of the story has only recently been unearthed, and how much remains to be discovered.

The period surveyed is necessarily a very long one, and it is significant that successive chapters cover an increasingly narrow span of time, from the half a million years of the first chapter to the 150 of the last. That is partly a function of the historical record, which shifts from the scattered evidence of archaeology to the plentiful records of modern social surveys. But it is also a reflection of the accelerating pace of change, particularly in the past millennium, as increasing density of population, urbanization, and the manipulation of new sources of energy and wealth reshaped both culture and environment. In the process Britain shifted from being marginal, on the outer edge of human developments whose focus lay elsewhere, to being central: in the eighteenth and nineteenth centuries Britain was the originator of changes which have transformed the globe since then.

That is one story, familiar enough in outline, but examined from new perspectives in the later chapters of this book. But there is also a second story, completed very much earlier, and forming the theme of the early chapters of this collection. It lies in the initial peopling of Britain by humans, and the stages by which biological evolution was replaced by cultural evolution as the main motor of change.

Together, the first two chapters cover a daunting expanse of time—from more than half a million years ago to a mere twenty thousand years in the past. During this long period, virtually all the major events that marked the biological formation of our species occurred. In the main, they took place far from Britain. For most of the period Africa and Asia were the theatres in which the unfolding drama was played out. In the first act, which saw the entrance of the first members of the genus *Homo*, Europe was essentially peripheral to the action. Nevertheless, important insights about these early evolutionary phases can be gleaned from a small number of critical sites in Europe. Moreover, while the most exciting biological evidence comes from sites on the fringes of Europe—in Spain, at the site of Atapuerca, and in the Caucasus, at Dmanisi—one of the most revealing perspectives on landscape use comes from the British site of Boxgrove. As Gamble points out in the first chapter, Boxgrove provides a snapshot of human activities that indicate how these humans interacted with each other and the landscape nearly half a million years ago. Boxgrove is by no means unique. By a happy combination of quirks of geological deposition and the intense activity of local archaeologists, Britain provides a remarkably detailed and comprehensive picture of landscape use by different groups of archaic humans.

While Britain remains somewhat peripheral to the events described in the second chapter, Europe now occupies centre stage for one of the more dramatic aspects of our evolutionary past: the replacement of archaic humans by the anatomically modern humans who were our immediate ancestors. While the evolutionary transition from archaic to modern forms most likely took place long ago and far away (in Africa, perhaps some 120,000 years ago), in Europe the key phenomenon was replacement. Replacement of Neanderthals was relatively sudden and dramatic, and occurred some 80,000 years after modern humans had evolved in Africa. It also occurred a considerable time after modern humans had expanded out of Africa to reach Australia, suggesting that despite its closer proximity to Africa, the colonization of Europe was impeded.

It is tempting to speculate that the successful exploitation of the European landscape by Neanderthal communities meant that it was difficult for early modern humans to find a sustainable niche within the ecosystem. Whether it was the presence of other competing human groups, or simply the difficulty of making a living in the extremes of Late Pleistocene Europe, it is clear that successful colonization of Europe was dependent on the development of a tool kit embodying a considerable degree of technological sophistication. As Mellars emphasizes, the westward spread of the Aurignacian tool kit from the Near East to the Atlantic margins represents the indelible trace of the movement of modern humans across the landscape. Sherratt notes the significance of the fact that the initial spread of Aurignacian culture across Europe seems to have avoided the areas in which the heaviest concentrations of Mousterian industries are found.

Thus it seems likely that during the 10,000 years 'replacement' period, Europe would have presented a variegated pattern, a mosaic of landscape use. The initial populations of modern humans appear to have filled the interstitial spaces between the landscape of habit occupied by Neanderthals. As time went on, the mosaic changed, with the increasing sophistication of modern humans leading to ever higher population densities and expansion of ecological range; and the Neanderthal niches shrank into small isolated pockets, until they finally disappeared. While the replacement itself is often characterized as the replacement of one morphological set of characters by another, or as the invasion of a different kind of technological industry, the underlying reality behind the process must have been ecological. Hence, understanding the differences in landscape use is the key to understanding the biological and cultural imperatives that dictated the outcome of competition between two highly advanced and successful groups of humans.

Archaic humans such as the Neanderthals had held sway in Europe for at least 300,000 years, and modern humans, while somewhat more recent, had also been successful for nearly 100,000 years. Both groups were therefore highly evolved. With both groups using essentially the same features of the landscape, only one could survive, and it is tantalizing to speculate on what gave modern humans the competitive edge. Probably not raw intelligence, but rather subtle differences in symbolic representation. Thus, of the twelve characteristics cited by Mellars, five involve the development of symbolic representations (art, jewellery, music, etc.). But even more important was the likely translation of symbolic representation into aspects of landscape use. As Gamble points out, increasing ability to symbolize not only leads to a more definitive focus on defining the landscape of habit. It also leads to wider and more effective trading networks and more focused use of specific environmental resources, such as specialized hunting techniques. The overall result is an increase in population density. The increasingly sophisticated cognition of landscape led inexorably to an increase in the success of modern humans at the expense of the last surviving Neanderthals.

Once that process was completed, 30,000 years ago, the main story—as Sherratt suggests—was in one sense over. After that date, there was no longer the ebb and flow of different human varieties (or species) across the global landscape. Indeed, as Mellars makes clear, shortly after that date the diversity of humankind, which had been a feature of the previous 2 million years, was suddenly reduced to a single variety—ourselves. All other forms of humans became extinct, driven by events that are largely unknown and certainly controversial. In the larger sense, however, the story of transformation of the landscape continued unabated, and with even greater vigour than in those very early days. Human populations continued to flow back and forth across the landscape, now distinguished by cultural attributes rather than biology. Cultural changes proceeded at an accelerated pace, leading to an increasingly dramatic interaction between human groups and with an increasing impact on landscape.

By far the most important of these was the advent of agriculture, which had a profound effect on society and, by virtue of changing patterns of subsistence, on local ecology. Once again this was a change that did not arise *de novo* in Britain, but rather spread from the outside. Roughly 7,000 years ago, when Britain was still a hunting foraging society, agriculture had become firmly established within the cold temperate regions of continental Europe, perhaps via a transitional zone in the Carpathian basin. As Whittle explains, the chronology and means of its transmission across the continent are still uncertain. Much depends on interpretation of the evidence for the spread of the LBK (Linear Pottery) culture, and overall the change was slow, though punctuated by accelerations, and accompanied by considerable continuity of population. There is therefore room for disagreement about whether population movement and colonization or the local acculturation of indigenous populations played a greater part in the process. Whittle and Renfrew strike different balances between the two below.

There is no disagreement, however, about the radical implications of the change. Renfrew stresses its demographic consequences, permitting population to rise by a factor of as much as 20 or 30 in inland areas. For Whittle the shift to cereals also brought with it the introduction of sheep, goats, and perhaps cattle to Britain, and—associated with the domestication of animals—a wholesale shift in attitudes towards the landscape and men's place in it. In the monuments which arose from about 4000 BC onwards Whittle finds reflections of self-representations and views of ancestors and the dead, and hence evidence of the importance of 'the realm of ideas' in the origins of the Neolithic.

The end of the 'monumentalizing' of the British landscape between 1500 and 1400 BC was therefore, as Cunliffe says, a dramatic turning-point. In place of henges, stone circles, and barrows there were now new forms of landscape manipulation which persisted for another thousand years and more. Prompted in part no doubt by population growth, boundaries of banks and ditches, and the laying out of large areas in patterns of rectangular fields, as in Wessex, brought fresh meanings and a new continuity to the countryside. There was no break in cultural and technological imports from outside. They came first through the Atlantic and continental exchange networks which Cunliffe reconstructs, and then through interactions with Rome, as the flag and the legions followed trade to Gaul and, in AD 43, to Britain. The Romans brought towns and roads, the sinews of trade and empire, and also new identities, as Millett argues, since Britain and its peoples were defined by outsiders and a new élite. Despite a probable doubling of the population, however, the countryside itself changed remarkably little.

Cunliffe's discussion of the 'Celtic' issue returns us again to the broad question which was raised with respect to the advent of agriculture: whether change was triggered essentially by a migration of peoples or by acculturation, perhaps helped by the movement of small groups, whether traders or rulers. It is now generally accepted that there were no major incursions of invading Celts, 'Celtic' being rather the *lingua franca* of trading communities along the Atlantic seaboard who carried distinctive artefacts with them. In the case of the Romans, military garrisons clearly augmented the gene pool, but *in toto* 'foreigners' probably numbered no more than 120,000 out of a population of around 4 million in Roman Britain. Precisely the same issues necessarily arise in the case of the Anglo-Saxon, Viking, and Norman invasions described by Härke's chapter. Here too, current wisdom tends to visualize static populations with only artefacts or small élite groups moving, but Härke rightly warns us that the pendulum of expert opinion may well have moved too far away from earlier hypotheses of massive population mobility.

The various groups collectively known as Anglo-Saxons must certainly have been large enough to have changed for good not only the place-names but also the language of southern and eastern England. Härke estimates their numbers at between 100,000 and 200,000, perhaps between 10 and 20 per cent of a now much reduced population, although all his population estimates (as he makes clear) are subject to large margins of error. The Vikings were probably fewer in number, since there is no evidence of massive language change, although Scandinavian place-names are common in areas where they settled in the north and the east. There they may have numbered 4 to 8 per cent of the population. The Normans, 1–2 per cent of the population, were the smallest group, but a ruling élite which replaced the Anglo-Saxon aristocracy in only twenty years, and—much like the Romans—marked the landscape with the symbols of a new regime: in this case castles, parks, and royal forests.

What is striking in Härke's discussion of the long period from the sixth to the eleventh centuries, however, is the evidence for continuity in the landscape, despite successive episodes of invasion and cultural adaptation.

The Anglo-Saxons introduced new technology and new means of exploiting the land: mouldboard ploughs, which allowed the cultivation of heavy soils, watermills, new crop rotations, and, from the tenth century, the open-field system, which encouraged nucleation of population in villages. There were new towns, from the seventh-century *wiks* or *emporia* like Ipswich, to the ninth-century Anglo-Saxon *burhs*. There was more horse traction and use of fibre crops and hence textile manufacture. The Scandinavians altered none of this, but rather contributed further to urbanization and the nucleation of rural settlement in eastern and central England, and these processes continued after the Norman Conquest of 1066. Demographic growth, colonization, and the reclamation of land were probably not continuous after the decline in population and economic activity which followed the withdrawal of the legions, and Härke rightly draws attention to the uncertainty which still surrounds the Anglo-Saxon economy, particularly in the seventh and eighth centuries. From the tenth century onwards, however, the tools and tactics which determined patterns of settlement and growth in Britain seem to have been set.

In his chapter on demographic change and its effects between the thirteenth and seventeenth centuries, therefore, Smith can analyse what was in essentials a relatively 'closed' set of relationships, certainly by comparison with what had gone before. Until the emigrations from Britain to Ireland and the New World in the seventeenth century, there were no great streams of migration, whether in or out. Even the Black Death of 1348–50—an extraneous import if ever there was one—needs to be set in context. It helped massively to cut a population which had risen to around 6 million in 1300 back to no more than 3 million by 1377. But population had been falling in the fifty years before 1348, and it remained low for nearly two centuries afterwards; and in explaining those phenomena Smith shows the importance of population pressing against resources, and so raising mortality, as in the Great Famine of 1315–17, and of economic and other factors determining fertility as much as mortality. The plagues of 1348 and afterwards were not the sole determinants of demographic change nor even its prime movers, any more than earlier epidemics in the Anglo-Saxon period had probably been.

This is not to say, however, that models of long-run economic change which stress cycles and successive 'equilibria' necessarily imply a return to some stationary state of balance between population and food supplies of a crudely Malthusian kind. As Smith shows, the equilibrium point reached in England in the later seventeenth century, after another period of population growth, was significantly different from that of 1300: the total population was lower (5 million as against 6 million) and, partly in consequence, it enjoyed substantially higher per capita standards of living. The same conditions did not apply in Scotland, where there was still famine in the later seventeenth century, nor, of course, in Ireland, where there was much worse famine in the 1840s. But in southern Britain it was a significant breakthrough. Urbanization, the expansion of foreign trade, and the growth of rural industry could all continue, fuelled by rising demand after the mid-seventeenth century, without the checks to economic growth which had occurred around 1300.

Wrigley's chapter shows some of the lasting consequences of this emancipation from past constraints by means of an analysis of the ways in which English people earned their living. The occupational structure, which can first be examined in detail for the early nineteenth century, reveals the importance of secondary and tertiary employments, in handicrafts and services, even before industrialization, and in areas little affected by it. In England in 1811 only 39 per cent of adult males were working in agriculture, compared with perhaps 60 per cent in the 1680s; and even 60 per cent was a low figure by comparison with most other European countries at the same time, given that England was then exporting corn as well as feeding a population of 5 million. Moreover, the country was able to tolerate the return of population growth from the 1760s without any shocks of a Malthusian or any other kind. Exceptional growth in per capita agricultural productivity was one essential precondition for that, and it dated back well into the seventeenth century and arguably owed much to the restructuring of the economy and its agrarian base which Smith shows occurred in the fourteenth and fifteenth centuries. The importance of rising agricultural productivity is vividly illustrated by the fact that more people were working in agriculture in England in 1300 than at any time since—or indeed before—that date.

A more recent and no less vital determinant of growth and change from the late eighteenth century was the shift from an organic to an energy-rich economy, which Wrigley has stressed elsewhere and which Langton emphasizes in this volume. It came, in the first place, from the exploitation of Britain's abundant resources of coal. Langton underlines the importance of the coalfields in shaping patterns of economic and industrial growth and creating 'enormous regional disparities' in per capita incomes, population densities, and hence landscape. By the middle of the nineteenth century Britain had been transformed. In agriculture the peasantry had disappeared, replaced by farmers and wage-labourers. There were new industries and wholly new kinds of town. The service sector, already large in 1700, had become more varied, with new functions. In 1851, as Peach shows, more than half the population was living in towns, and a third of adult males were employed in services and less than a third in agriculture.

Most of these trends continued for the next hundred years, though the dominant industrial and energy sectors shifted and so did the locations of particular growth. The chief focus of Peach's chapter, however, is the contrasting and rapid trajectory of change in the short period since 1950. In 1911 80 per cent of the population lived in towns, but the growth of megacities had peaked by the 1950s. Counter-urbanization has succeeded urbanization and suburbanization. With the demographic transition to low fertility as well as low mortality, population has stabilized and emigration to the Empire and North America been replaced by immigration, largely from the Commonwealth, to fill vacant niches in the economy and the urban landscape. The ethnic minority population has grown from 80,000 to 3 million, 5.5 per cent of the British population. The decline of staple industries and the international division of labour have left 80 per cent of the male labour force now in the services sector.

More multicultural than it has been for a millennium, Britain is once again on the periphery, responding to outside developments rather than leading them, as it did in the eighteenth and nineteenth centuries. But the human landscape is vastly different from what it was in the pre-industrial past: ten times more densely populated than in 1300, at least twenty times more than in 1066, its population employed and housed in different settings and concentrations, though still building monuments and leaving artefacts as evidence of its self-perception and its changing cultural mix.

Depending on the period they are discussing, the contributors to this book draw on different techniques and different kinds of expertise, from archaeology and history to demography and other forms of social analysis. One of the lessons learnt in the course of the lectures was the need for a 'creative interaction of disciplines', in Cunliffe's phrase, if we are to understand the processes of long-term change and to illuminate some of the several areas which are still obscure. This applies, for example, to the questions which Härke raises about levels of population and consequently the nature of settlement in the Anglo-Saxon period. That is an area where collaboration between archaeologists and historians promises to yield important new insights. On the vexed question of the size of migrant streams before the tenth century, much may be discovered (as Whittle and Härke point out) from studies of mitochondrial DNA in modern populations. Though still at any early stage, these and related studies of skeletal material and early diet may transform our picture of some of the topics discussed in early chapters. As for later chapters, the vital issue of what made Britain exceptional in the eighteenth and nineteenth centuries requires further comparative work on different societies, before the particular relationships between demography, culture, and environment in the British case can be properly understood.

In all these instances, however, it is essential that experts in different fields communicate and that they should be aware of the latest findings of their different disciplines. That was one of the purposes of bringing these contributions together, and one of the recurring themes of the discussions which followed the lectures on which they are based. There is still exciting work to be done on the interactions between humans and their landscape which are explored in the chapters which follow.

1

Early Beginnings 500,000–35,000 Years Ago

Clive Gamble

OUR understanding of the first peopling of Britain has recently undergone a transformation. On the one hand there have been fundamental advances in the investigation of Pleistocene environments and chronology, while on the other exceptionally well preserved archaeological sites of the period have now been investigated. These data are allowing us to reinterpret the society and palaeo-ecology of the people who inhabited this small corner of north-west Europe between 500,000 and 35,000 years ago.

In order to put these findings into their proper context I will, however, need to roam more widely across the Palaeolithic world and consider the evolutionary changes and geographical processes that were involved over such long time-spans. One aspect I will concentrate upon in this contribution is that, although these earliest inhabitants did not dramatically transform the landscape, in the manner that either prehistoric farmers did with fields and ritual monuments (see Whittle in this volume) or, later, more complex societies achieved through trade, cities and the military machine (see Cunliffe and Härke in this volume), we can, none the less, see the beginnings of such shaping in the way they went about their daily and lifetime routines. My point is that these early hominids (a term which includes ourselves and all our fossil ancestors) were not slaves to nature, ecological creatures determined in everything by the environment, but rather creative builders of social networks that linked their daily landscapes of habit into very different social worlds. Their act of living in the worlds of half a million years ago was every bit as transformative for those environments as our acts of living are today. In other words, the idea that our earliest ancestors lived solely in a natural landscape because they had very simple technologies, smaller brains, and tiny social groupings, while we by contrast create and inhabit a complex cultural world, needs to be revised.

Moreover, the second theme of this volume, population diversity and movement, is also illustrated in these early beginnings. The earliest peopling of Britain was not achieved once but instead was a repeated process. However, in spite of all the ebb and flow of population between 500,000 and 35,000 years ago these earliest inhabitants were not our direct ancestors (see Mellars in this volume).

In this contribution I will concentrate on three topics: human evolution and the earliest colonization of Europe; changing Pleistocene environments in Britain; and hominids in their landscapes.

HUMAN EVOLUTION AND THE EARLIEST COLONIZATION OF EUROPE

There is currently a debate concerning the age of the oldest Europeans. Three chronologies are on offer: the short, some time after 500,000 (Roebroeks and Kolfschoten 1995), the mature, back to about 1 million (Carbonell *et al.* 1996), and the very long of anything between 2 and 2.5 million years ago (Bonifay and Vandermeersch 1991). What is at issue is the timing of hominid dispersal out of Africa and the appearance of people in Asia and Europe. On present evidence it seems that Asia was colonized before Europe. Dates of 1.8 million years ago for hominid material from Java provides the evidence and is associated with the fossil species *Homo erectus*. Not so long ago *Homo erectus* was regarded as an African species which on reaching Asia developed into a distinctive regional population known as Asian *Homo erectus*. However, there is now a growing opinion that *Homo erectus* was never an African species but evolved solely in Asia as a result of an earlier hominid dispersal (Clarke 1990; Groves 1989). According to this model the appearance of *Homo erectus* in Africa, as represented for example by the fossil skull OH9 dated to 1.4 million years at Olduvai Gorge, Tanzania, records a movement into and not out of that continent. The find of *Homo erectus/ergaster* at Dmanisi in Georgia (Gabunia and Vekua 1995; Gabunia *et al.* 1999), now dated to 1.7 million years, appears to support this out of Asia movement by providing a signpost at an important crossroads in the Middle East. This dispersal was then followed by a later expansion into the Mediterranean. Here a skull showing *Homo erectus* features has been found at Ceprano in central Italy and dated to *c.*800,000 years ago (Ascenzi *et al.* 1996). The discovery of stone tools which are much older that this at Fuente Nueva in southern Spain (Gibert *et al.* 1998) and Monte Poggiolo in Italy (Peretto *et al.* 1998) are currently not matched by fossils. However, the finds suggest that southern Europe was possibly colonized by *Homo erectus* at the same time as

Georgia and East Africa, about 1.5 million years ago. The simple stone tools associated with these fossils and archaeological occurrences are invariably pebble tools and flakes. This basic technology has an antiquity of at least 2.6 million years and is first known from Gona in Ethiopia (Semaw *et al.* 1997).

But Africa is not to be outdone by this apparent role-reversal in the export-import trade of early hominid evolution. The period 1.8–1.5 million years ago was a particularly important 300,000 years in this continent for three reasons. Firstly there is the appearance of *Homo ergaster* (work man) best known from the almost complete skeleton of a 12-year-old boy from Nariokotome in Kenya dated to 1.6 million years ago and originally classed as African *Homo erectus* (Johanson and Edgar 1996). This remarkable find has a brain size almost two-thirds of our own (880 cc), a robustly built skeleton, and a precocious height, for one still apparently growing, of 4′ 9″. His estimated adult height would have been 5′ 9″ and a body weight of some 10 stone (68 kg.).

Secondly the oldest occurrence of fire (Brain and Sillen 1988) is known at 1.5 million years from the evidence of burnt bones in the South African cave of Swartkrans. And finally, *Homo ergaster* coincides with the appearance of a new form of stone technology employing bifaces (or handaxes) at 1.6 million years ago. These Acheulean artefacts in most cases replaced the pebble tools/hammerstones and simple cutting/scraping stone flakes of the preceding Oldowan. However, the pebble tools and flakes continued in Asia which may indicate something about the geographical dispersal of *ergaster's* descendants.

Now, while *Homo erectus* may hold the distinction of being the first fossil hominid to colonize southern Europe, it is a descendant of *ergaster* who conclusively cracks the problem of colonizing northern Europe particularly after 500,000 years ago. At this time all of the European fossils are regarded as *Homo heidelbergensis* previously known by the vaguer grouping of 'archaic' *Homo sapiens* (Stringer and Gamble 1993). While the fossil record is not completely clear on this point the likeliest ancestor for *Homo heidelbergensis* is an african *Homo ergaster*.

Half a million years ago also sees a dramatic change in the quality and quantity of the European archaeological record, as first pointed out by Roebroeks and van Kolfschoten (1994) in their short chronology model (Table 1.1).

An important element in this change is the widespread appearance of Acheulean biface industries which add another page to the story of European colonization. Considerable consensus now exists that these bifaces were used in meat butchery and experimental work has indicated their advantages. They appear at a time of increasing encephalization which, as

Table 1.1. *Changes in Palaeolithic archaeology before and after 500,000 years ago*

Europe before 500,000 years ago	Europe after 500,000 years ago
Very small artefact collections selected from a natural pebble background; few or no stone refits, suggesting natural fracture	Large collections of artefacts; excavated knapping floors with refitted stone nodules, indicating human manufacture
'Geofacts' found in coarse matrix, disturbed secondary contexts	Artefacts found in fine grained matrix, primary context locales
Contested 'primitive' looking assemblages of flakes and pebble tools	Uncontested Acheulean (biface) and non-Acheulean stone industries
Very few human remains	Human remains common

Source: After Roebroeks and van Kolfschoten 1994.

Aiello and Wheeler have argued (Aiello and Wheeler 1995; Aiello 1998), could only be achieved metabolically at the expense of another key organ. The shrinking stomachs of these early hominids freed up the metabolic budget to expand an expensive tissue such as the brain which, although only accounting for 2 per cent of our body weight uses up 20 per cent of all the energy we consume. The expensive tissue hypothesis therefore predicts a move to higher quality foods such as animal protein to compensate for the reduced processing capacity of the stomach and the energetic demands of the larger brain. Bifaces therefore arrive when expected, selected for by the changing environment of the hominids. The date for the oldest traces of fire is also pertinent. Such technology would, as Aiello points out, provide hominids with an 'external stomach' since burning and cooking food does some of the hard work of the gut.

These elements—bigger brains, a stone technology for meat butchery, higher protein diets, fire processing, smaller stomachs—must all have been key aspects in the colonization of northern latitudes including the British Isles. We can go further, however, and infer both group size and ranging patterns from these data.

Concerning group size, Dunbar (Dunbar 1993; Aiello and Dunbar 1993) has shown, using a large sample of primates, that a strong relationship exists between the size of the neocortex, the thinking part of the brain, and group size. The means of social interaction are crucial. When bonds depend upon physical grooming then interaction is limited to at most 50–5 individuals, as shown by chimpanzees and baboons. A critical threshold exists when more than 30 per cent of the waking day is spent grooming. Beyond that figure might lie a happy life but a very hungry one.

Humans have much larger neocortex ratios and consequently larger interaction networks. Dunbar argues that we managed this by shifting, gradually, from social interaction based on time-consuming grooming to a more time-effective vocal grooming—in short a form of language to negotiate and confirm ties within a fluid social network centred on the individual (Dunbar 1996). The 30 per cent threshold predicted from brain size was only surpassed after 500,000 years ago when group sizes in Dunbar's model reach 148 (Aiello 1998: figure 5.1). Steele (1996: table 8.8) using a group mass model has shown, however, that these predictions of group size can be highly variable. What is needed is some indication of the geographical area over which such groups roamed. This can be estimated by using the archaeological evidence of the raw materials which were used to make the stone tools. Their geological provenance allows us to estimate the maximum distances over which hominids ranged (Féblot-Augustins 1997). Moreover, when group mass data on modern carnivores and primates are used to establish a comparative framework for establishing hominid ranging patterns we see, as might be expected, that hominids exhibit the much larger carnivore scale ranging pattern. Steele (1996: table 8.8) provides estimates of home ranges between 33 and 98 km. diameter for relevant aged hominids while the average greatest distances which raw materials travelled range in Europe during the period 500,000–35,000 years ago from 28 to 58 km. (Gamble and Steele 1999: table 2). Support for a carnivore size home range also comes from the archaeology for their diet after 500,000 years ago. Not only do we now possess hunting spears, as at Schöningen (Thieme 1997), but also evidence from the age profiles of the prey that they were taking prime age animals. The expensive tissue hypothesis predicts these elements for a northern species. What remains to be seen is to what extent those much earlier incursions into southern Europe were based on similar strategies.

So, to return to Europe and those three chronologies. The very long chronology suggested by some finds in southern Spain, Mediterranean France, and Italy would have this part of the continent peopled well before these changes had come together as a recognizable package suggesting a move into a new niche. The finds are often hotly disputed. The open landscape around the village of Orce near Granada has, however, produced small collections of definite artefacts in deposits dated by geomagnetics to the Olduvai event between 1.76 and 1.98 million years ago (Gibert *et al.* 1998). Much depends on the reliability of the dating and the geology. The sparcity of finds before 500,000 indicates that hominids were not a regular component of the colonizing cycles of mammals that occurred in European latitudes on a regular basis. Extinctions were frequent.

This pattern would also be the case with the mature chronology (Carbonell *et al.* 1996). Here the prime evidence comes from Atapuerca in northern Spain where, since 1994 in the Gran Dolina deposits, a collection of eighty hominid remains representing six individuals and some 200 simple stone artefacts have been excavated. The level TD6 was at the same time redated using geomagnetics which moved the site from *c.*500,000 to 900,000 years old. On the basis of one of the finds from TD6, the fragmentary skull (ATD6-69) of a 10–11-year-old, a new species has been named *Homo antecessor* (Bermúdez de Castro *et al.* 1997). 'Pioneer man' has been put forward as the ancestor for both the much later *Homo neanderthalensis*, Neanderthal people, and *Homo sapiens*, who originated in Africa as shown both genetically and anatomically (see below).

Finally, the short chronology has, as we have seen, the bulk of the evidence and an important change in the quality of the archaeology. After 500,000 fossils become common as at Mauer and Steinheim in Germany, Arago in southern France, and Petralona in Greece. All of them regarded as *Homo heidelbergensis*. The Acheulean is commonly found, particularly in western and Mediterranean Europe. Excavations produce many artefacts together with the flakes and chips that indicate on the spot manufacture. Material is well preserved in fine grained sediments with little post-depositional disturbance (Table 1.1).

All of this forms, as Roebroeks and van Kolfschoten pointed out (1994), a remarkable contrast with the archaeology before 500,000 years ago. Atapuerca aside, the quantitative change in numbers, preservation, and frequency of the archaeology evidence is a powerful argument that we should be cautious about earlier claims. However, since then the weight of evidence from southern Europe, in particular Spain (Fuente Nueva) and Italy (Monte Poggiolo), has led to a rethink (Dennell and Roebroeks 1996) as reported above.

CHANGING PLEISTOCENE ENVIRONMENTS IN BRITAIN

This is where the British data are particularly important. Here a few supporters exist for a mature-age chronology based on artefacts in a gravel terrace at Fordwich in Kent and at Waverley Wood in Warwickshire (Roberts, Gamble, and Bridgland 1995). However, the majority view is that the earliest occupation dates to an interglacial warm phase that lasted from 524,000 to 478,000 years ago. This is Oxygen Isotope Stage (OIS) 13 in the record obtained from cores drilled into the muds on the ocean floor and whose contents chart the fluctuating signal of global climate (see Gamble 1993: ch. 3 for description). This is done by contrasting the changes between small and large oceans—ice ages and interglacial climates—as recorded in the isotopic ratios preserved in the skeletons of tiny foraminifera.

In the last twenty-five years the study of oxygen isotopes has revolutionized our understanding of ice age climates. This began with the landmark paper by Shackleton and Opdyke (1973). They described a continuous record of global climate change from a deep sea core drilled on the Solomon Plateau and dated by palaeomagnetic reversals of known age from terrestrial locations (Figure 1.1). The core covered the entire Middle Pleistocene back to almost 800,000 years ago. The revolution took three forms. Firstly it doubled the number of glacial/interglacial cycles in this

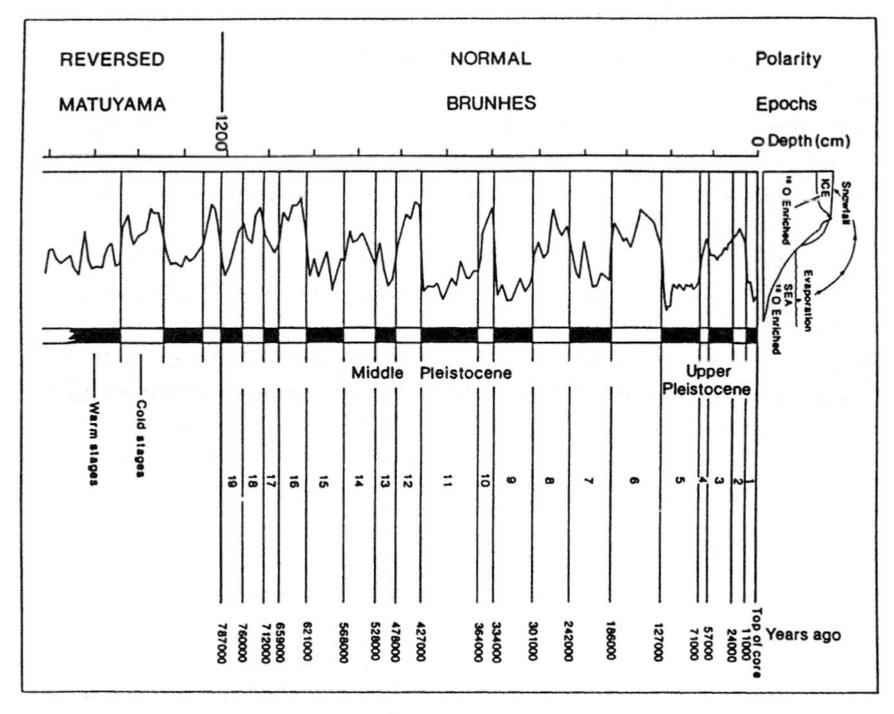

FIG. 1.1 The continuous oxygen isotope record for the Middle and Upper Pleistocene in Core V28-238.

Note: Odd numbers indicate interglacial and even glacial stages. A full cycle includes an odd and even stage and there have been eight since 787,000 years ago.

Source: Gamble 1993: figure 3.2.

period from four to eight. Secondly it showed that the transitions from ice cover to large oceans, such as we see in today's interglacial, were very rapid. Finally, the values of the isotopic curve allowed further comparisons to be made concerning the comparative severity of the various glaciations and the warming of the interglacials (see Lowe and Walker 1997 for review). Many hundreds of cores at varying degrees of resolution have now been analysed. An isotope record has also been obtained from ice cores drilled through the Greenland ice cap. The advantage of this record is that it lacks the mixing which took place among the ocean sediments and therefore provides a very high precision record of changes in ice cap and by inference ocean size.

The challenge for Quaternary scientists and Palaeolithic archaeologists has been to match the often fragmentary sequences they have from the terrestrial evidence to this continuous record. While we now know the shape of the interglacial/glacial curve it is another matter entirely to decide in which OIS an isolated geological section, a faunal assemblage, or a collection of artefacts should be placed. The last twenty-five years has seen much progress towards meeting this challenge and one site in particular, Boxgrove in West Sussex, has been important for the new British synthesis.

Excavations since 1983 by Mark Roberts at Boxgrove in West Sussex have revealed exceptional preservation in soft sediments that formed in front of a collapsing chalk sea cliff (Pitts and Roberts 1997; Roberts *et al.* 1997; Roberts and Parfitt 1999). 500,000 years ago the cliffs on this part of the Sussex coast stood as high as Beachy Head and in front of them were first a series of marine sands followed, as the coastal geography changed, by silts and lagoonal deposits. Close to the cliff the calcium carbonate in the sediment has preserved organic remains including animal bone and a robust hominid tibia and two teeth (Roberts, Stringer, and Parfitt 1994; Roberts and Parfitt 1999). The Boxgrove investigations have reconstructed a grassy coastal plain with woods on the chalk plateau above the cliff. The many animal and bird species preserved include several which, by comparison with other sites in Britain and Europe, allowed the excavators to build up a bio-stratigraphic assessment of the age (Table 1.2). This has been determined as OIS 13, an interglacial during the Cromerian complex of cold and warm stages.

One reason for placing Boxgrove and other British sites such as High Lodge, Mildenhall (Ashton *et al.* 1992) into OIS 13 at 500,000 years ago is the major glaciation, known as the Anglian, which followed in OIS 12. This is the great hinge in the British Pleistocene sequence since it was the most severe of all the eight glaciations which have taken place in the last 780,000 years. It resulted in a number of extinctions (Table 1.2) so that elements in the Boxgrove fauna including giant deer, a distinctive rhino,

TABLE 1.2. *Key species in the changing animal faunas during the warm, interglacial periods of the British Middle Pleistocene*

OIS		5e	7	9	11	12	13	pre 13
Mimomys savini	A water vole							*
Arvicola terrestris cantiana	A water vole	*	*	*	*		*	
Arvicola terrestris	Water vole	*						
Sorex savini	A giant shrew					†	*	*
Sorex runtonensis	An extinct shrew					†	*	*
Pliomys episcopalis	An extinct vole					†	*	*
Ursus deningeri	Deninger's bear						*	*
Ursus spelaeus	Cave bear	*	*	*	*			
Canis lupus mosbachensis	Mosbach wolf					†	*	*
Megaloceros dawkinsi	Giant deer					†	*	*
Stepanorhinus hundsheimensis	Hundsheim rhino					†	*	*
Trogontherium cuvieri	Extinct beaver			†	*		*	*
Talpa minor	Small mole			†	*		*	*
Microtus (Terricola) cf. subterraneus	Common pine vole				*		*	*
Macaca sylvanus	Macaque		*	*	*			*
Equus ferus	Horse		*	*	*		*	
Stephanorhinus kirchbergensis	Merck's rhino		*	*	*			
Stephanorhinus hemitoechus	Narrow-nosed rhino	*	*	*	*			
Bos primigenius	Aurochs	*	*	*	*			
Crocidura spp.	White-toothed shrew		*	*	*			
Ursus arctos	Brown bear	*	*	*				
Hippopotamus amphibius	Hippopotamus	*						

Note: Selected species are shown for extinction (†) and evolution among the bears and water voles. The OIS interglacial stages are as follows: 13 Cromerian, 11 Hoxnian, 9 Purfleet, 7 Aveley, 5e Ipswichian. Stage 12 is the Anglian glaciation.

Source: After Currant 1989: table 2; Parfitt 1998: figure 11.2; Pitts and Roberts 1997: figure 19.

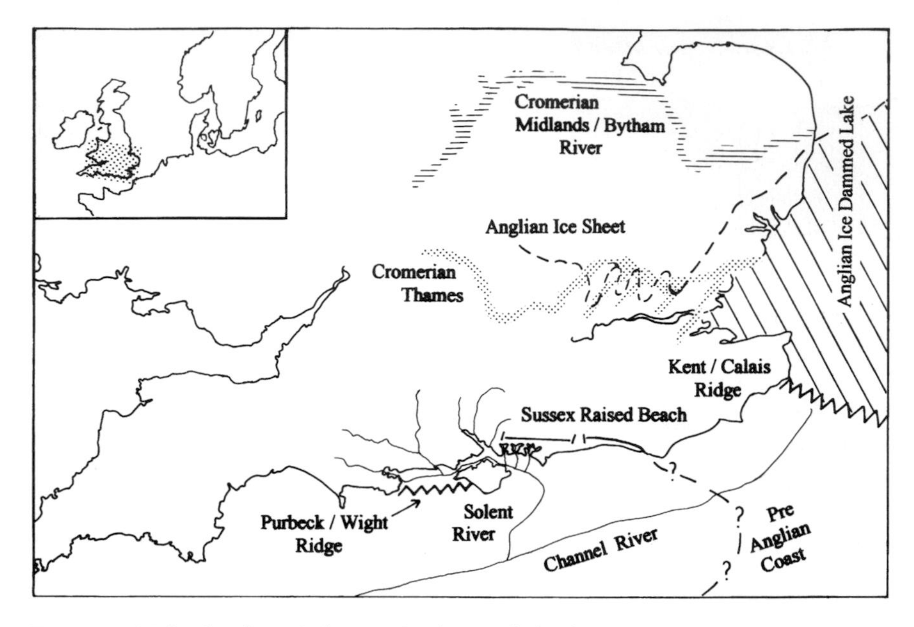

FIG. 1.2 Major landscape changes in the English Pleistocene.

Source: After Allen and Gibbard 1994; Bates, Parfitt, and Roberts 1997; Roberts, Gamble, and Bridgland 1995.

Stepanorhinus hundsheimensis, and several rodents failed to make the transition. Others did but in evolved form. These included the water vole *Arvicola* which evolved from *Mimomys*, and in so doing lost the roots on its molars, and the cave bear, *Ursus spelaeus*, which is represented at Boxgrove by Deninger's bear.

The Anglian also did two major things to the English landscape. Firstly it repositioned the major river system that drains east (Bridgland 1994). Without the Anglian London would have been further north and might even have been sited on the Midlands/Bytham river which flowed into the North Sea near Lowestoft (Figure 1.2). Instead the Thames developed in front of the Anglian ice sheet in southern England. Secondly, the Anglian ice sheet produced our island status in all subsequent interglacials (Preece 1995). The ice dammed lake which formed in front of it breached the chalk ridge connecting Dover and Calais. This allowed the rivers to drain south across the exposed continental shelf and out into the Atlantic somewhere beyond the Scilly Isles. But as White and Schreve have recently pointed out (2000) this did not result in permanent island status. Subsequent glacial stages lowered sea levels and re-established our continental status (for the most recent peninsular phase see Coles 1998). Indeed, they argue

TABLE 1.3. *The changing island status of Pleistocene Britain*

Period	Status of British Isles
Cromerian and Anglian complex	
Early Pleistocene to end of Anglian glaciation (OIS 12)	Peninsula joined by Kent-Artois chalk ridge. Severed during Anglian
427,000 Holsteinian Complex begins	
Early Hoxnian interglacial (OIS 11)	Status uncertain but probably peninsular which allowed human recolonization
Mid Hoxnian interglacial	Peninsula
Late Hoxnian interglacial	Island
Glacial (OIS 10)	Peninsula during low sea level glaciation
Purfleet interglacial (OIS 9)	Variable status
303,000 Saalian Complex begins	
Glacial (OIS 8)	Peninsula
Aveley interglacial (OIS 7)	Island status during early and late parts of the interglacial Short period of connection inferred from faunal turnover during the middle of the interglacial
Glacial (OIS 6)	Peninsula
128,000 Last interglacial/glacial cycle begins	
Ipswichian interglacial (OIS 5e)	High sea levels, island
Devensian glaciation (OIS 5d—3)	Predominantly peninsula

Source: After White and Schreve 2000 with additions.

that peninsular status was the default state for most of the last 500,000 years (Table 1.3).

HOLSTEINIAN COMPLEX 427,000–303,000 YEARS AGO

The Anglian glacial stage lasted 50,000 years and was followed by the Holsteinian complex, which lasted from 427,000 to 303,000 years ago. It consists of two interglacials (OIS 11 and 9) separated by a much weaker glacial episode (OIS 10). It is from this 120,000-year period that some of our most famous Lower Palaeolithic sites come. Swanscombe in the lower Thames valley (Conway, McNabb, and Ashton 1996) and Barnham (Ashton, Lewis, and Parfitt 1998) and Hoxne (Singer, Gladfelter, and Wymer 1993) in East Anglia. These are well preserved localities either in riverbank or lakeside settings. The Hoxne lake muds have particularly good preservation of pollen. From here and the nearby locality of Marks Tey comes the intriguing hint of hominid impact on the vegetation as revealed by a decline in tree pollen which can possibly be attributed to burning. In his original report West (1956: 338) was rightly cautious but pointed out that phenomena correlated with the later Neolithic forest clearance (see Whittle in this volume) are not necessarily confined to that period. Subsequently the ability of hunters and gatherers to transform their landscapes, particularly through the use of fire, has been widely recognized (Mellars 1976). The general interpretive trend in the last forty years has been to attribute Palaeolithic foragers with many of the landscape management skills previously only reserved for later periods. The Hoxne and Marks Tey evidence has always raised the possibility that the modification of the landscape was of very great antiquity and is now regarded as less surprising than in 1956.

The Holsteinian, and later Saalian, complexes saw some very different land forms and river systems in areas of southern England which were never glaciated. Of these the suite of five raised beaches in Sussex, of which Boxgrove at 43 m. is the oldest, indicate a complex history of coastal change, tectonic uplift, and subsequent erosion (Bates, Parfitt, and Roberts 1997: figure 13; Wenban-Smith *et al.* 2000). To the west of these cliffs and beaches the former Solent river (Allen and Gibbard 1994; Bridgland 1996) flowed in a chalk valley round the north of the Isle of Wight. Before the Purbeck–Wight ridge was breached, and when this happened is still disputed, the Solent river with its tributaries was one of the major rivers of England. Today the remnants of the Test, Itchen, Avon, Stour, Piddle, and Frome are indicators of its former importance. As we have seen at Boxgrove, the coastal plains formed productive landscapes for hunting during the interglacials. The Solent valley, as Hosfield (1996, 1998) has demonstrated in his GIS study of the Lower Palaeolithic artefacts and their relation to the terrace deposits, must have been a similarly productive region for human occupation in all but the most severe phases of the glacial periods.

During the Holsteinian complex we see the local evolution of what are best described as pre-Neanderthals. The best known example is the partial Swanscombe skull with its distinctive suprainiac fossa, a small depression on the back of the skull. This is a feature shared with the later Neanderthals but not with ourselves (Stringer and Gamble 1993).

SAALIAN COMPLEX 303,000–128,000 YEARS AGO

The next complex of glacials and interglacials, the Saalian, begins some 300,000 years ago with two glacial periods separated by an interglacial, OIS 7. There are marked faunal changes with the widespread appearance of reindeer and what has been termed by Guthrie the mammoth steppe (1990; Turner 1990). This mid-latitude biotope eventually stretched from western Europe to Alaska. The woolly mammoth, woolly rhino, reindeer, horse, and bison formed the key elements and their presence in great numbers points to the high productivity in this treeless but highly structured set of mosaic environments.

The cave site of Pontnewydd near Denbigh in North Wales (Aldhouse-Green 1995) was occupied by Neanderthals during the Aveley interglacial 220,000 years ago. The sediments which contain those teeth and stone tools were then pushed into the cave by a glacier in OIS 6 and were preserved as the ice sheet sat on Wales.

This period sees a change in stone technology as well as in hominids. Raw materials are gathered from further afield and then carefully knapped to produce more standardized shapes (Féblot-Augustins 1997; Roe 1981; Wymer 1968). This levallois technique is common in Middle Palaeolithic stone industries associated with Neanderthals.

THE LAST INTERGLACIAL–GLACIAL CYCLE

Finally we move into the last interglacial, OIS 5e, a short but very warm period from 128,000 to 118,000 years ago. This was a very high sea level interglacial (Shackleton 1987) and is reflected by pollen records for *Abies* (silver fir) extending as far north as southern England, well outside its present area of distribution in southern Europe (Zagwijn 1992: figure 10). The Scandinavian peninsula also became an island with the creation of the Eemian sea linking the Baltic to the White Sea (van Andel and Tzedakis 1996: figure 9).

The island status of Britain (Table 1.3) during this Ipswichian interglacial is interesting. *Hippopotamus* was a regular component of the fauna (Table 1.2) pointing to the warmer conditions during this 10,000 years. However, we can find no trace of humans (Gamble 1986) which rather contradicts the view that during the Pleistocene it was the cold glacial periods which alone controlled human settlement in northern Europe.

One explanation for the lack of hominids at a time when the fauna and flora of Britain were diverse might come from a closer reading of the ice core data from Greenland. Here the Summit core has subdivided OIS 5e into five further substages (GRIP 1993). This shows that far from being a stable 10,000 years the Ipswichian was marked by rapid oscillations in ice volume. One event at the end of OIS 5e1 lasted only an estimated seventy years but saw the oxygen isotope values plunge to mid-glacial levels (GRIP 1993: 206). These findings are confirmed by Dansgaard *et al.*'s (1993) study of the same core where they calculate that OIS 5e2 and OIS 5e4 lasted 2,000 and 6,000 years respectively. They note that these brief periods were as cool as subsequent substages in the Early Glacial which followed the Ipswichian. It appears therefore that the last interglacial, OIS 5e, was climatically unstable (Dansgaard *et al.* 1993: 220). These high resolution ice core data indicate that changes within interglacials of up to 10° C are possible in twenty years or even within a decade (White 1993: 186). This means that dramatic shifts in climate occurred within the lifetime of a hominid. Hominid adaptation to several millennia of constant climate, sea level, and presumably plant cover is looking less and less likely as a scenario for the period 300,000–35,000 years ago. Quaternary scientists are now considering why our present interglacial, which began 10,000 years ago, seems apparently so stable by comparison with OIS 5e, the Ipswichian.

However, these same rapid changes did not prevent human occupation in the more continental conditions of northern Europe (Roebroeks, Conard, and van Kolfschoten 1992). Perhaps there was an ecological constraint on island occupation by hominids even though Britain was a substantial land mass. Whatever the reason hominids returned with the cooler, less forested conditions after 118,000 years ago. These more open conditions persisted for a long time until rapid change initiated a glacial episode between 71,000 and 58,000 years ago. This severe climate was followed by a series of weak ameliorations in temperature down to 35,000 years ago. Indeed the dominant conditions which faced all hominids colonizing Britain were neither fully interglacial nor fully glacial but rather that rich mosaic of the highly productive mammoth steppe that accounted for over 50 per cent of the last interglacial/glacial cycle (Gamble 1986: ch. 3).

It is from this period, 71,000–35,000 years ago (OIS 4 and 3), that many of the classic Neanderthals (*Homo neanderthalensis*) have been excavated, particularly from caves in France and Germany (Stringer and Gamble 1993). The characteristic low forehead and long head containing a brain which on average is slightly larger than ours is widely considered to be the result of regional evolution from *Homo heidelbergensis.* Neanderthals continue that pattern of robustly built, powerful physiques that began with *Homo ergaster* and which characterizes the earliest Europeans such as Mauer and Boxgrove. The Neanderthal world was limited to Europe and parts of the Middle East. Britain was a part of this world although, with the possible exception of twelve poorly provenanced teeth from La Cotte, Jersey (Callow and Cornford 1986), there is no fossil evidence from this later (OIS 4) period.

In 1997 the bones of the original Neanderthal skeleton found in Germany in 1857 were successfully analysed for traces of ancient mtDNA (Ward and Stringer 1997). When compared with modern mtDNA the Neanderthal sequence consistently fell outside. The data also pointed to closer links between Neanderthals and Africans rather than modern Europeans indicating perhaps about half a million years of independent evolution for the Neanderthals. This suggests to Stringer (Comment at lecture 21 Jan. 1999) that *Homo antecessor* from Atapuerca TD6, dated to 900,000 years ago, predates by too much the last common ancestor for *Homo sapiens* and *Homo neanderthalensis*. Instead he suggests that the remarkable collection of thirty-two individuals from the Sima de los Huesos (Pit of the Bones) also at Atapuerca (Bermúdez de Castro and Nicolás 1997) but dated early in the Saalian complex (Table 1.3) might be much closer to the point of divergence. Whether the genetic evidence from the Neanderthal skeleton also supports the short chronology of 500,000 for the major settlement of Europe, we will have to wait and see.

HOMINIDS IN THEIR LANDSCAPES: CAMPSITES

Palaeolithic archaeology provides us with the evidence of the varied uses these early hominids made of their landscapes. The evidence may at first sight seem meagre, consisting mainly of stone artefacts and humanly modified animal bones, but these none the less allow us to reconstruct those habitual routines which made up most of their lives. Indeed, in this respect they do not differ much from ourselves where most of our consciousness works at a practical rather than a discursive level (Giddens 1984). Although we have acquired a very large brain during our evolution it could be argued that it allows us to do less rather than more thinking as usually supposed. Less thinking about those many habitual actions and routines which are coded into muscle memories and contained in patterns of movement and gestures. While these would include largely unthinking activities such as walking and eating such habitual routines can also be extended to encompass getting food, providing secure environments for raising young, travelling between resources, and using the varied affordances of the immediate habitat. Collectively such routines which are vital to survival, but for the most part undertaken in a practical rather than discursive frame of mind, can be grouped analytically as a landscape of habit (Gamble 1999; Gosden 1994). This is a regional concept which identifies a common structure in the space–time behaviour of people, past and present. The landscape of habit encompasses both subsistence and social behaviour. It contains other hominids, non-hominid competitors, and resources. It is centred on the individual and the decisions he or she must make. In this sense it is the wider spatial network for the negotiation and reproduction of social life.

Now we are very fortunate that the British Palaeolithic has some of the best preserved examples of such daily routines anywhere in the Palaeolithic world. As examples of this preservation I would cite the footprints of animals from Swanscombe; complete fish skeletons from the Hoxne lake muds; a recently discovered combustion feature at Beeches Pit, Suffolk; many flint knapping scatters at sites such as Barnham; an elephant and rhino drive over the headland at La Cotte, Jersey; and the use of the Boxgrove landscape in front of the collapsing sea cliff. Such detail provides us with accurate and very immediate information about the life of early hominids. In the rest of this volume you will rarely encounter such well preserved information about daily activity, even though it took place a mere one or two thousand years ago. For example, at Boxgrove are preserved the routines of flint working and the varied social performances which centred upon killing and butchering animals. The sequence of events can be broadly reconstructed as follows. In the first place a carcass was found or an animal, such as a horse, killed on those grassy plains beneath the cliffs (Pitts and Roberts 1997). Then it was secured against wolves and hyenas. Spears such as those recently found at Schöningen in Germany, 400,000 years old and 2.5 m. long (Thieme 1997), would have done this job efficiently as well as assisting in any hunting. The next step was to bring in blocks of flint grubbed from the collapsing cliff 200–300 m. away from the carcass. First the flint was tested at its source, then out on the plain an ovate biface was knapped and butchery undertaken. Afterwards the biface was thrown away and the hominids left the theatre.

I would emphasize three aspects of this remarkable footage of life 500,000 years ago. Firstly the evidence points to a short attention span. There was a rapid response to carcasses or stone as they became available. Very little seems to have been carried in anticipation, possibly some antler to assist in the flaking of the stone.

Secondly they did not stay for very long. There are no fireplaces. No huts and no postholes to indicate where they might have pitched a tent. Indeed this is a feature of landscape use in this early period. Although preservation is remarkable we are still waiting to find the first believable trace of architecture. It is not until the last few millennia of the Neanderthals that we find convincing artificial structures.

Thirdly, we underestimate the hominids of this period if we just concentrate on what we so obviously have—making wooden and stone tools to kill and butcher animals. It is time we moved away from such stomach-led pictures of the remote past. We need to remind ourselves that locales like Boxgrove were places where social life was performed. Hence my deliberate reference to it earlier as a theatre. Making bifaces was a social act, not just meeting a functional need or exploiting an affordance in the local environment. It was a social technology concerned with relationships between hominids as much as between the skill of the maker and the lump of flint in his or her hand. I would go further and propose that the act of making these stone tools was a form of visual grooming based on learned rhythms of manufacture and the doing of which had a powerful effect on the networks being negotiated by the individuals engaged in such repeated performances.

These networks are what we now need to investigate. At this time social life was principally constructed from two resources—emotional and material. The use of the former created intense bonds between small numbers of individuals, probably no more than three to seven, in what I refer to as an intimate network (Gamble 1998). Material resources such as food and stone were used to create larger, but less intense or permanent, effective networks of between ten and twenty-five members as seen in modern cross-cultural network studies (Milardo 1992). A third form of network, the extended, which we build depends on symbolic resources. This is the network which allows us to achieve that exaggerated extension of social relationships in time as well as space (Gamble 1998). The archaeological evidence for the earliest occupants of Britain strongly points to very little, if any, use of symbolic resources and hence their social worlds were local and predominantly exclusive in relation to individuals who were not closely networked through emotional and material resources.

These intimate and effective networks provided psychological security and a means for individuals to recruit others into social and economic projects, such as driving mammoth and rhino over the cliffs at La Cotte (Scott 1986). Most importantly they are part of our social heritage. The two networks underscore a creative society that is built by individuals, with personalities, from the bottom up, rather than imposed top down by existing institutions. As a result these hominids led highly complex social lives even though their artefacts and impact on the landscape seem from our perspective so unchanging and unremarkable. It is the emotional and material resources used to build these networks which explains why there was so little landscape change and alteration.

These social needs also explain the widespread similarity in the archaeology of the Lower Palaeolithic. From Olduvai Gorge (Leakey and Roe 1994) on the Equator to Barnham, in Suffolk, 51° N (Ashton, Lewis, and

Parfitt 1998) the archaeology is essentially the same. Ecological variation is not producing variation in hominid cultural response as it would, for example, on a similar transect among modern hunters and gatherers. What we have is a set of transferable *landscape* skills rather than *place* specific skills that promote such diversity.

HOMINIDS IN THEIR LANDSCAPES: THE REGION

Locales such as Boxgrove provide the polaroid pictures of short-term activity stuck within huge albums of Pleistocene time. How can we look at longer sequences and at wider geographical scales in the lifetime routines of these early hominids?

One approach recognizes that over such long timescales much of our data is time averaged (Stern 1993). The bulk of our evidence as Roe (1968) and later Wymer (1996, 1999) have documented at a national scale are stone tools recovered not from fine sediments, as at Boxgrove, but from coarse gravels laid down in river terraces. Cave deposits, that other sampling point for the Palaeolithic, are very rare in Britain when compared to their profusion in the limestone regions in continental Europe. Roe (1981) and Wymer (1999) provide a comprehensive survey of the other non-river finds such as open sites on the clay-with-flints of southern England. These discoveries suggest that there is still much to discover in terms of new Palaeolithic locations.

The time averaging involved in the accumulation of the terrace deposits is therefore of the order of a glacial or interglacial stage, approximately 70,000 to 100,000 years. While this contrasts markedly in temporal resolution with the fifteen minutes it took to knap a Boxgrove biface it is possible to use such data to determine long-term patterns of landscape use. Such off-site archaeology provides a signature of occupation density both between river systems and within them. The three major concentrations of stone artefacts from the Lower and Middle Palaeolithic are found in the catchments of the Ouse, Thames, and Solent rivers. Hosfield (1998) has analysed the Solent in detail taking into account the pattern of collection by antiquarians and the history of gravel extraction. Modelling the distributions and comparing them with the actual recovery of stone artefacts highlights particular segments of the valley system, particularly confluences, for hominid settlement. Moreover, when compared with the accumulation of stone tools of similar age in East Africa, Hosfield shows that the Solent data are consistently smaller. The inference must be that occupation of these northern latitudes was conditioned, as has always been suspected but never tested, by the rhythms of the interglacial–glacial cycles

TABLE 1.4. *The occurrence of raw materials on Middle Palaeolithic sites*

Km. radius from site	% of stone on site	% utilized, made into tools
'Local' = within 5 km.	55–98	1–5
Region = 5–20 km.	2–20	1–20
'Distant' = 30–80 km.	<5	74–100

Source: Geneste 1988.

(Figure 1.1). The pattern of landscape use was therefore one of repeated ebb and flow from 500,000 to 35,000 years ago. As White and Schreve (2000) point out, the source, either from southern or central Europe, of the various recolonizations might possibly be traced through the composition of the stone tool assemblages. Given the evidence from physical anthropology, which I reviewed above, the direction could be significant for the pattern of hominid evolution at a regional and continental scale.

These regional data give us some idea of where, over time, the landscapes of habit clustered. It is also possible to use raw material data, particularly once the levallois technique appears after 300,000 years ago, to estimate the scale. Based on the work of Geneste (1988) in south-west France we know that after this time stone was transferred over longer distances (Table 1.4). Sometimes 20 per cent in an assemblage comes from up to 20 km. away while less than 5 per cent comes from between 30 to 80 km.

The distance of 80 km. can be used to indicate the size of an individual's landscape of habit, which if treated as a diameter would be 5,000 km.^{2} Obviously at a regional scale the paths along which individuals traversed their landscapes of habit coincided with others in their social networks. Therefore even larger areas must have been known to network partners so that the density of paths produced a group, or network, landscape based on habitual use and movement.

A landscape of 5,000 km.^{2} for the Neanderthals of the Middle Palaeolithic, between 300,000 and 35,000 years ago, would result in some sixty such landscapes of habit in a combined United Kingdom and Ireland. This of course assumes maximum occupation in those unglaciated conditions that made up 50 per cent of any glacial–interglacial cycle (see above) and makes no allowance for the exposure of the continental shelf or heavily forested human deserts such as the last interglacial. This speculative assessment does, however, assume that the current absence of Lower or Middle Palaeolithic evidence from much of Scotland and all of Ireland is a result of glacial erosion.

TABLE 1.5. *Population estimates for Middle Palaeolithic hominids based on ethnographically observed densities*

Ethnographic densities	Persons per km^2	England 130,000 km^2	Wales 20,000 km^2	Scotland 78,000 km^2	Ireland 75,000 km^2	Total UK population
High	0.09	11,700	1,800	7,020	6,750	27,270
Low	0.05	6,500	1,000	3,900	3,750	15,150
UK, Early Palaeolithic estimate	0.035	4,515	630	2,730	2,625	10,500
Sparse	0.02	2,600	400	1,560	1,500	6,060

To continue the conjecture, what population numbers might we expect? If we assume that the sixty landscapes of habit were also largely self-sufficient breeding populations then we can derive some estimates. Wobst (1974) using a Monte Carlo simulation showed that a minimum equilibrium figure of 175 would be sufficient to overcome any long-term stochastic fluctuations in mate availability. Howell and Lehotay (1978) in their simulation found that 150–200 formed an effective breeding unit. Elsewhere small populations have been modelled and compared with ethnographic cases (Birdsell 1968). Here a mean of 500 is frequently cited although often disputed (Newell and Constandse-Westermann 1986). Using these figures (175 and 500) for our tentative sixty landscapes would produce a UK and Ireland population of either 10,500 or 30,000 hominids. When compared to ethnographic densities for mobile foragers (Table 1.5) the figure of 10,500 falls between the sparse and low population estimates while the breeding group of 500 exceeds the high values and is therefore best discounted. These coarse calculations do not take into account variation in regional ecology or the higher densities of finds along the Ouse, Thames, and Solent. Hence they should be treated with great caution. But in the absence of any alternative estimates they might serve as a point of departure for the development of more reliable figures.

CONCLUSION

The implication from these minimum estimates is that social life in the Lower and Middle Palaeolithic was very local and based on the principle of exclusion. This is borne out by the predominance of raw material obtained only 5 km. away from where they were eventually left (Table 1.4). There is also a complete lack of art and objects which transcend the local and exotic boundaries as determined from the stone data. This principle of exclusion would have implications for the pattern of gene flow in small populations particularly as they were subject to repeated ebb and flow. Moreover, even within these small populations and at a local scale within the 5,000 km.^{2} of their landscape of habit it is possible that considerable modification of the environment took place. This would have been selective and due to repeated activities.

These societies may look very similar to us because the stone tools they made, and the places where they were left in the landscape, persist, unchanged, for such huge periods of time. Consequently we have often, mistakenly, defined the essence of the earliest Palaeolithic society as limited and unrelentingly dull. However, I have argued here that while such persistence stemmed from their use of mainly emotional and material resources to create social life, at the same time the construction of their social lives through movement and making no doubt produced a range of subtly different performances which until now we have chosen not to look for. Long-term persistence was complemented by very different internal social histories.

What changed with the arrival of modern humans in Britain about 35,000 years ago was the construction of complicated social landscapes using symbols most readily identified by archaeologists in the form of representational art. Social relationships were intensified through the use of these largely novel symbolic resources and so stretched further across time and space. Such extension is the hallmark of modern humans and represents a very different form of networking. I would therefore expect that population numbers actually declined as a result of these changes to social life. Proximity to social partners no longer determined how networks were built. Rather, the construction of social landscapes with named places symbolically marked and dealing with absence of individuals rather than depending on their presence ushered in that transformation of the land that led eventually to monumentality and ritual.

But why should these changes appear so late in our story? Is it, as some would argue, that the new levallois technique and an increase in the scale of landscape use at 300,000 is an indication of the evolution of modern humans (Foley and Lahr 1997)? This would mean in archaeological terms that what we call the Middle Palaeolithic should actually be the Upper Palaeolithic with its implications of modernity. I do not agree and for a very simple reason based upon the use of resources for the construction of society and their preservation in the Palaeolithic record (Gamble 1999). Social landscapes and the extended networks which created them led, unintentionally, to the colonization of the rest of the world and the shaping of a global humanity. That is a story which begins late, only 60,000 years ago as people colonized Australia for the first time and then later the Americas, the Arctic, and the Pacific (Gamble 1993). Modern humans can be defined genetically and anatomically but it is what they did which makes them familiar to us. Only archaeology reveals when this happened. But to understand why, we need to spend much more time investigating how they created their social lives. The British data provide the opportunity to do just that and to see the first shaping of the landscape.

REFERENCES

Aiello, L., and Dunbar, R. (1993). 'Neocortex size, group size and the evolution of language', *Current Anthropology*, 34: 184–93.

Aiello, L., and Wheeler, P. (1995). 'The expensive-tissue hypothesis: the brain and the digestive system in human and primate evolution', *Current Anthropology*, 36: 199–221.

Aiello, L. C. (1998). 'The "expensive tissue hypothesis" and the evolution of the human adaptive niche: a study in comparative anatomy', in J. Bayley (ed.), *Science in Archaeology: An Agenda for the Future*. London: English Heritage, 25–36.

Aldhouse-Green, S. (1995). 'Pontnewydd Cave, Wales, a later Middle Pleistocene hominid and archaeological site: a review of stratigraphy, dating, taphonomy and interpretation', in J. M. Bermudez, J. L. Arsuaga, and E. Carbonell (eds.), *Evolución humana en Europa y los yacimientos de la Sierra de Atapuerca*. Vallodolid: Junta de Castilla y León, 37–55.

Allen, L. G., and Gibbard, P. L. (1994). 'Pleistocene evolution of the Solent River of Southern England', *Quaternary Science Reviews*, 12: 503–28.

Ascenzi, A., Biddittu, I., Cassoli, P. F., Segre, A. G., and Segre-Naldini, E. (1996). 'A calvarium of late *Homo erectus* from Ceprano, Italy', *Journal of Human Evolution*, 31: 409–23.

Ashton, N. M., Cook, J., Lewis, S. G., and Rose, J. (1992). *High Lodge: Excavations by G. de G. Sieveking 1962–68 and J. Cook 1988*. London: British Museum Press.

Ashton, N., Lewis, S. G., and Parfitt, S. (1998) (eds.). *Excavations at the Lower Palaeolithic site at East Farm, Barnham, Suffolk, 1989–1994*. London: British Museum Occasional Paper Number 125.

Bates, M. R., Parfitt, S. A., and Roberts, M. B. (1997). 'The chronology, palaeogeography and archaeological significance of the marine Quaternary record of the West Sussex coastal plain, southern England, UK', *Quaternary Science Reviews*, 16: 1227–52.

Bermúdez de Castro, J. M., Arsuaga, J. L., Carbonell, E., Rosas, A., Martinez, I., and Mosquera, M. (1997). 'A hominid from the Lower Pleistocene of Atapuerca,

Spain: possible ancestor to Neandertals and modern humans', *Science*, 276: 1392–5.

Bermúdez de Castro, J. M., and Nicolás, M. E. (1997). 'Palaeodemography of the Atapuerca-SH Middle Pleistocene hominid sample', *Journal of Human Evolution*, 33: 333–55.

Birdsell, J. B. (1968). 'Some predictions for the Pleistocene based on equilibrium systems among recent hunter-gatherers', in R. Lee and I. DeVore (eds.), *Man the Hunter*. Chicago: Aldine, 229–40.

Bonifay, E., and Vandermeersch, B. (1991) (eds.). *Les Prèmieres Européens*. Paris: CTHS.

Brain, C. K., and Sillen, A. (1988). 'Evidence from the Swartkrans cave for the earliest use of fire', *Nature*, 336: 464–6.

Bridgland, D. R. (1994). *Quaternary of the Thames*. London: Chapman and Hall.

Bridgland, D. R. (1996). 'Quaternary river Terrace deposits as a framework for the Lower Palaeolithic record', in C. S. Gamble and A. J. Lawson, *The English Palaeolithic Reviewed*. Salisbury: Trust for Wessex Archaeology, 23–39.

Callow, P., and Cornford, J. M. (1986) (eds.). *La Cotte de St. Brelade 1961–1978: Excavations by C. B. M. McBurney*. Norwich: Geo Books.

Carbonell, E., Mosquera, M., Rodriguez, X. P., and Sala, R. (1996). 'The first human settlement of Europe', *Journal of Anthropological Research*, 51: 107–14.

Clarke, R. J. (1990). 'The Ndutu cranium and the origin of Homo sapiens', *Journal of Human Evolution*, 19: 699–736.

Coles, B. (1998). 'Doggerland: a speculative survey', *Proceedings of the Prehistoric Society*, 64: 45–81.

Conway, B., McNabb, J., and Ashton, N. (1996) (eds.). *Excavations at Barnfield Pit, Swanscombe, 1968–1972*. London: British Museum Occasional Paper Number 94.

Currant, A. (1989). 'The Quaternary origins of the modern British mammal fauna', *Biological Journal of the Linnean Society*, 38: 23–30.

Dansgaard, W., Johnsen, S. J., Clausen, H. B., Dahl-Jensen, D., Gundestrup, N. S., Hammer, C. U., Hvidberg, C. S., Steffensen, J. P., Sveinbjörnsdottir, A. E., Jouzel, J., and Bond, G. (1993). 'Evidence for general instability of past climate from a 250-kyr ice-core record', *Nature*, 364: 218–20.

Dennell, R., and Roebroeks, W. (1996). 'The earliest colonization of Europe: the short chronology revisited', *Antiquity*, 70: 535–42.

Dunbar, R. I. M. (1993). 'Coevolution of neocortical size, group size and language in humans', *Behavioural and Brain Sciences*, 16: 681–735.

Dunbar, R. I. M. (1996). *Grooming, Gossip and the Evolution of Language*. London: Faber and Faber.

Féblot-Augustins, J. (1997). *La Circulation des matières premières au Paléolithique*. Liège: ERAUL, vol. 75.

Foley, R., and Lahr, M. M. (1997). 'Mode 3 technologies and the evolution of modern humans', *Cambridge Archaeological Journal*, 7: 3–36.

Gabunia, L., and Vekua, A. (1995). 'A Plio-Pleistocene hominid from Dmanisi, East Georgia, Caucasus', *Nature*, 373: 509–12.

Gabunia, L., Vekua, A., Lordkipanidze, D., Justus, A., Nioradze, M., and Bosinski, G. (1999). 'Neue Urmenschenfunde von Dmanisi (Ost-Georgien)', *Jahrbuch des Römisch-Germanischen Zentralmuseums Mainz*, 46: 23–38.
Gamble, C. S. (1986). *The Palaeolithic Settlement of Europe*. Cambridge: Cambridge University Press.
Gamble, C. S. (1993). *Timewalkers: The Prehistory of Global Colonization*. Stroud: Alan Sutton.
Gamble, C. S. (1998). 'Palaeolithic society, and the release from proximity: a network approach to intimate relations', *World Archaeology*, 29: 426–49.
Gamble, C. S. (1999). *The Palaeolithic Societies of Europe*. Cambridge: Cambridge University Press.
Gamble, C. S., and Steele, J. (1999). 'Hominid ranging patterns and dietary strategies', in H. Ullrich (ed.), *Hominid Evolution: Lifestyles and Survival Strategies*. Gelsenkirchen: Edition Archaea, 396–409.
Geneste, J.-M. (1988). 'Systemes d'approvisionnement en matières premières au paléolithique moyen et au paléolithique supérieur en Aquitaine', *L'Homme de Néandertal*, 8: 61–70.
Gibert, J., Gibert, L., Iglesias, A., and Maestro, E. (1998). 'Two "Oldowan" assemblages in the Plio-Pleistocene deposits of the Orce region, southeast Spain', *Antiquity*, 72: 17–25.
Giddens, A. (1984). *The Constitution of Society*. Berkeley: University of California Press.
Gosden, C. (1994). *Social Being and Time*. Oxford: Blackwell.
GRIP (1993). 'Climate instability during the last interglacial period recorded in the GRIP ice core', *Nature*, 364: 203–7.
Groves, C. P. (1989). *A Theory of Human and Primate Evolution*. Oxford: Oxford University Press.
Guthrie, R. D. (1990). *Frozen Fauna of the Mammoth Steppe*. Chicago: Chicago University Press.
Hosfield, R. T. (1996). 'Quantifying the English Palaeolithic: GIS as an approach', in C. Gamble and A. Lawson (eds.), *The English Palaeolithic Reviewed*. Salisbury: Trust for Wessex Archaeology, 40–51.
Hosfield, R. T. (1998). 'A GIS approach to the Lower Palaeolithic of the Solent River, Hampshire', Ph.D. diss., University of Southampton.
Howell, N., and Lehotay, V. A. (1978). 'Ambush: a computer program for stochastic microsimulation of small human populations', *American Anthropologist*, 80: 905–22.
Johanson, D., and Edgar, B. (1996). *From Lucy to Language*. New York: Simon and Schuster.
Leakey, M. D., and Roe, D. A. (1994). *Olduvai Gorge*, v. *Excavations in Beds III, IV and the Masek Beds, 1968–71*. Cambridge: Cambridge University Press.
Lowe, J. J., and Walker, M. J. C. (1997). *Reconstructing Quaternary Environments*. Harlow: Longman.
Mellars, P. A. (1976). 'Fire ecology, animal populations and man: a study of some

ecological relationships in prehistory', *Proceedings of the Prehistoric Society*, 42: 15–45.

Milardo, R. M. (1992). 'Comparative methods for delineating social networks', *Journal of Social and Personal Relationships*, 9: 447–61.

Newell, R. R., and Constandse-Westermann, T. S. (1986). 'Testing an ethnographic analogue of Mesolithic social structure and the archaeological resolution of Mesolithic ethnic groups and breeding populations', *Proceedings of the Koninklijke Nederlandse Akademie van Wetenschappen*, 89: 243–310.

Parfitt, S. A. (1998). 'The interglacial mammalian fauna from Barnham', in N. Ashton, S. G. Lewis, and S. Parfitt (eds.), *Excavations at the Lower Palaeolithic Site at East Farm, Barnham, Suffolk, 1989–1994*. London: British Museum Occasional Paper Number 125, 111–51.

Peretto, C., Amore, F. O., Antoniazzi, A., Bahain, J.-J., Cattani, L., Cavallini, E., Esposito, P., Falgueres, C., Gagnepain, J., Hedley, I., Laurent, M., Lebreton, V., Longo, L., Milliken, S., Monegatti, P., Ollé, A., Pugliese, N., Renault-Miskovsky, J., Sozzi, M., Ungaro, S., Vannucci, S., Wagner, J.-J., and Yokoyama, Y. (1998). 'L'industrie lithique de Ca'Belvedere di Monte Poggiolo: stratigraphie, matière première, typologie, remontages et traces d'utilisation', *L'Anthropologie*, 102: 343–65.

Pitts, M., and Roberts, M. (1997). *Fairweather Eden*. London: Century.

Preece, R. (1995) (ed.). *Island Britain*. London: Geological Society Special Publication No. 96.

Roberts, M. B., Stringer, C. B., and Parfitt, S. A. (1994). 'A hominid tibia from Middle Pleistocene sediments at Boxgrove, U.K.', *Nature*, 369: 311–13.

Roberts, M. B., Gamble, C. S., and Bridgland, D. R. (1995). 'The earliest occupation of Europe: the British Isles', in W. Roebroeks and T. van Kolfschoten (eds.), *The Earliest Occupation of Europe*. Leiden: European Science Foundation and University of Leiden, 165–91.

Roberts, M. B., Parfitt, S. A., Pope, M. J., and Wenban-Smith, F. F. (1997). 'Boxgrove, West Sussex: rescue excavations of a Lower Palaeolithic landsurface (Boxgrove project B, 1989–91)', *Proceedings of the Prehistoric Society*, 63: 303–58.

Roberts, M. B., and Parfitt, S. A. (1999). *Boxgrove: A Middle Pleistocene Hominid Site at Eartham Quarry, Boxgrove, West Sussex*. London: English Heritage.

Roe, D. A. (1968). *A Gazeteer of British Lower and Middle Palaeolithic Sites*. London: Council for British Archaeology Research Report 8.

Roe, D. A. (1981). *The Lower and Middle Palaeolithic Periods in Britain*. London: Routledge and Kegan Paul.

Roebroeks, W., Conard, N. J., and van Kolfschoten, T. (1992). 'Dense forests, cold steppes, and the Palaeolithic settlement of northern Europe', *Current Anthropology*, 33: 551–86.

Roebroeks, W., and van Kolfschoten, T. (1994). 'The earliest occupation of Europe: a short chronology', *Antiquity*, 68: 489–503.

Roebroeks, W., and van Kolfschoten, T. (1995) (eds.). *The Earliest Occupation of Europe*. Leiden: European Science Foundation and University of Leiden.

Scott, K. (1986). 'The bone assemblage from layers 3 and 6', in P. Callow and J. M. Cornford (eds.), *La Cotte de St. Brelade 1961–1978: Excavations by C. B. M. McBurney*. Norwich: Geo Books, 159–84.
Semaw, S., Renne, P., Harris, J. W. K., Feibel, C. S., Bernor, R. L., Fesseha, N., and Mowbray, K. (1997). '2.5 million-year-old stone tools from Gona, Ethiopia', *Nature*, 385: 333–6.
Shackleton, N. J. (1987). 'Oxygen isotopes, ice volume and sea level', *Quaternary Science Reviews*, 6: 183–90
Shackleton, N. J., and Opdyke, N. D. (1973). 'Oxygen isotope and palaeomagnetic stratigraphy of Equatorial Pacific core V28-238', *Quaternary Research*, 3: 39–55.
Singer, R., Gladfelter, B. G., and Wymer, J. J. (1993). *The Lower Palaeolithic Site at Hoxne, England*. London: University of Chicago Press.
Steele, J. (1996). 'On predicting hominid group sizes', in J. Steele and S. Shennan (eds.), *The Archaeology of Human Ancestry*. London: Routledge, 230–52.
Stern, N. (1993). 'The structure of the Lower Pleistocene archaeological record', *Current Anthropology*, 34: 201–25.
Stringer, C., and Gamble, C. (1993). *In Search of the Neanderthals: Solving the Puzzle of Human Origins*. London: Thames and Hudson.
Thieme, H. (1997). 'Lower palaeolithic hunting spears from Germany', *Nature*, 385: 807–10.
Turner, E. (1990). 'Middle and Late Pleistocene Macrofaunas of the Neuwied Basin region (Rhineland-Palatinate) of West Germany', *Jahrbuch des Römisch-Germanischen Zentralmuseums Mainz*, 37: 133–403.
van Andel, T. H., and Tzedakis, P. C. (1996). 'Palaeolithic landscapes of Europe and environs, 150,000–25,000 years ago: an overview', *Quaternary Science Reviews*, 15: 481–500.
Ward, R., and Stringer, C. (1997). 'A molecular handle on the Neanderthals', *Nature*, 388: 225–6.
Wenban-Smith, F., Gamble, C., and Apsimon, A. (2000). 'The Lower Palaeolithic site at Red Barns, Portchester: bifacal technology, raw material quality, and the organisation of archaic behaviour', *Proceedings of the Prehistoric Society*, 66: 209–57.
West, R. G. (1956). 'The Quaternary deposits at Hoxne, Suffolk', *Philosophical Transactions of the Royal Society of London, Series B*, 239: 265–356.
White, J. W. C. (1993). 'Climate change: don't touch that dial', *Nature*, 364: 186–220.
White, M. J., and Schreve, D. C. (2000). 'Island Britain—Peninsula Britain: palaeogeography, colonisation, and the Lower Palaeolithic settlement of the British Isles', *Proceedings of the Prehistoric Society*, 66: 1–28.
Wobst, H. M. (1974). 'Boundary conditions for palaeolithic social systems: a simulation approach', *American Antiquity*, 39: 147–78.
Wymer, J. J. (1968). *Lower Palaeolithic Archaeology in Britain, as Represented by the Thames Valley*. London: John Baker.
Wymer, J. J. (1996). 'The English rivers Palaeolithic survey', in C. S. Gamble and

A. J. Lawson (eds.), *The English Palaeolithic Reviewed*. Salisbury: Trust for Wessex Archaeology, 7–22.

Wymer, J. J. (1999). *The Lower Palaeolithic Occupation of Britain*. Salisbury: Wessex Archaeology.

Zagwijn, W. H. (1992). 'Migration of vegetation during the Quaternary in Europe', *Courier Forschungsinstitut Senckenberg*, 153: 9–20.

2

The *Homo Sapiens* Peopling of Europe

Paul Mellars

THE origin of our own species, *Homo sapiens*, has sometimes been described as 'the hottest topic in palaeoanthropology' (Shreeve 1995). Lively debate has surrounded this issue throughout this century and the debate continues, if in a slightly more muted form, down to the present. Indeed in some ways recent discoveries have tended to fuel the debate. Needless to say the issues extend far beyond the realms of Europe, but the evidence from Europe itself remains critical to many aspects of these debates, owing to the exceptional detail and clarity of the relevant archaeological and human skeletal records in many parts of the continent. The approach I wish to adopt here is to look first at the evidence for the initial appearance of fully *Homo sapiens* populations in Europe generally, and then to extend this focus, more briefly, to other regions. As we shall see, the evidence from Britain itself inevitably forms only a small part of this picture, but one which adds some important elements to the wider international perspective.

THE EVOLUTIONARY PERSPECTIVE

The long-running debates over modern human origins reduce essentially to two sharply polarized perspectives (Stringer and Gamble 1993; Stringer and McKie 1996; Wolpoff and Caspari 1997). On the one hand is the so-called 'multi-regional evolution' or 'regional continuity' model, which asserts that in effectively all parts of the old world there was an essentially continuous, gradual process of both biological and cultural evolution from the various *Homo erectus*-like populations which first spread from Africa over a million years ago, and which eventually led to the emergence of fully modern populations within each region—though with a good deal of peripheral gene flow between the different regional populations throughout this period (Wolpoff and Caspari 1997). On the other hand there is the more dramatic population dispersal or 'Garden of Eden' hypothesis. This posits an entirely separate and unique evolution of *Homo sapiens* populations in one specific region of the world (most probably Africa), followed by an eventual dispersal of these populations to all other regions—broadly between 100,000 and 40,000 years ago—which rapidly gave rise to the extinction and disappearance of the pre-existing 'archaic' populations (Stringer and McKie 1996; Lahr and Foley 1998). How far there may be room for some degree of compromise between these two positions—for example by allowing for varying degrees of mixing and interbreeding between the expanding modern and resident archaic populations in different regions—remains one of the more contentious points in the recent debates (e.g. Duarte *et al.* 1999; Tattersall and Schwartz 1999).

In terms of the hard evidence for choosing between these two very different perspectives there are clearly two different approaches we can adopt. To take the most direct approach, we can look at what one might term collectively the 'biological' evidence—i.e. evidence derived partly from the (sadly scarce) surviving skeletal remains of early human populations, and partly from more recent studies into the genetic aspects of biological evolution, derived from research into the DNA and related features of present-day populations in different regions of the world. The second approach, and the one on which I will mainly focus here, is to examine the archaeological evidence for the evolution of modern behavioural and cultural patterns associated with the appearance of biologically and anatomically modern populations in different regions. It is in the latter field that I believe the European evidence is particularly explicit, and has a central role to play in any analysis of the broader patterns of human evolution over this critical transition.

To take the biological evidence first, most authors would agree that most of the scientific developments and discoveries over the past two decades have tended to provide better support for the Garden of Eden, or population dispersal, model of modern human origins than for the competing regional continuity model. In terms of the skeletal evidence, for example, we can now show that essentially modern forms of anatomy, little different from those of most recent populations, emerged significantly earlier in parts of both Africa and the immediately adjacent parts of south-west Asia than in more peripheral areas such as Europe or south-east Asia. This is best documented perhaps by the abundant skeletal remains recovered from the sites of Mugharet es Skhul and Djebel Qafzeh in Israel (now well dated by two different dating methods to around 90–100,000 years ago) and by more isolated discoveries from African sites such as Omo in Ethiopia and Klasie's River Mouth and Border Cave in South Africa at a broadly similar date (Bar-Yosef 1994, 1998*a*; Stringer and McKie 1996; Valladas *et al.* 1998). Many of these finds must predate by at least 50–60,000 years the disappearance of characteristically archaic populations in other parts of the world, as represented for example by the classic Neanderthals of western and central Europe and by some of the latest *Homo erectus* populations in Indonesia (Lahr and Foley 1998).

Recent research into the patterns of genetic variation in modern (i.e. present-day) populations in different parts of the world seems to reinforce the same conclusion (Stoneking *et al.* 1992; Harpending *et al.* 1993; Cann *et al.* 1994; Tishkoff *et al.* 1996; Relethford 1998). The pattern which has emerged consistently from studies of both nuclear and mitochondrial DNA is that we are all extraordinarily similar in genetic terms. The only way in which we can explain this similarity would seem to be in terms of a relatively recent common origin for all present-day populations. Estimates of the likely date of this common ancestor remain controversial, but most studies of the patterns of mitochondrial DNA variation in recent populations (i.e. genetic material which is transmitted almost entirely through the maternal line of inheritance, and which is known to mutate at an exceptionally rapid rate) put the age at around 150–200,000 years ago (Relethford 1998). A second, and rather more controversial, conclusion from the recent DNA research is that this recent ancestral population most probably lived in Africa. The arguments in this case are more involved, but there seems to be an increasing convergence from many different studies of both mitochondrial and nuclear DNA (the latter inherited through both the male and female lines) that overall Africa represents the most likely point of origin of genetically—and presumably anatomically—modern populations (Stringer and McKie 1996; Harpending *et al.* 1993; Krings *et al.* 1997; Relethford 1998; Lahr and Foley 1998).

One of the most dramatic developments in this field was announced in 1997, when some remarkably well preserved mitochondrial DNA was recovered from a bone of the classic Neanderthal skeleton from the site of Neanderthal itself in south Germany (Krings *et al.* 1997). In this case the pattern of the DNA was found to be so different from that of modern European populations (differing by around 27 points in the particular segment of DNA recovered, as compared with an average of only 7 or 8 points between different individuals in modern European populations) that the authors concluded that the European Neanderthals must have evolved along an entirely separate lineage from that which eventually gave rise to modern European populations over a period of at least 500,000 years. The detailed patterns of the Neanderthal DNA once again seemed to fit better with the hypothesis of an ultimately African source for modern human populations than an origin elsewhere in the world. Assessed in these terms, an Out of Africa model of *Homo sapiens* human populations now appears to be the one which accords best with the totality of the strictly biological evidence for recent human evolution.

THE EUROPEAN PERSPECTIVE

No one would dispute that in Europe the whole issue of modern human origins centres on the period between *c.*45,000 and 30,000 years before present (i.e. BP), as measured in terms of the conventional radiocarbon timescale.[1] At this time Europe was approximately midway through the last major glacial period, with ice sheets covering at least the northern parts of Scandinavia, and with large parts of the middle latitudes of western, central, and eastern Europe covered by open, tundra, or steppe-like vegetation, not too different from that found in northern Norway or Alaska at the present day. Fully forested conditions would have existed only in the southern parts of Europe and, more sparsely, along the Mediterranean coast (Van Andel and Tzedakis 1996; Van Andel 1998). Actual temperatures around the middle of the last glaciation (the period of so-called 'oxygen-isotope stage 3') are known to have been highly unstable, with brief periods of very severe climate, with average annual temperatures up to 10–15°C below present-day values, interspersed between periods of much milder climate, perhaps only a few degrees cooler than the present day. But the predominantly open vegetation which covered large parts of the continent supported rich growths of grasses, mosses, and low-growing shrub vegetation which clearly provided ideal grazing conditions for large herds of reindeer, horse, bison, as well as now-extinct species such as mammoth and woolly rhinoceros—a walking larder for human groups who were well equipped to cope with severe winters and to hunt a range of large and fast-moving animals. Lowered sea levels at this time (resulting from the large amounts of water locked up in the continental ice sheets) would have expanded the coastal plains in many parts of Europe, and would have joined up Britain to the adjacent areas of the continent over a large part of what is now the English Channel and the southern part of the North Sea.

[1] There is now increasing evidence that within the time range under discussion here (mainly from 40,000 to 30,000 BP) radiocarbon measurements tend to underestimate the true ages of the dated samples by somewhere between 2,000 and 4,000 years (Laj *et al.* 1996; Van Andel 1998; Voelker *et al.* 1998). To convert these radiocarbon dates into absolute, calendrical ages it is therefore necessary to calibrate the radiocarbon figures by approximately this amount. Since the details of these calibrations remain at present uncertain, however, the usual convention is to cite radiocarbon dates in terms of the raw, uncalibrated figures.

Bracketed within this time range of 45,000–30,000 years ago we can identify two radical changes in the records of human occupation in Europe. In the first place there was the effective replacement (by whatever means) of the classic Neanderthal populations which had occupied the continent for at least the preceding 200,000 years by populations of fully *Homo sapiens* or anatomically modern form—the so-called 'Cro-Magnon' populations. As discussed in the preceding chapter, reasonably well preserved skeletal remains of Neanderthals have now been recovered from over a score of locations in Europe, and show these populations to have been much more heavily built than their Cro-Magnon successors, with a short, stocky body form which seems to have been specifically adapted to survive in the generally cold conditions of glacial Europe (Stringer and Gamble 1993; Tattersall 1995; Duarte *et al.* 1999). The distinctive facial form of the Neanderthals (with a generally flattened, oval cranial vault, heavy brow ridges, receding chins, and large noses) may have been exaggerated in some earlier caricatures, but was nevertheless strikingly different from that of modern populations. Nevertheless the Neanderthals had brains just as large as ours and, at least in terms of technology and economic practices, were clearly highly successful in surviving in a range of sharply varying climatic and environmental conditions across most areas of Europe. The succeeding Cro-Magnons (best represented by the finds from sites such as Vogelherd and Mladeč in central Europe) were skeletally perhaps slightly more 'robust' than modern Europeans but were otherwise effectively identical to ourselves. On the basis of both the striking skeletal differences and (above all) the nature of the DNA recently recovered from the original Neanderthal skeleton, most authors now incline to view the European Neanderthals as probably a separate species from the Cro-Magnons (i.e. taxonomically *Homo neanderthalensis* as opposed to *Homo sapiens*), though this whole area of the recognition of species differences in human evolutionary lineages remains fraught with controversy (Simmons 1994; Stringer and McKie 1996; Duarte *et al.* 1999; Tattersall 1995; Tattersall and Schwartz 1999). Some authors have seen the distinctively elongated, 'gracile' body-form of the Cro-Magnons as a possible reflection of their ancestry in more temperate or tropical regions, though this point again remains controversial.

The second and in some respects more dramatic feature of the human evolutionary record over the period between 45,000 and 30,000 BP in Europe is the appearance in the associated archaeological evidence of a whole range of radical technological and other behavioural innovations, which collectively define what archaeologists conventionally refer to as the 'Middle-to-Upper Palaeolithic transition' or (more colourfully) as the 'Upper Palaeolithic revolution'. The details of this transition have been so fully discussed in the earlier literature that they can perhaps be recalled fairly swiftly here (Mellars 1973, 1989*a*, 1989*b*, 1992, 1996*a*; White 1993; Knecht *et al.* 1993). They seem nevertheless to have embraced at least a dozen major behavioural innovations, extending into many different spheres of human cultural, social, and behavioural organization, all of which can be documented clearly in the surviving archaeological records. Briefly, these can be summarized as follows:

1. A quantitative shift from predominantly flake-based technologies to technologies based on the production of more regular and elongated blade forms—probably reflecting the introduction of indirect punch techniques of flaking.
2. The introduction of many new forms of stone tools (typical end scrapers, various forms of burins, retouched bladelet forms, etc.), apparently implying shifts in several other related aspects of technology, such as skin working, hunting weaponry, and more complex bone and antler technology.
3. The appearance of more standardized and visually distinctive tool forms—apparently reflecting a new element of a deliberately imposed form in tool production.
4. The sudden emergence of complex and extensively shaped bone, antler, and ivory tools, in a wide variety of forms. These again must reflect changes in other related aspects of technology (especially perhaps hunting projectiles) as well as new and more standardized norms of tool production (Knecht 1993).
5. The effective explosion of explicitly decorative or ornamental items. These range from carefully perforated animal teeth and marine shells to a wide variety of laboriously shaped bead and pendant forms in a variety of raw materials (ivory, steatite, schist, etc.) (Figure 2.1). The majority of these almost certainly represent items of personal decoration, probably reflecting new ways of signifying the social role or status of individuals in the societies.
6. The emergence of long-distance trading or exchange networks for the procurement of these ornamental items—in the case of both marine shells and certain varieties of stone beads extending in some cases up to distances of several hundred kilometres (White 1993; Taborin 1993).
7. The appearance of extensively and regularly notched or incised bone artefacts, possibly representing in some cases systematic numerical or notation systems (Marshack 1991).
8. The first emergence of varied and remarkably sophisticated forms of representational art. These range from representations of both male and female sex symbols, through elaborately carved statuettes of both

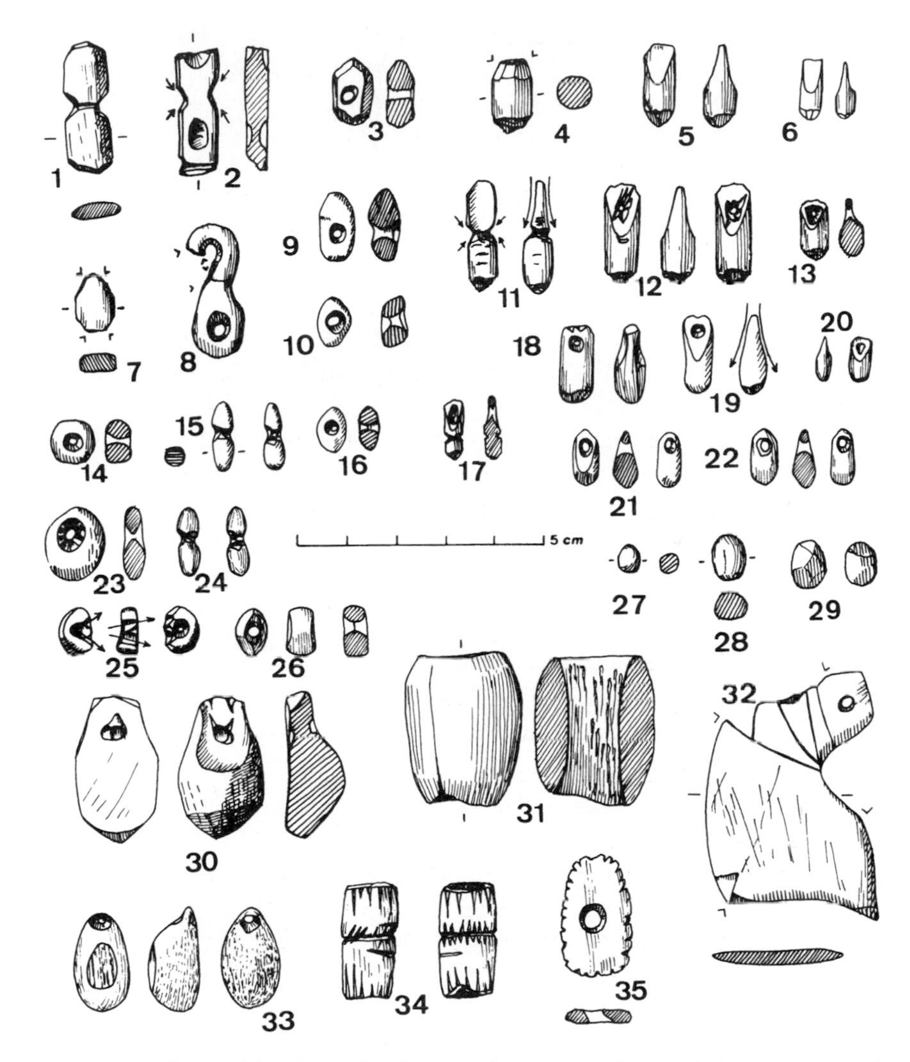

FIG. 2.1 Perforated beads and other pendants manufactured from mammoth ivory and stone, from the early Upper Palaeolithic levels of the Spy Cave, south Belgium.

animal and human figures (Figure 2.2), to the recently discovered animal drawings in the Chauvet cave in south-eastern France (Figure 2.3) (Hahn 1993; Chauvet *et al.* 1995).

9. The appearance of musical instruments—best represented by the newly discovered bird-bone flutes from the early Upper Palaeolithic levels of the Geissenklösterle cave in south Germany.

FIG. 2.2 Lion-headed human figure of mammoth ivory, from the early Aurignacian levels of the Hohlenstein-Stadel Cave, south Germany.

FIG. 2.3 Frieze of drawings of lions' heads from the recently discovered Chauvet Cave in Ardèche (France) dated directly by radiocarbon to *c.* 30–32,000 BP.

10. The first clear evidence in Europe of explicitly ceremonial burials, reflected by the presence of clearly associated decorative or other grave goods in association with human burials—as documented for example at Cro-Magnon in France, Cueva Morín in northern Spain, and apparently Mladeč in Czechoslovakia (Oliva 1993).
11. The emergence of what appear to be more selective and highly specialized hunting activities, focused on a single species of game. The best examples of this are provided by the highly specialized reindeer-dominated faunal assemblages from French sites, in some cases showing up to 99 per cent of this species in the early Upper Palaeolithic levels (Boyle 1988).
12. In at least some of the better documented areas of Europe (such as western France and Czechoslovakia) a sharp increase in the total numbers of occupied sites, apparently reflecting a marked increase in human population densities (Mellars 1973; Oliva 1993).

The spectrum of innovations listed above is impressive in both its range and in the dramatic nature of many of the innovations involved—especially perhaps those in the spheres of bone and antler technology, and in the extraordinary proliferation of new forms of personal ornamentation and remarkably sophisticated art. Many workers have characterized this transition as pre-eminently a 'symbolic explosion'. How far this transition reflects not merely a technological revolution, but also some fundamental restructuring in human cognitive and communication patterns—perhaps involving the emergence of much more highly structured language and related symbolic thought—has dominated much of the literature over the past decade (e.g. Donald 1991; Bickerton 1995; Mithen 1996; Pinker 1995; Mellars 1991, 1998*b*, etc.).

The central question in the present context, of course, is exactly how the two parallel developments outlined above—i.e. the biological transition from Neanderthal to anatomically modern populations, and the broadly synchronous archaeological transition from Middle to Upper Palaeolithic culture—were related. It is this question which lies at the heart of the current debate over the population-replacement versus regional-continuity models for the appearance of *Homo sapiens* populations throughout Europe. In my own view, the critical importance of the European evidence lies in our ability effectively to demonstrate beyond reasonable doubt that, at least in this part of the world, there was indeed a major episode of population dispersal—and ultimately population replacement—associated with the first appearance of characteristically modern human anatomy, and that the same episode of population dispersal was responsible for the massive sweep of radical cultural and behavioural innovations reflected so clearly in the archaeological evidence. What follows is a review of the relevant evidence to support this rather sweeping assertion (Mellars 1989*a*, 1992, 1996*c*, 1999*a*, 1999*b*).

Arguably the most striking feature of the European archaeological record is the close association of all the major behavioural innovations listed above with one specific and highly distinctive archaeological entity—the so-called 'Aurignacian'. In terms of the European evidence, the Aurignacian *is* the 'Upper Palaeolithic revolution'. The first appearance of many new forms of stone tools, improved methods of both blade and (more significantly) bladelet technology, complex and elaborate bone, antler, and ivory tools, literally thousands of perforated sea shells, animal teeth, and other forms of personal ornaments, bird-bone flutes, elaborately notched and incised bones, the first explicitly ceremonial burials, and the immensely impressive art reflected in the vulvar and phallic symbols of western France, the animal and human statuettes of southern Germany, and the extraordinarily sophisticated cave art from the recently discovered

Chauvet cave in south-east France (Chauvet *et al.* 1995), are all associated specifically with Aurignacian technologies (see Figures 2.1–2.3). In at least some areas these were associated with a sharp increase in the total numbers of occupied sites, the appearance of clearly structured occupation sites, and in some contexts the liberal use of powdered red ochre scattered across occupation surfaces. All these behavioural innovations appear within a time-span of at most 2,000–3,000 years in the individual regions of Europe, and in each case the first clearly documented archaeological associations are with the local occurrence of Aurignacian technologies (Mellars 1992, 1996*a*; Knecht *et al.* 1993).

Stated briefly, the reasons for believing that the Aurignacian represents the widespread dispersal of a new human population across Europe can be reduced to four basic observations (see Mellars 1992, 1996*a*, 1996*b*, 1999*b*; Kozlowski 1993, 1996):

1. Unlike any other subsequent phase of the European Upper Palaeolithic sequence, the distinctive features of Aurignacian technology (i.e. carinate and nosed scrapers, edge-retouched Aurignacian blades, small inversely retouched Font-Yves and Dufour bladelets, etc.) can be traced across effectively the entire span of western, central, and eastern Europe, extending from the Atlantic coasts of Spain and Portugal (and indeed southern Britain, as discussed below) in the west, to the Levantine coast of Lebanon and Israel in the east. As many workers have pointed out, the distinctive stone-tool industries recovered from sites such as Hayonim and Kebara in Israel and Ksar Akil in Lebanon are closely similar to those recovered from the classic Aurignacian localities in western France which were used to formulate the original definition of the Aurignacian in the last century (e.g. Bordes 1968; Bar-Yosef and Belfer Cohen 1988; Ohnuma and Bergman 1990). Most striking of all perhaps is the geographical distribution of the highly distinctive split-base bone and antler spear-head forms, which can be traced in a broad arc extending from Cantabria and the Pyrenees, through most areas of central, eastern, and south-eastern Europe, to at least three separate sites (Kebara, Hayonim, and El Q'esir) in northern Israel (see Figure 2.4). At no other point in the Eurasian Upper Palaeolithic sequence can we observe such a remarkable uniformity in technology extending across such a wide expanse of contrasting geographical and ecological zones.[2]

[2] A finer analysis of these early Aurignacian industries could be taken to suggest a division into two geographically separate subgroupings: an essentially classic Aurignacian distributed mainly to the north and west of the Alps, and a more southern or Mediterranean facies, characterized by high frequencies of small, retouched bladelet forms, distributed mainly along the Mediterranean coast (Kozlowski 1993, 1996). These could well reflect two separate routes of dispersal of the early *Homo sapiens* populations across Europe (Mellars 1999*b*).

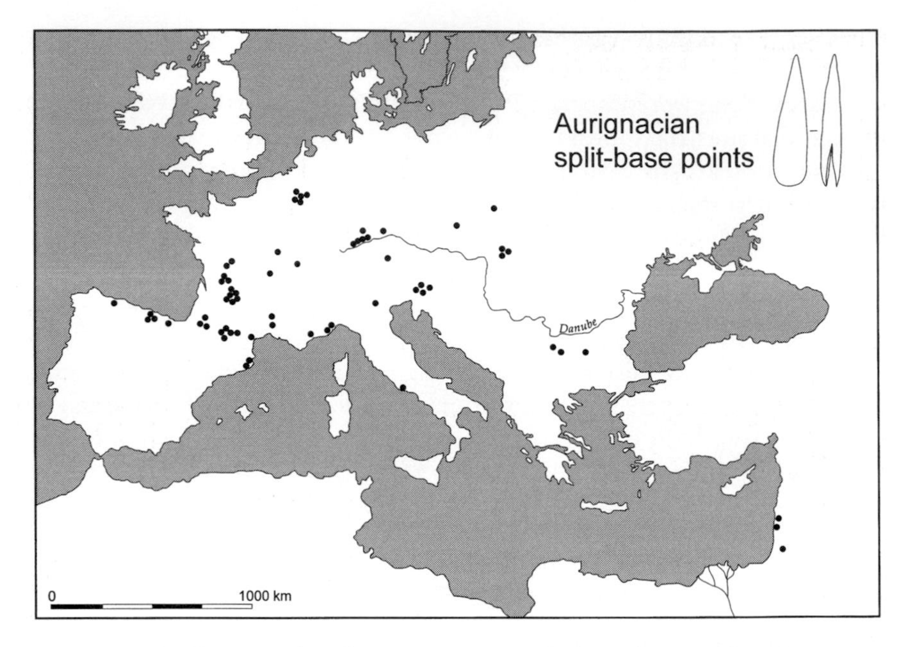

FIG. 2.4 Distribution of early Aurignacian split-base bone and antler points across Europe and the Near East, apparently reflecting strong continuities in technology across this region around 34–38,000 years ago.

2. In most if not all regions of Europe the first appearance of Aurignacian technologies appears to present an abrupt contrast with the preceding patterns of local (Middle Palaeolithic) technologies, and has been interpreted almost invariably by local workers as a clearly intrusive phenomenon (Mellars 1992, 1996*a*, with references; Kozlowski 1993, 1996, etc.). Certainly, no convincing case has ever been made out for a specifically local origin of Aurignacian technology in Europe. The contrast between the relative uniformity of Aurignacian technology and the highly variable character of the immediately preceding Middle Palaeolithic technologies within the different regions of Europe is especially significant in this context (Kozlowski 1992, 1993; Mellars 1992).

3. The available chronological evidence appears to reinforce the same pattern. While radiocarbon dating must be handled with great caution in the 30–45,000-year time range owing to the potentially dramatic effects of contamination by even miniscule quantities of intrusive modern carbon in these very old samples (Aitken 1990; Mellars 1999*b*) the overall pattern of the available radiocarbon and other dates summarized in Figure 2.5 is at

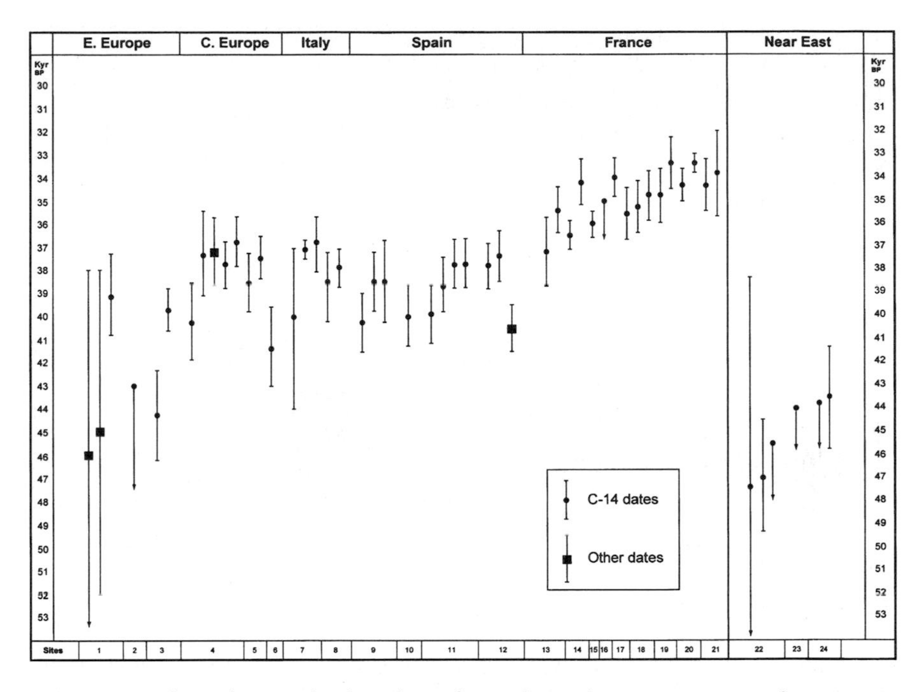

FIG. 2.5 Radiocarbon and other dates from the earliest appearance of Aurignacian and related technologies in different areas of Europe—apparently reflecting the spread of early *Homo sapiens* populations.

Note: Dates for the earliest Upper Palaeolithic industries in the Near East are shown on the right for comparison. Note that the dates produced by thermoluminescence (TL) and Uranium-series methods have been adjusted by between 1,000 and 4,000 years to allow direct comparison with radiocarbon ages over this time range, following the provisional calibration curves of Laj *et al.* (1966) and Voelker *et al.* (1998). The sites shown are as follows: 1. Temnata; 2. Bacho Kiro; 3. Istállósko; 4. Geissenklösterle; 6. Trou Magrite; 7. Riparo Fumane; 8. Grotta Paina; 9. El Castillo; 10. Reclau Viver; 11. L'Arbreda; 12. Abric Romani; 13. Abri Caminade; 14. Isturitz; 15. La Rochette; 16. La Ferrassie; 17. Combe Saunière; 18. Abri Castanet; 19. Roc de Combe; 20. Abri Pataud; 21. Le Flagéolet; 22. Boker Tachtit; 23. Ksar Akil; 24. Kebara.

Sources: Mellars 1992, 1999*a*, 1999*b*; Zilhao and d'Errico 1999; and other sources.

least consistent with a significantly earlier occurrence of this technology in the east European and Levantine areas than in areas further to the north and west. The precise origins of Aurignacian technology remain more controversial. However, there are strong grounds for looking for the earliest emergence of this technology in sites such as Ksar Akil in the Lebanon, or possibly Bacho Kiro in Bulgaria, than in any other areas further to the north or west (Ohnuma and Bergman 1990; Kozlowski 1992). Equally significant is the fact that in these east Mediterranean areas the earliest Aurignacian industries are preceded by a series of demonstrably earlier Upper Palaeolithic (or 'proto-Upper Palaeolithic') technologies, which seem to extend back to at least 45–47,000 BP, and which can provide a much more plausible ancestry for the eventual emergence of the Aurignacian in these areas than in any area of Europe (Marks 1993; Bar-Yosef 1994, 1998*b*).

4. Finally, whenever characteristically Aurignacian industries have been found in association with well documented human skeletal remains, these remains seem invariably to be of characteristically anatomically modern form. The best associations of this kind are those from Mladeč in Czechoslovakia and Vogelherd in south Germany, with similar associations apparently at La Crouzade, Les Rois, and (more questionably) Cro-Magnon itself in France (Stringer and Gamble 1993; Gambier 1993). It is debatable whether any of these finds date from the very earliest phases of the Aurignacian (before *c.*35,000 BP) but if all of the documented skeletal associations from the middle and later stages of the Aurignacian are of anatomically modern form, the reasonable assumption is that the same applies to the immediately preceding stages. Certainly no convincing case has ever been made out for a reliable association between the Aurignacian and distinctively Neanderthal skeletal remains, in either Europe or the Middle East.

COLONIZATION SCENARIOS

If we accept that the Aurignacian does indeed represent the archaeological signature of the *Homo sapiens* colonization of Europe, this in turn raises interesting questions of exactly how this colonization was achieved, in both demographic and ecological terms. A discussion of this whole topic would no doubt require an article, if not a monograph, in its own right, and raises questions comparable with those discussed in several of the other papers in this volume. In essence, however, I would suggest that two critical factors are likely to have been involved (Mellars 1992, 1996*b*, 1998*a*, 1999*b*). The first is the purely demographic issue of an increase in population numbers. Presumably any process of human population dispersal must involve some substantial increase in population numbers, not only to fuel the initial process of geographical expansion, but also to sustain this process throughout the whole period of colonization of new territories. The most obvious catalyst for such an expansion, as in the in many ways analogous dispersal of the earliest agricultural communities across Europe (Bar-Yosef 1998*b*), would be an increase in the efficiency and productivity of subsistence systems. At this point we delve largely into the realms of speculation, since one of the aspects of modern human origins on which we remain least well informed is that of the precise subsistence strategies, and the associated social systems to exploit and distribute essential resources. We do nevertheless have explicit evidence for a whole range of technological innovations associated with the dispersal of the earliest anatomically modern (i.e. Aurignacian) populations across Europe, several of which would almost certainly have had a major impact on the efficiency and reliability of subsistence activities. The most obvious of these perhaps are the sudden changes in the form and complexity of the armatures of hunting weapons, which would at least seem to indicate the emergence of more efficient forms of spears and conceivably (though still entirely speculatively) the first appearance of bows and arrows (Knecht 1993). Equally if not more important, however, could have been largely invisible changes in the social mechanisms for the organization of subsistence activities (such as the emergence of increasingly integrated and co-operative hunting parties) and similar processes for the more effective distribution of food resources or their storage over periods of seasonal or annual food scarcity. The emergence of more complex and efficient language could of course have had a dramatic effect on all these aspects of economic and social organization—for example by helping to disseminate information on the variable distribution and movements of animals or other resources, or for predicting the seasonal migrations of animals (Whallon 1989; Donald 1991; Mellars 1991, 1998*b*; Bickerton 1995; Pinker 1995). While all these aspects at present remain only dimly visible in the archaeological record, there is no reason to doubt that collectively they could have had a dramatic impact on the capacity of the earliest anatomically modern populations in Europe both to increase the quantities of food produced per unit area of land, and to distribute this more efficiently both between different social segments of the communities and over periodic episodes of food scarcity or failure. These developments in turn could have had a major impact on the potential rates of increase of population numbers, and their capacity to colonize a range of new and ecologically unfamiliar territories.

The second factor which is likely to have played a major role in the process of population dispersal lies in the pattern of climatic fluctuations around the middle of the last glaciation. We now have a battery of evidence derived from studies of climatic records in arctic and antarctic ice cores, detailed pollen sequences through extinct lake basins, studies of associated insect remains, etc., to show that among the complex sequence of climatic oscillations during this period (the period of so-called 'oxygen isotope stage 3') there were two closely spaced episodes of sharply warmer climate, dating in radiocarbon terms to between *c.*43,000 and 38,000 BP. These episodes are known to have seen a rapid increase in average annual temperatures by at least 5–7° C, and to have allowed the expansion of scattered coniferous or deciduous woodland along at least the Mediterranean coast of Europe, and perhaps along the Danube valley (Van Andel and Tzedakis 1996; Van Andel 1998; Voelker *et al.* 1998). For populations originating in the temperate, forested environments of the east Mediterranean zone, this would inevitably have made a process of population dispersal into areas to the north and west much easier to achieve. As I have suggested elsewhere, it might perhaps have amounted to little more than what we might refer to (slightly flippantly) as 'surfing the ecological tide' (Mellars 1996*b*, 1998*a*). In any event, there can now be no doubt that this period of climatic warming coincides closely with the initial dispersal of Aurignacian populations across Europe, and it is reasonable to see this as a major factor in the precise timing and geographical pattern of this population expansion. As discussed further below, the same episodes of rapid climatic and ecological change could well have acted to destabilize some of the local adaptations of the latest Neanderthal communities in Europe, perhaps creating large areas of effectively empty or very sparsely populated landscapes into which the new populations could expand. Certainly, all of the available radiocarbon and other dating evidence suggests this process of population dispersal was achieved very rapidly, reaching both the Atlantic coasts of northern Spain and the western parts of the Danube valley by, or very shortly after, 40,000 BP in radiocarbon terms (Cabrera Valdés *et al.* 1996; Mellars 1999*a*, 1999*b*). (See note added in press, page 61).

Exactly how these new populations impinged on, and interacted with, the pre-existing Neanderthal populations in the different regions of Europe raises a further range of intriguing and still highly controversial issues, which have stimulated some lively debate in the recent literature (Graves 1991; d'Errico *et al.* 1998; Mellars 1998*b*, 1999*a*; Duarte *et al.* 1999; Tattersall and Schwartz 1999). Stated briefly, the available dating evidence now leaves no realistic doubt that in at least certain regions of Europe the final Neanderthal populations did survive for a period of at least several thousand years broadly alongside the new, intrusive populations of modern humans. We can document this especially clearly in western Europe, where the final Neanderthals seem to have survived down to at least 35,000 BP in areas to the north of the Pyrenees (in the form of the so-called 'Chatelperronian' culture), while the earliest Aurignacian populations were already present in the rather milder and probably more forested environments immediately to the south of the Pyrenees (in both Catalonia and on the Cantabrian coast) by around 38–40,000 BP (Cabrera-Valdés *et al.* 1996; Mellars 1999*a*, 1999*b*). There may have been a similar survival of late Neanderthal populations in the southern parts of the Iberian peninsula, and perhaps in the analogous peninsular areas of Italy and Greece (d'Errico *et al.* 1998; Duarte *et al.* 1999). Interestingly—but hardly surprisingly—there is evidence that some of these final Neanderthal populations show strong elements of acculturation from the new and culturally intrusive Aurignacian populations, in both their technology (for example the appearance of new stone tool forms, some simple bone and ivory tools, and increased levels of blade technology) and even in the appearance at one well documented site (Arcy-sur-Cure, in north-central France) of a range of perforated animal-teeth and other decorative pendants (Hublin *et al.* 1996; d'Errico *et al.* 1998; Mellars 1999*a*). The skeletal remains recovered from Saint-Césaire (Charente-Maritime) and Arcy-sur-Cure show unquestionably that these acculturated technologies were manufactured by Neanderthals (Lévêque and Vandermeersch 1980; Hublin *et al.* 1996).[3] Similar patterns may be discernible in parts of central and eastern Europe, in the form of the various Szeletian and related leaf-point technologies (Allsworth-Jones 1990; Kozlowski 1996). All of this may well indicate that the European Neanderthals had significantly greater intellectual capacities for more complex behavioural patterns than some earlier authors have given them credit for. Nevertheless, all the available evidence indicates that the Neanderthals did eventually become extinct, probably as a direct result of the progressive increase in the population numbers of the anatomically modern populations and the consequent increasing competition for ecological space and economic resources (Zubrow 1989; Mellars 1996*b*, 1998*a*). The final *coup de grâce* for the Neanderthals may well have been delivered by a sudden return to very much colder climatic conditions around 35,000 BP—an episode referred to by palaeoclimatologists as 'Heinrich event 4' (Voelker *et al.* 1998; Van Andel 1998; Mellars 1998*a*). After over 200,000 years of highly successful adaptation to the harsh, glacial environments of western Europe, the adaptive capacities of the final Neanderthal populations ultimately seem to have been no match for those of their new, biologically and behaviourally modern human competitors in this final ecological challenge.

AFRICAN ORIGINS

However intriguing the dispersal of *Homo sapiens* populations across Europe may seem to a European audience, this is of course only one piece in the overall jigsaw of modern human origins on a world-wide scale. If we

[3] It has been suggested that the recently discovered human skeleton from the site of Lagar Velho in Portugal may indicate some interbreeding between the late Neanderthals and early modern humans in the Iberian peninsula—though this at present remains highly controversial (Duarte *et al.* 1999; Tattersall and Schwartz 1999).

accept all the arguments advanced from the recent studies of both human skeletal remains and the associated studies of DNA and other genetic variations in present-day world populations, then by far the most likely point of origin of our species lies in Africa (Stringer and McKie 1996; Lahr and Foley 1998). The challenge to archaeologists is obvious. How far can we identify evidence that distinctively modern patterns of technology and behaviour—broadly analogous to those reflected in the European Upper Palaeolithic—were indeed significantly earlier in Africa than in areas further to the north and west?

Here we immediately encounter the two interlinked problems of the sheer size and ecological diversity of the African continent (over three times the size of Europe) and the comparative scarcity of archaeological research focused specifically on the problems of modern human origins in most areas of Africa, compared to that in the intensively explored regions of Europe. The interpretation of the intriguing but very patchy archaeological record in Africa certainly remains more controversial than that in Europe (Deacon 1989; Thackeray 1992; Clark 1992; Yellen *et al.* 1995; Henshilwood and Sealy 1997; Ambrose 1998; Klein 1994, 1998). Nevertheless on one point there now seems to be a consensus: that at least in the southern parts of Africa there is evidence for the appearance of certain distinctively modern features of both technology and apparently increased symbolic behaviour at a substantially earlier date than in any areas of either Europe or Asia (though it should be recalled that large areas of Asia are still largely a blank on the archaeological map). The most explicit evidence at present comes from a number of sites close to the southern tip of Africa—notably those of Border Cave, Klasies River Mouth, Boomplaas Cave, and the newly excavated site of Blombos Cave, all in Cape Province. From the site of Klasies River Mouth, for example, we have evidence for stone-tool industries which are in most respects remarkably similar to those from the classic Upper Palaeolithic sites in Europe, provisionally dated by several dating methods to around 65–80,000 BP. These so-called 'Howiesons Poort' industries combine high levels of blade technology with typical small end-scraper forms, and a range of small, elegantly shaped trapeze and crescent forms which almost certainly represent the hafted inserts of either spears, or conceivably arrows (Singer and Wymer 1982; Deacon 1989). From the site of Blombos Cave we have a rather different industry, combining flake and blade tools with small, leaf-like, pressure-flaked projectile points, remarkably similar to those of the European Solutrian (Henshilwood and Sealy 1997). The age of the latter site may be closer to 90–100,000 BP. Equally if not more significant is the presence at both Klasies River Mouth and Blombos Cave of a number of simple but extensively shaped bone tools (far more advanced than anything ever recovered from a European Mousterian site) and the occurrence at the latter site of several large pieces of red ochre, evidently used to produce powdered pigment, including two with carefully incised criss-cross designs along their edges.

Further north in central and eastern Africa the archaeological records over the same time range remain rather poorly documented. From sites such as Mumba in Tanzania, and Enkapune ya Muto in Kenya, however, there is evidence that broadly similar, essentially Upper Palaeolithic (or Later Stone Age) industries were being manufactured by at least 50,000 BP, and at the latter site there is recently published evidence for the production of carefully shaped and perforated beads manufactured from segments of ostrich eggshell by around 40,000 BP (Ambrose 1998). Finally, immediately to the north of Africa, there is the crucially important evidence for what seem to be explicitly symbolic grave goods (including a large deer antler, and a complete boar's jaw reportedly 'clasped in the arms' of one of the skeletons) associated with the burials of the distinctively anatomically modern humans at the two sites of Djebel Qafzeh and Mugharet es Skhul in Israel, both securely dated to around 90–100,000 BP (Defleur 1993; Bar-Yosef 1994, 1998*a*). From the former site there is also evidence for the presence of deliberately perforated sea shells in the same occupation levels (Inizan and Gaillard 1978). If the latter items are indeed explicitly decorative or symbolic objects, as all the evidence suggests, they precede by at least 40–50,000 years the widespread appearance of similar perforated sea shells, animal teeth, and other forms of decorative pendants in the earliest Aurignacian levels in Europe, discussed above.

The African evidence therefore remains tantalizingly sparse and patchy, but is at least consistent with the view that many of the distinctive features of both technology and explicitly symbolic behaviour which in Europe we associate with the first appearance of anatomically modern populations, around 40,000 years ago, appeared in both Africa and apparently the immediately adjacent parts of south-west Asia in some cases 40–50,000 years earlier than this. All of this is clearly broadly consistent with the 'Out of Africa' model for the origin of our own species. The critical question remains exactly how and when these biologically and behaviourally modern populations first dispersed beyond the bounds of Africa. The initial appearance of anatomically modern populations in Israel at around 90–100,000 BP evidently did not extend into Europe—although it is conceivable that these populations expanded further to the south and east into south-east Asia and perhaps ultimately Australia (Lahr and Foley 1998; Thorne *et al.* 1999). The most likely scenario is that there was a *second* phase of dispersal of anatomically modern populations from eastern or northern Africa between 45,000 and 50,000 BP, which perhaps brought the distinctively Upper-Palaeolithic-like package of both technology and associated symbolic and ceremonial activity initially into south-west Asia (as represented for example at Boker Tachtit in Israel and Ksar Akil in Lebanon, both dated to *c.*45–47,000 BP) and subsequently into Europe (Ambrose 1998; Klein 1998; Bar-Yosef 1998*b*). In any event it is clear that all of the present evidence puts the spotlight firmly on to Africa as the most likely cradle for the emergence of the characteristically modern behavioural package which we see in the European Upper Palaeolithic. To what extent this process involved a radical restructuring not only in the actual *patterns* of human behaviour but also in the underlying mental and cognitive *capacities* for new forms of behaviour—including language—remains one of the critical questions in modern human origins research (Mellars 1991, 1998*b*; Donald 1991; Klein 1994, 1998; Pinker 1995; Bickerton 1995; Mithen 1996; Gibson 1996; Renfrew 1996; d'Errico *et al.* 1998).

THE *HOMO SAPIENS* PEOPLING OF BRITAIN

In the scenario of the *Homo sapiens* colonization of Europe outlined above, Britain of course remains a very distant and peripheral part of the picture—in the colourful words of Dorothy Garrod 'the Ultima Thule of Upper Palaeolithic Europe, a north-west cape, remote and inhospitable, bounded by the great ice sheets under which Scotland and Ireland still lay buried' (Garrod 1926: 191). Of course Garrod was working without the benefits of modern palaeoclimatic research, which as noted earlier has revealed a number of episodes of very much milder climate around the middle of the last glaciation, which at times may have brought temperatures close to modern post-glacial conditions. It is therefore not surprising to find evidence of a number of fairly short, but potentially quite intensive, episodes of Upper Palaeolithic occupation in southern Britain during these periods of sharply milder climate (Campbell 1977; Jacobi 1980).

The history of research into the British Upper Palaeolithic has unfortunately been blighted by the large-scale plundering of the available cave and rock-shelter deposits which occurred throughout the nineteenth century (especially following the publication of Darwin's *Origin of Species* in 1859), which has left only sparse and very poorly documented evidence of most of the essential finds (Garrod 1926; Campbell 1977; Jacobi 1980). In terms of the earliest evidence for Upper Palaeolithic occupation, however, we have access to three crucial pieces of information. The first has come from the application of direct radiocarbon dating (by the small-sample accelerator mass spectrometer technique) to a fragment of a human upper jaw containing two teeth recovered during the early excavations of William Pengelly in Kent's Cavern, South Devon, around 1870. The dating of this sample to around 30,900 ± 900 BP by the Oxford radiocarbon laboratory puts this firmly within the time range of the Aurignacian, as documented in the adjacent areas of western Europe, and the morphological features of the jaw fragment have been described as characteristically anatomically modern, as opposed to Neanderthal, in form (Aldhouse-Green and Pettitt 1998). If we accept that all radiocarbon dates in this age range should be regarded essentially as minimal estimates (for the reasons discussed earlier) then the true age of the sample could conceivably be rather older. Indeed, this could be seen as one of the earliest directly dated samples of *Homo sapiens* remains in Europe. The archaeological associations of this individual jaw fragment are unfortunately far from clear from the excavation records preserved at the time. There are, however, indications that at least some of the flint artefacts recovered from Pengelly's excavations at Kent's Cavern are of distinctively Aurignacian type, including several examples of carinate scrapers, and one or two specimens of busqué burin forms (Campbell 1977; Aldhouse-Green and Pettitt 1998).

Discoveries from some other nineteenth-century excavations reinforce the evidence for a definite episode of Aurignacian occupation in Britain. From the Paviland Cave in the Gower Peninsula of south Wales the early excavations of William Buckland, and subsequently William Sollas, produced a range of pieces which are typologically Aurignacian, though again in an extremely poorly documented stratigraphic context. The most explicit single piece of artefactual evidence is the absolutely classic busqué burin recovered during the early excavations in the Fynnon Beuno Cave in north Wales (Garrod 1926: 109). By analogy with comparable specimens from well excavated and well dated sites in France and Belgium, this piece almost certainly dates from the later stages of the Aurignacian, between *c.*32,000 and 30,000 BP (Sonneville-Bordes 1960). This of course could be seen to accord well with the dating of the jaw fragment from Kent's Cavern referred to above. Significantly, it is now known that a major episode of climatic warming occurred at precisely this time (the so-called 'Denekamp' or 'Arcy' interstadial) which would inevitably have facilitated an expansion of human settlement into these northern, periglacial areas of Europe (Van Andel 1998; Voelker *et al.* 1998). Indeed, the British finds stand at present as the most northerly evidence for Aurignacian occupation so far recorded in Europe—though not as yet from its very earliest phases.[4]

[4] Whether there was any human occupation in Britain during the earlier warm phases between *c.*43,000 and 35,000 BP remains more open to debate. There are certain sites characterized by large, bifacially thinned leaf-point forms, closely similar to those from sites in Belgium and central Europe, which may well belong to this period (Campbell 1977; Jacobi 1980; Aldhouse-Green and Pettitt 1998). On the present (rather sparse) evidence it seems more likely that the latter industries were produced by late Neanderthal rather than by early *Homo sapiens* populations (Allsworth-Jones 1990; Kozlowski 1996).

FIG. 2.6 Reconstruction of the human burial in the Paviland Cave, south Wales, dated to *c.*26,000 BP. The body is that of a male, liberally sprinkled with powdered red ochre and accompanied by a range of carved ivory ornaments.

The third and final piece in the British jigsaw is provided by the extraordinary discovery of the so-called 'Red Lady' skeleton in the Paviland Cave in south Wales (referred to above) encountered during the excavations by William Buckland (the first Professor of Geology at Oxford, and later Dean of Westminster) in 1823. A new programme of research into this discovery (Aldhouse-Green and Pettitt 1998) has shown that the skeleton is almost certainly that of a young male, rather than a 'lady' as originally thought, which was evidently interred in a grave containing large quantities of powdered red ochre which had subsequently coated the bones (Figure 2.6). In association with the burial was found an extraordinary collection of ornamental items, including an ivory egg-like pendant manufactured from a natural deformity in a mammoth tusk, two elaborately shaped bone rods or batons, a fragment of an ivory bracelet or ring-like form, and apparently several perforated animal teeth. Clearly, this was an elaborate ceremonial burial of the kind which is still very rare in the European Upper Palaeolithic. In view of the virtual lack of stratigraphic information surrounding the original discovery, the precise age and wider archaeological associations of the find have remained uncertain. Direct radiocarbon dating recently carried out on the actual bones of the skeleton by the Oxford laboratory, however, has produced two dates of 25,840 ± 510 and 26,350 ± 430 BP (Aldhouse-Green and Pettitt 1998). If these results are regarded once again as essentially minimum age estimates, then the original interment of the skeleton could conceivably be related to the traces of typically Aurignacian occupation in the cave referred to above. But in either case, this is clearly one of the earliest examples of a fully ceremonial human burial so far recorded from the European Upper Palaeolithic, not too far removed in time from the initial colonization of the continent by early anatomically modern human groups. The evidence for the early *Homo sapiens* occupation of Britain may therefore not be abundant, but it does add some important new dimensions to our understanding of this first great peopling of Europe by members of our own species.

Note added in press: Since the present article was written, Zilhao and d'Errico (1999) have questioned the dating of Aurignacian sites in Europe prior to *c*.36,500 (radiocarbon years) BP, and many of the associated ideas of acculturation between anatomically modern and Neanderthal populations. This contradicts the dating accepted unequivocally in an immediately preceding publication by the same authors (d'Errico *et al.* 1998: 19) as well as the interpretations proposed by the excavators of the sites themselves. A full discussion of these ideas will appear in a later publication.

REFERENCES

Aitken, M. J. (1990). *Science-Based Dating in Archaeology*. London: Longmans.

Aldhouse-Green, S., and Pettitt, P. (1998). 'Paviland Cave: contextualising the "Red Lady"', *Antiquity*, 72: 756–72.

Allsworth-Jones, P. (1990). 'The Szeletian and the stratigraphic succession in Central Europe and adjacent areas: main trends, recent results, and problems for solution', in P. Mellars (ed.), *The Emergence of Modern Humans: An Archaeological Perspective*. Edinburgh: Edinburgh University Press, 160–243.

Ambrose, S. H. (1998). 'Chronology of the Later Stone Age and food production in East Africa', *Journal of Archaeological Science*, 25: 377–92.

Bar-Yosef, O. (1994). 'The contribution of southwest Asia to the study of the origins of modern humans', in M. T. Nitecki and D. V. Nitecki (eds.), *Origins of Anatomically Modern Humans*. New York: Plenum, 23–66.

Bar-Yosef, O. (1998*a*). 'The chronology of the Middle Paleolithic of the Levant', in

T. Akazawa, K. Aoki, and O. Bar-Yosef (eds.), *Neandertals and Modern Humans in Western Asia*. New York: Plenum, 39–56.

Bar-Yosef, O. (1998*b*). 'On the nature of transitions: the Middle to Upper Palaeolithic transition and the Neolithic revolution', *Cambridge Archaeological Journal*, 8: 141–63.

Bar-Yosef, O., and Belfer Cohen, A. (1988). 'The early Upper Palaeolithic in the Levantine Caves', in J. F. Hoffecker and C. A. Wolf (eds.), *The Early Upper Palaeolithic: Evidence from Europe and the Near East*. Oxford: British Archaeological Reports International Series 437, 23–42.

Bickerton, D. (1995). *Language and Human Behavior*. Seattle: University of Washington Press.

Bordes, F. (1968). *The Old Stone Age*. London: Weidenfeld and Nicolson.

Boyle, K. V. (1988). *Upper Palaeolithic Faunas from South-west France: A Zoogeographic Perspective*. Oxford: British Archaeological Reports International Series 557.

Cabrera-Valdés, V., Valladas, H., Bernaldo de Quiros, F., and Gomez, M. H. (1996). 'La Transition Paléolithique moyen-Paléolithique supérieur à El Castillo (Cantabrie): nouvelles datations par le carbone-14', *Comptes Rendus de l'Académie des Sciences de Paris*, 322 (ser. IIa): 1093–8.

Campbell, J. B. (1977). *The Upper Palaeolithic of Britain: A Study of Man and Nature in the Later Ice Age*. Oxford: Clarendon Press.

Cann, R. L., Rickards, O., and Koji Lum, J. (1994). 'Mitochondrial DNA and human evolution: our one lucky mother', in M. H. Nitecki and D. V. Nitecki (eds.), *Origins of Anatomically Modern Humans*. New York: Plenum, 135–48.

Chauvet, J.-M., Deschamps, E. B., and Hillaire, C. (1995). *La Grotte Chauvet*. Paris: Seuil.

Clark, J. D. (1992). 'African and Asian perspectives on the origins of modern humans', in M. J. Aitken, C. Stringer, and P. Mellars (eds.), *The Origin of Modern Humans and the Impact of Chronometric Dating*. London: Royal Society (Philosophical Transactions of the Royal Society, series B, 337, no. 1280), 210–16.

Deacon, H. J. (1989). 'Late Pleistocene palaeoecology and archaeology in the Southern Cape, South Africa', in P. Mellars and C. Stringer (eds.), *The Human Revolution: Behavioural and Biological Perspectives on the Origins of Modern Humans*. Princeton: Princeton University Press, 547–64.

Defleur, A. (1993). *Les Sépultures Moustériennes*. Paris: CNRS.

d'Errico, F., Zilhao, J., Julien, M., Baffier, D., and Pelegrin, J. (1998). 'Neanderthal acculturation in western Europe? A critical review of the evidence and its interpretation', *Current Anthropology*, 39: S1–S44.

Donald, M. (1991). *Origins of the Modern Mind: Three Stages in the Evolution of Culture and Cognition*. Cambridge, Mass.: Harvard University Press.

Duarte, C., Maurício, J., Pettitt, P. B., Souto, P., Trinkaus, E., Van der Plicht, H., and Zilhao, J. (1999). 'The early Upper Paleolithic human skeleton from the Abrigo do Lagar Velho (Portugal) and modern human emergence in Iberia', *Proceedings of the National Academy of Sciences (USA)*, 96: 7604–9.

Gambier, D. (1993). 'Les Hommes modernes du début du Paléolithique supérieur en France: bilan des données anthropologiques et perspectives', in V. Cabrera-Valdés (ed.), *El Origen del Hombre Moderno en el Suroeste de Europa*. Madrid: Universidad Nacional de Educacion a Distancia, 409–30.

Garrod, D. A. E. (1926). *The Upper Palaeolithic Age in Britain*. Oxford: Clarendon Press.

Gibson, K. R. (1996). 'The biocultural human brain, seasonal migrations, and the emergence of the Upper Palaeolithic', in P. Mellars and K. Gibson (eds.), *Modelling the Early Human Mind*. Cambridge: McDonald Institute for Archaeological Research, 33–46.

Graves, P. (1991). 'New models and metaphors for the Neanderthal debate', *Current Anthropology*, 32: 513–41.

Hahn, J. (1988). *Die Geissenklösterle-Hohle in Achtal bei Blaubeuren I*. Forschungen und Berichte zur Vor- und Fruhgeschichte in Baden-Wurttemberg 26. Stuttgart: Theiss.

Hahn, J. (1993). 'Aurignacian art in Central Europe', in H. Knecht, A. Pike-Tay, and R. White (eds.), *Before Lascaux: The Complex Record of the Early Upper Paleolithic*. Boca Raton, Fla.: CRC Press, 229–42.

Harpending, H., Sherry, S., Rogers, A., and Stoneking, M. (1993). 'The genetic structure of ancient human populations', *Current Anthropology*, 34: 483–96.

Henshilwood, C., and Sealy, J. (1997). 'Bone artefacts from the Middle Stone Age at Blombos Cave, Southern Cape, South Africa', *Current Anthropology*, 38: 890–5.

Hublin, J.-J., Spoor, F., Braun, M., Zonneveld, F., and Condemi, S. (1996). 'A late Neanderthal associated with Upper Palaeolithic artefacts', *Nature*, 381: 224–6.

Inizan, M.-L., and Gaillard, J. M. (1978). 'Coquillages de Ksar-'Aqil: éléments de parure?', *Paléorient*, 4: 295–306.

Jacobi, R. M. (1980). 'The Upper Paleolithic of Britain with special reference to Wales', in J. A. Taylor (ed.), *Culture and Environment in Prehistoric Wales*. Oxford: British Archaeological Reports 76, 15–100.

Klein, R. G. (1994). 'The problem of modern human origins', in M. T. Nitecki and D. V. Nitecki (eds.), *Origins of Anatomically Modern Humans*. New York: Plenum, 3–17.

Klein, R. G. (1998). 'Why anatomically modern people did not disperse from Africa 100,000 years ago', in T. Akazawa, K. Aoki, and O. Bar-Yosef (eds.), *Neandertals and Modern Humans in Western Asia*. New York: Plenum, 509–21.

Knecht, H. (1993). 'Splits and wedges: the techniques and technology of early Aurignacian antler working', in H. Knecht, A. Pike-Tay, and R. White (eds.), *Before Lascaux: The Complex Record of the Early Upper Paleolithic*. Boca Raton, Fla.: CRC Press, 137–62.

Knecht, H., Pike-Tay, A., and White, R. (1993) (eds.). *Before Lascaux: The Complex Record of the Early Upper Paleolithic*. Boca Raton, Fla.: CRC Press.

Kozlowski, J. K. (1992). 'The Balkans in the Middle and Upper Palaeolithic: the gateway to Europe or a cul-de-sac?', *Proceedings of the Prehistoric Society*, 58: 1–20.

Kozlowski, J. K. (1993). 'L'Aurignacien en Europe et au Proche Orient', in L. Banesz and J. K. Kozlowski (eds.), *Aurignacian en Europe et au Proche Orient*. Bratislava: Acts of 12th International Congress of Prehistoric and Protohistoric Sciences, 283–91.

Kozlowski, J. K. (1996). 'Cultural context of the last Neanderthals and early modern humans in central-eastern Europe', in M. Piperno (ed.), *The Lower and Middle Palaeolithic: Colloquia*. Forlí (Italy): XIII International Congress of Prehistoric and Protohistoric Sciences, 205–18.

Krings, M., Stone, A., Schmitz, R. W., Krainitzki, H., Stoneking, M., and Paabo, S. (1997). 'Neandertal DNA sequences and the origin of modern humans', *Cell*, 90: 19–30.

Lahr, M. M., and Foley, R. (1998). 'Towards a theory of modern human origins: geography, demography and diversity in recent human evolution'. *Yearbook of Physical Anthropology*, 41: 137–76.

Laj, C., Mazaud, A., and Duplessy, J.-C. (1996). 'Geomagnetic intensity and 14C abundance in the atmosphere and ocean during the past 50 kyr', *Geophysical Research Letters*, 23: 2045–8.

Lévêque, F., and Vandermeersch, B. (1980). 'Découverte de restes humains dans un niveau castelperronien à Saint-Césaire (Charente-Maritime)', *Comptes Rendus de l'Académie des Sciences de Paris*, 291: 187–9.

Marks, A. E. (1993). 'The early Upper Paleolithic: the view from the Levant', in H. Knecht, A. Pike-Tay, and R. White (eds.), *Before Lascaux: The Complex Record of the Early Upper Paleolithic*. Boca Raton, Fla.: CRC Press, 5–22.

Marshack, A. (1991). *The Roots of Civilization*. Mount Kisco: Moyer Bell.

Mellars, P. A. (1973). 'The character of the Middle-Upper Palaeolithic transition in south-west France', in C. Renfrew (ed.), *The Explanation of Culture Change: Models in Prehistory*. London: Duckworth, 255–76.

Mellars, P. A. (1989*a*). 'Major issues in the emergence of modern humans', *Current Anthropology*, 30: 349–85.

Mellars, P. A. (1989*b*). 'Technological changes across the Middle-Upper Palaeolithic transition: technological, social and cognitive perspectives', in P. Mellars and C. Stringer (eds.), *The Human Revolution: Behavioural and Biological Perspectives on the Origins of Modern Humans*. Edinburgh: Edinburgh University Press, 338–65.

Mellars, P. A. (1991). 'Cognitive changes and the emergence of modern humans in Europe', *Cambridge Archaeology Journal*, 1: 63–76.

Mellars, P. A. (1992). 'Archaeology and the population-dispersal hypothesis of modern human origins in Europe', in M. J. Aitken, C. B. Stringer, and P. A. Mellars (eds.), *The Origin of Modern Humans and the Impact of Chronometric Dating*, London: Royal Society (Philosophical Transactions of the Royal Society, series B, 337, no. 1280), 225–34.

Mellars, P. A. (1996*a*). *The Neanderthal Legacy: An Archaeological Perspective from Western Europe*. Princeton: Princeton University Press.

Mellars, P. A. (1996*b*). 'Models for the dispersal of anatomically modern populations across Europe: theoretical and archaeological perspectives', in M. Piperno (ed.), *The Lower and Middle Palaeolithic: Colloquia*. Forlí (Italy): XIII International Congress of Prehistoric and Protohistoric Sciences, 225–37.

Mellars, P. A. (1996*c*). 'The emergence of biologically modern populations in Europe: a social and cognitive "revolution"?', in W. G. Runciman, J. Maynard-Smith, and R. I. M. Dunbar (eds.), *Evolution of Social Behaviour Patterns in Primates and Man*. London: The British Academy (Proceedings of the British Academy, vol. 88), 179–202.

Mellars, P. A. (1998*a*). 'The impact of climatic changes on the demography of late Neanderthal and early anatomically modern populations in Europe', in T. Akazawa, K. Aoki, and O. Bar-Yosef (eds.), *Neanderthals and Modern Humans in Western Asia*. New York: Plenum, 493–507.

Mellars, P. A. (1998*b*). 'Neanderthals, modern humans and the archaeological evidence for language', in N. G. Jablonski and L. C. Aiello (eds.), *The Origin and Diversification of Language*. San Francisco: California Academy of Sciences, 89–115.

Mellars, P. A. (1999*a*). 'The Neanderthal problem continued', *Current Anthropology*, 40: 341–50.

Mellars, P. A. (1999*b*). 'Radiocarbon dating and the origins of anatomically modern populations in Europe', in A. Harding (ed.), *Experiment and Design: Essays in Honour of John Coles*. Oxford: Oxbow, 1–12.

Mithen, S. (1996). *The Prehistory of the Mind: A Search for the Origins of Art, Religion and Science*. London: Thames and Hudson.

Ohnuma, K., and Bergman, C. A. (1990). 'A technological analysis of the Upper Palaeolithic levels (XXV–VI) of Ksar Akil, Lebanon', in P. Mellars (ed.), *The Emergence of Modern Humans: An Archaeological Perspective*. Edinburgh: Edinburgh University Press, 56–80.

Oliva, M. (1993). 'The Aurignacian in Czechoslovakia', in H. Knecht, A. Pike-Tay, and R. White (eds.), *Before Lascaux: The Complex Record of the Early Upper Paleolithic*. Boca Raton, Fla.: CRC Press.

Pinker, S. (1995). *The Language Instinct*. Harmondsworth: Penguin Books.

Relethford, J. H. (1998). 'Genetics of modern human origins and diversity', *Annual Review of Anthropology*, 27: 1–23.

Renfrew, C. (1996). 'The sapient behaviour paradox: how to test for potential?', in P. Mellars and K. Gibson (eds.), *Modelling the Early Human Mind*. Cambridge: McDonald Institute for Archaeological Research, 11–14.

Shreeve, J. (1995). *The Neandertal Enigma: Solving the Mystery of Human Origins*. Harmondsworth: Penguin/Viking.

Simmons, T. (1994). 'Archaic and modern *Homo sapiens* in the contact zones: evolutionary schematics and model predictions', in M. T. Nitecki and D. V. Nitecki (eds.), *Origins of Anatomically Modern Humans*. New York: Plenum, 201–25.

Singer, R., and Wymer, J. (1982). *The Middle Stone Age at Klasies River Mouth in South Africa*. Chicago: University of Chicago Press.

Sonneville-Bordes, D. de. (1960). *Le Paléolithique Supérieur en Périgord*. Bordeaux: Delmas.

Stoneking, M., Sherry, S. T., Redd, A. J., and Vigilant, L. (1992). 'New approaches to dating suggest a recent age for the human DNA ancestor', in M. Aitken, C. B. Stringer, and P. A. Mellars (eds.), *The Origin of Modern Humans and the Impact of Chronometric Dating*. London: Royal Society (Philosophical Transactions of the Royal Society, series B, 337, no. 1280), 167–76.

Stringer, C., and Gamble, C. (1993). *In Search of the Neanderthals: Solving the Puzzle of Human Origins*. London: Thames and Hudson.

Stringer, C. B., and McKie, R. (1996). *African Exodus: The Origins of Modern Humanity*. London: Jonathan Cape.

Taborin, Y. (1993). 'Shells of the French Aurignacian and Gravettian', in H. Knecht, A. Pike-Tay, and R. White (eds.), *Before Lascaux: The Complex Record of the Early Upper Paleolithic*. Boca Raton, Fla.: CRC Press, 211–28.

Tattersall, I. (1995). *The Last Neanderthal: The Rise, Success and Mysterious Extinction of our Closest Human Relative*. New York: Macmillan.

Tattersall, I., and Schwartz, J. H. (1999). 'Hominids and hybrids: the place of Neanderthals in human evolution', *Proceedings of the National Academy of Sciences (USA)*, 96: 7117–19.

Thackeray, A. I. (1992). 'The Middle Stone Age south of the Limpopo River', *Journal of World Prehistory*, 6: 385–440.

Thorne, A., Grün, R., Mortimer, G., Spooner, N. A., Simpson, J. J., McCulloch, M., Taylor, L., and Curnoe, D. (1999). 'Australia's oldest human remains: age of the Lake Mungo 3 skeleton', *Journal of Human Evolution*, 36: 591–612.

Tishkoff, S. A., Dietzsch, E., Speed, W., Pakstis, A. J., Kidd, J. R., Cheung, K., Bonné-Tamir, B., Santachiara-Benerecetti, A. S., Moral, P., Krings, M., Paabo, S., Watson, E., Risch, N., Jenkins, T., and Kidd, K. K. (1996). 'Global patterns of linkage disequilibrium at the CD4 locus and modern human origins', *Science*, 271: 1380–7.

Valladas, H., Mercier, N., Joron, J.-L., and Reyss, J.-L. (1998). 'GIF laboratory dates for Middle Paleolithic Levant', in T. Akazawa, K. Aoki, and O. Bar-Yosef (eds.), *Neandertals and Modern Humans in Western Asia*. New York: Plenum, 69–76.

Van Andel, T. H. (1998). 'Middle and Upper Palaeolithic environments and the calibration of 14C dates beyond 10,000 BP', *Antiquity*, 72: 26–33.

Van Andel, T. H., and Tzedakis, P. C. (1996). 'Palaeolithic landscapes of Europe and environs, 150,000–25,000 years ago', *Quaternary Science Reviews*, 15: 481–500.

Voelker, A. H. L., Sarnthein, M., Grootes, P. M., Erlenkeuser, H., Laj, C., Mazaud, A., Nadeau, M.-J., and Schleicher, M. (1998). 'Correlation of marine 14C Ages from the Nordic seas with the GISP2 isotope record: implications for 14C calibration beyond 25 ka BP', *Radiocarbon*, 40, 1: 517–34.

Whallon, R. (1989). 'Elements of cultural change in the later Palaeolithic', in P. Mellars and C. Stringer (eds.), *The Human Revolution: Behavioural and Biological Perspectives on the Origins of Modern Humans*. Edinburgh: Edinburgh University Press, 433–54.

White, R. (1993). 'Technological and social dimensions of "Aurignacian age" body ornaments across Europe', in H. Knecht, A. Pike-Tay, and R. White (eds.), *Before Lascaux: The Complex Record of the Early Upper Paleolithic*. Boca Raton, Fla.: CRC Press, 277–300.

Wolpoff, M. H., and Caspari, R. (1997). *Race and Human Evolution*. New York: Simon & Schuster.

Yellen, J. E., Brooks, A. S., Cornelissen, E., Mehlman, M. J., and Stewart, K. (1995). 'A Middle Stone Age worked bone industry from Katanda, upper Semliki valley, Zaire', *Science*, 268: 553–6.

Zilhao, J., and d'Errico, F. (1999). 'The chronology and taphonomy of the earliest Aurignacian and its implications for the understanding of Neandertal extinction', *Journal of World Prehistory*, 13: 1–68.

Zubrow, E. (1989). 'The demographic modelling of Neanderthal extinction', in P. Mellars and C. Stringer (eds.), *The Human Revolution: Behavioural and Biological Perspectives on the Origins of Modern Humans*. Princeton: Princeton University Press, 212–31.

COMMENT

End of Story?

Andrew Sherratt

WITHOUT wishing to dissuade the reader from penetrating further into this volume, there is a sense in which the story it tells is now almost over. By this I mean that with the arrival of behaviourally complex human beings, the potential was present for all the complicated arrangements of human society, and their increasing impacts on the natural world, which we shall see unfolding in the next 20–30,000 years. The cultural developments will indeed be remarkable: the formation of farming communities numbered in hundreds and thousands, beginning by 10,000 years ago; or the first cities and manufacturing communities which appeared 5,000 years later; and the industrial and electronic revolutions which came about 5,000 years after that. But the people responsible for these massive changes were in biological terms practically identical, and were only trivially different genetically either from each other, or from the creators of the cave-paintings and engravings which are illustrated in this chapter. So the biological part of the story of human emergence is largely over; and the rest, if not history, very soon will be—from now onwards we are looking at a process of culturally driven change. Genetics does not become irrelevant, but it is not what is making the running: it is helping to track the consequences of changes which are primarily the result of social decisions.

What makes the changes described in this chapter so fascinating, but at the same time so intellectually challenging, is the fact that the problem is at the same time both a biological and a cultural one. It is not just a straight handover from the biological to the social sciences, it is the most complicated possible mixture of both. This is immediately evident in the different lines of evidence, from at least three different disciplines, which converge on the reconstruction which Paul Mellars has put forward. It is only by combining both the genetic evidence, the anatomical evidence, and the archaeology, that we can understand what was going on. But my point is really a more fundamental one, and is not just about the methodologies used in reconstructing it, but about the nature of the process itself. The transition to modern *Homo sapiens* was a unique and unrepeatable kind of change, for which there is literally no comparison. We can study the genetic evolution of primates and other mammals; and we can study the further cultural development of humanity; but never again will we encounter the intensity of co-evolution between biology and culture which gave rise to modern humans.

Geneticists have given special attention in recent years to what is called the Baldwin Effect, which is the way in which organisms offer themselves (as it were) as candidates for natural selection, through the flexibility of their behavioural patterning (Dennett 1991: 182–7; Deacon 1997: 322–8). It is a perfectly respectable Darwinian process, but it is the point which Lamarck was trying to grasp and did not quite get right, that behavioural plasticity helps to set the parameters within which natural selection and genetic assimilation take place. Behaviour is, in effect, part of the created environment of complex organisms: they play a part in constructing their own niches.

Now it was precisely this kind of interaction between behavioural complexity and genetic change which lay behind the very rapid evolutionary processes which took early hominids from the African savannas to the British Isles in a little over 2 million years. Although biological anthropologists and archaeologists study different kinds of evidence, in the form of anatomical changes and the development of stone tools, they do not doubt that what they are studying are parts of the same process, which is one of feedback between biology and culture. But, at some point, this process came to an end. A couple of years ago, the geneticist Steve Jones gave a lecture in Oxford under the title of 'Is human evolution over?'; and he came to the conclusion that the answer was, effectively, 'yes'. Of course there are still fascinating phenomena such as the evolution of lactose tolerance or sickle-cell anaemias, but in broad terms the major design changes are over, and what is left is fine tuning. If you suffer, as I do from time to time, with back problems, you may think the process was left half completed—and, in a way, you are right. Because although for 2 million years there was an intensifying feedback process between biology and culture, there came a time when culture became so complex that instead of intensifying natural selection it came instead to buffer it. Neanderthals adapted to glacial conditions by their stocky physique, their hairiness, and the anatomy of the face; but modern humans adapted to the cold by putting on fur coats. So the feedback loop which had accelerated the human lineage from *Homo habilis* to *Homo sapiens* was effectively broken, and, while culture and behaviour became progressively more complex, these changes were not assimilated genetically, except in very subtle and ultimately not very important ways. After all, even if you are not lactose-tolerant, you can still make milk into more digestible forms such as yoghurt and cheese.

This is why the emergence of modern humans presents itself as such a fascinating and challenging problem, because it is essentially on the cusp between these two situations. After an accelerating period of bio-cultural interaction, culture effectively took off on its own.

But this formulation leaves many critical questions unanswered. Did the interaction just fizzle out, or did it come to a decisive stop? In a word, was it a punctuated transition? I do not think that we necessarily have to align this question with the big ideological disputes within biology concerning punctuated or gradual evolution, and choose between the different pictures of the overall pattern of evolutionary change offered by Stephen Jay Gould and John Maynard Smith, because the transition we are considering here was such a unique phenomenon; but there is, I think, a difference in perception between biologists and archaeologists on this question, arising from their different kinds of evidence. The kind of terminology which Paul Mellars has employed, in talking of a 'human revolution' or 'symbolic explosion' in the Upper Palaeolithic, aptly summarizes how most of us (and I speak as an archaeologist) would tend to see it; and in recent years archaeologists like Steven Mithen (1996) or Iain Davidson (Noble and Davidson 1996) have carried the idea of punctuated change into the realm of evolutionary psychology, and argued for a decisive breakthrough in the human capacity for language, for instance. But, on the other hand, a very excellent recent book by the neurobiologist Terence Deacon (1997), appropriately entitled *The Symbolic Species*, argues for a gradualist scenario in which the use of symbolic modes of communication must have been present right from the very beginning, from *Homo habilis* onwards. The account which Deacon offers is in many ways a very compelling one, and I hesitate to take issue with it; but he is really rather scathing about archaeologists. In particular, he argues (Deacon 1997: 370–2) that the appearance of art and ornaments in the Upper Palaeolithic is really just a sampling problem, because of the better chances of survival of these items on stone, and particularly in caves.

That is obviously true (and very familiar to archaeologists), but I do not think it will quite do to dismiss the very marked acceleration and transformation which we see in the archaeological record. If we take just the stone tools, which are what survive best and give a fairly consistent level of representation, then it is the whole character of typology which changes—not just in terms of functional differentiation, but in terms of idiosyncratic local variation, and in the rate at which these new types change. It really does look as if culture, in the singular, gave way to cultures, in the plural; and if this is any mirror of what was going on in human minds, then potentially it reflects the emergence not just of language but of languages: i.e. localized speech communities, implying a change from a rather generalized system of oral or gestural communication to a much more complex one that had particular local expressions. All this would argue for a rather specific transition from proto-human to human.

The obvious danger in generalizing from this work is in treating what may be a special case as if it were representative of the process as a whole. I mean that what was happening in Europe, with the replacement of Neanderthals by *sapiens* populations (and this is now clearly the majority opinion) is inevitably going to look like a dramatic shift. But in many ways it now seems rather like a sideshow in the whole process. When I studied biological anthropology with David Pilbeam at Cambridge many years ago, Neanderthals were still being seen as fairly directly ancestral to modern populations—but then that was in the era of comprehensive education and equal opportunity, when everyone had to be given their chance of getting on in the world. The picture looks very different today, and Neanderthals are seen not as a stage in the emergence of modern humanity, but as a very interesting localized adaptation to the northern, glaciated world, separated from the line of direct human ancestry by half a million years. Of course, therefore, their replacement by modern human populations in Europe is going to look like a punctuated event.

So the focus of interest has swung further south, to regions where the archaeological record is much less full than it is in Europe, after 200 years of intensive investigation. Africa offers only a few regional spotlights by comparison with this general illumination, and there is as yet no definitive answer to the crucial question of if, and where, a punctuated transition to modern humanity took place. The evidence from South Africa of anatomically modern humans dating to 80,000 years ago is very suggestive, both in the technologically advanced character of the associated stone tools, and in the hints of culturally specific differences between microlithic and pressure-flaked bifacial industries at this time; but at the moment there does not seem to be the cumulative momentum which characterizes the very rapid spread and proliferation of advanced types of tools which we see in the Upper Palaeolithic of western Asia and Europe, beginning around 40,000 years ago; and there is little that we could call art in Africa until much later. But we need very much more information, especially from the last 100,000 years in east Africa, where so many of the most important transitions in earlier human evolution seem to have occurred (Bar-Yosef 1998).

The question may also be considered, however, in the wider context of when and where the major transitions in later human culture have taken place, and how the pattern of these Palaeolithic developments fits into the geography of subsequent patterns of change. For the very use of the term 'Human Revolution' is an echo of historical terminology, with its ultimate ancestor Arnold Toynbee,[1] who in a set of lectures published posthumously in 1884 first used the phrase the 'Industrial Revolution' to describe what happened in Britain in the eighteenth and nineteenth centuries. It was the great prehistorian V. Gordon Childe who generalized this terminology, and gave us the idea of a 'Neolithic Revolution' which produced farming, and an 'Urban Revolution' which marked the beginning of life in cities (Greene 1999). Neither of these great transitions took place in Europe, and interestingly they were both multiple occurrences, in that they took place, independently but in parallel, at different times in western Asia, China, and the Americas. But both farming and city life made their earliest appearance in western Asia—the Neolithic Revolution took place in the Levant, and the Urban Revolution in nearby Mesopotamia. As soon as post-glacial conditions came about, around 11,500 years ago, farming began in the Jordan valley. It was the first major manifestation of that potential for cultural complexity which was inherent in modern human behaviour; and it took place in the area which maintained its lead as a centre of cultural innovation down to the sixteenth century AD.

It remains a possibility that this was also the area in which a critical episode in the development of *Homo sapiens* took place. If we look at the record of those stone tools, then we see a rather suggestive pattern. The first consistent appearance of the blade tools which consistently accompanied modern human populations into Europe was in the Negev desert around 50,000 years ago. There is as yet no evidence for art or for ornaments at this stage, but there is subsequent evidence in Israel for what was arguably the first manifestation of the Upper Palaeolithic culture which spread across Europe, the Aurignacian. So (as with the later spread of farming and urbanization) Europe was apparently revolutionized from western Asia. What we are uncertain about, in the case of Upper Palaeolithic, is whether this was itself just the echo of what was happening further south, in Africa—so that the Levantine developments are simply the first imprint in Eurasia of what was still essentially an African focus of innovation—or whether the Levant had already assumed the innovative role which it was to play in the post-glacial period. Since the onset of Upper Palaeolithic developments occurred more or less in the middle of the last glaciation,

[1] 1852–83: father of Arnold J. Toynbee, the author of *A Study of History* (1934–61).

when the Sahara was even larger and more forbidding an obstacle to north–south contacts than it is today (or had been in the last interglacial), the existence of an independent focus of change in the Levant is not implausible; and I have sketched a possible scenario for such a process in a recent paper (Sherratt 1997*a*), on the direct analogy of the changes which took place there 40,000 years later with the beginnings of farming. It would thus be possible to imagine a situation in which *anatomically* modern humans spread from Africa to the Levant in the last interglacial, around 100,000 years ago, but only came to exhibit distinctively modern patterns of *behaviour* some 50,000 years later. These then rapidly led to the snowballing pattern of expansion which carried modern human populations into Europe and around the world, and to the manifestation of complex behaviour in artistic representation and bodily adornment. Whether this was a purely cultural change on the basis of an already existing potential for complex behaviour, or whether it was the last manifestation of the Baldwin Effect and involved some kind of neurological reorganization, is the very heart of the problem. As I said at the beginning, the transition from biocultural evolution to culture is likely to have been one of the most complex phenomena known to science, and we need to deploy analogies both from biology and from archaeology—while recognizing that they are both inadequate on their own, or even in combination.

There is one further analogy from later prehistory which may be helpful, and which points the way to a more general principle. Accounts of the origins of agriculture often fall prey to the temptation of triumphalism, in suggesting an inexorable pattern of spread once a major innovation has been achieved. But detailed reconstructions of phenomena such as the spread of farming show that this is very far from being the case; initially, it was a very discontinuous process, and rather than being a wave-like advance it notably avoided the existing heartlands of indigenous hunting and fishing populations, such as those around the Black Sea and the Baltic (Sherratt 1997*b*: 22–5). In very much the same way, as Paul Mellars has described, early *sapiens* immigrants to Europe spread from east to west (along rather similar routes) in such a way as to fit themselves around Neanderthal heartlands such as south-west France. Such a pattern of interdigitating penetration would explain why the earliest Upper Palaeolithic dates from northern Spain are significantly earlier than those from the Dordogne. It is a feature which we might describe in a colloquial phrase as the 'new kid on the block' syndrome; and it is worth recognizing specifically because it counteracts the general tendency to hindsight, in seeing something which ultimately became the successful general model as necessarily dominant from the beginning.[2] It applies equally to earlier episodes in human evolution: *Homo habilis* was apparently far less numerous than the contemporary robust varieties of australopithecines, and it was only with the successor species *Homo erectus* that hominines expanded into the niches formerly occupied by australopithecines, who were thus driven to extinction. The principle is also manifested in later periods, in the patterns of expansion of early states and empires: Phoenician colonies fitted themselves around powerful local chiefdoms such as those of the Etruscans and the Iberians, preferring to occupy relatively underpopulated areas in north Africa (thus founding Carthage); and Celtic tribes for many years successfully resisted incorporation in the Roman Empire.

There is a specific lesson which might be learned from all this, which arises from the essentially dialectical nature of the process. Neolithic (farming) and Mesolithic (foraging) cultures transformed each other by their coexistence, producing novel phenomena such as megalithic monuments as a result of their interaction (Sherratt 1997*b*: ch. 13). Romans and Celts co-evolved, sociologically speaking. Successive hominid species emerged in the context of contemporary collateral lineages. Each side influenced the other, by its very existence. So was the presence of Neanderthals really just a sideshow on the road to modern humanity, or could it in fact have been an active element in the emergence of modern human culture? After all, it was precisely in those parts of the distribution area of anatomically modern humans which were adjacent to Neanderthal populations that their potential for the elaboration of material culture first became evident. Was this behavioural complexity elicited by interaction?

Of course due allowance must be made for cultural adaptation to cold, as *sapiens* populations moved into Europe: knives and needles would have been needed for skin clothing to substitute for Neanderthal layers of fur and fat, leading to an emphasis on blades and bonework; hunting and survival technologies would have to be modified to exist in a more northerly climate during a glaciation. Upper Palaeolithic tool assemblages were performing more functions than the Mousterian toolkits of the Neanderthals. But what of art and ornament? While these, too, could be seen as in some sense adaptive to the challenge of cold conditions, by some role in social organization they could equally be seen as responses to a social environment which included a related competitor-species, and were elaborated in opposition to an existing way of life. That some form of interaction occurred between the two is indicated by the existence of what are plausibly interpreted as very late Mousterian assemblages with Upper Pal-

[2] It is a pattern widely recognized in fairy-tales, of course, in which the younger son succeeds his initially more powerful elder brother to the crown.

aeolithic technological features, although associated with the remains of Neanderthals: evidence of the acculturation of natives by newcomers. Were the newcomers equally influenced by the presence of the natives? Was the cultural complexity of the Aurignacian in some way stimulated by the presence of competitors, provoking the appearance of elaborate systems of visual symbols? This would explain the otherwise puzzling feature that the florescence of artistic activity—the 'symbolic explosion'—seems to have occurred earliest and most extensively on the outer margin of the distribution of anatomically modern humans in the late Pleistocene.

However uncertain the details of the Human Revolution, the broad pattern is clear. The initial episodes of human emergence took place in Africa; but the focus of cultural innovation shifted at some point to western Asia, where the major cultural changes of the post-glacial period took place. The British Isles were deeply affected by these developments, but played no part in initiating them. Only when the larger human community was linked by sea-routes rather than land-routes, as sailing-ships crossed the Atlantic and rounded the Cape, were these islands to attain the temporary prominence that they achieved in the Industrial Revolution.

REFERENCES

Bar-Yosef, O. (1998). 'On the nature of transitions: the Middle to Upper Palaeolithic and the Neolithic revolution', *Cambridge Archaeological Journal*, 8: 141–63.
Deacon, T. (1997). *The Symbolic Species: The Co-evolution of Language and the Human Brain*. Harmondsworth: Penguin Books.
Dennett, D. (1991). *Consciousness Explained*. Harmondsworth: Penguin Books.
Greene, K. (1999). 'V. Gordon Childe and the vocabulary of revolutionary change', *Antiquity*, 73: 97–109.
Mithen, S. (1996). *The Prehistory of the Mind*. London: Thames and Hudson.
Noble, W., and Davidson, I. (1996). *Human Evolution, Language and Mind: A Psychological and Archaeological Inquiry*. Cambridge: Cambridge University Press.
Sherratt, A. (1997*a*). 'Climatic cycles and behavioural revolutions: the emergence of modern humans and the beginning of farming', *Antiquity*, 71: 271–87.
Sherratt, A. (1997*b*). *Economy and Society in Prehistoric Europe: Changing Perspectives*. Edinburgh: Edinburgh University Press.

3

The Coming of Agriculture

People, Landscapes, and Change *c.*4000–1500 BC

Alasdair Whittle

This chapter reviews the development of agriculture in Britain and Ireland from the Neolithic period to the middle of the Bronze Age (approximately 4000 to 1500 BC in calendar years), and the associated questions of the identity of the people involved, the density of populations, and their effect on the landscape. This brief account is set in the context of the wider development of an agricultural way of life on the adjacent continental mainland, going as far back as 6000 BC in central Europe. I hope to raise questions as much as to answer them, and to concentrate wherever possible on new evidence and approaches. I should like to frame my discussion by setting out four hypotheses:

1. Overall, change was slow, but punctuated by spurts or accelerations (notably around 5500 BC, 4000 BC, and 1500 BC), whose nature is still poorly understood. This hypothesis stands in opposition to a general tendency to envisage a steadily intensifying evolution of subsistence methods, population levels, and landscapes.
2. There was much continuity of population both in continental Europe and in Britain and Ireland, but the role of colonization still needs seriously to be considered. This hypothesis seeks to re-examine both the assumption in continental research of major colonization with the onset of the Neolithic and the recent British consensus that the beginnings of the Neolithic were essentially to do with the acculturation of an indigenous population.
3. Although some landscapes had been cleared of substantial tracts of

I am very grateful to many colleagues for discussion and information, including Tim Allen, Terry Brown, Serge Cassen, Detlef Gronenborn, Karin Riedhammer, Mark Robinson, Anne Tresset and Bryan Sykes, and to Rick Schulting for comments on an earlier draft.

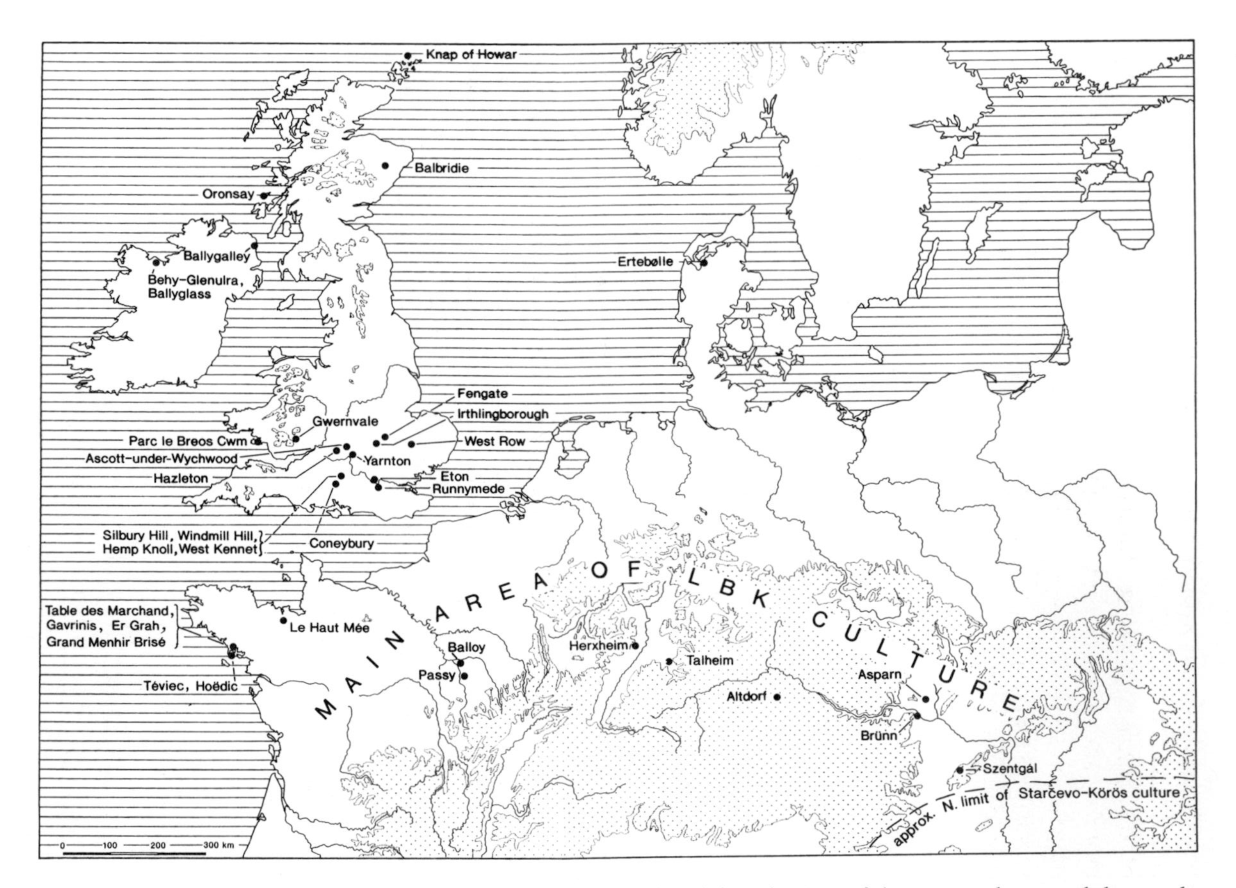

Fig. 3.1 Location of principal sites discussed, with generalized distribution of the LBK culture and the northern limits of the Starčevo-Körös culture.

woodland by about 2500–2000 BC, population levels in most parts of Britain and Ireland remained relatively low at least until the middle of the Bronze Age, and the lifestyle can be characterized by continuing mobility and/or short-term sedentism. This hypothesis restates recent opposition to the notion that the introduction of agriculture entailed sedentary existence, rapidly growing population, and intensifying production right from the start.

4. The coming of agriculture in a more familiar guise, although preceded in Britain and Ireland by herding and piecemeal cultivation from about 4000 BC, was not seen till as late as about 1500 BC onwards. This hypothesis draws attention to the recently relatively neglected changes of the middle part of the Bronze Age.

COLONIZATIONS IN THE HEART OF EUROPE?: SOME PROBLEMS AND POSSIBILITIES

It has long been widely assumed that the Neolithic way of life, involving the new subsistence technologies of cereal cultivation and animal husbandry, and associated practices of woodland clearance, sedentary existence, and craft manufacture including pottery and polished stone tools, spread across temperate Europe from south-east to north-west principally by means of colonization fuelled by population growth. This has been challenged for some regions, for example in south-east Europe from time to time (e.g. Dennell 1983) and regularly now in north-west Europe (e.g. Thomas 1991, 1996), with the alternative of indigenous acculturation mooted instead. Much less questioned has been the long held view that the first Neolithic culture of central and western Europe, the LBK (*Linienbandkeramische Kultur*), which spread from western Hungary to the Low Countries and northern France from about 5500 BC to after 5000 BC, was an intrusive population. This striking archaeological manifestation, with its substantial timber-framed longhouses, seems to set a benchmark for subsequent Neolithic developments and its status is in many ways critical to our understanding. In fact now both new questions and new methods of analysis are possible, and the LBK will form the first detailed case study of the chapter.

Carpathian basin background

Some authors have indeed questioned the status of the LBK as an intrusive pioneer agricultural population (e.g. Modderman 1988; Tillmann 1993; Whittle 1996) and more subtle readings of the evidence, involving both indigenous and external population, are beginning to emerge (e.g. Lüning

1988; Gronenborn 1997, 1998, 1999). A first step is to consider the conditions in which the LBK may have emerged.

One recurrent assumption has been that population growth or the conditions for expansion could be sought in the Neolithic populations to the immediate south, in the northern Starčevo and Körös cultures, which are to be found respectively now far up the Drava valley and as far north as Lake Balaton, and in the southern part of the Great Hungarian Plain, east of the Danube, from about 6000 to 5500 BC. On the Plain, or rather in the valley systems of this tectonic depression, there are very numerous locations with Körös culture occupation, characterized by pits and occasional above-ground structures, with rich inventories of pottery, and varied residues of animal husbandry, cereal cultivation, fishing, hunting, fowling, and shellfish collection. Formally, this population can be seen as agricultural since both cereals and domesticated animals were used, but this is to oversimplify a very broad spectrum of resource use. Moreover, the lifestyle may not have entailed a wholly sedentary existence, since site stratigraphies are generally thin, the evidence for permanent structures is relatively rare (though that may be in part a product of excavation methods), and many occupations were in riverside locations liable to flooding. There has been a tendency to treat the Körös culture settlement system as an undifferentiated whole (e.g. Sherratt 1982), but in fact it is possible to distinguish between use of old Pleistocene channels, Holocene channels, and backswamps (current research by the author, Pál Sümegi, and Kathy Willis), and it is a plausible hypothesis that occupations moved between these zones at least in part according to season. The population in question could be the product of northwards colonization by a population intrusive into south-east Europe as a whole, but could also be some kind of fusion between that source and more local population, evidence for which has been recently discovered on the northern edge of the Plain (see Whittle 1998*a*).

Another possible source for the LBK may lie west of the Danube, in the area from the middle and upper Drava up to Lake Balaton and on into eastern Austria (Kalicz *et al.* 1998; Bánffy 1996, 2000). Recent research has established the presence of a northern Starčevo culture or something resembling it in this area, but again both the lifestyle and the density of population are as yet far from clear.

The LBK expansion

The clear implication is that it is in fact very difficult to prove the hypothesis of LBK colonization when the evidence is examined in detail. The evidence can perhaps be grouped into three categories. First, there is some support for cultural and demographic continuity. LBK flint-working traditions may overlap, contrary to what is often stated, with indigenous styles in the broad area of eastern Austria, Moravia, Slovakia, and northern Hungary. Current analysis of earliest (*älteste*) LBK lithic assemblages from Brünn in Vienna will be particularly important in this respect. The physical types within LBK cemetery assemblages are said to be rather varied (Modderman 1988: 73–4), which may be at odds with the model of population intrusion from a single source. Secondly, there are substantial changes whose significance is ambiguous. The great LBK longhouses are both larger and laid out differently from such preceding structures as have been found in the Starčevo–Körös zone, and this includes now examples from the earliest phase of the LBK (e.g. in eastern Austria: Lenneis 1997). These represent therefore something very new, but innovation could have arisen as much through some process of acculturation as the inevitable outcome of colonization. There are broad distributions westwards of lithic raw materials, such as of radiolarite from a source in Szentgál north of Lake Balaton, which have been taken to signal an initial burst of colonization (Gronenborn 1997, 1998, 1999), but which could also signal new patterns of interaction and exchange in a rapidly acculturating indigenous population. Thirdly, there remains some evidence for things and some people coming in from the outside. Cereals and legumes used in the LBK are foreign to the area. There have been claims for precocious clearance and perhaps cultivations among hunter-gatherers in the Alpine zone as early as the seventh millennium BC (e.g. Erny-Rodmann *et al.* 1997; Gronenborn 1998), but even if the phenomenon can be supported it might show a Mediterranean rather than south-easterly connection. DNA analysis of early cereals is at a preliminary stage (Brown 1999), though the indications of a second phase of emmer development might be connected in some way to the LBK phenomenon. There is no specific DNA analysis yet of LBK cattle, though broader studies (e.g. Bailey *et al.* 1996) may be compatible with the introduction of new stock into central Europe from outside. It seems to remain the case that a gross distinction in size can be seen between domesticated and wild cattle in LBK contexts, from early stages (e.g. Arbogast 1998; Benecke 1994; cf. Kreuz 1990). Had local populations of cattle been domesticated *in situ*, by the indigenous population, then there should be a greater overlap of sizes. (It remains possible that indigenous people chose to obtain new domesticated stock from the outside, for a variety of reasons.) There is finally new DNA evidence for LBK human samples (Sykes 1999). Studies of mitochondrial DNA (passed through the mother) in the blood groups of modern European populations suggest that the great majority (80 per cent) are of indigenous type. Accepting current assumptions about mitochondrial mutation rates, there may have been intrusions with the arrival of anatomically modern people, then again somewhere within the late glacial period, and finally—haplotype J, with similarities to Near Eastern types—coinciding or at least overlapping with the LBK phenomenon around the sixth millennium BC; this might account for some 20 per cent of modern variation. Initial but so far limited studies of ancient DNA from LBK human samples are compatible with this picture of population of mixed descent. It remains to be seen whether this general DNA-based picture can be fitted to emerging archaeological hypotheses for an initial LBK colonization (roughly coinciding with the distribution of the *älteste LBK*) followed by a merging with local populations further to the north and west, represented among others by users of La Hoguette and Limburg pottery (Lüning 1988; Gronenborn 1997, 1998, 1999).

Much may therefore change with future research, but it is worth noting the complexities already evident once the long-assumed great colonization of central and western Europe is examined in more detail and with multiple approaches. The picture perhaps emerging now of much continuity of population but with external inputs and stimuli makes attention to the question of why the indigenous population should have changed now and so quickly—producing the first of the spurts noted above—all the more pressing. There is not the space here to deal with this in full. I have set out elsewhere a case for change among indigenous mobile hunter-gatherers, for some degree of convergence of lifestyles, and for the importance of changes in world-view as well as in subsistence methods and resources (Whittle 1996), and some of the reflections below on the situation around 4000 BC may also apply to this earlier situation. Modelling of these dimensions will be at least as important as tracking the descents of flints, cattle, cereals, and people.

FIRST FOREST FARMERS

Major characteristics of the settlement and subsistence of the LBK have been described and discussed many times (e.g. Modderman 1988; Lüning 1988, 2000; Bogucki 1988; Kreuz 1990; Bogucki and Grygiel 1993). The basic environment was of woodland, little modified by clearance. Settlement was preferred on fertile soils in the river valley systems, and took the form of ribbons and clusters of longhouses. Some sites were used again and again for rebuildings, but even in these the number of houses in use at any one time may have been relatively limited. People concentrated on the use of domesticated resources, though there was some hunting (and occasionally fishing). It is not my intention to discuss this again in full, but to highlight some key characterizations and some new evidence.

Principally because of the presence of reassuringly solid and large

FIG. 3.2 Reconstruction of an LBK longhouse (after Keefer)

buildings, the LBK engenders a dangerous sense of familiarity. It is easily and almost universally assumed that because of the presence of longhouses this way of life was fully sedentary. Its subsistence regime is often characterized as forest farming or horticulture (e.g. Bogucki 1988; Sherratt 1997); primacy is often given to cultivations, seen as small but intense and prolonged, year after year on fertile and resilient soils, with animal keeping regarded as a supplement in neighbouring woodland. In this recurrent view, agriculture arrives in a very familiar guise right from the outset, and later developments (especially by the fourth millennium BC) form a puzzling divergence or degeneration from the prototypical Eden. I have challenged these assumptions elsewhere (Whittle 1996, 1997*a*) and want to restate some of these doubts here. One alternative which I do not espouse, however, is that the uptake of new resources was primarily symbolic (Thomas 1996). Stable isotopic analysis of LBK human bone has yet to be carried out on any scale but it seems clear from the main subsistence residues that a shift to domesticated resources was made early and then routinely maintained.

Key questions for the future are degrees of mobility and permanence of settlement, the role of animals in subsistence and other spheres, and the scale and rate of change. It is obvious that longhouses, including those of less robust construction and smaller size, lasted for substantial periods of time. What we do not know is how they were used. Analogies can suggest both competitive, ceremonial, and short-term use, as well as long-term residence (Strathern and Stewart 1999). Some studies suggest very patterned use of the space around and between LBK longhouses for different activities and different kinds of deposition (e.g. Last 1996 and references; cf. Hachem 2000). It remains to be seen whether this is indeed a product of prolonged and permanent occupation by the whole population of a settlement, or whether it is compatible with the marking of comings and goings, either by segments of the population from season to season or by whole groups of inhabitants in a cycle of abandonment and reoccupation. Virtually all LBK settlements lack their original soil surfaces, and such questions can only be addressed by examination of subsoil features which have escaped erosion. One important exception has been recently found and partially examined at Altdorf, near Landshut in Bavaria, though even here it is becoming clear that the upper part of the original soil is lacking (Meixner 1998; Engelhardt *et al.* 1998). An even better opportunity has emerged in the Paris basin at Jablines, Seine-et-Marne, where two post-LBK houses had an original occupation surface 10cm. deep (Hachem 2000). For the first time it will be possible to study the deposition of artefacts and other residues in a preserved soil contemporary with an LBK-related settlement.

Equally important for future research is the question of the balance of resources. My suggestion is that the keeping of animals, especially cattle, was more important than cereal cultivation. The structure of longhouses, and indeed perhaps their first appearance, is at least compatible with this suggestion, and we know from the transport of raw materials that people moved widely in this period. Woodland herding is also a better explanation of the limited scale of clearance detectable in such pollen diagrams as are available through the LBK distribution; it is otherwise surprising that there was not a steady increase in the size of cleared areas through time, which appears generally not to be the case at this date. These questions could now be addressed by methods such as stable isotope analysis of human bone and analysis of lipids (or fatty acids) in pottery.

The last difficulty with the conventional model of LBK lifestyle that I want to discuss here is the question of lack of change. The LBK begins somewhere around 5500 BC and lasts, in culture historical terms, till after 5000 BC. Over the areas of its distribution it has a variety of cultural successors, which last from about 4900–4800 BC till towards 4000 BC (see Whittle 1996 for a more detailed picture). In older terminology these post-LBK groupings can largely be seen as a continuation of the same initial Danubian tradition. There is substantial continuity also in terms of settlement and subsistence, with similar wooded environments, choice of fertile soils and valley-edge locations, use of timber longhouses, and reliance on plant and animal domesticates; and the frontier with adjacent hunter-gatherer populations remains largely stable. Some change is represented in the layout, form, and grouping of longhouses; trapezoidal longhouses in more marked concentrations behind palisades in Rhineland Grossgartach and Rössen contexts from the fifth millennium BC are obviously not quite the same as their LBK predecessors. The western edge of the post-LBK distribution in northern France seems also to expand in this phase, with the Villeneuve-St Germain site of Le Haut Mée in Ille-et-Vilaine representing an extension to the eastern part of Brittany (Cassen *et al.* 1998). Animal bone assemblages from the Paris basin itself in this phase, however, show massive continuity, in terms of dominant species, kill-off patterns, and so on (Tresset 1997). It is curious to say the least that a system so often seen as predominantly intrusive and fuelled by population growth should then have stabilized for a period of well over a thousand years.

One other set of new evidence might be taken as counter to this claim for stability and continuity. This takes the form of evidence for fighting, injury, and killing in LBK contexts. The example of the pit from Talheim has been known for some years (Wahl and König 1987), containing the bodies of men, women, and children. The location of injuries from axes predominantly on their heads suggests that victims may have been bound.

The capacity of this find to shock seemed all the greater since it seemed a complete aberration from normal social behaviour in the LBK. Now two other substantial finds of people with injuries from interpersonal violence have been made. Both are from later LBK settlements with ditched enclosures, Asparn-Schletz in Lower Austria and Herxheim in Rheinland-Pfalz (Windl 1996; Teschler-Nicola 1996; Häusser 1998). Here bodies with injuries have been found in the ditches of the enclosures, deposited both with and without care or ceremony in a variety of positions. Younger women are said to be numerically underrepresented. A model is emerging of not only killing but raiding for women or even slaves, and a broader model still posits population build-up in the later LBK, intensifying competition for key resources such as land, and a widespread breakdown in social order resulting in the cultural reformations of the post-LBK phase (Windl 1999; Gronenborn 1999).

This scenario is not lightly to be dismissed, but it is premature to accept it without reservations. While new discoveries have changed the picture, it remains the case that many other sites lack this kind of evidence. It is hard in my view to see these early ditched enclosures in general as defensive arrangements. Some at least of the Herxheim human remains appear to have been carefully deposited, and ritual or other explanations may apply. If there was social breakdown, there was also evidently subsequent social recovery. Another pertinent observation is that some evidence for interpersonal violence nearly always seems to appear as the database expands, and this may apply as far back as the Upper Palaeolithic period. It certainly holds true among the reasonably documented later hunter-gatherer populations of the southern Baltic, chiefly in the Kongemose and Ertebølle cultures. The incidence of healed wounds, however, may be higher in Late Mesolithic contexts than later, so that the nature of interpersonal violence certainly need not have been stable in time or space (Schulting 1998*a*). My general assertion would be that such violence was not restricted to agricultural communities, and that there is not yet clear evidence for an intensification of such acts through time.

AROUND 4000 BC: THE CONTEXT OF NEOLITHIC BEGINNINGS IN BRITAIN AND IRELAND

It has already been seen that the LBK and post-LBK systems inhabited much the same parts of central and western Europe. The evidence of settlement and subsistence in the post-LBK world does not suggest either territorial expansion to any marked degree or significant population growth within its distribution. The extension of Neolithic lifestyles from

4500 to 4000 BC (into Brittany perhaps around 4500 BC, and into southern Scandinavia and Britain and Ireland around 4000 BC) is therefore prima facie hard to ascribe to the expansive nature of the Neolithic economy or the capacity for population to increase. This does not exclude the operation of demographic pressures of some subtler kind, which might hypothetically have produced the conditions for limited fission or budding off, the spur for restricted or filtered colonization. On the whole, however, most archaeologists currently agree that the beginnings of the Neolithic in southern Scandinavia and in estuarine and coastal parts of the Netherlands were largely the result of the acculturation of indigenous people, without population transfer from outside (e.g. Hvass and Storgaard 1993; Stafford 1999; Louwe Kooijmans 1993). In Brittany it is possible that there was some kind of fusion between indigenous coastal people and others both from the Paris Basin and from the western part of France south of the Loire, the latter connected perhaps ultimately to a Mediterranean world beyond the scope of this chapter. In Britain too most scholars currently argue for indigenous acculturation, on the basis partly of the difficulties in tracking migrations of people and partly of claimed continuities in use of the landscape and in basic traditions of flint tool manufacture (e.g. Edmonds 1999). These kinds of explanation in favour of indigenous people are certainly in tune with the modern spirit of self-determination, but they push archaeological interpretation to its limits. Detailed understanding of the beginnings of the Neolithic in these terms is more challenging than in the older terms of evolutionary progression, technological superiority, and expansion and growth. I will try to indicate some of the kinds of explanation appropriate for the indigenous model, but will suggest also that we may still have to do with an element of restricted or filtered colonization. The case for at least small-scale colonization has been recently restated for Ireland (Cooney 2000).

In the case of Britain and Ireland the indigenous people in question were hunter-gatherers or foragers. Their resource base was probably very varied, but we remain embarrassingly ignorant of the details of later Mesolithic diet or of the balance between animals, plants, fish, and other resources in the couple of millennia before 4000 BC. There is some evidence in some areas for clearance or interference with woodland cover, and it is normal to assume by way of ethnographic analogy that these people were knowledgeable and skilled agents. In southern Scandinavia, where the later Mesolithic is far better documented in nearly every respect, it is clear that hunter-gatherers must have known of farming populations not far to their south for over a millennium, and were in contact with them, but chose not to adopt agriculture until around 4000 BC. In many parts of southern Scandinavia the hunter-gatherer population seems to have been concentrated on the coast. There have been arguments for the very restricted mobility of such a coastal population, and even semi-sedentary existence, supported by rich natural resources, and intensifying systems of fishing, hunting, and plant collecting or even tending. The most recent studies may suggest, however, that coastal locations, seen by some as the bases for a near-sedentary existence, were in fact used on a seasonal basis (Rowley-Conwy 1998). In Britain, the situation looks different (though some archaeologists have tried to model the situation here as though it were indeed Scandinavian). There were people inland as well as on the coasts, and in neither zone is there surviving evidence to suggest substantial sites or population as in the southern Baltic. Hunter-gatherers in Britain may still have been mobile, moving through wide territories on seasonal, annual, and lifetime scales. Recent stable isotopic analyses of human bone from the Late Mesolithic shell middens on the small west Scottish island of Oronsay are certainly compatible with the model of seasonal movement, because of the presence in one individual of a mixture of terrestrial and marine protein (Richards and Mellars 1998; cf. Mithen 2000).

How quickly did such people change long established patterns of subsistence, and why? As part of the consensus about indigenous acculturation, it is often assumed that change was gradual: that acculturating indigenous people continued to move around their landscapes while adopting the use of domesticated animals and cereals, and that these adoptions were set alongside a very broad and continuing spectrum of other, traditional resources still in use (e.g. Thomas 1996; Whittle 1996). I should like to assert that mobility of varying kinds did indeed continue to be a feature of early Neolithic lifestyle, but that we may need to rethink the speed of change in subsistence, as Schulting has argued (1998*a*, 1998*b*, 2000). I will deal with details of the early Neolithic economy in the next section, but it is useful to the argument to anticipate some of these here. The radiocarbon dating evidence need not show significant overlap between Mesolithic and Neolithic around 4000 BC, and—making allowance for the imprecision of radiocarbon dating—the transition from Mesolithic to Neolithic was swift, though perhaps a little varied from region to region, but with no obvious south–north or east–west trend (Schulting 1998*a*; contrast Williams 1989). In both Britain and southern Scandinavia, stable isotope analysis of human bone samples from coastal areas indicates a marked shift from a strong marine component in Mesolithic diet to a terrestrial component from the start of the Neolithic (Schulting 1998*b*; Richards 1998; Richards and Hedges 1999). This clearly implies, accepting for the time being that there are no factors complicating the stable isotope values, that indigenous people not only adopted new resources but favoured these strongly over their existing ones. Why should this have come about?

Various traditional kinds of model are inadequate explanations of such a development. One variety posits again population pressure or resource stress. There is no obvious sign of an increase in Mesolithic sites (though their chronology is very badly understood). In the case of southern Scandinavia, it was argued that changes in the salinity of the Baltic at this period affected the crucial late winter resource of oysters, leading to unmanageable stress on the subsistence system and a willingness at last to take up agriculture instead to cope (Rowley-Conwy 1985). It is unlikely, however, that shellfish alone were responsible for carrying late Ertebølle populations through the end of winter, or that there was not the ability to find a substitute even if they did. Nor does this style of explanation seem convincing in the case of Britain. Another kind of model has been based around the notion of social competition (Bender 1978). According to this, pressure could have emerged to intensify production in order to provide food, through feasting, as a means of enhancing social position. Such competition has been widely envisaged, even for seemingly remote areas of north-west Scotland (e.g. Armit and Finlayson 1992), but can hardly be documented independently in the archaeological evidence. Even where a wider range of late Mesolithic evidence exists than in Britain, such as in the cemeteries and burials of Brittany (Schulting 1996; Thomas and Tilley 1993) or southern Scandinavia (Hvass and Storgaard 1993; Larsson 1993), the case for marked social difference within mortuary groups is weak.

For good reason therefore another kind of explanation has emerged, to do with changes in the general outlook or world-view of indigenous people (e.g. Thomas 1991; Bradley 1993, 1998; Whittle 1996). This need not be incompatible with the knowledgeability of foragers, or their general ability to have seen advantages (as well as disadvantages) in adopting new changes. There is ethnographic support for the likelihood that foragers would make rational choices of this kind (e.g. Bird-David 1992). This leaves unanswered, however, the question of time-scale. In the absence of population pressure, resource stress, or intensifying social competition, why should indigenous foragers have changed at all?

One answer lies in the realms of how people saw themselves in the world, how they regarded their identity, their origins, and their relationship with their surroundings. Two aspects in particular can be considered here from this broad field of speculation. First, the Neolithic lifestyle as it emerged and developed from region to region involved frequent reference to the past, and it may be supposed that part of the Neolithic phenomenon was a strong sense of where people were thought to have come from. For example, it has long been considered that there is a strong link between the eventual disappearance of the timber longhouse in the LBK and post-LBK worlds and the subsequent emergence of the long barrow or cairn in the areas of north-west Europe around these (Hodder 1984; Bradley 1993,

1998), which is often connected with human remains. For example, in Kujavia in central-north Poland the trapezoidal longhouses of the late Lengyel culture give way to the first long barrows of the region nearby, perhaps before 4000 BC (Midgley 1992). It has been suggested that the collapsed longhouse was itself mound-like (Bradley 1996), and some kind of equation between household of the living and house of the dead may have emerged. This seems to have been widespread through the post-LBK area, since there is newer evidence from the Paris Basin for long mortuary enclosures or mounds of Passy type in the fifth millennium BC (Duhamel and Prestreau 1991), whose form is plausibly again an echo of the longhouse. At Balloy-Les Réaudins, in the Seine valley, there is dramatic new evidence that Passy-type mortuary enclosures were actually built on the site of former longhouses, at least three directly above the traces of longhouses (Mordant 1997). Long cairns were part of the repertoire of new monumental forms in Brittany at the start of the Neolithic (e.g. Boujot and Cassen 1993; Thomas and Tilley 1993), as well as in Britain and southern Scandinavia. Accepting therefore the arguments set out above for continuities of population, part of what was new among indigenous people must have been a set of ideas from outside their own worlds, bound up in part with former social ties (the household) and the dead or the past.

There is another element, which introduces the second consideration: animals and the wider meaning of domestication. It is dangerous to construct universal models of how hunter-gatherers may have regarded animals but there are recurrent indications among modern hunter-gatherers of attitudes which included people and animals in the same scheme of things. In north-west Europe, greatest symbolic attention seems to have been given in the late Mesolithic to red deer (e.g. Schulting 1996 for Brittany, or Tilley 1996 for southern Scandinavia), whether or not this was the prime economic resource. Both in the LBK and post-LBK world of the sixth–fifth millennia BC and in the wider north-west European Neolithic world of the fourth millennium BC it was cattle which were of both central economic and symbolic importance. Domestication brings control over animals, and thereby economic advantages, but it also entails new relationships with creatures of a kind previously perhaps regarded as equals or partners. On the criterion of size, there again does not seem to have been a process of local domestication of cattle in Britain (Grigson in Whittle *et al.* 1999; Serjeantson forthcoming), though preliminary DNA analysis may allow for the possibility of some (Bailey *et al.* 1996). Another ambiguity may have arisen from the fact that although cattle would have been familiar because they were part of the local fauna (unlike sheep and goats which were introduced), much of the domestic stock may have been introduced, again from the outside.

One important clue to the central importance of animals comes from one of the decorated menhirs in Brittany. One of these was broken up and its three sections reused in the tombs or shrines of La Table des Marchand, Gavrinis, and Er Grah (Le Roux 1984). Originally this tall menhir had a series of motifs or representations inscribed on it. Lower down there are what appear to be an axe and a crook, then above two horned animals, and at the top a motif commonly seen as an 'axe-plough' but which I believe is a representation of a whale (Whittle 2000). I believe that these representations are part of a mythic narrative, and to do with contrasting and perhaps contested views of origins and creation. Their special interest resides in the juxtaposition of a sea creature which was certainly encountered and occasionally used by late Mesolithic people, and new animals and things from outside. The menhir in question may originally have stood somewhere in the Locmariaquer complex, where the even larger *Le Grand Menhir Brisé* was also decorated with a 'whale' motif. Both were dismantled. They should alert us, in a way that little other evidence can, to the power of ideas. People may have chosen or been persuaded to alter their way of life under the influence of myths and legends about the beginnings of things and the place of people in the world.

This discussion may imply that the Mesolithic–Neolithic transition in north-west Europe was wholly a process of acculturation. It may be wise to continue to entertain the possibility of some filtered colonization. Cereals, sheep and goats, and perhaps cattle were introduced into Britain. They could have been acquired by indigenous people, who could also have taken up the use of pottery, but the speed of the spread of these new elements remains impressive. Irish archaeologists have maintained for some time that processes may have been different in Ireland, since the character of material assemblages seems to change so much and since the Neolithic presence appears so much wider than that of the Mesolithic (e.g. Cooney and Grogan 1994; Cooney 1997, 2000). In particular, Ireland seems to have lacked large fauna in the post-glacial period, and even red deer could have been a Neolithic introduction (Cooney 2000). The impact of cattle in such a setting could have been considerable. Some animals might have been brought in first into indigenous contexts, as perhaps at Ferriter's Cove, Co. Kerry, in the later fifth millennium BC (Woodman *et al.* 1999), but that leaves open the possibility of incomers with their own animals. Future DNA analysis may help to support or refute this general view. On a final note of caution, it has been customary to see colonizers as more active and purposeful than indigenous people. We do not understand the conditions in which filtered, small-scale colonization could have taken place. It is possible that at least some would have been opportunistic, as the major systems of late Mesolithic north-west Europe altered.

EARLY NEOLITHIC LANDSCAPES

By one or other of these processes, or by a combination of them, changes came into Britain and Ireland about 4000 BC. The initiation of changes may have been rapid. There were now more clearances of woodland. Domesticated animals were kept, including cattle, pigs, and sheep and goats, and cereals were cultivated, principally wheats and barleys. Some post-framed above-ground structures were built, which are commonly seen as residential houses, and material culture included now pottery and polished stone tools. The construction of barrows and cairns, many housing human remains, was widespread, and mainly in the southern part of Britain, where there were considerable numbers of ditched enclosures. It has been easy to assume that change was extensive from the outset, that settled agricultural life was rapidly established, and that the trajectory of subsequent change was steadily intensifying towards social and economic complexity and specialization. It is the aim of this section to repeat recent challenges to this view, focusing principally on the early Neolithic between roughly 4000 and 3000 BC. While there were clearly elements of agriculture present from 4000 BC, we cannot talk of a full coming until much later, in my view around 1500 BC onwards.

The environment remained predominantly wooded. Some openings may have been natural clearings as much as clearances created by people (Brown 1997). Some tree-throw pits made by falling trees were used for occupation (Evans *et al.* forthcoming). Clearances appear to have been mostly quite small, and few were long lasting. The impression is of a mosaic of openings of the woodland canopy, older ones closing in by natural regeneration as others were started. Archaeologists have traditionally concentrated their thinking on what went on in the clearances, neglecting woodland itself. At Runnymede in the lower Thames, an unusual combination of pollen and insect evidence suggests that cattle began to be used more intensively before the woodland canopy had been much altered at all (Robinson forthcoming; supplementing Robinson 1991). Cattle and pigs presumably continued to be managed in woodland even when clearances were created. Wild cattle, which were present in small numbers at sites like the Windmill Hill causewayed enclosure in Wiltshire (Grigson in Whittle *et al.* 1999), were presumably hunted in woodland, along with red deer, roe deer, and wild boar. Other woodland products have been shown to be in use, including honey (Needham and Evans 1987), nuts, berries, roots, and tubers (Moffett *et al.* 1989). Assuming that it was indeed mainly the same indigenous population involved, the setting would have seemed still very familiar, and other natural features and places could have framed the landscape. Some new monuments at least were built on places where there had been earlier, Mesolithic occupations, such as Gwernvale, Ascott-under-Wychwood, and Hazleton (Saville 1990), though it cannot be demonstrated that there was direct continuity of use. Just as with animals as discussed above, it remains a moot point whether people now regarded the land in different ways or whether they continued to see themselves as part of the landscape. It is possible, by analogy, that an ambiguous relationship emerged, people thinking of the land and woodland on the one hand as an indivisible part of the world and a source of good things but on the other hand as a now more separate realm of spirits, the dead, and dangerous forces (Whittle *et al.* 1999).

A wide range of resources was used in the early Neolithic: domesticated and wild animals, cereals and wild plants, and some fish and birds. The challenge is to understand the balance between them. There was probably no uniformity and the evidence from archaeological sites can seem contradictory. At causewayed enclosures like Windmill Hill, animal bone seems the dominant residue, with domesticated cattle predominant among the animals and few wild animals, but the charred remains of cereals also occurred (Whittle *et al.* 1999). Since these sites were the arena for rituals of various kinds, it is possible that feasting and other debris from them does not reflect everyday practices. In the large Coneybury Anomaly pit on Salisbury Plain, both similarity and difference can be seen (Richards 1990). Here there were few cereal remains, but many animal bones. These included the remains of at least ten cattle, which would have provided the most meat, but there were also several roe deer, and red deer, pig, and beaver were also represented. The roe may have been eaten on the spot but parts at least of cattle and red deer carcasses were probably taken off for use elsewhere. Might this suggest that cattle were of central ritual and symbolic importance and emphasized accordingly at important ritual loci, but that from day to day a much more varied use was made of animals including wild ones? Other non-enclosure sites, however, including Runnymede in the lower Thames valley and Knap of Howar on Orkney suggest that cattle were indeed the most numerous domesticated animal and that domesticated animals were more important than wild ones.

At Windmill Hill, cattle were often kept until their third or fourth year, and sheep and goats into their second, while most pigs were killed within a year (Grigson in Whittle *et al.* 1999). Pigs especially and also sheep and goats may have been kept for meat, but the greater age which cattle routinely reached suggests more varied uses. They may have been kept for meat, and also milk, given the substantial numbers of cows represented in many assemblages (despite the claim that milk was a product developed only later, in the second millennium BC: Sherratt 1981). Initial lipid analysis of early pottery from Orkney suggests the use of both beef and milk

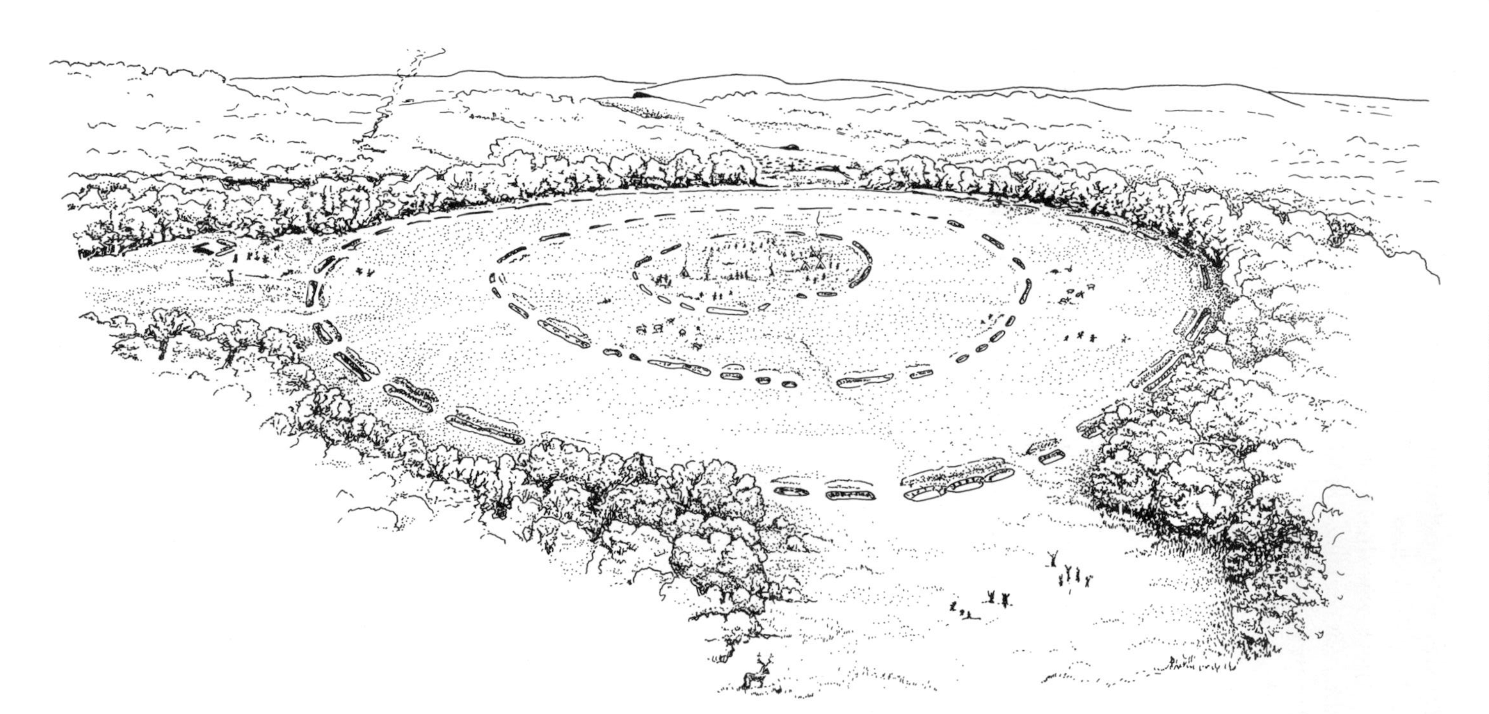

Fig. 3.3 Reconstruction of the form and setting of the causewayed enclosure at Windmill Hill, Wiltshire (after a drawing by Joshua Pollard).

(Jones 1999). Cattle may also have been valued in their own right, given their importance in enclosure sites and at some shrines or tombs. Recent stable isotope analysis suggests some diversity of practice, with some sites oriented more to meat eating and others reflecting a more mixed diet, but it is striking that none seems to reflect a predominantly plant-based diet (Richards 1998; Richards and Hedges 1999). There is little evidence for a marked increase in the rate of caries in human teeth across the Mesolithic–Neolithic transition in north-west Europe (Schulting 1998*a*; Wysocki and Whittle 2000), as might be expected from a marked shift to carbohydrates in the diet. Cereal pollen, though a poor disperser, especially through wooded environments, is infrequent in the pollen diagrams. There is also new evidence for variation between the sexes and between different assemblages of human remains in terms of kinds of strenuous activity and the resulting impact on the human skeleton (as 'musculo-skeletal stress markers'). Some males, for example at Parc le Breos Cwm, in south Wales, may have had much more active lifestyles than some women, compatible perhaps with men ranging more widely for herding and hunting (Whittle and Wysocki 1998). Given now the radiocarbon dating of the stone-walled enclosures or fields at Behy-Glenulra, Co. Mayo (Caulfield 1983) and other locations in western Ireland to the early Neolithic (Caulfield *et al.* 1998; Cooney 2000), it is again significant that their use seems to have been for grazing not cultivation. It is also important to stress, however, the evident differences within Ireland (Cooney 2000), and diversity can be seen even within small regions, such as parts of south-east Wales (Wysocki and Whittle 2000).

Overall, the evidence suggests a very considerable importance for animals. Whether this reflects direct continuity from the late Mesolithic is not known, since it is quite possible that the role of plants in that period has been underestimated (Zvelebil 1994). Wild plants certainly went on being used in the early Neolithic (Moffett *et al.* 1989). Apart from the patchy presence of cereal pollen, charred cereals themselves occur in irregular quantities and rarely in large amounts. Emmer, einkorn, hulled, and naked barley recur, and there may be instances of bread wheat, but surprisingly so far no legumes, in contrast to earlier continental assemblages. There is well known evidence for cultivation by ard or scratch plough, under South Street long barrow, Wiltshire (Ashbee *et al.* 1979). There are occasional larger finds of cereals, as at Balbridie on Deeside (Fairweather and Ralston 1993). Overall, cereal cultivation may have been widespread, and perhaps an important signifier of people's allegiance to new ways (Fairbairn in Whittle *et al.* 1999), but it may also have been episodic and generally small-scale. It has been easy to assume that cereal cultivation would have tied people permanently to one place, but this assumption is now being questioned. Some growing crops may have been left to fend for themselves, or watched only by certain segments of a community.

Several other lines of evidence suggest that people may have continued to move about, or not to settle in one place for long; tethered mobility or very short-term sedentism may have been characteristic. The existence of above-ground structures has long been recognized: normally post- or stake-framed, stone-footed in northern and western areas, and usually rectangular and up to 10 m. or a little more in length, but sometimes circular (Darvill and Thomas 1996). Archaeologists have until recently been content to call these 'houses' and assume domestic residence, but their duration, numbers, and contents call this into question. Few structures have significant signs of renewal; they might have lasted for a generation or so, but perhaps hardly more. The prime exception to this are the stone-footed and stone-walled examples, as at Knap of Howar in an outlying part of the Orkneys (Ritchie 1984), which could of course have endured much longer. Most structures occur singly, even when, as more recently, large areas have been opened in excavation around them, as at Yarnton in the upper Thames valley (Hey 1997) or Fengate on the west side of the Fens (Pryor 1974); a recent example comes from White Horse Stone in Kent (Anon. 2000). Recent exceptions to this are some of the new Irish discoveries (Cooney 1997, 2000; Grogan 1996). There is little sense of village or even hamlet. The roles of these structures may have varied. The structure recently investigated at Ballygalley, Co. Antrim (Simpson 1996), was associated with large quantities of debris from stone tool manufacture; the structure under the court cairn at Ballyglass, Co. Mayo, appears to have been deliberately dismantled (Ó'Nualláin 1972); and that at Balbridie was unusually massive. Some might therefore have been used for short-term permanent residence or periodic occupation, but others might have served as something akin to meeting houses, cult houses, or the locale for special activities. Much of the population may have lived in or used flimsier shelters, appropriate to lives on the move.

The situation may have varied. Large regional surveys and open-area excavations in southern Britain have not found many new structures. Instead, there are signs of patterned use of chosen parts of the landscape, for example certain channel edges in the flood plain of the upper Thames at Yarnton and of the lower Thames at the Eton Rowing Lake (Allen and Welsh 1997), and it is striking how people seem to have returned again and again to these locations, with a frequency apparently far greater than visible at house sites. Qualitative studies of flint working have also suggested that raw material was still carefully used, compatible with people being on the move and consistent with preceding Mesolithic traditions (Brown and Edmonds 1987). In Ireland there have certainly been more recent discoveries of structures in pipeline and other developments (Cooney 1997, 2000). In neither case is there overwhelming evidence for substantial levels of population. It continues to be very difficult to suggest specific figures for population size or density. I would assert in more general terms that population was scattered, often mobile, sometimes attached to particular places for longer periods but more often as part of patterned cycles of movement, and of low density. Where short-term sedentism was achieved, this was rarely for longer than a generation, and perhaps often rather less.

In contrast to an older view of change brought about by incoming, colonizing people who rapidly established sedentary lives and practised a recognizable form of mixed agriculture almost from the outset, which then steadily intensified with time, a different picture is emerging of continuity of population for the most part, with indigenous people maintaining occupation of the land and patterns of movement across it, supporting themselves in part by old staples but shifting also rapidly to new ways, dominated by the keeping of domestic cattle, guided in part by practical reason but led in large measure also by new beliefs and attachment to a sense of identity and beginnings which came from the past of elsewhere. The domain of beliefs can best be investigated by looking at monuments (in the jargon of archaeologists), that variety of built constructions to do with self-representation, views of the world, the past, ancestry, and the dead, which come into being from about 4000 BC onwards. Many monuments, though not all, had the physical capacity to endure. These were some of the most important and permanent marks which people created in the landscape, far longer lasting than occupations, clearances, structures, and houses, and perhaps invested with much greater significance. There is a contrast between the relative mobility and transience of daily lives and the stability of built monuments, and it is no accident that monuments finally lapsed in the very different world of the mid-second millennium BC.

This is not the place to set out the great variety of early Neolithic monuments (and subsequent ones); there has been a prolific and enquiring recent literature on them (e.g. Bradley 1993, 1998; Edmonds 1999; Thomas 1991; Barrett 1994; Cooney 2000; and many others). That literature has often seemed content to use monuments to construct a sense of Neolithic context, whereas wider studies of context and daily lives (cf. Cooney 2000) are needed to put monuments themselves into context. I want here, to conclude this discussion of the early Neolithic, briefly to consider some recurrent aspects of monuments, which further illustrate the central position of concepts and ideas in Neolithic landscapes.

Monuments were involved with a wide range of concerns. Their construction brought people together, possibly from far afield in some cases, and these initial gatherings may be one of their most significant aspects, especially when new ways of doing things were being created. The use of many monuments also involved the gathering of people, who were variously engaged in eating and feasting, burial and other treatment of the dead, and deposition, the placing of things in the ground. The form that monuments took, their position in the landscape, and the materials used to construct them were all significant. Long mounds and long cairns are generally agreed to have played on the memory of the longhouse, as discussed already, but other sources may be relevant, including earlier linear shell middens, while round cairns may have drawn on circular dwellings. Ditched enclosures seem related to earlier ditched enclosures going as far back as the later stages of the LBK, which in turn may have been created out of a sense of shared space between longhouses; their circular form may also have drawn on arrangements in occupations or the form of clearances and clearings in woodland. In both cases, long mounds and ditched enclosures in Britain were created quite long after their likely prototypes. Long mounds and other shrines or tombs appeared from early in the Neolithic, but ditched enclosures may not have been started till after a few centuries. This indicates the power of memory of the past, and it appears that different kinds of memory were deemed appropriate for different times and purposes. Many monuments appear to have been positioned carefully in the landscape, to mark previously significant places, to capture or frame views, or to merge with and perhaps represent the landscape itself, and the varied use of stone, large timbers, chalk, and earth drew upon elements from the earth and the surroundings.

The scope of concerns expressed and played out by people at monuments seems to have varied. Shrines or tombs were clearly not just to do with the disposal and treatment of the dead, but that is a recurrent aspect of many, and a more specialized theme than is evident in many enclosures, where a wider range of ideas and activities can be seen, overlapping with the world of the everyday, animals, relations with neighbours, and so on. Monuments stood for things other than themselves, and their symbolic references included the past, nature or the surrounding world (the distinction may have been ambiguous as discussed above), animals, other people, social existence, identity, and ancestors (both imagined and real). These seem to have been the sorts of central concepts which guided early Neolithic existence. Subsistence techniques and resources are not to be excluded from this frame of reference, but people may have thought about cattle for example not only as sources of food but also (and perhaps far more) as ambiguous partners, as definers of identity and value, and as indicators of mythical origins. If this kind of reconstruction can be accepted, it indicates once more how the beginnings of the Neolithic may best be understood in the realm of ideas.

RATES OF CHANGE: FROM THE LATE NEOLITHIC TO THE MIDDLE BRONZE AGE WATERSHED

The conventional expectation seems to be that as time went on, so the economy intensified, population grew, and society became steadily more complex and hierarchical. With regard to the Late Neolithic (*c.*3000–2000 BC) and the Early Bronze Age (*c.*2000–1500 BC), there has been frequent reference in discussions of monuments, burials, and material culture to chiefdoms and 'the rise of the individual' (e.g. Renfrew 1973; Parker Pearson 1993; cf. Earle 1997), and in discussions of the economy to the emergence of a 'secondary products revolution' and pastoral specialization (Sherratt 1981; Fleming 1971, 1972). Thus, for example, the very large monuments of the Late Neolithic are seen as the products of a strongly differentiated society, while the lack of settlement evidence in the Early Bronze Age has been taken to support a new shift to a specialized pastoral economy, with which the general notion of an evolutionary shift to greater emphasis on the secondary products of milk and wool is compatible. Neither kind of hypothesis is satisfactory.

Large and complex monuments are the only demonstrable criterion for chiefdoms (assuming anyway that that is a meaningful analytical category) in the Late Neolithic. The climax of monument building may have other explanations, in the sacred imperatives of the ritual tradition (Whittle 1997*b*, 1997*c*; Parker Pearson and Ramilisonina 1998). In other spheres there is much less obvious change. At ritual and ceremonial sites the predominant animal was now pig, presumably for feasting, but in other contexts this preference is not so marked (Serjeantson forthcoming). In some Beaker contexts, it was cattle which were still emphasized, such as the 'head and hooves' deposit in the grave pit at Hemp Knoll near Avebury in Wiltshire (Robertson-Mackay 1980) or the many cattle skulls above the grave at Irthlingborough in the Nene valley (Davis and Payne 1993). Cultivation was still practised. Depending on context, charred cereal remains may be infrequent, as in the West Kennet palisade enclosures near Avebury (Whittle 1997*b*), though in Beaker pits, in the upper Thames, cereal remains appear to become now more frequent (Hey 1997), and residue analysis of Late Neolithic sherds from Orkney also suggests now the more regular presence of cereals (Jones 1999). Settlement sites remain elusive in the Late Neolithic, with the obvious exception of the Orkneys, and there is no clear increase in the number of known structures ('houses') or their size and complexity. There is an argument that flint working processes and raw material choices suggest less mobile lifestyles (Bradley 1987), but large-scale projects in southern Britain have failed (at least so far) to come up with the corresponding structures or deposits. There are clear signs in some areas of a reduction in woodland cover, and the establishment of grassland, principally on areas of the southern Chalk and around the major monument complexes (e.g. Evans 1993; cf. Edwards 1993). This may be in part the specialized effect of the conditions in which the great monuments were constructed, rather than an index of general development. Even in these complexes the environment may still be characterized as a mosaic. The unusually wide range of evidence from under Silbury Hill indicates a mix of open and less open environments, and the palisades in the nearby West Kennet complex show the continued existence of oak woodland (Whittle 1997*b*). There is no certain evidence yet for permanent fields or plots, though cases of ardmarks can be documented. The fen-edge paddocks at Fengate (Pryor 1980) can best be assigned to the middle of the Bronze Age rather than the Late Neolithic or Early Bronze Age.

Older arguments for some kind of mobility and reliance on animals in the Early Bronze Age are not in themselves to be dismissed. Rather, these cannot now be seen as a development peculiar to this phase but should be regarded as part of a much longer history. Occupations, when they can be found, as at West Row, Mildenhall, Suffolk, on the fen-edge (Martin and Murphy 1988), are small, perhaps still quite short lived, and linked to animal husbandry and small-scale cultivation (see also Brück 1999).

The horizon of marked and extensive change falls in the middle of the Bronze Age from about 1500 BC onwards, from the Middle to the Late Bronze Age, as the next chapter will also describe. From this sort of date it becomes possible to find many more settlement sites, with some rectangular and more often circular structures, of which many seem more surely now domestic houses (also with signs of renewal), pits, and other ancillary features; some are open, some enclosed by palisades or ditches. There is variety, perhaps now of a hierarchical kind, in the size and complexity of sites, from individual open households or very small hamlets, to ditched and palisaded enclosures containing several buildings; there are also enigmatic midden sites. This evidence is chiefly southern, but there is related evidence too from the uplands of northern England, southern Scotland, and elsewhere. The distribution of pot styles becomes increasingly regionalized through the later part of the Bronze Age, in contrast to the Early Bronze Age and Late Neolithic, suggesting greater attachment to more local identities. At the same time, a greater interdependence between sites may have emerged, and the evidence of the movement of bronzes suggests much more extensive contact with continental Europe. Also predominantly in southern Britain, there is good evidence now for enclosed land, in the varied form of reaves or stone walls on Dartmoor which constitute both boundaries and fields for grazing and cultivation (Fleming 1988), linear ditches in Wessex (Bradley *et al.* 1994), and fields of both more and less regular kinds on the Chalk.

In total, these changes can at last be taken to represent the full coming of agriculture. How quickly did they come about, and why? This landscape was not necessarily an instant creation, since linear ditches may precede field systems in some areas, and there are differences in the extent of field system layout. On the other hand, substantial tracts of reave field systems, covering thousands of hectares, were evidently planned at the same time, since they share common, strong axes (Fleming 1988). The shift can be characterized again as rapid, even if there were centuries of subsequent development, and the challenge, as earlier at *c.*5500 BC and *c.*4000 BC, is to understand why it could have come about in these ways. This period of British prehistory has been comparatively neglected in recent theoretical debates, curiously so since it offers many opportunities to investigate the everyday and individual agency, which have been stressed as in general desirable (Dobres and Robb 2000), but perhaps because fields and houses lack the interpretive glamour of ancestral tombs and ritual enclosures. I suggest that perspectives developed for earlier periods may be critical for understanding this horizon too.

Other factors have of course to be considered. Since the 1970s, prehistorians in Britain have tended to neglect detailed studies of population, and it could be that subtle increases in population in the end encouraged the process of settling down. On the other hand, there is no obvious sign of population increase in the period preceding 1500 BC (just as this was lacking in the periods before 5500 BC and 4000 BC), and population increase may rather be a development *after* settling down had occurred. Agricultural production likewise may have been intensified *after* this horizon, rather than before it. Models of social competition can seriously be considered, though the evidence for differentiation in the mortuary assemblages of the Late Neolithic and Early Bronze Age has been much exaggerated, and it is far too glib and simplistic to talk of the 'rise of the individual', since individuality and individualism are complex and varying, and individuals (rather than 'the individual') had important roles to play in all periods (see Whittle 1998*a*, 1998*b*).

My last assertion therefore is that these shifts were the outcome of gradual shifts in social values; in this sense yet another major horizon of change can be explained in terms of the realm of ideas. We need perhaps broader perspectives, since few scholars study both sides of this claimed watershed. Two phenomena need to be linked: the decline of monument building in the Early Bronze Age and its restriction to much smaller burial monuments, and the emergence of a much more settled and bounded landscape, from the Middle Bronze Age onwards (e.g. Last 1998; Thomas 1997). The great Late Neolithic monuments were still of obvious and perhaps still central importance in the Early Bronze Age, since round barrows cluster so densely around them. It is as though the aftermath of the great feats of the Late Neolithic was to have settled things with regard to the spirits or ancestors (see Parker Pearson and Ramilisonina 1998) or other driving forces of the powerful sacred tradition. There then emerged a concern not so much for the individual as for the relative ranking of *groups* of people (whether kin groups or something different) whose burials formed the cumulative collectivities of so many round barrows. The attention to genealogy and social memory (see Last 1998) was in itself perhaps not new, but it gained new importance with reference to a fixing of ancestral and other conceptual realms. The Early Bronze Age interest in descent may have been a key precondition for the emergence of Middle Bronze Age landscapes, since it may have fostered a shift in values which incorporated a sense of smaller group identity, particular belongings, and the expression of these through the private (rather than individual) deposition of bodies and valued goods. This is not to claim that the full adoption of agriculture was itself predominantly individualistic, since there are clear signs through the Middle to Late Bronze Age, and indeed into the Iron Age of the first millennium BC, of strongly communal decisions and actions, though kinship relations may have become more prominent (Thomas 1997). After a long history of co-operation especially in central conceptual spheres, of ambiguous partnership with animals, of attachment to particular places but continued fluidity and mobility in their daily lives, people had first to begin to think differently before they would adapt agriculture to something resembling its more familiar modern guise.

REFERENCES

Allen, T., and Welsh, K. (1997). 'Eton Rowing Lake, Dorney, Buckinghamshire. Second interim report', *South Midlands Archaeology*, 27: 25–34.

Anon. (2000). 'White Horse Stone: a Neolithic longhouse', *Current Archaeology*, 168 (XIV, 12): 450–3.

Arbogast, R. (1998). 'Haustiere und Wildtiere der Bandkeramiker', *Archäologie in Deutschland*, 4: 36–9.

Armit, I., and Finlayson, B. (1992). 'Hunter-gatherers transformed: the transition to agriculture in northern and western Europe', *Antiquity*, 66: 664–76.

Ashbee, P., Smith, I. F., and Evans, J. G. (1979). 'Excavation of three long barrows near Avebury, Wiltshire', *Proceedings of the Prehistoric Society*, 45: 207–300.

Bailey, J. F., Richards, M. B., Macaulay, V. A., Colson, I. B., James, I. T., Bradley, D. G., Hedges, R. E. M., and Sykes, B. C. (1996). 'Ancient DNA suggests a

recent expansion of European cattle from a diverse wild progenitor species', *Proceedings of the Royal Society of London*, B 263: 1467–73.
Bánffy, E. (1996). 'Neolithic and Copper Age settlements at Hahót and Zalaszentbalász (Zalaszentbalász-Pusztatető, Hahát-Szartóri I–II)', *Antaeus*, 22: 35–50.
Bánffy, E. (2000). 'Starčevo und/oder LBK? Die ersten Ergebnisse der westungarischen Ausgrabungen aus der Entsheungsphase der Bandkeramik', *Varia Neolithica*, 1: 47–60.
Barrett, J. C. (1994). *Fragments From Antiquity.* Oxford: Blackwell.
Bender, B. (1978). 'Gatherer-hunter to farmer: a social perspective', *World Archaeology*, 10: 204–22.
Benecke, N. (1994). *Archäologische Studien zur Entwicklung der Haustierhaltung in Mitteleuropa und Südskandinavien von den Anfängen bis zum ausgehenden Mittelalter.* Berlin: Akademie Verlag.
Bird-David, N. (1992). 'Beyond "the hunting and gathering mode of subsistence": observations on the Nayaha and other modern hunter-gatherers', *Man*, 27: 19–44.
Bogucki, P. (1988). *Forest Farmers and Stockherders.* Cambridge: Cambridge University Press.
Bogucki, P., and Grygiel, R. (1993). 'The first farmers of central Europe: a survey article', *Journal of Field Archaeology*, 20: 399–426.
Boujot, C., and Cassen, S. (1993). 'A pattern of evolution for the Neolithic funerary structures of the west of France', *Antiquity*, 67: 477–91.
Bradley, R. (1987). 'Flint technology and the character of Neolithic settlement', in A. G. Brown and M. R. Edmonds (eds.), *Lithic Analysis and Later British Prehistory.* Oxford: British Archaeological Reports, 181–6.
Bradley, R. (1993). *Altering the Earth.* Edinburgh: Society of Antiquaries of Scotland.
Bradley, R. (1996). 'Long houses, long mounds and Neolithic enclosures', *Journal of Material Culture*, 1: 239–56.
Bradley, R. (1998). *The Significance of Monuments: On the Shaping of Human Experience in Neolithic and Bronze Age Europe.* London: Routledge.
Bradley, R., Entwistle, R., and Raymond, F. (1994). *Prehistoric Land Divisions on Salisbury Plain: The Work of the Wessex Linear Ditches Project.* London: English Heritage.
Brown, A. G., and Edmonds, M. R. (1987) (eds.). *Lithic Analysis and Later British Prehistory.* Oxford: British Archaeological Reports.
Brown, T. (1997). 'Clearances and clearings: deforestation in Mesolithic/Neolithic Britain', *Oxford Journal of Archaeology*, 16: 133–46.
Brown, T. A. (1999). 'How ancient DNA may help in understanding the origin and spread of agriculture', *Proceedings of the Royal Society of London*, B 354: 89–98.
Brück, J. (1999). 'What's in a settlement? Domestic practice and residential mobility in Early Bronze Age southern England', in J. Brück and M. Goodman (eds.), *Making Places in the Prehistoric World.* London: UCL Press, 52–75.
Cassen, S., Audren, C., Hinguant, S., Lannuzel, G., and Marchand, G. (1998). 'L'habitat Villeneuve-St-Germain du Haut Mée (St-Etienne-en-Conglès, Ille-et-Vilaine)', *Bullétin de la Société Préhistorique Française*, 95: 41–76.

Caulfield, S. (1983). 'The Neolithic settlement of north Connaught', in T. Reeves-Smyth and F. Hamond (eds.), *Landscape Archaeology in Ireland.* Oxford: British Archaeological Reports, 195–215.

Caulfield, S., O'Donnell, R. G., and Mitchell, P. I. (1998). 'Radiocarbon dating of a Neolithic field system at Céide Fields, County Mayo, Ireland', *Radiocarbon*, 40: 629–40.

Cooney, G. (1997). 'Images of settlement and the landscape in the Neolithic', in P. Topping (ed.), *Neolithic Landscapes.* Oxford: Oxbow, 23–31.

Cooney, G. (2000). *Landscapes of Neolithic Ireland.* London: Routledge.

Cooney, G., and Grogan, E. (1994). *Irish Prehistory: A Social Perspective.* Dublin: Wordwell.

Darvill, T., and Thomas, J. (1996) (eds.). *Neolithic Houses in Northwest Europe and Beyond.* Oxford: Oxbow.

Davis, S., and Payne, S. (1993). 'A barrow full of cattle skulls', *Antiquity*, 67: 12–22.

Dennell, R. (1983). *European Economic Prehistory.* London: Academic Press.

Dobres, M.-A., and Robb, J. (2000) (eds.). *Agency in Archaeology.* London: Routledge.

Duhamel, P., and Prestreau, M. (1991). 'La Nécropole monumentale néolithique de Passy dans le contexte du gigantisme funéraire européen', *Actes du 14e colloque interrégional sur le Néolithique (Blois 1987)*, 103–17.

Earle, T. (1997). *How Chiefs Come to Power: The Political Economy in Prehistory.* Stanford: Stanford University Press.

Edmonds, M. (1999). *Ancestral Geographies of the Neolithic: Landscape, Monuments and Memory.* London: Routledge.

Edwards, K. (1993). 'Models of mid-Holocene forest farming in north-west Europe', in F. M. Chambers (ed.), *Climate Change and Human Impact on the Landscape.* London: Chapman and Hall, 133–45.

Engelhardt, B., Meixner, G., and Schaich, M. (1998). 'Linearbandkeramische Siedlung und Paläoboden von Aich, Gemeinde Altdorf, Landkreis Landshut, Niederbayern', *Das archäologische Jahr in Bayern 1997*, 32–5.

Erny-Rodmann, C., Gross-Klee, E., Haas, J. N., Jacomet, S., and Zoller, H. (1997). 'Früher "human impact" und Ackerbau im Übergangsbereich Spätmesolithikum-Frühneolithikum im schweizerischen Mitteland', *Jahrbuch der Schweizerischen Gesellschaft für Ur- und Frühgeschichte*, 80: 27–56.

Evans, C., Pollard, J., and Knight, M. (forthcoming). 'Life in woods: tree-throws, "settlement" and forest cognition', *Oxford Journal of Archaeology*.

Evans, J. G. (1993). 'The influence of human communities on the English chalklands from the Mesolithic to the Iron Age: the molluscan evidence', in F. M. Chambers (ed.), *Climate Change and Human Impact on the Landscape.* London: Chapman and Hall, 147–56.

Fairweather, A. D., and Ralston, I. B. M. (1993). 'The Neolithic timber hall at Balbridie, Grampian Region, Scotland: the building, the date, the plant macrofossils', *Antiquity*, 67: 313–23.

Fleming, A. (1971). 'Territorial patterns in Bronze Age Wessex', *Proceedings of the Prehistoric Society*, 37: 138–66.

Fleming, A. (1972). 'The genesis of pastoralism in European prehistory', *World Archaeology*, 4: 179–91.

Fleming, A. (1988). *The Dartmoor Reaves: Investigating Prehistoric Land Divisions.* London: Batsford.

Grogan, E. (1996). 'Neolithic houses in Ireland', in T. Darvill and J. Thomas (eds.), *Neolithic Houses in Northwest Europe and Beyond.* Oxford: Oxbow, 41–60.

Gronenborn, D. (1997). *Silexartefakte der ältestbandkeramischen Kultur.* Bonn: Rudolf Habelt.

Gronenborn, D. (1998). 'Ältestbandkeramische Kultur, La Hoguette, Limburg, and . . . what else? Contemplating the Mesolithic-Neolithic transition in central Europe', *Documenta Praehistorica*, 25: 189–202.

Gronenborn, D. (1999). 'Variations on a basic theme: the transition to farming in southern central Europe', *Journal of World Prehistory*, 13: 123–210.

Hachem, L. (2000). 'New observations on the Bandkeramik house and social organization', *Antiquity*, 74: 308–12.

Häusser, A. (1998) (ed.). *Krieg oder Frieden? Herxheim vor 7000 Jahren.* Herxheim: Landesamt für Denkmalpflege.

Hey, G. (1997). 'Neolithic settlement at Yarnton, Oxfordshire', in P. Topping (ed.), *Neolithic Landscapes.* Oxford: Oxbow, 99–111.

Hodder, I. (1984). 'Burials, houses, women and men in the European Neolithic', in D. Miller and C. Tilley (eds.), *Ideology, Power and Prehistory.* Cambridge: Cambridge University Press, 51–68.

Hvass, S., and Storgaard, B. (1993) (eds.). *Digging into the Past: 25 Years of Archaeology in Denmark.* Copenhagen and Aarhus: Royal Society of Northern Antiquaries and Jutland Archaeological Society.

Jones, A. (1999). 'The world on a plate: ceramics, food technology and cosmology in Neolithic Orkney', *World Archaeology*, 31: 55–77.

Kalicz, N., Virág, Z., and Bira, K. (1998). 'The northern periphery of the Early Neolithic Starčevo culture in south-western Hungary: a case study of an excavation at Lake Balaton', *Documenta Praehistorica*, 25: 151–87.

Kreuz, A. M. (1990). *Die ersten Bauern Mitteleuropas—eine archäobotanische Untersuchung zu Umwelt und Landwirtschaft der ältesten Bandkeramik.* Leiden: Leiden University Press.

Larsson, L. (1993). 'The Skateholm project: late Mesolithic coastal settlement in southern Sweden', in P. Bogucki (ed.), *Case Studies in European Prehistory.* Boca Raton, Fla.: CRC Press, 31–62.

Last, J. (1996). 'Neolithic houses—a central European perspective', in T. Darvill and J. Thomas (eds.), *Neolithic Houses in Northwest Europe and Beyond.* Oxford: Oxbow, 27–40.

Last, J. (1998). 'Books of life: biography and memory in a Bronze Age barrow', *Oxford Journal of Archaeology*, 17: 43–53.

Lenneis, E. (1997). 'Houseforms of the Central European Linear Pottery culture and of the Balkan Early Neolithic—a comparison', *Poročilo o raziskovanju paleolitika, neolitika in eneolitika v Sloveniji*, 24: 143–50.

Le Roux, C.-T. (1984). 'A propos des fouilles de Gavrinis (Morbihan): nouvelles données sur l'art mégalithique Armoricain', *Bulletin de la Société Préhistorique Française*, 81: 240–5.

Louwe Kooijmans, L. (1993). 'The Mesolithic/Neolithic transformation in the Lower Rhine basin', in P. Bogucki (ed.), *Case Studies in European Prehistory.* Boca Raton, Fla.: CRC Press, 95–145.

Lüning, J. (1988). 'Frühe Bauern in Mitteleuropa im 6. und 5. Jahrtausend v. Chr.', *Jahrbuch des Römisch-Germanischen Zentralmuseums Mainz*, 35: 27–93.

Lüning, J. (2000). *Steinzeitliche Bauern in Deutschland: die Landwirtschaft im Neolithikum.* Bonn: Habelt.

Martin, E., and Murphy, P. (1988). 'West Row Fen, Suffolk: a Bronze Age fen-edge settlement site', *Antiquity*, 82: 353–8.

Meixner, G. (1998). 'Paläoboden und Siedlungsbefunde der Linearbandkeramik von Altdorf, Lkr. Landshut', *Vorträge des 16. Niederbayerischen Archäologentages*, 13–40.

Midgley, M. (1992). *TRB Culture: The First Farmers of the North European Plain.* Edinburgh: Edinburgh University Press.

Mithen, S. (2000). 'Mesolithic sedentism on Oronsay: chronological evidence from adjacent islands in the southern Hebrides', *Antiquity*, 74: 298–312.

Modderman, P. J. R. (1988). 'The Linear Pottery culture: diversity in uniformity', *Berichten van de Rijksdienst voor het Oudheidkundig Bodemonderzoek*, 38: 63–139.

Moffett, L., Robinson, M., and Straker, V. (1989). 'Cereals, fruits and nuts: charred plant remains from Neolithic sites in England and Wales and the Neolithic economy', in A. Milles, D. Williams, and D. Gardner (eds.), *The Beginnings of Agriculture.* Oxford: British Archaeological Reports, 243–61.

Mordant, D. (1997). 'Le Complexe des Réaudins à Balloy: enceinte et nécropole monumentale', in C. Constantin, D. Mordant, and D. Simonin, *La Culture du Cerny: nouvelle économie, nouvelle société au Néolithique.* Nemours: Mémoires du Musée de Préhistoire d'Ile de France, 449–77.

Needham, S., and Evans, J. (1987). 'Honey and dripping: Neolithic food residues from Runnymede Bridge', *Oxford Journal of Archaeology*, 6: 21–8.

Ó'Nualláin, S. (1972). 'A Neolithic house at Ballyglass, Co. Mayo', *Journal of the Royal Society of Antiquaries of Ireland*, 102: 49–57.

Parker Pearson, M. (1993). *Bronze Age Britain.* London: Batsford.

Parker Pearson, M., and Ramilisonina (1998). 'Stonehenge for the ancestors: the stones pass on the message', *Antiquity*, 72: 308–26.

Pryor, F. (1974). *Excavation at Fengate: The First Report.* Toronto: Royal Ontario Museum.

Pryor, F. (1980). *Excavation at Fengate: The Third Report.* Toronto: Royal Ontario Museum.

Renfrew, C. (1973). 'Monuments, mobilization and social organization in Neolithic Wessex', in C. Renfrew (ed.), *The Explanation of Culture Change: Models in Prehistory.* London: Duckworth, 539–58.

Richards, J. (1990). *The Stonehenge Environs Project.* London: English Heritage.

Richards, M. P. (1998). 'Paleodietary studies of European human populations using bone stable isotopes', D.Phil. diss., Oxford University.

Richards, M. P., and Mellars, P. A. (1998). 'Stable isotopes and the seasonality of the Oronsay middens', *Antiquity*, 72: 178–84.

Richards, M. P., and Hedges, R. E. M. (1999). 'A Neolithic revolution? New evidence of diet in the British Neolithic', *Antiquity*, 73: 891–7.

Ritchie, A. (1984). 'Excavation of a Neolithic homestead at Knap of Howar, Papa Westray, Orkney', *Proceedings of the Society of Antiquaries of Scotland*, 113: 40–121.

Robertson-Mackay, M. E. (1980). 'A "head and hooves" burial beneath a round barrow, with other Neolithic and Bronze Age sites, on Hemp Knoll, near Avebury, Wiltshire', *Proceedings of the Prehistoric Society*, 46: 123–76.

Robinson, M. (1991). 'The Neolithic and late Bronze Age insect assemblages', in S. Needham, *Excavation and Salvage at Runnymede Bridge, 1978.* London: British Museum, 277–326.

Robinson, M. (forthcoming). 'Coleopteran evidence for the elm decline, Neolithic activity in woodland, clearance and the use of the landscape', in A. Fairbairn (ed.), *Plants in Neolithic Britain and Beyond.* Oxford: Oxbow.

Rowley-Conwy, P. (1985). 'The origin of agriculture in Denmark: a review of some theories', *Journal of Danish Archaeology*, 4: 188–95.

Rowley-Conwy, P. (1998). 'Cemeteries, seasonality and complexity in the Ertebølle of Southern Scandinavia', in M. Zvelebil, R. Dennell, and L. Domańska (eds.), *Harvesting the Sea, Farming the Forest.* Sheffield: Sheffield Academic Press, 193–202.

Saville, A. (1990). *Hazleton North: The Excavation of a Neolithic Long Cairn of the Cotswold-Severn Group.* London: English Heritage.

Schulting, R. J. (1996). 'Antlers, bone pins and flint blades: the Mesolithic cemeteries of Téviec and Hoëdic, Brittany', *Antiquity*, 70: 335–50.

Schulting, R. J. (1998*a*). 'Slighting the sea: the Mesolithic-Neolithic transition in northwest Europe', Ph.D. diss., Reading University.

Schulting, R. J. (1998*b*). 'Slighting the sea: stable isotope evidence for the transition to farming in northwestern Europe', *Documenta Praehistorica*, 25: 203–18.

Schulting, R. J. (2000). 'New AMS dates from the Lambourn long barrow and the question of the earliest Neolithic in southern England: repacking the Neolithic package?', *Oxford Journal of Archaeology*, 19: 25–35.

Serjeantson, D. (forthcoming). 'Neolithic and Early Bronze Age', in D. Serjeantson (ed.), *A Review of Archaeological Animal Bone Studies in Southern Britain.*

Sherratt, A. (1981). 'Plough and pastoralism: aspects of the secondary products revolution', in I. Hodder, G. Isaac, and N. Hammond (eds.), *Pattern of the Past.* Cambridge: Cambridge University Press, 261–305.

Sherratt, A. (1982). 'The development of Neolithic and Copper Age settlement in the Great Hungarian Plain', *Oxford Journal of Archaeology*, 1: 287–316.

Sherratt, A. (1997). 'Changing perspectives in European prehistory', in A. Sherratt, *Economy and Society in Prehistoric Europe.* Edinburgh: Edinburgh University Press, 1–34.

Simpson, D. (1996). 'Ballygalley houses, Co. Antrim', in T. Darvill and J. Thomas (eds.), *Neolithic Houses in Northwest Europe and Beyond.* Oxford: Oxbow, 123–32.

Stafford, M. (1999). *From Forager to Farmer in Flint: A Lithic Analysis of the Prehistoric Transition to Agriculture in Southern Scandinavia.* Aarhus: Aarhus University Press.

Strathern, A., and Stewart, P. (1999). 'Dangerous woods and perilous pearl shells: the fabricated politics of a longhouse in Pangia, Papua New Guinea', *Journal of Material Culture*, 5: 69–89.

Sykes, B. (1999). 'The molecular genetics of European ancestry', *Proceedings of the Royal Society of London*, B 354: 131–9.

Teschler-Nicola, M. (1996). 'Anthropologische Spurensicherung—Die traumatischen und postmortalen Veränderungen an den linearbandkeramischen Skelettresten von Asparn/Schletz', in *Rätsel um Gewalt und Tod vor 7,000 Jahren: eine Spurensicherung.* Asparn a.d.Zaya: Museum für Urgeschichte, 47–64.

Thomas, J. (1991). *Rethinking the Neolithic.* Cambridge: Cambridge University Press.

Thomas, J. (1996). 'The cultural context of the first use of domesticates in central and north-west Europe', in D. R. Harris (ed.), *The Origins and Spread of Agriculture and Pastoralism in Eurasia.* London: UCL Press, 310–22.

Thomas, J., and Tilley, C. (1993). 'The axe and the torso: symbolic structures in the Neolithic of Brittany', in C. Tilley (ed.), *Interpretative Archaeology.* Oxford: Berg, 225–324.

Thomas, R. (1997). 'Land, kinship relations and the rise of enclosed settlement in first millennium B.C. Britain', *Oxford Journal of Archaeology*, 16: 211–18.

Tilley, C. (1996). *An Ethnography of the Neolithic.* Cambridge: Cambridge University Press.

Tillmann, A. (1993). 'Kontinuität oder Diskontinuität? Zur Frage einer bandkeramischen Landnahme im südlichen Mitteleuropa', *Archäologische Informationen*, 16: 157–87.

Tresset, A. (1997). 'L'Approvisionnement carné Cerny dans le contexte néolithique du bassin Parisien', in C. Constantin, D. Mordant, and D. Simonin (eds.), *La Culture du Cerny: nouvelle économie, nouvelle société au Néolithique.* Nemours: Mémoires du Musée de Préhistoire d'Ile de France, 299–314.

Wahl, J., and König, G. (1987). 'Anthropologisch-traumatische Untersuchung der menschlichen Skelettreste aus dem bandkeramischen Massengrab bei Talheim, Kreis Heilbronn', *Fundberichte Baden-Württemberg*, 12: 65–186.

Whittle, A. (1996). *Europe in the Neolithic: The Creation of New Worlds.* Cambridge: Cambridge University Press.

Whittle, A. (1997*a*). 'Moving on and moving around: Neolithic settlement mobility', in P. Topping (ed.), *Neolithic Landscapes.* Oxford: Oxbow, 15–22.

Whittle, A. (1997*b*). *Sacred Mound, Holy Rings. Silbury Hill and the West Kennet Palisade Enclosures: A Later Neolithic Complex in North Wiltshire.* Oxford: Oxbow.

Whittle, A. (1997*c*). 'Remembered and imagined belongings: Stonehenge in its traditions and structures of meaning', *Proceedings of the British Academy*, 92: 145–66.

Whittle, A. (1998*a*). 'Fish, faces and fingers: presences and symbolic identities in the Mesolithic-Neolithic transition in the Carpathian basin', *Documenta Praehistorica*, 25: 133–50.

Whittle, A. (1998*b*). 'Beziehungen zwischen Individuum und Gruppe: Fragen zur Identität im Neolithikum der ungarischen Tiefebene', *Ethnographisch-Archäologische Zeitschrift*, 39: 465–87.

Whittle, A. (2000). '"Very like a whale": menhirs, motifs and myths in the Mesolithic-Neolithic transition of north-west Europe', *Cambridge Archaeological Journal*, 10: 243–59.

Whittle, A., and Wysocki, M. (1998). 'Parc le Breos Cwm transepted long cairn, Gower, West Glamorgan: date, contents, and context', *Proceedings of the Prehistoric Society*, 64: 139–82.

Whittle, A., Pollard, J., and Grigson, C. (1999). *The Harmony of Symbols: The Windmill Hill Causewayed Enclosure, Wiltshire*. Oxford: Oxbow.

Williams, E. (1989). 'Dating the introduction of food production into Britain and Ireland', *Antiquity*, 63: 510–21.

Windl, H. (1996). 'Archäologie einer Katastrophe und deren Vorgeschichte', in *Rätsel um Gewalt und Tod vor 7,000 Jahren: eine Spurensicherung*. Asparn a.d.Zaya: Museum für Urgeschichte, 7–29.

Windl, H. J. (1999). 'Makabres Ende einer Kultur?', *Archäologie in Deutschland*, 1: 54–7.

Woodman, P. C., Anderson, E., and Finlay, N. (1999). *Excavations at Ferriter's Cove, 1983–95: Last Foragers, First Farmers in the Dingle Peninsula*. Bray: Wordwell.

Wysocki, M., and Whittle, A. (2000). 'Diversity, lifestyles and rites: new biological and archaeological evidence from British Earlier Neolithic mortuary assemblages', *Antiquity*, 74: 591–601.

Zvelebil, M. (1994). 'Plant use in the Mesolithic and its role in the transition to farming', *Proceedings of the Prehistoric Society*, 60: 35–74.

COMMENT

Significant Transitions

Colin Renfrew

'Erst kommt das Fressen, dann kommt die Moral'
(Bertholt Brecht)

DR WHITTLE's account of the Neolithic makes a number of illuminating points which are well worth pondering. In the first place, he rightly stresses the complexity and variety in each region of Europe, where local adaptations to the environmental take different courses, and the trajectories of development can shape and enhance emerging local traditions.

He is right to stress the local particularities of the *Linearbandkeramik*, as well as to recognize the rapidity of the LBK spread. To my mind, however, he is too reluctant to accept the possibility that this represents the expansion of a population of mixed farmers who may ultimately be the descendants, at least in part, of immigrants to the area in question, representing (and in genetic terms in part replicating) a population with origins further afield, to the south-east. One may envisage a series of transformations, from region to region (Thessaly to Macedonia, Macedonia to the Danube Valley, the Serbian Plain to the Hungarian Plain, etc.), each drawing on and transforming (and adapting to local circumstances) the economy and practices of its predecessor, and each based in part on an immigrant population which soon intermarries with the indigenous locals. That is the traditional view, often associated with the demic diffusion model of Ammerman and Cavalli-Sforza (1973). Its blanket application to Europe as a whole has justifiably been criticized (Zvelebil 1995), but widely accepted for the Balkans and the *Linearbandkeramik* spread, although not necessarily beyond those limits. Most scholars would see the development of farming in Scandinavia as one of acculturation, but for Whittle to speak of 'the recent British consensus that the beginnings of the Neolithic were essentially to do with the acculturation of an indigenous population' seems very much an overstatement.

I am again very much in agreement with his general emphasis upon continuities in local tradition. Indeed after the inception of the Neolithic it seems likely to me that there was very little further immigration to the British Isles on any very significant scale until the Roman invasion (itself perhaps not a very significant episode in demographic terms) and then the adjustments of population following the collapse of Roman Britain, which certainly brought the new Germanic language, Anglo-Saxon, to these shores, and some further infiltration of population at the same time.

But I feel that the transition from a hunter-gatherer way of life to that of Neolithic farmers was a much more significant one than he has suggested. Indeed in the whole story of human history, this same transition, in its various manifestations, may have been the most significant of all. Even the change which accompanied the so-called 'Human Revolution' in Europe, the transition some 40,000 years ago to *Homo sapiens sapiens*, does not have so dramatic an impact upon material culture. To a non-specialist in the study of lithic industries the change from a Mousterian industry (associated with the Neanderthalers) to an Aurignacian one (associated with our own species, *Homo sapiens sapiens*) is not overwhelmingly impressive. And which among you could unerringly distinguish (as I might fail to do) a 'Châtelperronian industry'? It should be remembered that Franco-Cantabrian cave art, the astonishing creation of these hunter-gatherers, is in global terms a very restricted phenomenon.

The transition to the Neolithic, while it may not have been occasioned by strong demographic pressure—and here I concur with Whittle that there need have been no 'overcrowding' in the earlier Neolithic—must certainly have produced a very significant rise in population. There is some agreement among students of hunter-gatherers that, unless there is access to abundant aquatic and marine resources, a population density of one person per 10 square kilometres is an acceptable average figure for a region like north-western Europe. It may have been more in coastal regions but for inland Europe the figure seems reasonably generous. With a population practising simple agriculture a figure of two or three persons per square kilometre will be usual (at least for those parts of the landscape which are occupied), and even ten persons per square kilometre is not a high population density for simple farmers on suitable land. There may well have been extensive uncultivated areas at first, but the number and distribution of burial monuments in the Wessex area, and of megalithic monuments, for instance in Arran, in Orkney, and in parts of Ireland, supports such a figure at least for those areas.

This figure represents an increase in population density by a factor of at least 20 or 30 in inland areas, possibly by as much as 100, perhaps in the course of just a few centuries, as a consequence of the coming of farming.

This is a very significant figure indeed—more than an order of magnitude. It elucidates one of the factors underlying the transformed nature of social relations in the Neolithic period.

Such a change was made possible mainly by the introduction of cereal crops—principally wheat and barley—as well as pulse crops and flax (from which the earliest European textiles were woven). Dr Whittle has emphasized the importance of sheep and goat, and particularly cattle and he is right. But I am sceptical when he asserts that livestock played a much more important role than cereals in the diet. Certainly in Greece today meat is not a daily occurrence at the rural table, often not even a weekly occurrence, and I am not sure why it should be proposed that there was such a preponderance in the British Isles.

The farming package of cereals and pulses (and flax) along with sheep, goat, and cattle came to Europe from Anatolia, accompanied or soon followed by pottery-making and probably by weaving (although this may have reached northern Europe later than the cereal complex). The almost complete lack of evidence for a Greek Mesolithic (as recently reasserted by Curtis Runnels) combined with the stratigraphic record of the Franchthi Cave suggests that this was, at least in Greece, in the main a discontinuous transition, occasioned by the advent of immigrant Neolithic farmers. The limited evidence for the Mesolithic period so far attested in south-east Europe may in part be a feature of less-intensive research, but in some areas there is at present little evidence of a Mesolithic population for adjacent groups to acculturate.

While it is true that in south Britain we have very little evidence for the form of houses in the Neolithic period, this is not the case for some of the Scottish islands, notably the Orkney Islands. The famous Neolithic village of Skara Brae is only one of the settlement sites known, and the concentration of chambered cairns, notably on the island of Rousay, has long been taken as an indicator of a substantial population density. When we add to this the circumstance that no Mesolithic occupation is yet securely documented in Orkney (and certainly no indication of year-round occupation) then the notion of 'the acculturation of an indigenous population' seems highly questionable, just as it does (as Whittle himself discreetly hints) in Ireland. It does not of course follow that the Orcadian case is typical: certainly the absence of wood and the presence of laminar flags of sandstone made easy the construction of stone buildings. But those are local constructional aspects which help to explain the preservation of the Orkney evidence: they do not in themselves explain the evident population density. There is no special reason to imagine this to have been exceptionally high. I find it difficult to accept for this context Whittle's dictum that 'the coming of agriculture in a more familiar guise, although preceded in

Britain and Ireland by herding and piecemeal cultivation from about 4000 BC, was not seen till as late as about 1500 BC onwards'.

There are many refreshing aspects to Whittle's sympathetic approach to the Neolithic period. It makes sense to see it in part as the product of acculturation, and to view the transition in large measure from the standpoint of the indigenous population. He is right to stress the symbolic aspects of the society, as exemplified so well by the chambered tombs and the other monuments. Indeed the emphasis upon the internal processes within the local societies at this time which have been so thoughtfully considered in Julian Thomas's *Rethinking the Neolithic* (Thomas 1991) and Whittle's own *Europe in the Neolithic: The Creation of New Worlds* (Whittle 1996) is an altogether refreshing one, and a splendid antidote to the diffusionist thought which has for so long pervaded the study of prehistoric Europe. But while it is indeed true that man does not live by bread alone, it may also be the case that the coming of agriculture was a decisive factor in facilitating the demographic, social, and spiritual transformations which followed. The Marxist notion that the mode of production is of crucial significance was one of the sources upon which Gordon Childe drew in formulating his concept of a 'Neolithic revolution'. As Thomas and Whittle rightly show, it is not obligatory to take on this model unthinkingly. But to bear in mind that the Neolithic did indeed represent a new mode of production may not be untimely.

REFERENCES

Ammerman, A. J., and Cavalli-Sforza, L. L. (1973). 'A population model for the diffusion of early farming in Europe', in C. Renfrew (ed.), *The Explanation of Culture Change, Models in Prehistory.* London: Duckworth, 344–58.

Thomas, J. (1991). *Rethinking the Neolithic.* Cambridge: Cambridge University Press.

Whittle, A. (1996). *Europe in the Neolithic: The Creation of New Worlds.* Cambridge: Cambridge University Press.

Zvelebil, M. (1995). 'Agricultural origins and the agricultural transition in Europe', *Journal of European Archaeology*, 3, 1: 33–70.

4

Tribes and Empires *c.*1500 BC–AD 500

Barry Cunliffe

THE period of two thousand years or so which we set out to cover here—roughly 1500 BC to AD 500—begins at a time when the evidence available to us is purely archaeological, untainted by the vagaries of history, and ends when the gleanings from archaeology have to be reconciled with a rich historical tradition and the varied interpretations of linguists. Thus, in spanning the millennia, we bridge the disciplines. The first historian to consider the tribes of the British Isles from a truly informed position was Tacitus. Writing towards the end of the first century AD he had access not only to the vague and anecdotal writings of the Posidonian tradition and the observations of Julius Caesar on the tribal situation in the south-east, but he was also able to draw upon the reminiscences of his father-in-law, Julius Agricola, who had spent many seasons campaigning in Britain first as a legionary commander and later as governor of the province. Agricola travelled from one end of the island to the other and, incidentally, was probably responsible for killing more Britons than any other Roman. Assessing the varied array of evidence available to him in an attempt to characterize the British population,[1] Tacitus showed the commendable restraint of an historian in his famous summation

> who the first inhabitants of Britain were, whether native or immigrant remains obscure: one must remember, we are dealing with barbarians. (*Agricola*, 11)

After several centuries of hard archaeological endeavour the situation has changed little.

[1] The textual sources referring to Britain before the invasion of AD 43 are few. The works of Posidonius, compiled in the early first century BC from a wide range of earlier texts, are lost but fragments survive quoted by later sources such as Diodorus Siculus, Athenaeus, and Strabo. These have been collected and assessed by Tierney 1960, Edelstein and Kidd 1972, and Kidd 1988. Julius Caesar gives lengthy descriptions of Britain and the Britons in *De Bello Gallico*, Books IV and V. These are based on the writings of Posidonius and upon personal observations (discussed in Nash 1976). Tacitus' book *Agricola* was completed in AD 98.

Forty years ago, in considering the formation of the British people, we would have been much more confident. We would have talked of a series of 'invasions' bringing in successive waves of new people from the Continent—Deverel-Rimbury folk in the Late Bronze Age about 1000 BC, Hallstatt overlords resplendent on their horses and wielding long slashing swords in the seventh century, invaders from the Marne region around 400 BC and Belgae first raiding and then settling in the south-east in the first century BC (Hawkes and Dunning 1931). We would have debated the exact chronology and would have spent some time considering by whom, and along what routes, the Celtic language groups—the archaic Q Celtic and the more recent P Celtic—were introduced.[2] All this, we now realize, is the stuff of historical romance! Archaeology has moved far on since then. The data now available to us are far more complex and intricately textured and our perceptions are, we believe, rather less naïve. I make this point not to pour scorn on previous generations of scholars—all vital disciplines necessarily change their paradigms from time to time—but as a warning that much of the outdated thought is still believed to be valid by those in the kindred disciplines of linguistics, biological anthropology, and history. In any study which involves the creative interaction of disciplines it is necessary for us all to be aware of current thought and debate in the relevant subject areas.

In the last chapter, Alasdair Whittle brought the story down to the middle of the second millennium BC. The century or two around 1500–1400 BC was a period of quite dramatic change in the British landscape. Until this time much of society's energy had been invested in monumentalizing the landscape by creating ritual structures like the henges of Wessex (Wainwright 1989) and the alignments and circles of standing stones in the west and north (Burl 1993) and by building prominent tombs for ancestors, the great long barrows and chambered tombs of the fourth and third millennia giving way to the round barrows in the third and second. But by the middle of the second millennium this tradition of monumentalization had passed. In its place came a new form of landscape manipulation. The surface of the land was now divided—and thus controlled—by boundaries often in the form of banks and ditches continuous for many kilometres (Bradley, Entwistle, and Raymond 1994) and in some areas huge tracts of land were laid out in a systematic manner in patterns of rectangular fields. A number of these early field systems are known, particularly in Wessex. Near Quarley Hill, in the west of Hampshire, one such system has been traced by aerial photography covering an area of some 90 hectares. Other

[2] The old literature is massive but the mood of the time is best caught by Hawkes 1959. The development of Iron Age studies in Britain is summed up (with references) in Cunliffe 1991: 1–20.

early systems of comparable size have been identified in the same general region near the later Iron Age hillforts of Danebury and Woolbury. It would appear that once the land was divided and bounded these focal areas retained their social significance over many centuries. At Quarley it is possible to show that the boundaries laid out in the mid-second millennium BC were still being renewed a thousand years later. Certain lengths of the principal boundary ditch still persist as a property boundary today![3]

How to interpret this shift to controlling the land by containing it within boundaries is not entirely clear. A simple explanation would be to suppose that population increase was beginning to create new demands making it necessary to control more carefully the food producing capacity of the land, this becoming manifest in the social apportionment of the more productive regions. Such a model is oversimple in that it takes no account of regional variations but as an overarching explanation it can be refined to accommodate the many variables—decrease in the fertility of fragile soils through overuse, climatic deterioration, and the special demands of local élites.[4] These are all matters of high interest but not of direct relevance to our main theme. What is of importance is that the systems of controlling the landscape, which developed in the middle of the second millennium BC, set the scene for the next two thousand years. There were, of course, different regional trajectories but above these there lies an impressive continuity evident in the social and technical systems controlling land use and settlement spanning the two millennia of the Late Bronze Age, the Iron Age, and the Roman period. To do justice to such a crucial time in the history of Britain in the space available is difficult. However, by selecting certain themes—continuity, external contacts, regionalism, and mobility—something of the richness of the evidence can be demonstrated.

It is conventional to think of the British Isles as simply an offshore part of Europe. At one level this is, of course, true but the statement belies the true complexity of the situation. It is far more in tune with reality to conceive of Britain as belonging to two very different Europes—Atlantic Europe and continental Europe—as the map (Figure 4.1) will make clear. In both cases the sea bonds the island zone to its mainland counterpart while the land between divides. Thus the Atlantic zone of Britain shares far more in common with the Atlantic zone of France and Iberia than it does

[3] The evolution of the Wessex landscape in the second and first millennia BC has been the focus of several recent fieldwork programmes among them Gingell 1992, Bradley, Entwistle, and Raymond 1994, and Cunliffe 1999.

[4] Another intriguing possibility that has recently been put forward is that a near encounter with a comet in the twelfth century BC led to a rapid but brief environmental change which might have affected the fertility of fragile soils (Baillie 1999).

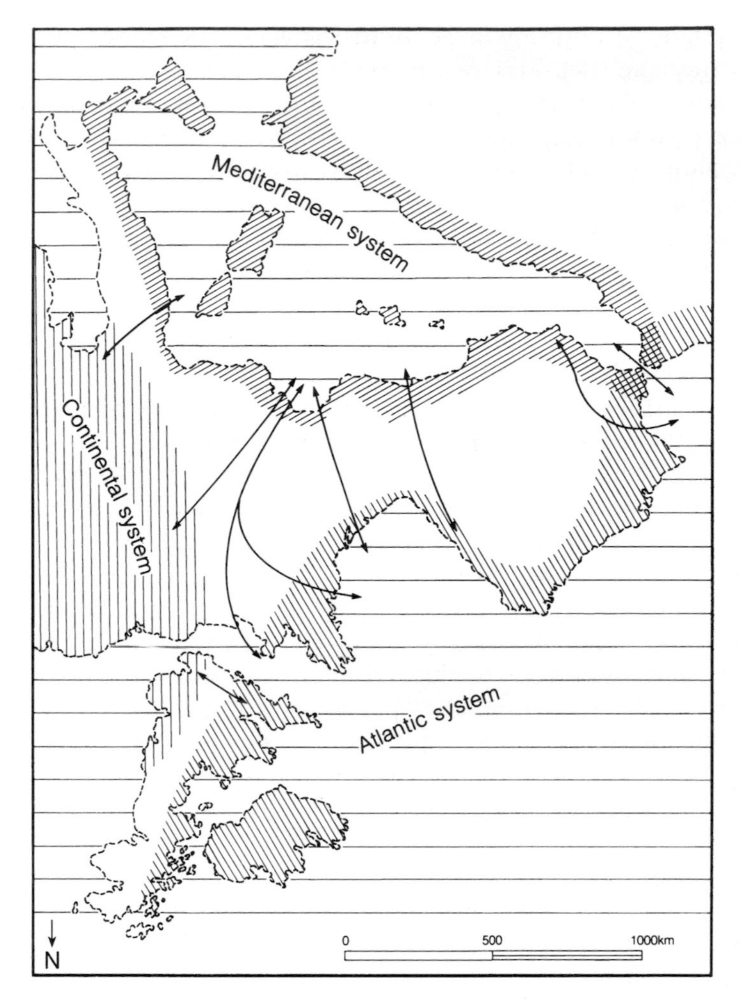

FIG. 4.1 A cognitive view of Europe indicating Britain's position in relation to major cultural systems.

with the eastern, continental, zone of Britain. It could even be argued that the land between (Wessex and the Midlands), far from being a cultural core for early Britain, was really little more than an intermediate zone between two stable systems. The intriguing possibility of this view of geography cannot be pursued here: what is of significance to the present discussion is to understand the geographical divide between east and west and the vital importance of the sea in maintaining close and consistent links between Britain and the adjacent continental systems (Cunliffe 1991: 405–43).

Atlantic Britain, stretching from the Northern Isles to Cornwall, is a zone of broadly similar micro-regions sharing in common a geomorphology of old hard rocks and a moist climate created by a predominantly westerly air stream. Without being too overtly geographically determinist we may say that these factors give rise to environments sharing similar constraints and opportunities which, inevitably, condition the nature of the socio-economic systems developing within them. Thus the zone is one dominated by scattered, single family or extended family units: larger agglomerations of population were, until comparatively recently, rare.

Behind this general similarity lies an intensely regional vernacular 'architecture'.[5] In the later first millennium BC the typical settlement in Cornwall and south-west Wales was the roughly circular embanked enclosure protecting the house and ancillary buildings of a single family. These *rounds* as they are known in Cornwall (Johnson and Rose 1982) and *raths* in Wales (Williams 1988), found in considerable numbers in the south-west (Figure 4.2), have many similarities to contemporary settlement in Brittany. Further north, in Atlantic Scotland and the Western and Northern Isles, the same kind of social unit practising much the same type of economy engineered more sophisticated stone-built structures known as *duns* and *brochs* and within these groups regional variations are apparent (Rivet 1966; Armit 1990; Armit and Ralston 1997). What we are witnessing in these patterns is, on the one hand, a basic similarity caused by a limited range of human responses to the constraints of environment and, on the other, a regionalization borne of different degrees of remoteness.

Another characteristic of these Atlantic settlements is the longevity of some of the basic settlement structures. In Cornwall rounds were being built from the Late Bronze Age well into the early Middle Ages. While the majority of the Atlantic settlements known from excavation were occupied for only a few centuries at a time before being rebuilt at new locations, a few remained in use over considerable periods. One of the best known examples, Jarlshof on the island of Shetland, was first settled in the Late Bronze Age around 1000 BC and thereafter was continuously occupied, though rebuilt on a number of occasions, until the later Middle Ages. This exceptional record is likely to be more a reflection of the site's highly favoured littoral environment than of any thread of inherited continuity.[6]

[5] A review of Iron Age settlement types in Britain with extensive references to the detailed literature will be found in Cunliffe 1991 to which may be added Armitt 1990 for more recent work in Scotland.

[6] For Jarlshof the definitive (and highly detailed) excavation report is Hamilton 1956. Another of the well excavated Shetland sites, Clickhimin (Hamilton 1968), shows a continuous sequence over centuries though without the medieval phases.

Fig. 4.2 Tregeare Round, St Kew, Cornwall. The Iron Age settlement area probably lay in the central enclosure with the outer enclosures used to keep animals. (Steve Hartgroves: Cornish Archaeological Unit.)

The principal characteristic of the Atlantic zone is that it looks to the ocean. The individual regions may have been remote one from another over land but by sea they could communicate and in this way ideas were transmitted. An impressive example of this is provided by the two island communities—Shetland to the far north of Scotland and the Aran Islands off the Atlantic coast of Galway. Both islands were small and without exceptional resources yet at Jarlshof on Shetland and Dún Aonghasa on Inis Mór excavations have produced clear evidence that bronze was being cast by skilled bronzesmiths about 1000 BC.[7] In all probability the archaeological deposits are the remnants of the workings of itinerant craftsmen who visited the islands from time to time, but even if the communities had

[7] For Shetland, Hamilton 1956. The recent excavations at Dún Aonghasa have not yet been published in full but for an interim account see Cotter 1996.

been large enough to support their own full-time specialists the metal alloy would have had to be imported.

That sea journeys of this kind were made need occasion no surprise. Efficient exploitation of the maritime resources underpinned the Atlantic economy. In the five millennia before the Bronze Age the Atlantic communities had learned to sail in search of fish: by 1000 BC maritime technology was highly developed. The principal type of vessel seems to have been the skin boat made of a light wattle framework with animal skins stretched across. Hide boats of this kind are mentioned on several occasions by Greek and Roman writers describing maritime communities from Iberia to Britain while a remarkable gold model boat dating to the first century BC, found at Broightar, Co. Derry in Ireland, seems to depict just such a vessel large enough for nine rowers and powered, in addition, by a square rigged sail. It was skin boats of this kind that were later used by the Irish saints in ocean-going journeys that took them into the far North Atlantic to the Faroes and to Iceland. Similar vessels known as currachs, built of tarred canvas stretched on a wooden skeleton, are still used for sea voyages from the Aran Islands today.[8] We need, therefore, have no doubt that the Atlantic communities had the technology necessary to make long sea journeys from the earliest times and it was as the result of constant short haul trafficking that these communities kept in contact and exchanged ideas.

Most of the journeys made along the western seaways were probably over no great distance yet commodities and concepts spread widely by being passed from one community to another in a system of down-the-line exchange. Such processes are evident in the distribution of Neolithic polished stone axes made from distinctive and sought-after stone (Cummings 1979). After the middle of the second millennium, when bronze came widely into use, sparsely distributed metals like copper, tin, and gold, often found close together in many regions of Atlantic Europe, were extensively exploited and widely traded. Archaeological distribution maps show that exchange networks developed all along the Atlantic seaways and large quantities of metal—as ingots, scrap, or finished items—were moved by sea, some of it over considerable distances. In one case spearheads of Irish manufacture—a type with distinctive basal loops—were found with much other material in a large deposit dredged from the estuary of Huelva in southern Spain more than 1,000 miles from their place of manufacture.

The European-wide demand for bronze may well have intensified maritime activity in the late second and early first millennium BC but by then the Atlantic routes had been in active operation for several thousand years.

[8] For a convenient summary of hide boats in the Atlantic region with copious references see McGrail 1998: 173–87.

In other words the contacts evident in the Late Bronze and Iron Age were part of the *longue durée* of maritime contact by means of which values, beliefs, and technological knowledge were exchanged. Such cultural similarities as there are can best be understood against this background.

The other axis by means of which Britain shared in continental European culture was across the southern North Sea and the Channel. These routes, like the Atlantic networks, were long established and may indeed have developed from the seasonal migrations of hunting groups in the early Mesolithic period before isostatic readjustment severed Britain from the Continent. Thereafter continuous contact between Britain and the mainland is evident in the archaeological record and becomes particularly visible in the distribution of manufactured bronze items in the Mid and Late Bronze Age. The underwater discovery of a quantity of bronze scrap of French origin at Langdon Bay, just beneath the cliffs east of Dover harbour, may reasonably be taken as evidence of a wrecked vessel engaged in transporting scrap bronze across the Channel.[9]

In the eighth and seventh centuries a large area of west central Europe, roughly from Burgundy to Bohemia, developed an élite social system dominated by a horse-riding aristocracy. The broad cultural continuum within which the élite zone developed is generally known after the archaeological type site of Hallstatt. Among the status-related luxury goods by which the paramounts distinguished themselves were horses, with all the trappings that went with them, and a distinctive type of long slashing sword. Four-wheeled vehicles also seem to have played a significant rôle and in western central Europe usually accompanied the dead leader to his grave. It has long been noticed that many of the different types of élite artefacts are to be found distributed far more widely than the core area within which the élite system developed and for many years this was conventionally interpreted as evidence of invasions by warrior élites. Thus the discovery of Hallstatt swords and horse gear in Britain was seen as evidence of an incursion of warriors in the seventh century crossing the southern North Sea and fighting their way across the island. Those who favoured such views no doubt had in mind the Norman invasion eighteen hundred years later.[10]

Such a simple model is no longer generally accepted. There are many reasons for this not least the fact that the alien artefacts are invariably found in cultural contexts characteristic of British belief systems and unlike those of the Continent. For example the élite burial practices of the west central

[9] The evidence for the Bronze Age Langdon Bay wreck at Dover and another broadly contemporary site at Moor Sands, Salcombe, Devon, is summarized in Muckelroy 1981.

[10] The European background to this is summed up in Cunliffe 1997: ch. 3. The British finds are considered in Cunliffe 1991: 405–24 and the Irish in Waddell 1998: 279–83.

Hallstatt province were not adopted in Britain. Instead the swords and horse gear were generally deposited in ritual contexts demanded by local tradition. There was also the growing awareness that many of the swords were made by British craftsmen and some were actually exported to the Continent. In parallel with these observations came a greater understanding of the processes of social interaction borne of a wider appreciation of the relevant anthropological literature. In short, it is now widely believed that the spread of Hallstatt style artefacts outside the west central core is best explained in terms of gift exchange and élite emulation in the context of long-established patterns of contact and has nothing to do with the incursion of invaders.

The fifth century BC saw the development, in the innovative centre of west central Europe focused on the Marne and Moselle region, of a vigorous and highly distinctive art style generally known as La Tène or Celtic art. The principal motifs used were derived from the Greek and Etruscan worlds but were interpreted with a much greater freedom and energy. La Tène art began as the art of the élite adorning the grave goods of the aristocracy but soon came to be adopted for enlivening humbler goods such as widely used safety-pin brooches and domestic pottery and woodwork.

The spread of the La Tène art style to Britain in the fourth century BC used to be interpreted as the manifestation of another invasion emanating in the Marne region and spreading across Britain eventually to reach Ireland. Such a simplistic model is now discounted. It is far more in tune with the fast-growing body of archaeological data to see the concepts and values embedded in La Tène art spreading through the traditional networks of contact to be adopted and adapted by local communities at will. One of the routes used was the southern North Sea route which brought knowledge and appreciation of sword and shield decoration to the east of Britain where skilled craftsmen developed distinct local schools. Another route lay along the Loire to Brittany and, by way of the Atlantic sea lanes, to south-west Britain, Wales, and Ireland. The axis had long been used to carry Atlantic commodities, principally metals to west central Europe. Armorica played a focal role in these networks both as a producer of copper, tin, and gold and as a geographical focus for the meeting of the maritime and river routes. The local communities no doubt had access to decorated metalwork brought in in cycles of gift exchange and it was not long before local potters began to adapt the motifs of the metalworker to ornament their own products. One of the masterpieces of this interaction, which still survives miraculously largely intact, is the elegant jar from St-Pol-de-Leon enlivened with motifs closely echoing those found on metalwork of the Marne region and beyond. These same motifs were used by metalworkers who made a bronze vessel (or vessels) that finally ended up in a burial cist at Cerrig-y-Drudion in north Wales.[11] From evidence of this kind, incomplete though it is, something of the complex patterns of social interaction can dimly be discerned.

We have seen that archaeologists have long since abandoned invasionist theories to explain culture change in Britain in the first millennium BC (Clark 1966) but this said it is as well to remember that swords don't swim. Items and concepts of continental European origin had to be brought to Britain by people: what the archaeological record suggests is that these interactions were probably geographically extensive and temporally continuous. In social terms we must be witnessing, in our artefact distributions, a wide variety of individual acts—a fisherman unsuccessfully attempting to land a cargo of bronze scrap at Dover in an off season, emissaries from the courts of continental élites bringing gifts of horses and armour to establish diplomatic relations, further ratified by the exchange of women or craftsmen, entrepreneurs setting themselves up at agreed ports-of-trade during the summer months to acquire native products, and even small-scale settlement from time to time. All of these are likely models but it is seldom that the coarse-grained archaeological evidence will allow us to distinguish between them with any degree of certainty. We can, however, be reasonably sure that there were no major incursions of invaders. That said, the population of Britain—some million or two people—while remaining largely of indigenous origin, was constantly being refreshed by social interaction with the European mainland.

If this perception of Britain in the first millennium BC is correct we must attempt to tackle a favourite debating issue of the earlier part of this century, 'When did the Celts arrive in the British Isles?'[12] That tribal confederacies, known to Classical writers as Celts or Gauls, emerged in west central Europe in the middle of the first millennium and that some part of them were involved in large-scale folk movements, south through the Alps to the Po valley and east along the Danube to Transdanubia and beyond, is generally accepted (Rankin 1987) but the frequently made assumption that migratory bands entered the British Isles at this time is entirely without foundation. 'But then', a disbeliever may ask, 'how is it that Celtic languages are still spoken in Wales, Scotland, Ireland, and Brittany?' Between such a question and the available evidence lies a thick crust of scholarly assumption which we need to penetrate.

It began with Edward Lhuyd, Keeper of the Ashmolean Museum from

[11] The literature on La Tène or Celtic art is legion but by far the most convenient source, well illustrated and thoroughly referenced, is Megaw and Megaw 1989. For the Atlantic sea routes as a means of contact in this period see Cunliffe 1990. An up-to-date assessment of the Cerrig-y-Drudion find is given by Stead 1982.

[12] The whole question of the validity of the concept of the Celts is the subject of lively debate. Entrenched attitudes bolstered by bold *credos* are currently being published almost daily. For a perceptive and balanced overview see Sims-Williams 1998.

1691 to 1709. Lhuyd was a polymath but one of his great interests was language and in 1695 he presented a prospectus for a scholarly work he intended to produce called *Archaeologia Britannica* in which, together with other studies, he proposed to compare his native language Welsh with other European languages among them Irish, Cornish, and Armorican. The first volume of *Archaeologia*, which appeared in 1707, presented the grammar and vocabularies of Irish, Breton, and Cornish, Lhuyd noting that these languages had close similarities to Gaulish and Welsh. He referred to the group as Celtic, and in the preface to *Archaeologia* went on to suggest that the differences between them could be explained in terms of successive waves of colonization. The first he saw as Irish Britons from Gaul who settled in Britain but were later driven northwards into Scotland and westwards to Ireland by a second Gaulish wave who settled in Britain. This hypothesis gained wide acceptance and was soon to be formalized into the Q-Celtic/P-Celtic model, Q-Celtic being thought of as the earliest form of Celtic spoken in Ireland and Scotland, with P-Celtic being a more recent introduction forming the basis of the Welsh, Cornish, Breton, and Gaulish. Given such a model it was inevitable that attempts should be made to integrate the archaeological data bringing them into line with the linguistic hypothesis, hence the question 'When did the Celts arrive in Britain?'

To untangle this web of preconceptions it is necessary to be clear about the use of the word 'Celtic'. No Classical writer uses the word about the British. Strabo and Caesar were both clear that much of Gaul, between the Seine and the Garonne, was inhabited by Celti and other writers use the term for the bands migrating into Italy and eastern Europe but the Britons are never thus described. Strictly therefore the languages spoken in the British Isles and Ireland ought not to have been called 'Celtic'. Had we been attempting to name them today we would have used a less ethnically loaded term such as, perhaps, 'Atlantic'. The only justification the early linguists had for coining the term Celtic was that the early Insular languages belonged to the same family as Gaulish and most of the Gaulish tribes were referred to as *Celti* in the first century BC. The question 'When did the Celts arrive in Britain?' is therefore an irrelevance based on misconceptions. The only way to rephrase it and still to retain the spirit of the enquiry is 'At what stage and by what process did the language group, commonly referred to as "Celtic", reach, or emerge in, western Europe?' This is a fertile ground for speculation but it is now widely believed, at least among archaeologists, that the Celtic language was spoken in the west from a very early stage quite possibly as early as the Neolithic period (Renfrew 1987: 211–49). What is tolerably certain is that the intensity of the exchange networks along the Atlantic seaways and along the rivers flowing into the Atlantic, from the Neolithic period onwards, which saw the spread of belief systems and technological knowledge as well as commodities, will have ensured that a high level of communication was maintained. By the first millennium BC Celtic would have been the *lingua franca* common to all these regions in much the same way as Swahili developed as the language of the east African littoral.

In the first century BC Britain was drawn increasingly into the expanding sphere of the Roman world and, as a result, found itself in the shadowy fringes of the recorded history, sparse and anecdotal though it was.[13] We may distinguish three phases in the interaction of Rome and the Britons.

The first, from about 120 BC to 55 BC, saw increased trading activity mainly along the Atlantic seaways initiated by the annexation of southern Gaul. Into the newly created province of Transalpina Roman merchants moved, eager to develop profitable commerce with the large and largely untapped market of Gaul. A new impetus was generated by these entrepreneurs. Slaves and raw materials from the Barbarian north were much in demand by the consuming societies of the Mediterranean. In return for these, surplus Roman wine from the huge north Italian estates together with a range of consumer durables—flashy tableware and the like—poured into Gaul (Tchernia 1983). Roman traders set themselves up in the nearer native market centres while deeper in barbarian territories the native networks adapted to the new opportunities. In this way Roman items including amphorae of wine found their way to Britain.

The second stage saw the flag following the trade as Julius Caesar and his massive Roman army swept through Gaul up to the Rhine. In a single decade the entire territory had been subdued and a substantial Roman force had twice braved the Channel, in 55 and 54 BC, to make a brief show in the south-east of Britain.

That Gaul was now Roman changed the economic situation entirely. Roman and native traders from Gaul now had easy access to south-east Britain and no doubt the Roman authorities were anxious to maintain diplomatic relations with the British élite building upon treaties negotiated by Caesar. One of the clearest archaeological manifestations of all this activity, both economic and political, is the appearance of Roman luxury goods in the burials of the British chieftains in Kent, Essex, and Hertfordshire. When, eventually, the invasion of Britain was launched by Claudius in AD 43 the south-east had been in close contact with the Roman world for ninety years.

During this century and a half of contact with the Roman world, first at a comfortable remove, then briefly immediate, and finally at close range,

[13] Convenient summaries of the historical evidence for Britain in the first century BC and early first century AD are given in Frere 1987: 1–47 and Salway 1981: 20–61.

there were discernible changes in British society particularly in the south-east of the country. The data, now available, are rich (Cunliffe 1991: 107–79). Not only is the archaeological record unusually prolific but to it can now be added a body of historical anecdotes and a full numismatic sequence reflecting, albeit obscurely, the dynastic changes and shifting allegiances of the southern British tribes. From this it is possible to sketch out a political, social, and economic history for the period.

Since our present concerns are with demographic changes we must be selective. The period of early contact, from *c.*120 BC to the time of Caesar's Gallic Wars, provides three clear examples of different kinds of population interaction. The first, direct trade, is nicely demonstrated by the site of Hengistbury Head in Dorset examined on various occasions this century (Cunliffe 1987). Hengistbury Head is a coastal promontory protecting a large sheltered harbour (Christchurch harbour) into which flow two of the major rivers of Wessex, the Avon and the Stour. It is admirably sited to perform the functions of a port-of-trade: it lies on an interface between two tribes; it is isolated but easily accessible by sea and river; and it has direct access to desirable local resources such as salt, iron, and Kimmeridge shale (for making armlets). The rich archaeological assemblage derived from the excavations shows that it formed the focus of a complex trading network (Figure 4.3). Metals were brought to the headland from different parts of south-west Britain—silver-rich lead from Mendip, tin from Cornwall, and

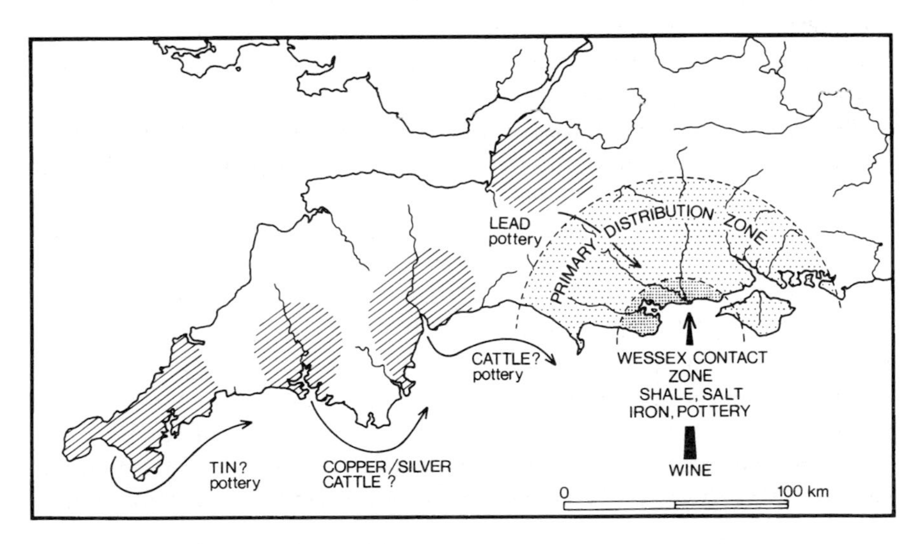

FIG. 4.3 South-western Britain about 100 BC outlining the exchange system operating through the port at Hengistbury Head.

copper-silver alloy from the western fringes of Dartmoor, together with scrap gold in the form of broken torcs and bracelets. From nearer at hand corn was imported from the Wessex hinterland and there is evidence to suggest that cattle were driven to the site in some numbers, perhaps to be killed and salted or to provide hides, or both. A number of commodities brought in from the Continent are also evident in the archaeological record. The most bulky were the north Italian amphorae used for importing wine. Of less volume, but of no less value, were lumps of raw glass, both purple and yellow, and figs, represented now by seeds preserved in the organic deposits. Pottery from Brittany was also found in considerable quantity indicating that the ships may have sailed from the north Armorican coast possibly from a port in the bay of St Brieuc. The presence of so much Breton pottery raises interesting questions. One possibility is that it may have arrived as containers carrying some local delicacy but another is that it was brought by Armorican traders for their own use during the summer season when they lived on the headland and exchanged their goods for those accumulated by their British counterparts from Wessex and the south-west. The Greek geographer Strabo, who wrote in the early years of the first century AD, mentioned regular trading expeditions to Britain where, he said, a range of useful things could be acquired, among them metals, hides, corn, hunting dogs, and slaves.

The opening up of this Armorica–Solent axis eventually brought a number of foreigners to the shores of Britain but while the contact exacerbated social and economic changes in central southern Britain it is unlikely that the numbers of incomers added significantly to the gene pool.

A rather different kind of social interaction linked the south-east of Britain with the adjacent coastal region of Gaul. In this case it seems as though we are dealing with a network of political allegiances between élites.[14] The clue is given by Caesar. Writing about the Suessiones he mentions one of their previous kings, Diviciacus, who, within living memory, was 'the most powerful ruler in the whole of Gaul' and 'had control not only over a large area of this region but also of Britain' (*De Bello Gallico*, II. 4). The implication here is that Diviciacus was recognized as a high king to whom some at least of the British rulers offered homage. The close relationship is further demonstrated by the way in which the British rulers adopted Gallo-Belgic coinage and used it as a model for their own mintings. The most prolific of the Gallo-Belgic types to be found in Britain, known as Gallo-Belgic E, may have been minted to reward troops fighting Caesar at the time of the Gallic Wars. Its occurrence in the island in such

[14] The overviews in Salway 1981 and Frere 1987 provide conventional accounts largely from an historical point of view. A rather different approach, focusing on the nature of the societies involved, is presented in Nash 1984.

quantity is an indication that British troops may well have fought in Gaul as Caesar himself implies. It is impossible to quantify these movements but during the eight years or so of hostilities it is quite likely that large numbers of Britons crossed to Gaul to fight and Britain, no doubt, received many refugees. The one whom we know by name was the Gaulish noble Commius, once a friend of Caesar and now a sworn enemy, who escaped to Britain and established his authority in north Hampshire and Berkshire where he founded the dynasty of the Atrebates. In this time of all out war, on a scale probably never before experienced, there would have been much mobility of population.

Caesar provides one further enigmatic reference to mobility which has been the subject of active debate for more than a century. Referring to the Belgae—a general name which he used to describe the tribes occupying northern Gaul between the Seine and the Rhine—he mentions that some time in the past some of them had migrated to Britain—'They came to raid and stayed to sow.' Much has been built on this sparse observation and the 'Belgic invasion' of the British Isles came to be regarded as one of the established facts of history, the general belief being that the entire south-east of the country was overrun by invaders some time around 100 BC. More recently doubts have been expressed for a variety of sound archaeological reasons. While the debate continues a good case could be made out for there having been a limited incursion in the Solent region (Figure 4.4). The fact that the town which developed on the site of Winchester was known to the Romans as *Venta Belgarum* adds support to this view.[15]

The three examples so briefly considered here—organized trade, diplomatic interaction, and limited incursion—all founded on reliable archaeological, historical, and numismatic evidence, give some idea of the complexity of the intercourse binding the populations facing each other across the Channel. Interactions of this kind no doubt occurred in the many centuries before but the proximity of Rome gives them a heightened visibility as well, one suspects, as being a catalyst to greater activity.

The establishment of Roman control throughout Gaul, culminating in the careful administrative systems put in place by Augustus after the end of the Civil War, brought a new stability to the country allowing trade to flourish. This in turn had a direct impact on Britain. The cross-Channel routes, including those which had long linked Britain and Armorica, seem to have declined in importance while the Thames estuary began to take on a new significance as an axis of communication. The Roman luxury goods that now flowed in—amphorae of wine, silver and bronze drinking vessels, ceramic tableware and the like—frequently ended up in the burials of the

[15] The conventional interpretation is summed up in Frere 1987: 9–15. The view favoured here is argued in Cunliffe 1991: 107–29.

FIG. 4.4 The Late Iron Age enclosure at Nettlebank Copse near Stockbridge in Hampshire during excavation in 1993. (Danebury Trust.)

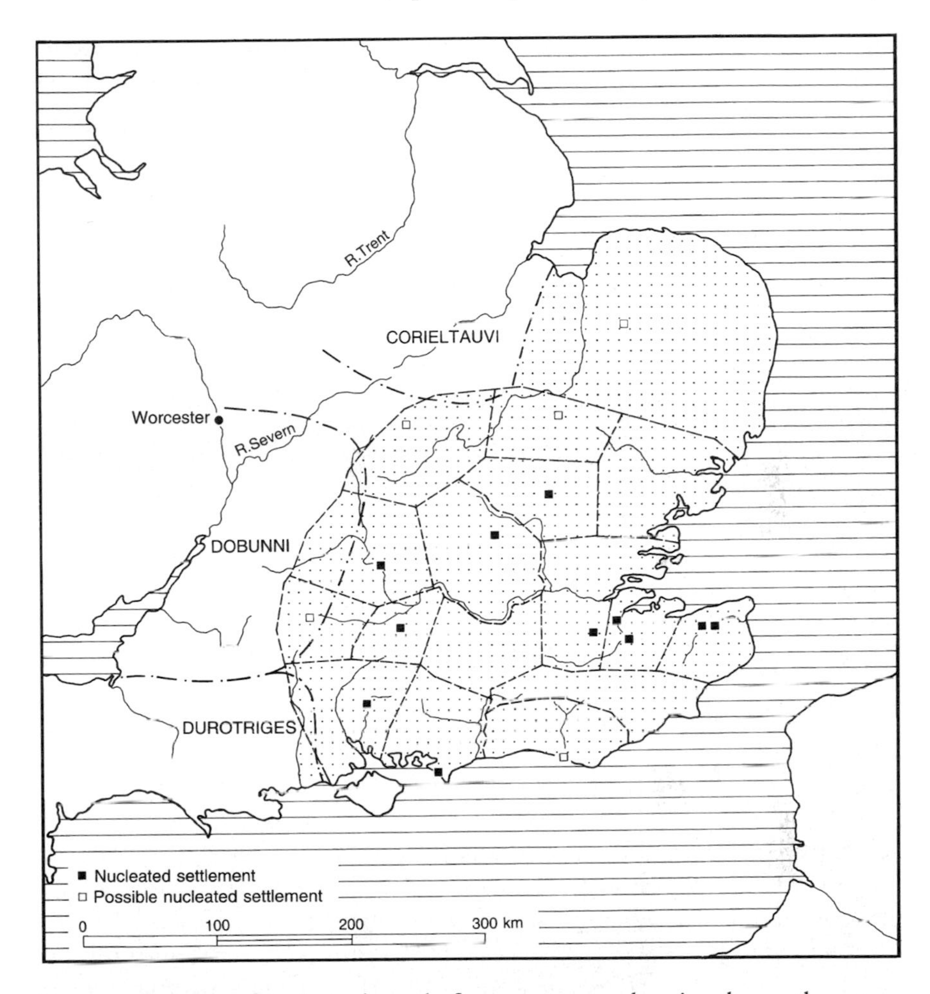

FIG. 4.5 Southern Britain in the early first century AD showing the south-eastern economic zone with its constituent socio-economic territories based on *oppida* and the three peripheral tribes.

élite under whose auspices trade with the Roman and Gaulish entrepreneurs developed apace. Such was its volume that it seems highly likely that enclaves of traders from the Continent were resident in the main urban centres of south-eastern Britain—places like Canterbury, *Verulamium* (St Albans), and *Camulodunum* (Colchester).

By the time of the Claudian invasion in AD 43 the socio-economic structure of Britain had crystallized into three broad zones (Figure 4.5). In the south-east, closest to Gaul, large nucleated settlements had developed with many of the characteristics of urban centres. In this zone successive rulers, dominated by the two principal dynasties, the Catuvellauni north of the Thames and the Atrebates to the south, were issuing a complex coinage in bronze, silver, and gold suitable both for diplomatic and commercial exchanges. Beyond this lay an inner periphery, stretching from Dorset to Lincolnshire, composed of three large tribal agglomerations, the Durotriges, the Dobunni, and the Corieltauvi each issuing their own distinctive coinage for circulation within their own territory. Within this zone nucleated settlements had begun to develop but none is known to have reached the proportions of those in the south-east. Beyond this lay the outer periphery—essentially the rest of Britain—a zone without coinage and with no evidence of the kind of complex economic organization that gave rise to the larger settlements. It is tempting to argue that this simple threefold division was, in large part, the result of intensified trading contacts between the now-Roman Continent and Britain. In this model the south-east functioned as a core zone, serving as an interface with the Continent while the tribes of the inner periphery acted as middle men in articulating exchanges between the core and the metal-rich west and north. These more remote areas may also have been a convenient source of slaves always much in demand among Roman entrepreneurs, the more so after Gaul had ceased to be a ready source following its absorption into the Roman empire.

The early course of the Roman invasion of Britain initiated by Claudius in AD 43 was to a large extent conditioned by the existing socio-political structure of Britain. The immediate cause of the invasion, if we are to believe Roman propaganda, was the plea, by one of the Atrebatic leaders, for Roman help against aggressive neighbours (Salway 1981: 65–99; Frere 1987: 48–80). At any event the initial plan seems to have been simply to contain the more civilized core zone by creating a military frontier, linked by a road known as the Fosse Way, slicing across the tribal territories of the inner periphery (Figure 4.6). The system was anchored by a fortress at each end at Exeter and Lincoln, with another in the centre at Gloucester and troop detachments stationed in smaller forts along the line. It was an elegant solution to the problem. The frontier protected the settled and agriculturally productive core zone from the wilder tribes of the outer periphery while at the same time providing an effective control over the movement of commodities from one zone to another. It could not, however, be maintained and within a comparatively few years the Roman army was drawn first into the west Midlands and Wales and then further and further north eventually reaching the fringes of the Scottish Highlands.

The impact of the 400 years or so of Roman rule on the landscape and population of Britain is as complex as it is fascinating—a fascination

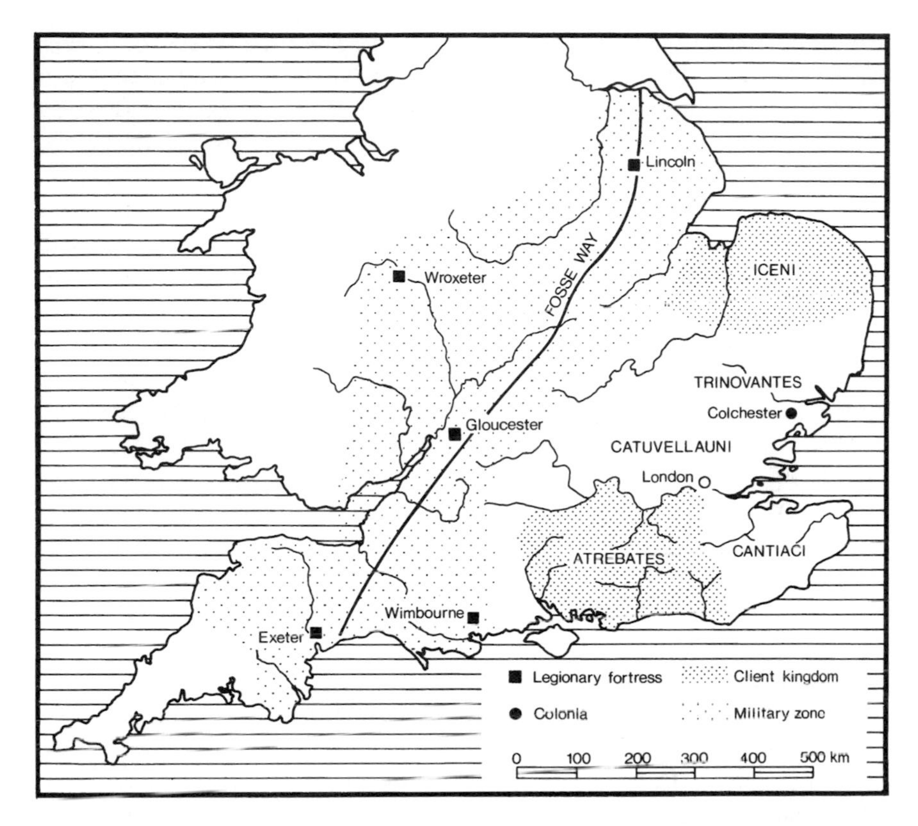

FIG. 4.6 Southern Britain in the decade following the Roman invasion of AD 43. The peripheral tribes (Figure 4.5) have become a military zone protecting the more economically advanced south-eastern region.

greatly enhanced by the high quality of the scholarship focused on the problem and the considerable effort that has been expended on the excavation of Roman sites over the last century. It was, undoubtedly, a period of change. Large numbers of foreigners came to Britain, in the army, as administrators, and as traders, and many Britons left the islands for the most part to fight in the Roman army abroad.[16] Quantification is very difficult but it is fair to say that the mobility of population was very much greater in the Roman period than at any time in Britain's prehistory. There have been many attempts to estimate the population of Roman Britain, the general consensus now being that it probably lay in the order of about four million

[16] The most accessible source for studying the ethnic and social mix in Britain is Birley 1979 which provides a detailed commentary on the historical and epigraphical evidence for the people of Roman Britain.

of whom perhaps as many as 120,000 at any one time were 'foreigners' mostly serving in the army or the administrative support services.[17] Many of the army personnel were stationed in Britain for years and it is probable that most of those who reached retiring age chose to remain in the province. In this way, over the 350 or so years of the occupation, the gene pool will have been constantly augmented. Inscriptions provide many insights into this process. One records the death at the age of 30 of an Essex girl, Regina, who had married a standard maker, Barates from Palmyra, and lived with him at South Shields on Hadrian's Wall. But not all of the foreigners were men. At Chester a Greek woman, Curatia Dionysia, was provided with an elaborate tombstone. It is possible that she arrived in Britain as a slave. In the same town another Greek, Thesaeus, erected a memorial inscription for his brother and son.

In addition to the inscriptions there are occasional historical references to contingents of foreign auxiliaries being sent to the province. In AD 175 5,500 Sarmatian cavalry from the Great Hungarian Plain arrived in Britain. Where they were stationed and how long they remained is unclear but in the third century a detachment of Sarmatians is recorded to have been at Ribchester and Sarmatian horse gear has been discovered at Chesters on Hadrian's Wall. It is not unlikely that during their term of military service in Britain Sarmatian genes were added to the British.

The new mobility that came with Roman rule affected all parts of the Roman province. In the frontier zones of the north and Wales the cosmopolitan mix would probably have been at its greatest but the trading centres and major cities like London, teaming with traders and merchants, as Tacitus reminds us, would also have been centres of mixed population. Bath, with its sanctuary and healing springs, was also a focus for travellers as the many inscriptions found there remind us. This said it is, however, as well to remember that the bulk of the population of Britain, perhaps as many as three and a half million, lived in rural settlements in the countryside and a high percentage of these were concentrated in the south-east: intensive field surveys have suggested that the density of rural settlement may, in some favoured areas, have been as high as one or two per square kilometre. It was in these areas that the indigenous British population remained largely untouched by foreign incomings, deeply rooted in its pre-Roman stock.

The countryside seems to have changed remarkably little (Hingley 1989; Millett 1990). The most noticeable feature were the roads, running in

[17] The question of the size of the population of Roman Britain has been considered many times this century and varying estimates have been offered. A summary of all this together with a new estimate, and a clear statement of the data on which it is based, is given by Millett 1990: 181–6.

unvarying straight lengths cleared across the face of the countryside cutting indiscriminately through earlier settlements and boundaries alike. Unerring and determined, these roads were a potent and ever present reminder of the new order. But elsewhere the changes were much slighter. There seems to have been much continuity in the locations chosen for settlements throughout the country. Many sites can be shown to have been several hundred years old by the time of the invasion. The tenurial system was probably largely unchanged and landownership may have remained within the same extended family for many generations. Even in the south-east, where masonry buildings, some with sophistications such as mosaic floors and bath suites, were to be found it is often the case that the farms did not begin to take on the visible trappings of Romanization until the late second or third century and then only gradually (Figure 4.7). Outside this villa zone native styles of building continued. In Cornwall, which had been within the civilized region of the province since the end of the first century AD, the round remained the norm even for establishments like Tregarthy not established until the third century. Throughout the remoter regions of the west—the Atlantic zone of Britain—little changed over a thousand years.

FIG. 4.7 An aisled hall of the third century AD: one of the buildings of a Roman villa complex at Grateley, Hampshire. Excavated in 1998. (Danebury Trust.)

Roman Britain shared in the homogenized culture of the Roman empire. It contributed to the Roman economy, was subject to Roman laws, and its élites espoused Roman value systems, yet by far the greatest bulk of the population was of indigenous descent and lived in a manner and in an environment which had changed little for hundreds of years. When, in the fifth century, the Roman administrative infrastructure collapsed, the rapid reversion to a fragmented system of rival enclaves led, with varying degrees of success, by warrior overlords, turned the clock back to a situation not unlike that of the Middle Iron Age six or seven hundred years before. It is a reminder that the façade of Romanization was more fragile and superficial than at first appears.

In this brief survey of Britain in the period 1500 BC–AD 500 we have suggested that the population, perhaps about a million at the beginning, trebling or quadrupling over two millennia, was refreshed by a constant trickle of new people arriving from the Continent but never was it overwhelmed or even significantly modified by invaders in the manner that scholars used to imagine forty years or more ago. The Celtic languages remained dominant over much of the region and even in the Romanized south-east where Latin was commonly spoken there are hints that Celtic may have remained far more widespread than was once thought (Tomlin 1988). That there was a massive continuity of population throughout is not in doubt but there were also changes with the gene pool constantly being augmented. To quantify these oppositions through time is not yet possible. While the archaeological evidence is imperfect and the historical evidence perhaps even more so, considerable advances have been made in the last forty years. It remains to be seen what new insights the study of ancient DNA and the mapping of genotypes will bring.

REFERENCES

Armit, I. (1990) (ed.). *Beyond the Brochs: Changing Perspectives on the Atlantic Scottish Iron Age*. Edinburgh: Edinburgh University Press.

Armit, I., and Ralston, I. B. M. (1997). 'The Iron Age', in K. J. Edwards and I. B. M. Ralston (eds.), *Scotland: Environment and Archaeology 8000 BC–AD 1000*. Chichester: Wiley, 169–93.

Baillie, M. (1999). *Exodus to Arthur: Catastrophic Encounters with Comets*. London: Batsford.

Birley, A. (1979). *The People of Roman Britain*. London: Batsford.

Bradley, R., Entwistle, R., and Raymond, F. (1994). *Prehistoric Land Divisions on Salisbury Plain*. London: English Heritage.

Burl, A. (1993). *From Carnac to Callanish*. New Haven: Yale University Press.

Clark, G. (1966). 'The invasion hypothesis in British archaeology', *Antiquity*, 40: 172–89.

Cotter, C. (1996). 'Western Stone Fort Project: interim report', *Discovery Programme Reports* 4, 1–14.
Cummings, W. A. (1979). 'Neolithic stone axes: distribution and trade in England and Wales', in T. H. McKClough and W. A. Cummings (eds.), *Stone Axe Studies*. London: CBA Research Report 23, 5–12.
Cunliffe, B. (1987). *Hengistbury Head, Dorset*, i. *Prehistoric and Roman Settlement, 3500 BC–AD 500*. Oxford: OUCA Monograph 13.
Cunliffe, B. (1990). 'Social and economic contacts between western France and Britain in the early and middle La Tène period', *Rev. archéol. Ouest Supplément*, 2: 245–51.
Cunliffe, B. (1991). *Iron Age Communities in Britain*. 3rd edn., London: Routledge.
Cunliffe, B. (1997). *The Ancient Celts*. Oxford: Oxford University Press.
Cunliffe, B. (1999). *The Danebury Environs Programme: A Prehistoric Wessex Landscape*, i. Oxford: OUCA Monograph 48.
Edelstein, L., and Kidd, I. G. (1972). *Posidonius: The Fragments*. Cambridge: Cambridge University Press.
Frere, S. S. (1987). *Britannia: A History of Roman Britain*. 3rd edn., London: Routledge.
Gingell, C. (1992). *The Marlborough Downs: A Later Bronze Age Landscape and its Origins*. Devizes: Trust for Wessex Archaeology.
Hamilton, J. R. C. (1956). *Excavations at Jarlshof, Shetland*. Edinburgh: HMSO.
Hamilton, J. R. C. (1968). *Excavations at Clickhimin, Shetland*. London: HMSO.
Hawkes, C. F. C. (1959). 'The ABC of the British Iron Age', *Antiquity*, 33: 170–82.
Hawkes, C. F. C., and Dunning, G. C. (1931). 'The Belgae of Gaul and Britain', *Archaeological Journal*, 87: 150–335.
Hingley, R. (1989). *Rural Settlement in Roman Britain*. London: Seaby.
Johnson, N., and Rose, P. (1982). 'Defended settlements in Cornwall—an illustrated discussion', in D. Miles (ed.), *The Romano-British Countryside*. Oxford: BAR British Series 103, 151–207.
Kidd, I. G. (1988). *Posidonios II: The Commentary*. Cambridge: Cambridge University Press.
McGrail, S. (1998). *Ancient Boats in North-West Europe*. 2nd edn., London: Longman.
Megaw, R., and Megaw, V. (1989). *Celtic Art: From its Beginnings to the Book of Kells*. London: Thames and Hudson.
Millett, M. (1990). *The Romanization of Britain*. Cambridge: Cambridge University Press.
Muckelroy, K. (1981). 'Middle Bronze Age trade between Britain and Europe: a maritime perspective', *Proceedings of the Prehistoric Society*, 47: 275–98.
Nash, D. (1976). 'Reconstructing Poseidonios' Celtic Ethnography: some considerations', *Britannia*, 7: 111–26.
Nash, D. (1984). 'The basis of contact between Britain and Gaul in the Late pre-Roman Iron Age', in S. Macready and F. H. Thompson (eds.), *Cross-Channel Trade between Gaul and Britain in the Pre-Roman Iron Age*. London: Society of Antiquaries, 92–107.

Rankin, H. D. (1987). *Celts and the Classical World*. London: Croom Helm.
Renfrew, C. (1987). *Archaeology and Language*. London: Jonathan Cape.
Rivet, A. L. F. (1966) (ed.). *The Iron Age in Northern Britain*. Edinburgh: Edinburgh University Press.
Salway, P. (1981). *Roman Britain*. Oxford: Oxford University Press.
Sims-Williams, P. (1998). 'Celtomania and Celtoscepticism', *Cambrian Medieval Celtic Studies*, 36: 1–35.
Stead, I. M. (1982). 'The Cerrig-y-Drudion "hanging bowl" ', *Antiquaries Journal*, 62: 221–34.
Tchernia, A. (1983). 'Italian wine in Gaul at the end of the Republic', in P. Garnsey, K. Hopkins, and C. R. Whittaker (eds.), *Trade in the Ancient Economy*. London: Chatto and Windus, 87–104.
Tierney, J. J. (1960). 'The Celtic Ethnography of Posidonius', *Proceedings of the Royal Irish Academy*, 60 (Section C, no. 5): 189–275.
Tomlin, R. (1988). 'The curse tablets' [from the Roman spring at Bath], in B. Cunliffe (ed.), *The Temple of Sulis Minerva at Bath*. ii. *The Finds from the Sacred Spring*. Oxford: OUCA Monograph 16, 59–277.
Waddell, J. (1998). *The Prehistoric Archaeology of Ireland*. Galway: Galway University Press.
Wainwright, G. (1989). *The Henge Monuments*. London: Thames and Hudson.
Williams, G. (1988). 'Recent work on rural settlement in later prehistoric and early historic Dyfed', *Antiquaries Journal*, 68: 30–54.

COMMENT

Questions of Identities

Martin Millett

PROFESSOR CUNLIFFE has provided us with a magisterial overview of a formative period in the history of the British Isles. Rather than provide a critique of his lecture, I prefer to draw out a few complementary themes concentrating on the later part of the period. As archaeologists we are prone to think of long-term trends. In doing this we should be careful not to neglect the human dimensions of both continuity and change. To put this into perspective, the period under discussion from 1500 BC to AD 500 represents over sixty generations and is equivalent to the period separating us today from the reign of the Roman Emperor Augustus. In taking an archaeological overview of such a period Professor Cunliffe has shown that there were considerable underlying continuities. I would lay particular emphasis on Britain's primarily agrarian character with the modes of cultivation changing comparatively slowly from the Bronze Age through to the later Roman period. Even at the height of the Roman period, perhaps only 10 per cent of the population were employed in anything other than farming (Millett 1990: 181–5). The vast majority of individuals lived their whole lives in communities within very limited localized regions having little contact with outsiders.

Such continuity should not lead us to neglect changes in the world which had an immediate impact on only a minority of the populus. I would like to focus in particular on changing aspects of social identities, an area in which there has been considerable recent interest amongst archaeologists.

I would argue that Britain witnessed a series of changes in aspects of social identity especially in the latter part of the period. In the Bronze and Iron Ages, the primary emphasis was on self-conscious, localized group identities defined by such features as pottery styles and settlement forms. These parochial groups were interconnected and their linkages created overarching regional and broader identities such as those described by Professor Cunliffe which united the peoples of the Atlantic coast or those on either side of the English Channel. At some stages these commonalities were defined by features such as common artistic styles, burial traditions, or the exchange of commodities all of which were arguably shared by only a minority of the population. The archaeological complexes known as Hallstatt, La Tène (Cunliffe 1991: 26–7), and Celtic art (Megaw and Megaw 1989) should thus be seen as expressions of identity adopted by these peoples rather than evidence for population movements.

We can, however, detect an increasing opening up of the world especially in the Iron Age and Roman periods. Although the bulk of the population probably rarely strayed from the region where they were born there were more frequent movements of both individuals and groups into and around Britain. This perhaps led some social groups increasingly to emphasize their own identities. Such local groupings came to place more emphasis on their identities when under external threat. So, for instance, a number of peoples across Britain first emerge as named entities when they came into conflict with Roman expansion (eg. Breeze 1996: 115–17 on Scotland). The Roman way of devolving power to local populations within her empire also reinforced this trend although it was Roman generals and administrators who identified the leaders of peoples with whom they would treat. Thus Iron Age peoples became Roman *civitates* (Millett 1990: 65 ff.). To some extent this reinforced existing power structures within society, but the firm establishment of social groupings within the administrative structure probably gave them greater permanence than they would otherwise have enjoyed. This reinforced the power of the élites within their groups as they were legitimized by Rome. Their political control facilitated increasing social differentiation and encouraged their adoption of distinctive Roman symbols of prestige such as construction and use of villas. Roman power thus reinforced and accentuated patterns of social differentiation which were already present within later prehistoric Britain.

The quality of the evidence from the Roman period allows us to provide reasonably reliable population estimates. Current evidence suggests a fourth-century population of *c*.3.6 million (Millett 1990: 185). Although there is some suggestion of an increase in the population size over that achieved in later prehistory, this is very difficult to demonstrate because of the differences in available evidence.

Incorporation into the Roman world also forged a series of new identities within a society which was becoming increasingly differentiated although there was arguably considerable social mobility. Some of the class distinctions, such as that between citizen and non-citizen, were of vital significance but remain almost impossible to identify through archaeology alone. Other important demarcations, such as those between age groups and by gender, are only glimpsed through the study of cemeteries. The growth of larger urban centres probably provided a significant means by which people from both Britain and elsewhere in the empire could escape the social control of their local groups and adopt new identities. Such mixing can be argued to have provided a key crucible for social change.

Equally, the Roman army represented a self-conscious identity group with important social power and influence. By the time Britain became part of the empire the army was made up of a mixture of men recruited from across the already conquered provinces. Despite the soldiers' diverse biological origins, they shared institutions, religions, routines of life, building styles, dress, and power structures which turned the Roman army into the equivalent of a separate ethnic group. It had a major impact in the areas of northern and western Britain where most of its units eventually settled as the frontier emerged in the second century AD. This social grouping provides a strong self-identifying group which, in northern England, seems to have remained consciously Roman down to at least the early fifth century.

The incoming army also brought a large new population to Britain from a diverse range of places across Europe, the Near East, and North Africa. The incomers at the time of the invasion numbered 50–55,000 men, who were followed by other units later as the constant process of troop withdrawls and reinforcements took place (Frere 1987). Although some of them retired to their places of origin, many others probably intermarried locally and were absorbed into the populations of the areas in which they were stationed. At the same time, although the patterns of recruitment are difficult to reconstruct, it is clear that large numbers of British males were recruited to the army and moved abroad to serve and settle (Dobson and Mann 1973). Integration into the Roman world thus not only created new identities and provided the impetus for restructuring the old, but it also probably had a major impact on the gene pool of the population.

In considering the changes in identity which took place during this period we should perhaps not overlook one fundamental issue. The idea of Britain itself seems to have been a creation of the Graeco-Roman world looking in upon these islands. For the peoples living here the important distinctions had been between their groups. It was only when described from outside by those who had sufficient geographical knowledge to perceive of the islands as an entity that the terms Britain or the Britons could have any meaning. In this sense, although the linguistic origin of the term is Celtic, the concept is entirely a product of the Classical world (cf. Rivet and Smith 1979: 280–2).

Finally, I would like to argue that the aggregate result of Britain's inclusion in the Roman world resulted in a gradual but fundamental reorientation of society. In the area of East Yorkshire in which I have been doing fieldwork, a Roman road symbolically cuts across a valley at the foot of the Wolds occupied by a string of Iron Age farms (Halkon *et al.* 1998). On the one hand the Roman road united hitherto separate areas and peoples. Thus, it joined that part of Yorkshire with Northumbria and thence Scotland in one direction, and Lincoln, London, and ultimately Rome in another. These connections were real, opening up a new world and new opportunities for the local people. This contact brought new goods, ideas, and people from outside and probably allowed others to escape the constraints of their rural upbringing. By cutting across the valley community, the road cut it open for ever. Saxon settlements and cemeteries follow the route; even today the road and not the inward looking valley structures the landscape.

Equally the social processes of Roman control in Britain arguably stimulated two contrasting changes. Firstly, the linkages created between areas and the unifying structures of Roman power brought about the breakdown of vertical (i.e. ethnic) distinctions within society. By the fourth century one arguably thought of oneself as a Briton and a Roman rather than as a member of a tribe like the Dobunni or Catuvellauni. At the same time, Roman control enhanced the horizontal (i.e. class) distinctions within society as there was increased social differentiation and wealth was progressively concentrated in the hands of small groups over a long period. This wealth brought with it social connections and access to learning. Thus the villa occupier in the fourth-century Cotswolds or those who admired, read, and understood the classical mythological imagery on the Mildenhall Treasure had more in common (culturally and politically) with their social equivalents in Gaul or Africa, than with the person cultivating the fields on the surrounding estates. Integration into Rome's empire gradually undermined the very continuities which had permitted it to take place. This provided the new opportunities for the invaders who followed.

REFERENCES

Breeze, D. J. (1996). *Roman Scotland*. London: Batsford.

Cunliffe, B. W. (1991). *Iron Age Communities in Britain*. 3rd edn., London: Routledge.

Dobson, B., and Mann, J. C. (1973). 'The Roman army in Britain and Britons in the Roman army', *Britannia*, 4: 191–205.

Frere, S. S. (1987). *Britannia: A History of Roman Britain*. 3rd edn., London: Routledge.

Halkon, P., Millett, M., and Taylor, J. (1998). 'Fieldwork and excavation at Hayton, East Yorkshire', *Universities of Durham and Newcastle upon Tyne Archaeological Reports*, 21, *for 1997*, 71–3.

Megaw, M. R., and Megaw, J. V. S. (1989). *Celtic Art from its Beginnings to the Book of Kells*. London: Thames and Hudson.
Millett, M. (1990). *The Romanization of Britain: An Essay in Archaeological Interpretation*. Cambridge: Cambridge University Press.
Rivet, A. L. F., and Smith, C. (1979). *The Place-Names of Roman Britain*. London: Batsford.

5

Kings and Warriors

Population and Landscape from Post-Roman to Norman Britain

Heinrich Härke

MOVING our story forward into the first millennium AD, we are able, for the first time in Britain's past, clearly to identify populations and estimate their sizes, and we begin to see not just some details of the cultural landscape and its uses, but also changing patterns of landownership and other determinant factors. The full elucidation of the processes and interactions requires the combined use of historical, archaeological, and environmental data, and while the emphasis here will be on archaeological approaches, historical and environmental evidence will be drawn on. The regional emphasis is on the south and east of the island, but parallel developments in the west and north will be referred to.

The period covered in this contribution can be divided into three distinct phases, each with its own characteristics: the 'Dark Ages' of the fifth to early seventh centuries AD; the phase of urbanization and agricultural expansion of the later seventh to eleventh centuries; and the Norman period from AD 1066 onwards. While their differences make a chronological treatment by phases necessary, there are a number of common themes which have all been subject to intense ideological pressures, and which have undergone profound changes in thinking over the last several decades. The cultural landscape is not usually thought of as an ideological

The brief for this chapter is dauntingly wide for somebody whose specialism is in early Anglo-Saxon archaeology. I am much indebted to my Reading University colleagues Martin Bell, Anne Curry, Petra Dark, and Edward James for kind help with information on aspects outside my own field of expertise, and in particular to Grenville Astill who did not only supply helpful information, but also read, and commented in detail on, the entire draft of this paper. It is only fair to stress that they should not be blamed for any mistakes and errors I may have made. Paul Slack (Oxford) kindly drew my attention to Maddicott's reassessment of the plagues of the late seventh century.

battlefield. But as early as 1890, Seebohm wrote in the introduction to his weighty tome on *The English Village Community* that the question of land management and ownership tackled in his book is fundamental to the 'experiment . . . of freedom and democracy' undertaken by the English-speaking nations (Seebohm 1890: pp. vii–viii). More recent work has highlighted this ideological link between the cultural landscape and identity (e.g. Schama 1995).

The earlier part of the period covered in this chapter is crucial to the question of identity because many regional or national identities in Europe go back, or are believed to go back, to the middle centuries of the first millennium AD. Around the time when Seebohm wrote, a debate (later known as the Germanist debate; cf. Biddiss 1979) was raging in England: were the English descended from Germanic immigrants or from a largely indigenous population of Celtic stock? Curiously enough, this debate is being rerun right now in Anglo-Saxon archaeology and history.

But the key point here is that the question of English identity hinges on the question of immigration from the Continent. This touches on the wider debate on migrations which has been played out here in previous contributions (cf. Whittle, Renfrew, and Cunliffe, in this volume). We have seen, over the last three or so decades, a profound change in the perception of European prehistory and early history, from seeing it as a series of population movements to believing in largely static populations, with only artefacts, or at best small élite groups, moving. There can be little doubt that the role of past migrations was overestimated until the early 1960s. But there is a danger now that the pendulum is swinging too far in the opposite direction, to a denial of population movements even in reasonably well documented cases. Mobility and the interplay of indigenous and intrusive populations will, therefore, be paid particular attention here.

THE POST-ROMAN TRANSFORMATION

The end of the Roman period in Britain in the early fifth century was marked by the withdrawal of the Roman army (or, at least, the Mobile Field Army) to the Continent in 407, and a possibly more gradual end to the Roman administration. This collapse had profound social and economic consequences which, in turn, had an impact on population and landscape throughout most of Britain.

Population in England

From an archaeological point of view, the most striking consequence is that the population becomes archaeologically 'invisible'. This phenomenon is the result of an end to the import and production of Roman goods, and the gradual dereliction and abandonment of towns and rural estates (Esmonde Cleary 1989; Jones 1996). This gap ends with the appearance of the remains of intrusive populations from the Continent around the middle of the fifth century: Angles, Saxons, Jutes, Frisians, Franks, and others—collectively called Anglo-Saxons.

The evidence for these immigrant populations is wide-ranging (cf. Hills 1993): the testimony of textual sources; an intrusive material culture of continental type; the appearance of a new funerary rite (cremation); the introduction of a new language (Old English) of continental origin; and skeletal remains of a population which is different from native types, but shows close similarities to populations in northern and south-western Germany.

The distributions of early Old English place-names (Cameron 1961; Gelling 1978) and of cemeteries with diagnostic Anglo-Saxon material culture of the fifth to seventh centuries (Figures 5.1 and 5.2) indicate the settlement areas of the immigrants: they are in southern and eastern England, which is essentially the Lowland Zone of Britain. The Highland Zone to the west and north remained for centuries, in some areas right down to the early modern period, the domain of native, Celtic-speaking populations. It is intriguing how this geological divide shows up time and again in the patterns of prehistoric and early historical cultures of Britain (Fox 1947). In the Roman period, the Highland Zone (as far as it was under Roman control) had been a military zone, with a scattered rural population, while the Lowland Zone had been the zone of towns and villae (large farms and rural estates)—and it is exactly this zone of relatively high population density and high agricultural productivity which was taken over by the immigrants.

The few historical sources depict the process of settlement in terms of what would now be termed 'ethnic cleansing' of the native Britons by large-scale immigration of Anglo-Saxons (Stenton 1971; Myres 1986). The main problem for accepting these reports at face value is the question of what happened to the large numbers of natives. Estimates of the probable size of the Romano-British population have varied over time, but recent calculations put it somewhere between 2 and 4 million in the later Roman period (Millett 1990: 182–5; Jones 1996: 13–17). The full realization of the implications of these new, high estimates has contributed substantially to the popularity of a minimalist model: that there were only small groups of immigrants who set themselves up as the new élite, with the native Britons following élite tastes and fashions, and thus becoming Anglo-Saxons themselves (Arnold 1984; Hodges 1989; Higham 1992; Dark 1994). The minimalist estimates for the influx from the Continent range from 25,000 (Laing and Laing 1990) down to less than 10,000 (Higham 1992). The biggest problem with this model, though, is to explain how such a small

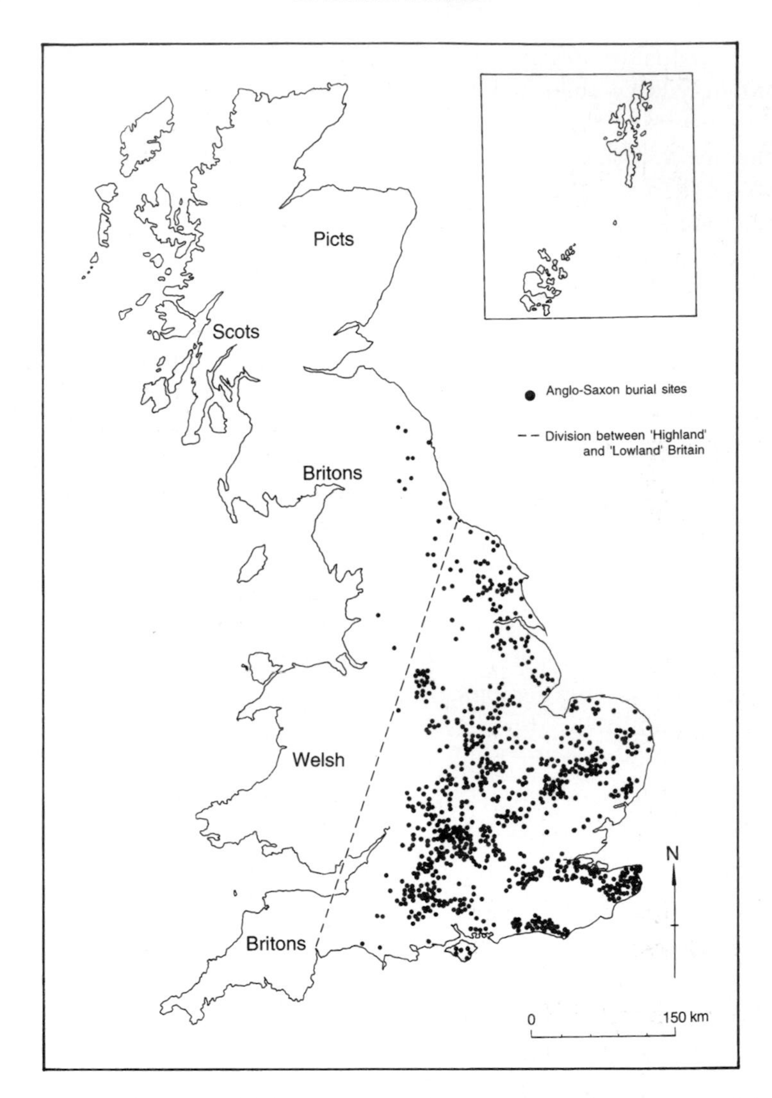

FIG. 5.1 Distribution of fifth- to seventh-century Anglo-Saxon burial sites (after L. Alcock and S. C. Hawkes), with the approximate boundary between the Highland and Lowland Zones (after D. K. C. Jones).

number of immigrants could have permanently changed the language of several millions of natives, and given names to almost every place and field in England.

We therefore need a model which reconciles the extensive evidence for large-scale immigration with the less clear, but still persuasive, evidence of

Fig. 5.2 Seventh-century inhumation grave 172 in the Anglo-Saxon cemetery at Butler's Field, Lechlade (Glos.), containing an adult male with seax (single-edged battle knife), two spears, knife and bucket, and a small child with a bead necklace and garnet-in-gold pendant. (Copyright Oxford Archaeological Unit.)

substantial survival of a large native population (Härke 1998). The end of Roman Britain would have been followed by rapid population decline, as can be observed in other cases of state and empire collapse, most recently in the 1990s right across Eastern Europe. After some two generations of such decline, Britain would have experienced a gradually increasing influx of warbands from the Continent, closely followed by complete family groups or even communities. Their settlement would have been interspersed with that of the natives who assumed the position of a lower-status population. This initial phase (later fifth/sixth centuries) would be followed by the assimilation of Britons living within the Anglo-Saxon settlement areas, and the acculturation of British enclaves during the seventh/eighth centuries. At the same time, the Anglo-Saxon expansion would have continued by a series of conquests and élite takeovers in adjacent areas of western and northern Britain, which would have imposed English culture and language on the Britons without much further population movement. The process of assimilation was probably completed, to a large extent, by the eighth or ninth centuries.

This still begs the question of the scale of the immigration, and the relative sizes of the populations. Archaeological and skeletal data suggest an immigrant–native proportion of 1 : 3 to 1 : 5 in the Anglo-Saxon heartlands of southern and eastern England (Härke 1999), but a much smaller proportion of Anglo-Saxons (1 : 10 or less) is likely in the later expansion areas of south-west, northern, and north-west England. Assuming a British population which had declined to about 1 to 2 million by the second half of the fifth century, the proportions translate into an immigration of up to 250,000, although a figure between 100,000 to 200,000 is more likely. This is perfectly compatible with the preliminary results of recent work on mytochondrial DNA which suggest an upper limit of 20 (+) per cent for the proportion of immigrants in the female population of post-Roman England (personal communication with M. Richards, Oxford).

Landscape in England

Large numbers of immigrants may be expected to have had a significant impact on the landscape, and this was, indeed, the old view which became influential through Hoskins's seminal work on landscape history (Hoskins 1955). According to this view, there was a rapid regrowth of forest after the end of Roman rule in Britain, and the Anglo-Saxons were pioneers moving into a wilderness and taming it through forest clearance and the introduction of the mouldboard plough.

However, new palaeobotanic work has shown that there was little woodland regeneration after the Roman period (Bell and Dark 1998; Dark 2000; Dark and Dark 1997). Working back from the Domesday survey and taking into account the slowly declining size of forest cover over the Anglo-Saxon period, one may estimate that woodland covered probably not much more than 20 per cent of the total area of England (cf. O. Rackham 1976, 1994: 38–9). The post-Roman period would, therefore, have been characterized by an open landscape with pockets of forest, and a few large forests, mainly of oak, on chalk also of lime and beech. The new settlements of this period were small affairs, consisting of two to five farmsteads each in an irregular layout although a few larger sites are known (Powlesland 1997).

But while the landscape was kept open at nearly the Roman level, the use of the open spaces appears to have changed in many cases from arable to pasture (cf. J. Rackham 1994)—a shift which may have started in the late Roman period when large tracts of downland were turned over to sheep rearing (Cunliffe 1985: 65). An important implication of this change is a lower population density than in Roman times because pastoral husbandry can support only a tenth of the population which could be fed by growing cereal on the same land. A similar shift from tillage to pasture happened in the fourteenth to sixteenth centuries, and population decline may have been one of the factors behind it (Smith in this volume).

Other new work on the Anglo-Saxon landscape has been inspired by recent approaches in prehistoric archaeology to focus on perceptions of the landscape. A recent study (Williams 1997) shows that the reuse of older monuments, Roman as well as prehistoric, for Anglo-Saxon burial sites was a widespread phenomenon of this period. Williams has interpreted this custom as an appropriation of the landscape by the immigrants who continued their continental custom of monument reuse. An interesting aspect of this phenomenon is its marked increase in the seventh century which appears to be, on other evidence, a period of increased assimilation of native British and immigrant Anglo-Saxon populations. This may be seen as the invention of a common tradition for both groups; alternatively, it may be a pagan reaction against the Christianization which was under way during the seventh century (Van de Noort 1993). Whichever way we look at the reuse phenomenon, it is an example of how the landscape could be, and was, used in a social and ideological context.

Western and northern Britain

Although the Celtic-speaking societes of Britain's Highland Zone had undergone little or no Romanization, they, too, were affected by some population shifts and settlement discontinuities around the middle of the first millennium AD. The population movements include immigration from Ireland to the west of Scotland, south Wales, and parts of south-west England (Ritchie and Ritchie 1981; Davies 1982; Pearce 1978), and British emigration from the latter two regions to Brittany (Chadwick 1965) and beyond. While these migrations are historically and linguistically attested, they have left hardly a trace in the archaeological record; this makes it impossible to check independently the impression of large-scale movements given in the historical sources for some of these migrations.

In Scotland, a reorganization of population and landscape in this period may be implied by the end of the brochs (stone-built living towers), and the emergence of small élite hillforts (Alcock 1981). Hillforts were also reoccupied or newly built in the late Roman and post-Roman period in south-west England and Wales (Alcock 1987). Overall, though, the pattern of a dispersed settlement of single farmsteads continued here and in mainland Scotland, although a few larger settlements of hamlet size are known (Laing 1975).

Through trading connections, the Justinian plague of the mid-sixth century reached western Britain from the Mediterranean. In Wales, it killed at least one king, Maelgwn of Gwynedd, and may have had wider effects on the population (Davies 1982: 31, 41). Baillie has speculated about a link between this plague and his 540 event, a volcanic eruption with catastrophic, global consequences for climate and harvest (Baillie 1995: 129). There is, however, no evidence for a population decline in other parts of Britain at this time, and only the second wave of plague in the late seventh century may have led to a sharp, albeit temporary population decline in England (Maddicott 1997). But the effects of these plagues may have varied regionally, and they seem to have been overcome rapidly. The early medieval phase of forest clearance in Scotland and Ireland, some of it extensive and as early as the fifth/sixth centuries (Rackham 1976: 52), might even imply population expansion.

INTENSIFICATON AND NUCLEATION

The story of the seventh to eleventh centuries was one of intensification of agricultural production, which led to a reorganization of the landscape, and of nucleation of population in new villages and towns, which included two successive waves of urbanization.

Intensification and the landscape

The intensification of production involved several elements: new crops and food sources; new agricultural techniques; and colonization and reclamation of new land. In addition, there was a process of concentration and expansion of industrial production.

Agricultural production witnessed a shift in emphasis, with bread wheat and rye, both introduced during the Roman period, becoming dominant, and barley and oats making their appearance (J. Rackham 1994; Fowler 1997; Dark 2000). Rye is more resistant to unfavourable conditions; oats were needed as fodder for horses, the use of which for traction became ever more important; and barley is an indication of brewing, supported by evidence for hop cultivation by the tenth century. A systematic widening of food sources is suggested by dams and fish weirs which appear in significant numbers in the archaeological record by the ninth/tenth centuries (Aston 1988).

The cultivation of fibre crops, such as hemp and flax, became an important element in the expansion of textile production. Significantly, their evidence is abundant in the towns emerging during this period; and they are often found together with remains of plants used for dyeing textiles, such as madder, dyer's greenweed, and woad (e.g. at York Coppergate; cf. Kenward and Hall 1995).

Among the new agricultural technologies, probably the most important was the mouldboard plough which came into use by the late tenth century (Astill, in Astill and Langdon 1997), and is famously depicted on the eleventh-century Bayeux Tapestry. This plough can work heavier soils than the simple scratch plough (ard) used before, and it can create the characteristic ridge-and-furrow fields which survive in many parts of the English landscape. It also increased the demand for horse traction which is more flexible than the use of oxen (Langdon 1986); and its greater productivity made a greater reliance on cereal production possible. The result was a significant shift in diet, and the effects of this 'cerealization' may just be reflected in a slight drop in stature in Late Saxon non-aristocratic populations (cf. White 1988: fig. 31).

These two innovations were supplemented by crop rotation which may have been used since the Iron Age. Continental documentary evidence suggests that it was being applied in early medieval Europe by the eighth century, although it may not yet have been the fully developed cycle of winter crop–summer crop–fallow. Crop rotation counteracts soil exhaustion, which is crucial given the low yields of this period: a typical harvest would produce about three times the quantity of the seed corn used, in contrast to modern yields which average thirty-five times the seed corn (information supplied by the Crop Research Unit, University of Reading). Crop rotation increased productivity, but it also required a reorganization of the landscape.

The greater quantities of grain being produced required more efficient mill technology than the hand quern. Water mills appear in the historical and archaeological record from the seventh century across western

Europe. The earliest examples in England are the seventh/eighth-century water mills of Old Windsor and Tamworth, the latter significantly located on a royal estate (Rahtz and Meeson 1992). By the eleventh century, the Domesday survey lists some 6,000 mills in England (Holt 1988). But while Ireland has produced some of the earliest water mills in the British Isles, similar evidence is lacking from Scotland and Wales, and there is virtually no evidence to suggest that these Highland Zone regions participated in the process of intensification.

In the upland regions of England, though, colonization expanded the extent of land in agricultural use. In the Peak District, the Yorkshire Dales, and Dartmoor, uplands which had been given up since the Bronze Age were again permanently settled and exploited from the eighth century onwards (cf. Coggins *et al.* 1983). In a parallel development, wetlands were reclaimed in the Fens, Essex, the Pevensey and Somerset Levels, Gwent, and elsewhere by the ninth or tenth century (Rippon 1994).

While colonization was facilitated by a climatic improvement from the eighth century onwards (Lamb 1981: 57–63), the possible reasons for the entire process of intensification include population increase for which there is indirect evidence by the tenth century; the supply of the emerging towns; and increasing aristocratic control of agricultural production, requiring surplus production for food renders (Astill, in Astill and Langdon 1997: 198; Hodges 1989: 63; Faith 1997).

The aristocracy was certainly involved in the creation of a new concept of landownership: that of permanent, individual ownership. This concept originated in the seventh century with the need of the newly established Church for land as a source of income. As the existing concept of landownership—that of royal or family land held by an individual for a specified time or for life, before falling back to king or family—could not be made to fit the particular needs of a corporate body, kings began to issue charters which specified permanent land grants to churches and monasteries (Stenton 1971: 141, 307–10; Whitelock 1979). From the early eighth century, similar charters were issued to laymen (and some women), establishing the principle of individual ownership. This might well have contributed to the development of 'multiple' estates which are so typical of this period: pieces of property scattered over various environments and landscape settings so as to provide a range of foods and products for their owner (Jones 1976; Hooke 1989, 1997). The reorganization of the landscape resulting from these two processes may be reflected in the seventh- to ninth-century settlement shift in England (Welch 1985; Hamerow 1991).

The second reorganization of the English landscape was under way from the tenth century as a result of the introduction of the open field system (Rowley 1981). In this system, each local community had two to four common fields divided into narrow strips, with each strip being farmed by one peasant family, and crop rotation being carried out by fields, not by strips (O. Rackham 1994: 74–9). In essence, it was the pooling of land in order to facilitate crop rotation and the use of the new plough. Its origin in the Midlands and its spread from there were closely linked to nucleated villages: both were the outcome of the reorganization of the landscape by aristocratic landowners attempting to increase the productivity of their estates. But it is worth noting that this reorganization spanned the Anglo-Saxon and the Norman periods, and that Viking lords and settlers appear to have played a key role in its implementation.

Nucleation of settlement and population

The nucleated village is one of the two key elements of the nucleation process. It seems to have originated in the ninth or tenth century, with villages replacing hamlets in the Midlands and parts of the north and south (Taylor 1983; Hooke 1988; Lewis, Mitchell-Fox, and Dyer 1997). This process is best documented in the archaeological record by the case of Wharram Percy (East Yorks.) where six Saxon farms of irregular layout were replaced, between the tenth and twelfth centuries, by a nucleated village, with regular, planned arrangement of houses, a green, two manor houses, and a stone church (Beresford and Hurst 1990). (See Figure 5.3.) The latter is also an illustration of the appearance on the scene of parish churches during this period (Blair 1988).

The introduction of open fields and nucleated villages created a broad division within England: an 'ancient countryside' of hamlets and single farmsteads located in irregular fields, with considerable woodland; and a 'planned countryside' of large villages in large regular fields, with straight roads and only small clumps of trees. These 'two Anglo-Saxon landscapes' (Rackham 1985: 69–70, 94–105) survive in the landscape to the present day.

The second element of nucleation, urbanization, came in two successive waves. The first of these was represented by the *wiks* or *emporia*: coastal and riverine trading stations of the seventh to ninth century of which Hamwic (Saxon Southampton) and Ipswich are the best-explored cases in England (Barley 1977; Hodges and Hobley 1988; Scull 1997). These were new foundations on greenfield sites, with regular layout suggesting royal planning and initiative. Their population, typically around 4,000 to 5,000, may (on parallel continental evidence) have been international and multi-ethnic, but skeletal evidence from their cemeteries shows that men were outnumbering women by two to one (Hinton 1990: 57; cf. Morton 1992). These towns were part of an international network of trading sites spanning north-west Europe (Hodges 1982), but apart from trade and craft

FIG. 5.3 Aerial photograph of the deserted medieval village of Wharram Percy (East Yorks.), showing layout of nucleated village. (Cambridge University Collection of Air Photographs: copyright reserved, ref. CFM 30.)

production, their other urban functions appear to have been limited or absent. Perhaps for this reason, they turned out to be a dead end of urbanism: none of them developed directly into a medieval town, and they went into decline before the Viking raids finally cut off their trade in the ninth century.

Urbanism finally took hold in England with the second wave: the Late Saxon towns from the ninth or tenth century onwards (Ralegh Radford 1978; Haslam 1984). They emerged on a variety of sites, including former Roman towns (such as Winchester; Biddle 1983) and the defensive sites built by King Alfred and his sucessors against Viking raids (*burhs*; Biddle and Hill 1971). In contrast to the previous trading sites and to some proto-urban population clusters around minsters and royal centres (Astill 1991), these were towns in the medieval sense, with walls, a street grid, tenements, aristocratic residences, craft production, and a minster. Their population is shown by cemetery evidence to have been composed of communities with a balanced gender ratio (Hinton 1990: 130).

The two waves of urbanization reintroduced townscapes to England, after a lapse of several centuries since the end of Roman towns in the fifth century. But they did not spread to Wales and Scotland until the early second millennium AD. Even in England, the development of urbanism was a slow process: by AD 1066, only five towns had more than 1,000 households, and only between 7 and 10 per cent of the overall population of England lived in towns.

The concentration of non-agricultural populations in towns had implications for consumption and communication. The annual meat consumption by the 4,000 inhabitants of tenth-century Lincoln has been calculated as requiring 500 cattle, 700 sheep, and 400 pigs (O'Connor 1982). Their production would, in turn, have required pasture in excess of 8,000 hectares (20,000 acres) and additional woodland for pigs. Towns would have also required a communication network, and it is surely no coincidence that the oldest Anglo-Saxon timber bridge, recently found across the river Trent, dates to the eighth century (Salisbury 1995).

Urban life would also have made an impact on human populations (Mays 1998). Life expectancy remained as low (between 30 and 35 years) as it had been in the rural communities of the previous period. However, skeletal studies have shown that people living in the early towns suffered fewer fractures and more infectious diseases and dietary problems; and while increasing sexual dimorphism and a much higher incidence of osteoarthritis in men suggest an increasing sexual division of labour in Late Saxon and early Norman towns, urban women were still dying at a younger age than men (V. Jenkins and J. Rogers, in Graham and Davies 1993: 120–7; White 1988).

THE SCANDINAVIAN IMPACT

The period discussed in the previous section also sees the appearance on the British scene of a Scandinavian population. The Vikings' first impact was on the Scottish isles from the late eighth century onwards. Further south, their arrival was slightly later, but, by the tenth century, Scandinavians were active participants in landscape reorganization and urbanization in England, and they may even have been initiators of both processes.

Yet their popular image of 'rape, plunder, and pillage' is very different from this constructive role. This image, though, has long been known to be distorted: it has its origins in the contemporary chronicles written and kept by the victims of their raids. Having said this, there can be little doubt that Viking raids (recorded from AD 793) seriously disrupted cultural, economic, social, and political activities in large parts of Britain and elsewhere. There was a smooth transition from raids to settlement, via winter camps, permanent bases, to grabbing land and sharing it out. Even settlers might have gone on raids between harvests, as the Orkneyinga Saga describes. The first Viking Age settlement in Scotland is dated archaeologically to around AD 800; settlement in England is recorded from the 860s to the 880s. The settlers in northern Scotland, the Scottish isles, the Isle of Man, and north-west England mostly came from Norway, while the settlement in the Midlands, east, and north-east England was dominated by Danes. But both groups spoke a common language, Old Norse, elements of which survive in place-names and the English language.

The Scandinavian population

The number of Scandinavian settlers has been the key question in a debate which was started by Sawyer (1962). As a result, there has been a shift of opinion, as there has been on the question of other migrations, from the conventional idea of large numbers of retired Viking raiders and immigrants taking land (Stenton 1971: 252–5), to the minimalist perspective of small numbers of Scandinavian chieftains setting themselves up by force as lords and landowners, possibly followed by small-scale immigration (Sawyer 1971; cf. Richards 1991; Loyn 1994).

Two kinds of evidence have led to the idea of mass immigration from Scandinavia following the initial Viking conquest: the sizes of Viking raiding armies mentioned in the written sources, and the numbers of Old Norse place-names in England and Scotland. Both types of evidence have their problems. While the historical sources for Britain do not mention concrete figures, continental sources give the size of the Viking 'Great Army' of the late ninth century as under 10,000 to 40,000 (Brooks 1979). However, the Viking camps known in Denmark and Britain, like that at Repton (Biddle and Kjølbye-Biddle 1992), do not appear to be designed for such large armies. Scandinavian place-names are, indeed, found in abundance in Scotland and England (Figure 5.4; Cameron 1975, 1976; Fellows-Jensen 1975, 1978; Nicolaisen 1982). Yorkshire alone has 744 Scandinavian place-names (typically ending in -by and -thorpe); in the East and North Riding, almost half of all place-names recorded for that period are Scandinavian. But this need not mean that these places were inhabited by Scandinavians—they could have been named by Viking lords sharing out the lands of the dispossessed native aristocracy (Hodges 1989: 154), or some of them (at least in England) might even go back to fifth/sixth-century Anglo-Saxon immigrants of Scandinavian origin (Richards 1991: 35).

Other evidence relating to the scale of Viking settlement is inconclusive or absent. Apart from place-names, there is no evidence of massive language change, except in Shetland. Some rural settlement sites with layout or finds of Scandinavian character are known from Scotland (Graham-Campbell and Batey 1998), the best known of which is Jarlshof on Shetland, a pioneer farmstead of the late eighth or early ninth century, growing into a fishing village by the eleventh century (Hamilton 1956). But there are no unambiguously Viking rural sites known in England, which means either that they do not exist, or that they are indistinguishable from Anglo-Saxon farmsteads or hamlets. There were no Viking towns in Scotland or Wales, but quite a few in Ireland and the north and east of England, the best explored of which is the trading town of York (Hall 1984). Graves should be the best indicator of immigrant settlers, but Viking graves in Britain are few and far between, with a concentration in the Isle of Man, an entire cemetery at Ingleby, and a scatter of individual graves all over the island (Figure 5.4; Wilson 1976). This could mean that there were, indeed, very few Viking settlers, or that many Vikings were buried in cemeteries of the native populations. It also means that there is not enough skeletal evidence from Viking graves to compare with series from native burial sites. The evidence from the mass grave at Repton where it has been claimed that the male individuals are probably of Scandinavian type (Biddle and Kjølbye-Biddle 1992), still awaits full publication.

Comparison with other areas of Scandinavian settlement in Europe during this period does not help, except to confirm that we do have a problem. Using the probably inflated figure of 40,000 Vikings in the Great Army, ignoring the possibility of further immigration from Scandinavia, and assuming a native population of 1 to 2 million in all of England, we arrive at an immigrant proportion of about 2 to 4 per cent, or something like double that proportion in the actual settlement areas of northern and eastern England.

If the Scandinavian settlers were small élite groups who soon became 'invisible' through acculturation and intermarriage, the clues for this process should be found in the interrelation between immigrant and native populations. In Scotland, it is noticeable that Scandinavian place-names are concentrated in the north and west while Pictish place-names are found in the south and east of the mainland (Hill 1981: 46; Nicolaisen 1982), which may indicate that the immigrant settlers avoided native population concentrations. On the other hand, the Viking settlement of Jarlshof was located on the site of a former Pictish settlement. In the Isle of Man, the evidence for interaction ranges from possible human sacrifice on top of a

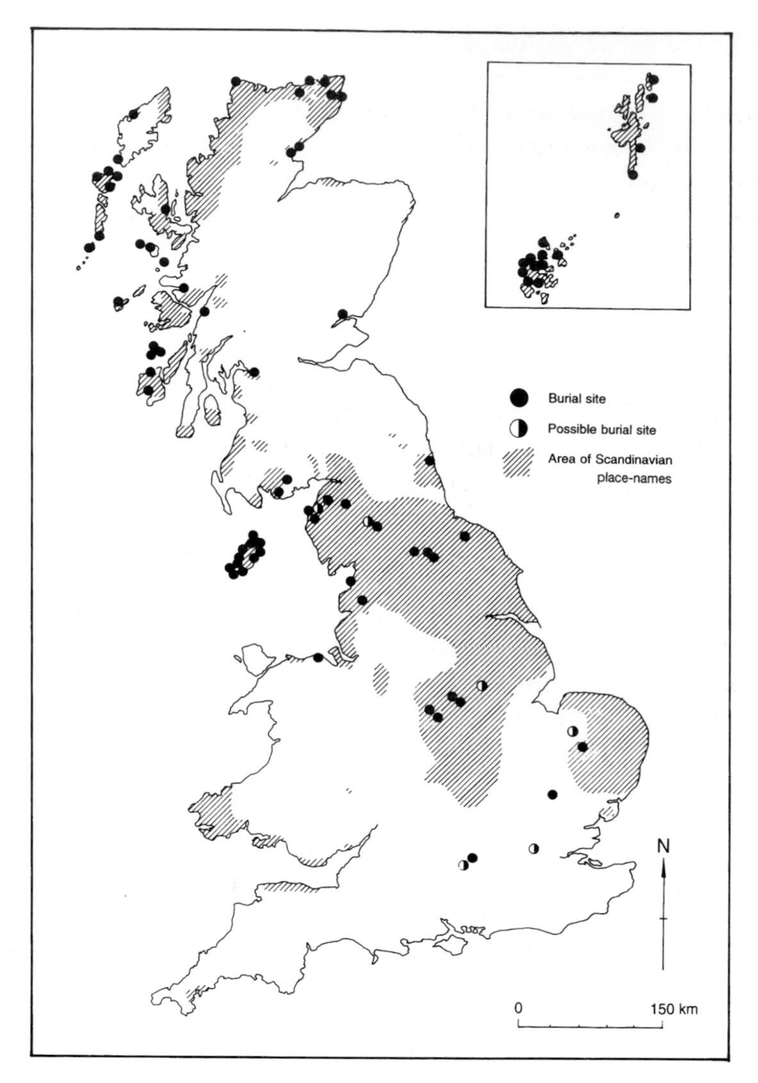

FIG. 5.4 Distribution of Viking burial sites in Britain (after D. Wilson), with areas of Scandinavian place-names (after D. Hill).

Viking burial mound (Wilson and Bersu 1966) to probable intermarriage suggested by a mixture of Scandinavian and native names and motifs on Manx crosses (Kermode 1907). In England, the scarcity of pagan Viking graves has been explained in terms of the rapid Christianization of the incomers (Richards 1991: 118), which would imply interaction between the populations, and acculturation of the settlers.

The Scandinavian impact on the landscape

The traditional image of the Scandinavian settlement has been that of 'demobilized Danish soldiers' bringing over their families and founding new villages on uncleared and untilled land (Hoskins 1955: 72). The prevailing view today is that this old image may be true in some areas, like parts of Scotland, some upland areas of northern England, and around Coventry (Gelling 1976: 209–11). But, on the whole, it is thought unlikely that vast tracts of empty land were available in the ninth and tenth centuries for colonization by the immigrants; and, anyway, colonization was a process going on in many parts of Britain at that time.

This reassessment clears the way for the idea that the main Scandinavian impact on the landscape was, in fact, in the more densely settled areas of central and eastern England: in the Scandinavian contributions to the ongoing processes of urbanization, nucleation of rural settlement, and creation of open-field systems. Certainly, the towns in the Danelaw develop a fully urban character at least as early as their Anglo-Saxon counterparts further south. The earliest evidence of nucleated villages and open fields, probably of ninth-century date, has been found in the Scandinavian-controlled Midlands where the reorganization of the landscape would have been easier to achieve for the new foreign lords than for the established Anglo-Saxon aristocracy (Hodges 1989: 168; Unwin 1988). Even the mouldboard plough has been claimed as a Scandinavian introduction into Britain (cf. Myrdal, in Astill and Langdon 1997).

The Scandinavian population was rapidly absorbed and assimilated into the English population after the Danelaw lost its independent status in the tenth century, although the Scandinavian populations of the Scottish isles retained their cultural and political autonomy for a considerably longer time (Graham-Campbell and Batey 1998). In the first half of the eleventh century, England was briefly incorporated into the short-lived North Sea Empire created by the conquests of the Danish king Knut (Canute). Some of Knut's Scandinavian followers became large landowners in England (Fleming 1991), but the two and a half decades from AD 1017 to 1042 left virtually no permanent mark on Britain.

THE NORMAN TAKEOVER

William's conquest of England in AD 1066 followed within a generation of the end of Knut's empire, and, like the previous conquest, it was essentially the story of one state taking over another. But, unlike Knut, the Norman conquest had quite an impact on population and landscape in England, parts of Wales, and indirectly on Scotland.

The population of Norman England

Ultimately, the Normans were of the same Scandinavian origin as the Vikings who had settled in eastern and northern England about two centuries earlier. But the Normans had been thoroughly acculturated in the course of the one and a half centuries they had lived in northern France, and they had essentially become French in language and culture. The incoming Normans were a military aristocracy, not peasant settlers; this situation was carried over from Normandy, but the conquest of England created opportunities for the promotion of lower-ranking followers.

With the Norman lords, there was an influx of other populations, mainly French, Bretons, and Flemings (Golding 1994). French lords and peasants arrived in substantial numbers, most of them from Normandy. Many French settlers were inserted into English towns, probably as part of Norman control mechanisms over the newly conquered country. Separate French boroughs developed in many towns, including London, Norwich, Nottingham, and Southampton. Breton and Flemish lords and lesser men made up a considerable part of the army of conquest, and they were settled in regional concentrations, with Bretons in south-west England and Yorkshire, and Flemings in Lincolnshire, Somerset, and particularly Pembrokeshire (Davies 1987). Jews also arrived in England, but some time after the conquest; Jewish communities are documented by the twelfth/thirteenth centuries, and some finds attest to their presence in towns (cf. Hinton 1990: 146).

Estimates of the overall scale of the influx have varied widely, from the older idea of 200,000 settlers to a more recent suggestion of less than 10,000 (Sawyer 1978: 253). Exact figures are impossible to calculate, but it is probably safe to say that the total immigration was in five rather than six figures—in other words, in the low 10,000s. An immigration on that scale would not have amounted to more than 1 or 2 per cent of the native population of England.

This relative estimate is possible because we have, for the first time, a large-scale census which allows a broad reconstruction of the population size of England: the Domesday Book of AD 1086 which lists about a quarter of a million households across Norman England (Darby 1952, 1977; Sawyer 1985; Holt 1987). This has been the basis of the widespread calculation of an overall population of 1 to 1.25 million (cf. Miller and Hatcher 1978). The underlying assumption of this calculation is an average household size of four to five (cf. Hallam 1981: 246–8). This assumption may actually be on the low side: earlier continental sources suggest average family sizes of 5.5 to 5.8 (Herlihy 1985: 69, 70 table 3.2). A much more serious problem, though, is the gaps in the Domesday Book: neither are all regions covered, nor are all groups of people. Because these gaps can only be closed by guessing, some historians now reject the Domesday Book altogether as a basis for population calculations (personal communication with S. Reynolds, London). The gaps imply, at any rate, that a population size of up to 2.5 million or more is entirely feasible.

Given the proportion of native population to numbers of incomers, the process of Norman conquest and settlement was not one of population replacement, but one of socio-ethnic change: some 4,000 to 5,000 Anglo-Saxon aristocrats were completely replaced, within a mere twenty years, by 144 Norman barons (Fleming 1991: 109, 220). Although there was considerable institutional continuity, there was a total discontinuity of personnel at the highest levels of society and Church. Loyn (1962: 327) has, therefore, compared the Norman conquest to a 'business take-over bid' while Fleming (1991: 210) has called the Norman barons a 'kleptocracy'.

The consequences for the Anglo-Saxon lords were dire: they lost status, or ended up dispossessed and in exile (Golding 1994: 68). Some intermarriage is recorded, but this may have been for Normans an alternative access to English lands. The social differences between conquerors and conquered were highlighted, and probably deliberately so, by a linguistic divide: Norman French was spoken by the aristocracy, while Latin became the language of government business because the clerks and churchmen understood it. English remained the language of the vast majority of the population, but was relegated to a position of inferiority (Loyn 1962: 317–18). Bilingualism took some time to develop, and only emerged slowly during the twelfth century. Normans and English were even treated differentially in law, at least in some aspects (Garnett 1985).

Post-conquest society, then, was an ethnically divided society, with profound social differences between immigrants and natives along ethnic lines, reinforced and signalled by linguistic and legal status differences. This situation appears in some ways remarkably similar to that of Saxon–British relations in seventh-century Wessex as reflected in the laws of King Ine (Whitelock 1979: 398–407). Both early Saxon Wessex and early Norman England were essentially conquest societies. The difference between them seems to have been the higher proportion of immigrants in the Anglo-Saxon case, resulting in a more permanent transformation of culture and language.

The Norman landscape

The conquest also had a profound impact on the landscapes and townscapes of England. Of all the Norman impositions on countryside and towns, the castle is probably the most significant colonial monument, not least because England had few castles before 1066. The early motte type, an earthen mound with palisade as built at Hastings right after the landing of the Norman invasion force, was soon superseded by stone castles of various designs (Brown 1984, 1989; McNeill 1992; Pounds 1990). Norman castles were political statements, and their wide distribution represented the symbolic as well as *de facto* appropriation of landscape and townscape (Figure 5.5). They were built in strategic places controlling lines of communication; in former Anglo-Saxon lords' residences, such as Goltho and Portchester (Beresford 1987; Cunliffe 1977); and in towns where their purpose was to hold down the population and to control the towns' central functions.

In towns, the building of a castle could require the destruction of tenements or entire quarters, such as at Norwich (Hinton 1990: fig. 4.2, 73; fig. 6.3, 117). But this was only one of several features of urban development in the centuries following the Norman conquest: others are the extensive construction of cathedrals and monasteries, and the settlement *en bloc* of French burgesses. The consequences for the layout and appearance of existing towns were profound, and amounted to a 'revolution in urban topography' (Fleming 1991: 197). This was complemented by the foundation, in a 'fever of borough creation' (Hoskins 1955: 110), of a series of towns, mostly smaller market towns such as Newbury, Stratford-upon-Avon, and Salisbury. This shift of emphasis may have led to an increasing economic separation between town and country (Astill, in Astill and Langdon 1997: 209; Hinton 1990: 119, 139); but even so the proportion of the urban population hardly rose above 10 per cent in the Norman period.

In the countryside, the reorganization of landownership into concentrated blocks, in contrast to the Anglo-Saxon pattern of dispersed estates, led to a 'period of jarring and violent territorial discontinuity' (Fleming 1991: 185; cf. Golding 1994: 75). But, to an extent, it could be argued that the Norman reorganization carried on the processes begun in the late Saxon period. There were other continuities, too: the village nucleation process continued (Sawyer 1976; Aston, Austin, and Dyer 1989; Lewis, Mitchell-Fox, and Dyer 1997); the replacement of country timber churches in stone (the 'Great Rebuilding'; cf. Blair 1988) and the construction of new parish churches were accelerated; and colonization and reclamation efforts continued, probably driven (as in late Anglo-Saxon England) by taxation and population increase, and facilitated by the so-called 'early medieval warmth' of the eleventh to thirteenth centuries (Lamb 1981: 57–63).

Monasteries continued to play a crucial role in the colonization process. Hundreds of monasteries were built during the Norman period, and

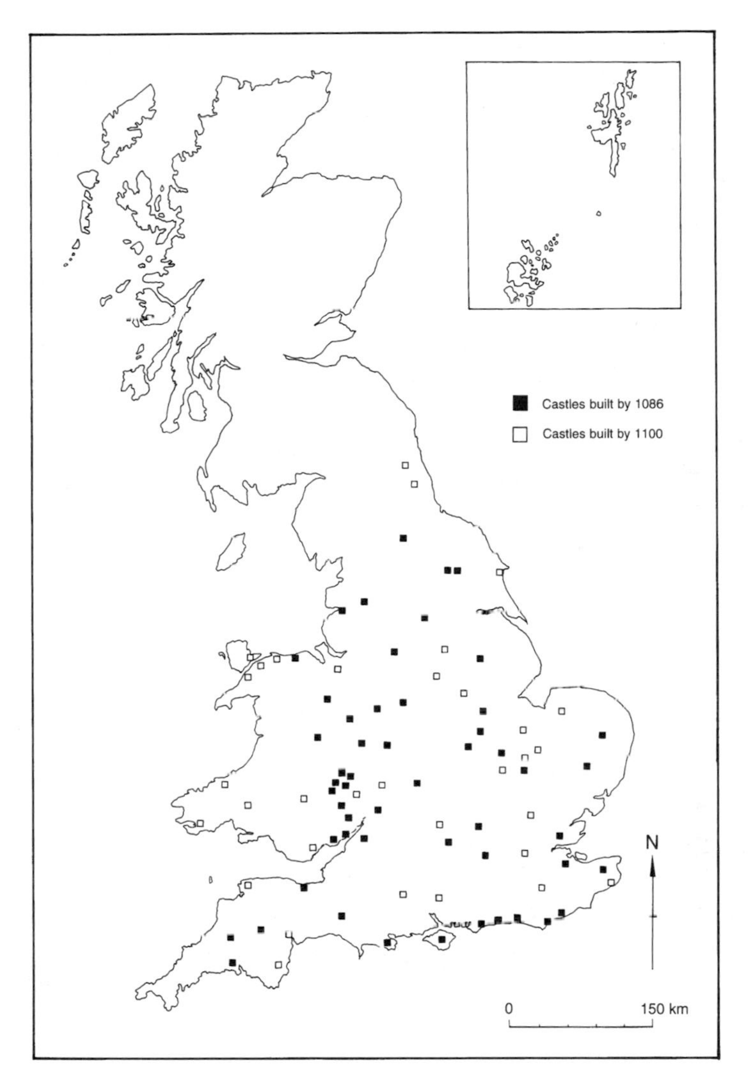

FIG. 5.5 Distribution of Norman castles in England and Wales (after B. Golding).

prominent among them from the twelfth century were the houses of the Cistercians, a new monastic order (Coppack 1998) whose preference for remote locations has not only left spectacular ruins in the landscape (such as Fountains Abbey; Coppack 1993), but also had a serious impact on previously less transformed landscapes.

Other Norman plantations in the landscape included deer parks and rabbit warrens (fallow deer and rabbits were introduced after the Norman conquest), fishponds and dovecotes, increasing the variety of food for the lords (Bettey 1993; Bond 1994; cf. Astill and Grant 1988). But the core elements of Norman food production were bread wheat and wine. Aristocratic consumption led to an expansion of viticulture; by 1086, the Domesday Book recorded fifty-five vineyards in England (Bettey 1993: 17). Bread wheat may even have influenced the course of the Norman conquest in the north. Kapelle (1979: 213–28) has pointed out that the first wave of Norman settlement in northern England only went as far as wheat could be cultivated (i.e. east of the Pennines and south of Durham); it was only the second wave which went beyond this 'oat bread line', and it was dominated by settlers from the rye and oats-growing regions of Lower Normandy and Brittany.

But probably the most notorious Norman imposition on the English landscape was the Royal Forest (Bettey 1993: 18–20; Bond 1994; O. Rackham 1994: 62–4). These royal hunting preserves operated under special forest law, and their creation and maintenance imposed on the local population hardships which were exaggerated in popular mythology. By the middle of the twelfth century, as much as half of the country was under forest law, but disafforestation—releasing land from forest law—took place from the early thirteenth century. In addition, there were more than thirty chases, the aristocratic equivalent of the Royal Forest, in England (Bettey 1993).

Wales and Scotland

In this period, the main process in the west and north of Britain was urbanization which so far had been limited to England. In Scotland, urbanization started in the early twelfth century, without permanent Norman occupation but clearly stimulated from the south (Spearman 1988; Kapelle 1979). In Wales, the building of towns and castles was a direct consequence of the Norman occupation: castles were key elements of military control, while towns were founded to serve castles (Soulsby 1983).

The conquest of Wales also brought in various groups of colonists, including Normans, Bretons, Flemings, and English, and their respective languages (Davies 1987). Despite some intermarriage at aristocratic level, social and cultural distinctions along ethnic lines developed even more markedly than in England, and by the end of the twelfth century, Wales had become a 'land of two peoples' (Davies 1987: 100). Within a further century, this socio-cultural division had become enshrined in the administrative and legal recognition of Welshries and Englishries. While this was a clear departure from the political and social development in England, it is somewhat reminiscent of the Danelaw, the distinct legal status of the areas of Scandinavian settlement in late Anglo-Saxon England.

CONCLUSIONS

The key processes of the interrelation between human populations and landscapes in first- and early second-millennium Britain are (*a*) migrations and the subsequent interactions between native and immigrant populations; and (*b*) the intensification of production and nucleation of population.

While the period under consideration offers four cases of immigration and/or conquest, their contexts and scales are rather different, although some of their outcomes may be considered surprisingly similar. The Anglo-Saxon and Scandinavian (Viking) cases are those of fringe barbarians progressing from raiding to permanent settlement, but the Anglo-Saxons moved into peripheral provinces of a collapsed empire while the Scandinavians moved into the territories of smaller, emergent states. Knut's North Sea Empire and the Norman conquest are cases of states taking over another state. In early Anglo-Saxon and Norman England, and possibly in the Danelaw, the result was a conquest society in which power and status were, at least temporarily, divided along ethnic lines, but the outcomes were different: in the Anglo-Saxon case, the British natives were acculturated and assimilated by the immigrants, while, in the other cases, the immigrants were eventually absorbed into the culture and population of the native societies, although on varying time scales. It is tempting to relate the different outcomes to the different sizes of the immigrant populations, but this might get us dangerously close to a circular argument because the known cultural and linguistic outcomes of the various immigrations play some role in the inference of the relative sizes of the immigrant populations.

Two of these four cases present us with the problem of part of the overall population being almost 'invisible' in archaeological terms: in the case of the Anglo-Saxon immigration, it is the native Britons; in the case of the Scandinavian settlement, it is the immigrants. Minimalists who try to play down or even deny the role of migrations in this period use these two problem cases in different ways, arguing that the invisible Britons must be there somewhere in substantial numbers, while the near-invisibility of the Scandinavian settlers is taken to demonstrate their small numbers. In this debate, progress will only be achieved if we adopt more interdisciplinary approaches (environmental, genetic, socio-linguistic), if we use more sophisticated models to interpret the data thus generated—and if we are more honest about our own preconceptions.

Whatever the sizes of immigrant populations suggested so far, it seems clear they had no significant impact on the overall population sizes of their respective periods. Even the Anglo-Saxon immigration suggested here to

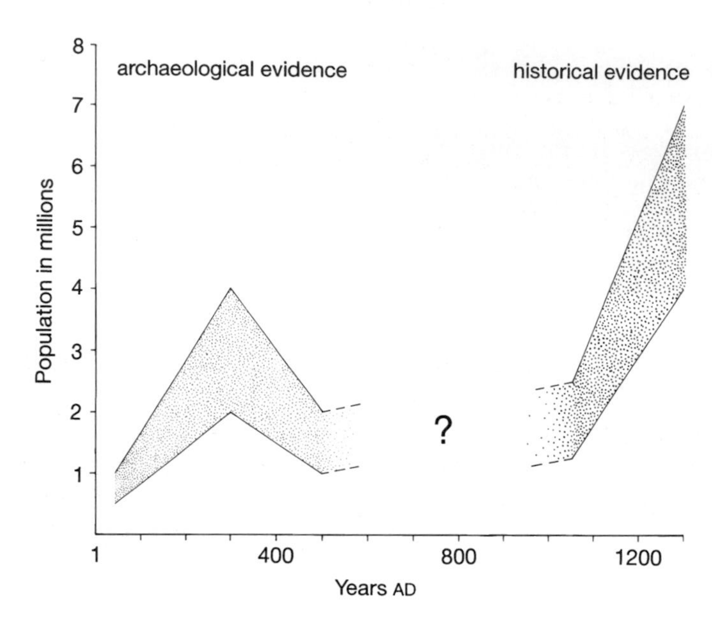

FIG. 5.6 The population of England *c.*AD 1–1300, based on archaeological and historical evidence.

have been the largest in relative terms (perhaps up to 20 per cent of the total population) is unlikely to have led to a sudden increase in population because it extended over the best part of a century, and it coincided with a post-collapse slump in the native population.

Population figures for the first half of the first millennium can be estimated, or even calculated, on the basis of archaeological evidence, and figures for the beginning of the second millennium may be extrapolated from historical information for England (Figure 5.6). Our problem is in between: both types of evidence suggest population growth in the seventh to tenth centuries, but, on that assumption, the curves do not link up. Either the archaeological estimates for the earlier (Roman) period are too high, or the historical information (i.e. the Domesday Book) for the later period gives figures which are too low. Part of the explanation might be a severe population decline as a result of the seventh-century plague, but it would have had to be nothing short of catastrophic for the two curves to link up. This compatibility problem has yet to be confronted by both disciplines. Population estimates for the north and west of Britain are even more difficult, but they are unlikely to add substantially to the overall total.

The beginnings of the intensification of production fall exactly into the gap in the population curve, and may well be linked to the population increase during that time. However, intensification was clearly also stimulated by social change: the rise of the aristocracy, centralizing tendencies of kingship, the appearance and growth of the Church, and urbanization. Intensification must be assumed to have had an impact on the landscape, and in the case of colonization and reclamation it demonstrably had. But by the time covered here, there was little, if any, pristine environment left—the key transformations of the British landscape seem to have happened in later prehistory and the Roman period (cf. Whittle and Cunliffe in this volume).

The nucleation of population in towns and villages, like intensification, was probably the result of social and economic change as much as of population increase, but the debate on the causes of this fundamental process is continuing. It is worth noting that urbanization required four attempts before it took hold in Britain: the late prehistoric tribal centres (*oppida*), Roman planned towns, the trading stations (*emporia*) of the seventh to ninth centuries, and finally the late Saxon and Norman towns from the ninth or tenth century onwards. The respective reasons for failure and success are as yet far from certain. Here, as in the case of population movements and population figures, we still need more data, but, even more urgently, we need more sophisticated models in order to advance our understanding of the process, and we need a more balanced debate which extends across disciplinary boundaries.

REFERENCES

Alcock, L. (1981). 'Early historic fortifications in Scotland', in G. Guilbert (ed.), *Hill-Fort Studies: Essays for A. H. A. Hogg.* Leicester: Leicester University Press, 150–201.

Alcock, L. (1987). *Economy, Society and Warfare among the Britons and Saxons.* Cardiff: University of Wales Press.

Arnold, C. J. (1984). *Roman Britain to Saxon England.* London: Croom Helm.

Astill, G. G. (1991). 'Towns and town hierarchies in Saxon England', *Oxford Journal of Archaeology*, 10: 95–117.

Astill, G. G., and Grant, A. (1988) (eds.). *The Countryside of Medieval England.* Oxford: Blackwell.

Astill, G. G., and Langdon, J. (1997). *Medieval Farming and Technology.* Leiden: Brill.

Aston, M. (1988) (ed.). *Medieval Fish, Fisheries and Fishponds in England.* Oxford: British Archaeological Report 182.

Aston, M., Austin, D., and Dyer, C. (1989) (eds.). *The Rural Settlements of Medieval England.* Oxford: Blackwell.

Aston, M., and Lewis, C. (1994) (eds.). *The Medieval Landscape of Wessex.* Oxford: Oxbow Monograph 46.

Baillie, M. G. L. (1995). *A Slice Through Time.* London: Batsford.

Barley, M. (1977) (ed.). *European Towns: Their Archaeology and Early History.* London: Academic Press.

Bayley, J. (1998) (ed.). *Science in Archaeology: An Agenda for the Future.* London: English Heritage.

Bell, M., and Dark, P. (1998). 'Continuity and change: environmental archaeology in historic periods', in J. Bayley, *Science in Archaeology: An Agenda for the Future.* London: English Heritage, 179–93.

Beresford, G. (1987). *Goltho: The Development of an Early Medieval Manor c. 850–1150.* London: Historic Buildings and Monuments Commission for England, English Heritage Archaeological Report 4.

Beresford, G., and Hurst, J. (1990). *Wharram Percy Deserted Medieval Village.* London: Batsford.

Bettey, J. H. (1993). *Estates and the English Countryside.* London: Batsford.

Biddiss, M. (1979) (ed.). *Images of Race.* New York: Holmes & Meier.

Biddle, M. (1983). 'The study of Winchester: archaeology and history in a British town', *Proceedings of the British Academy*, 69: 93–135.

Biddle, M., and Hill, D. (1971). 'Late Saxon planned towns', *Antiquaries Journal*, 51: 70–85.

Biddle, M., and Kjølbye-Biddle, B. (1992). 'Repton and the Vikings', *Antiquity*, 66: 36–51.

Blair, J. (1988) (ed.). *Minsters and Parish Churches: The Local Church in Transition, c. 950–1200.* Oxford: Oxbow Monograph 17.

Bond, J. (1994). 'Forests, chases, warrens and parks in medieval Wessex', in M. Aston and C. Lewis, *The Medieval Landscape of Wessex.* Oxford: Oxbow, 115–58.

Brooks, N. P. (1979). 'England in the ninth century: the crucible of defeat', *Transactions of the Royal Historical Society*, 5th series, 29: 1–20.

Brown, R. Allen (1984). *The Architecture of Castles: A Visual Guide.* London: Batsford.

Brown, R. Allen (1989). *Castles From the Air.* Cambridge: Cambridge University Press.

Cameron, K. (1961). *English Place-Names.* London: Batsford.

Cameron, K. (1975) (ed.). *Place-Name Evidence for the Anglo-Saxon Invasion and Scandinavian Settlements.* Nottingham: English Place-Name Society.

Cameron, K. (1976). 'The significance of English place-names', *Proceedings of the British Academy*, 62: 135–55.

Chadwick, N. (1965). 'The colonisation of Brittany from Celtic Britain', *Proceedings of the British Academy*, 51: 235–99.

Coggins, D., Fairless, K. J., and Batey, C. E. (1983). 'Simy Folds: an early medieval settlement site in Upper Teesdale, Co. Durham', *Medieval Archaeology*, 27: 1–26.

Coppack, G. (1993). *Fountains Abbey.* London: Batsford.

Coppack, G. (1998). *The White Monks.* London: Tempus.

Cunliffe, B. (1977). *Excavations at Portchester Castle, iii.* London: Reports of the Research Committe of the Society of Antiquaries of London, 34.

Cunliffe, B. (1985). 'Man and landscape in Britain 6000 BC–AD 400', in S. R. J. Woodell (ed.), *The English Landscape*. Oxford and New York: Oxford University Press, 48–67.

Cunliffe, B., and Munby, J. (1985). *Excavations at Portchester Castle, iv.* London: Reports of the Research Committe of the Society of Antiquaries of London, 43.

Darby, H. C. (1952). *The Domesday Geography of England.* Cambridge: Cambridge University Press.

Darby, H. C. (1977). *Domesday England.* Cambridge: Cambridge University Press.

Dark, K. (1994). *Civitas to Kingdom: British Political Continuity, 300–800.* Leicester: Leicester University Press.

Dark, K., and Dark, P. (1997). *The Landscape of Roman Britain.* Stroud: Sutton.

Dark, P. (2000). *The Environment of Britain in the First Millennium AD.* London: Duckworth.

Davies, R. R. (1987). *The Age of Conquest: Wales 1063–1415.* Oxford and New York: Oxford University Press.

Davies, W. (1982). *Wales in the Early Middle Ages.* Leicester: Leicester University Press.

Esmonde Cleary, S. A. (1989). *The Ending of Roman Britain.* London: Batsford.

Faith, R. (1997). *The English Peasantry and the Growth of Lordship.* London and Washington: Leicester University Press.

Fellows-Jensen, G. (1975). 'The Vikings in England: a review', *Anglo-Saxon England*, 4: 181–206.

Fellows-Jensen, G. (1978). 'Place-names and settlement in the North Riding of Yorkshire', *Northern History*, 14: 21–46.

Fleming, R. (1991). *Kings and Lords in Conquest England.* Cambridge: Cambridge University Press.

Fowler, P. (1997). 'Farming in early medieval England: some fields for thought', in J. Hines (ed.), *The Anglo-Saxons from the Migration Period to the Eighth Century.* Woodbridge: Boydell, 245–61.

Fox, C. (1947). *The Personality of Britain.* 4th edn., Cardiff: National Museum of Wales.

Garnett, G. (1985). 'Franci et Angli: the legal distinctions between peoples after the conquest', *Anglo-Norman Studies*, 8: 109–37.

Gelling, M. (1976). 'The evidence of place-names', in P. Sawyer (ed.), *Medieval Settlement.* London: Edward Arnold, 200–11.

Gelling, M. (1978). *Signposts to the Past.* London: Dent.

Gem, R. (1988). 'The English parish church in the 11th and early 12th centuries: a great rebuilding?', in J. Blair (ed.), *Minsters and Parish Churches.* Oxford: Oxbow Monograph 17, 21–33.

Golding, B. (1994). *Conquest and Colonisation: The Normans in Britain, 1066–1100.* New York: St Martin's Press.

Graham, A. H., and Davies, S. M. (1993). *Excavations in the Town Centre of Trowbridge, Wiltshire 1977 and 1986–1988.* Salisbury: Trust for Wessex Archaeology, Wessex Archaeology Report 2.

Graham-Campbell, J., and Batey, C. E. (1998). *Vikings in Scotland.* Edinburgh: Edinburgh University Press.

Härke, H. (1998). 'Briten und Angelsachsen im nachrömischen England', *Studien zur Sachsenforschung*, 11: 87–119.

Härke, H. (1999). 'Sächsische Ethnizität und archäologische Deutung im frühmittelalterlichen England', *Studien zur Sachsenforschung*, 12: 109–22.

Hall, R. (1984). *The Viking Dig: The Excavations at York.* London: Bodley Head.

Hallam, H. E. (1981). *Rural England 1066–1348.* Brighton: The Harvester Press, and New Jersey: Humanities Press.

Hamerow, H. (1991). 'Settlement mobility and the "Middle Saxon Shift": rural settlements and settlement patterns in Anglo-Saxon England', *Anglo-Saxon England*, 20: 1–17.

Hamilton, J. R. C. (1956). *Excavations at Jarlshof, Shetland.* Edinburgh: HMSO.

Haslam, J. (1984) (ed.). *Anglo-Saxon Towns in Southern England.* Chichester: Phillimore.

Herlihy, D. (1985). *Medieval Households.* Cambridge, Mass., and London: Harvard University Press.

Higham, N. (1992). *Rome, Britain and the Anglo-Saxons.* London: Seaby.

Hill, D. (1981). *An Atlas of Anglo-Saxon England.* Oxford: Blackwell.

Hills, C. (1993). 'The Anglo-Saxon settlement of England: The state of research in Britain in the late 1980s', in M. Müller-Wille and R. Schneider (eds.), *Ausgewählte Probleme europäischer Landnahmen des Früh- und Hochmittelalters.* Sigmaringen: Thorbecke, Vorträge und Forschungen 41, 303–15.

Hines, J. (1997) (ed.). *The Anglo-Saxons from the Migration Period to the Eighth Century.* Woodbridge: Boydell, Studies in Historical Archaeoethnology 2.

Hinton, D. E. (1990). *Archaeology, Economy and Society: England from the Fifth to the Fifteenth Century.* London: Seaby.

Hodges, R. (1982). *Dark Age Economics.* London: Duckworth.

Hodges, R. (1989). *The Anglo-Saxon Achievement.* London: Duckworth.

Hodges, R., and Hobley, B. (1988) (eds.). *The Rebirth of Towns in the West AD 700–1050.* London: Council for British Archaeology Research Report 68.

Holt, J. C. (1987) (ed.). *Domesday Studies.* Woodbridge: Boydell.

Holt, R. (1988). *The Mills of Medieval England.* Oxford: Blackwell.

Hooke, D. (1988) (ed.). *Anglo-Saxon Settlements.* London: Blackwell.

Hooke, D. (1989). 'Early medieval estate and settlement patterns: the documentary evidence', in M. Aston, D. Austin, and C. Dyer (eds.), *The Rural Settlements of Medieval England.* Oxford: Blackwell, 9–30.

Hooke, D. (1997). 'The Anglo-Saxons in England in the seventh and eighth centuries: aspects of location in space', in J. Hines (ed.), *The Anglo-Saxons from the Migration Period to the Eighth Century.* Woodbridge: Boydell.

Hoskins, W. G. (1955). *The Making of the English Landscape.* London: Hodder and Stoughton.

Jones, G. R. J. (1976). 'Multiple estates and early settlement', in P. Sawyer (ed.), *Medieval Settlement.* London: Edward Arnold, 15–40.

Jones, M. E. (1996). *The End of Roman Britain.* Ithaca, NY: Cornell University Press.

Kapelle, W. E. (1979). *The Norman Conquest of the North.* London: Croom Helm.

Kenward, H. K., and Hall, A. R. (1995). *Biological Evidence from 16–22 Coppergate.* York: Council for British Archaeology, The Archaeology of York 14/7.

Kermode, P. M. C. (1907). *Manx Crosses.* London.

Laing, Ll. (1975). *The Archaeology of Late Celtic Britain and Ireland c.400–1200 AD.* London: Methuen.

Laing, Ll., and Laing, J. (1990). *Celtic Britain and Ireland, AD 200–800.* Dublin: Irish Academic Press.

Lamb, H. H. (1981). 'Climate from 1000 BC to 1000 AD', in M. Jones and G. Dimbleby (eds.), *The Environment of Man.* Oxford: British Archaeological Report 87, 53–65.

Langdon, J. (1986). *Horses, Oxen and Technological Innovation.* Cambridge: Cambridge University Press.

Lewis, C., Mitchell-Fox, P., and Dyer, C. (1997). *Village, Hamlet and Field: Changing Medieval Settlements in Central England.* Manchester: Manchester University Press.

Loyn, H. R. (1962). *Anglo-Saxon England and the Norman Conquest.* Harlow: Longman.

Loyn, H. R. (1994). *The Vikings in Britain.* Oxford: Blackwell.

McNeill, T. E. (1992). *English Heritage Book of Castles.* London: Batsford and English Heritage.

Maddicott, J. R. (1997). 'Plague in seventh century England', *Past and Present,* 156: 7–54.

Mays, S. (1998). 'The archaeological study of medieval human populations, AD 1066–1540', in J. Bayley (ed.), *Science in Archaeology: An Agenda for the Future.* London: English Heritage, 195–210.

Miller, E., and Hatcher, J. (1978). *Medieval England: Rural Society and Economic Change 1086–1348.* London: Longman.

Millett, M. (1990). *The Romanization of Britain.* Cambridge: Cambridge University Press.

Morton, A. (1992). 'Burial in middle Saxon Southampton', in S. Bassett (ed.), *Death in Towns.* Leicester: Leicester University Press, 68–77.

Myres, J. N. L. (1986). *The English Settlements.* Oxford: Clarendon.

Nicolaisen, W. F. H. (1982). 'The Viking settlement of Scotland: the evidence of place-names', in R. T. Farrell (ed.), *The Vikings.* London and Chichester: Phillimore, 95–115.

O'Connor, T. (1982). *Animal Bones from Flaxengate, Lincoln c.870–1500.* London: Council for British Archaeology, Archaeology of Lincoln XVIII-1.

Pearce, S. (1978). *The Kingdom of Dumnonia.* Padstow: Lodenek.

Pounds, N. J. G. (1990). *The Medieval Castle in England and Wales.* Cambridge: Cambridge University Press.

Powlesland, D. (1997). 'Early Anglo-Saxon settlements, structures, form and layout', in J. Hines (ed.), *The Anglo-Saxons from the Migration Period to the Eighth Century.* Woodbridge: Boydell, 101–17.

Rackham, J. (1994) (ed.). *Environment and Economy in Anglo-Saxon England.* York: Council for British Archaeology Research Report 89.

Rackham, O. (1976). *Trees and Woodland in the British Landscape.* London: Dent.

Rackham, O. (1985). 'Ancient woodland and hedges in England', in S. R. J. Woodell (ed.), *The English Landscape: Past, Present, and Future.* Oxford and New York: Oxford University Press, 68–105.

Rackham, O. (1994). *The Illustrated History of the Countryside.* London: BCA.

Rahtz, P., and Meeson, R. (1992). *An Anglo-Saxon Watermill at Tamworth.* London: Council for British Archaeology Research Report 83.

Ralegh Radford, C. A. (1978). 'The pre-conquest boroughs of England, ninth to eleventh centuries', *Proceedings of the British Academy*, 64: 131–53.

Richards, J. (1991). *English Heritage Book of Viking Age England.* London: Batsford and English Heritage.

Rippon, S. (1994). 'Medieval wetland reclamation', in M. Aston and C. Lewis (eds.), *The Medieval Landscape of Wessex.* Oxford: Oxbow, 239–53.

Ritchie, G., and Ritchie, A. (1981). *Scotland: Archaeology and Early History.* London: Thames and Hudson.

Rowley, T. (1981) (ed.). *The Origins of Open-Field Agriculture.* London: Croom Helm.

Salisbury, C. (1995). 'An 8th-century Mercian bridge over the Trent at Cromwell, Nottinghamshire, England', *Antiquity*, 69: 1015–18.

Sawyer, P. (1962). *The Age of the Vikings.* London: Edward Arnold.

Sawyer, P. (1971). *The Age of the Vikings.* 2nd edn., London: Edward Arnold.

Sawyer, P. (1976) (ed.). *Medieval Settlement.* London: Edward Arnold.

Sawyer, P. (1978). *From Roman Britain to Norman England.* London: Methuen.

Sawyer, P. (1985) (ed.). *Domesday Book: A Reassessment.* London: Edward Arnold.

Schama, S. (1995). *Landscape and Memory.* London: Fontana.

Scull, C. (1997). 'Urban centres in pre-Viking England?', in J. Hines (ed.), *The Anglo-Saxons from the Migraton Period to the Eighth Century.* Woodbridge: Boydell, 269–98.

Seebohm, F. (1890). *The English Village Community.* 4th edn., London: Longmans, Green & Co.

Soulsby, I. (1983). *The Towns of Medieval Wales.* Chichester.

Spearman, M. R. (1988). 'Early Scottish towns: their origins and economy', in S. T. Driscoll and M. R. Nieke (eds.), *Power and Politics in Early Medieval Britain and Ireland.* Edinburgh: Edinburgh University Press, 96–110.

Stenton, F. M. (1971). *Anglo-Saxon England.* 3rd edn., Oxford: Oxford University Press.

Taylor, C. (1983). *Village and Farmstead: A History of Rural Settlement in England.* London: George Philip.

Unwin, T. (1988). 'Towards a model of Anglo-Scandinavian rural settlement in

England', in D. Hooke (ed.), *Anglo-Saxon Settlements.* London: Blackwell, 77–98.
Van de Noort, R. (1993). 'The context of early medieval barrows in western Europe', *Antiquity*, 67: 66–73.
Welch, M. (1985). 'Rural settlement patterns in the Early and Middle Anglo-Saxon periods', *Landscape History*, 7: 13–25.
Welch, M. (1992). *English Heritage Book of Anglo-Saxon England.* London: Batsford and English Heritage.
White, W. J. (1988). *Skeletal Remains from the Cemetery of St Nicholas Shambles, City of London.* London: London and Middlesex Archaeological Society.
Whitelock, D. (1979). *English Historical Documents, i* (repr.). London: Eyre Methuen.
Williams, H. (1997). 'Ancient landscapes and the dead: the reuse of prehistoric and Roman monuments as Early Anglo-Saxon burial sites', *Medieval Archaeology*, 41: 1–32.
Wilson, D. (1976). 'The Scandinavians in England', in D. Wilson (ed.), *The Archaeology of Anglo-Saxon England.* Cambridge: Cambridge University Press, 393–403.
Wilson, D., and Bersu, G. (1966). *Three Viking Graves in the Isle of Man.* London: Society for Medieval Archaeology Monograph Series, 1.
Woodell, S. R. J. (1985) (ed.). *The English Landscape.* Oxford and New York: Oxford University Press.

6

Plagues and Peoples

The Long Demographic Cycle, 1250–1670

Richard Smith

THE following discussion is focused around a consideration of what will be termed a 'long population cycle' from the late thirteenth century through to the late seventeenth century. In so far as this consideration is directed towards a society that may be unambiguously categorized as 'preindustrial' throughout this era, it is unavoidable that at various stages of the argument it will be necessary to engage with the classical Malthusian model of the relationship between living standards and population growth rates, although some assessment will be made of the role played by epidemic disease in determining both the width and depth of the cycle. In addition an attempt will be made to chart the principal changes to the economy and society relating to shifting numbers and geographical distribution of persons on the land during the extensive phases of demographic decline and recovery.

MEASURING THE POPULATION CYCLE

Before engaging with theory and explanations of long-term trends some mundanely empirical steps will be taken so that the broad dimensions of the 'cycle' might be established. Empiricism is no straightforward endeavour in the absence of serial census records of any kind, let alone individual census counts for randomly distributed moments, over this extensive four-century period. It is at least fortunate that the final 150 years of the cycle yield evidence from parish registers, which in recent years have been exploited by historical demographers in ways that make it possible to establish annual population totals and vital rates from 1541. In attempting to establish population trends and totals before a system of parochial registration of baptisms, marriages, and burials was in place, historians succumb to what Sir Michael Postan (1966: 561) once termed the 'lure of aggregates' by engaging in decidedly problematic, although unavoidable, exercises. In this present discussion we are in danger of incurring Postan's wrath since we employ one central and vital source that relates to demographic conditions in one year only, around which a key argument in this discussion revolves. That source is the poll tax of 1377—a tax, supposedly, on all lay persons 14 years of age and above. It is far from perfect since there are reasons to suppose that genuine paupers were omitted from those taxed (Fenwick 1998: pp. xxiii–xxiv). In addition, some allowance has to be made for the clerical population and the most uncertain factor of all—evasion. By utilizing on a vill-by-vill basis tax returns from four English counties in 1377—Essex, Cambridgeshire, Leicestershire, and the West Riding of Yorkshire—an attempt will be made to reconstruct population totals, first for counties and then nationally, in 1377 and 1300.[1] The estimates of population totals for 1300 will then be compared with those which obtained at the time of the first census of England in 1801.

Such an approach begins with the surviving totals of taxpayers recorded for vills in these selected counties in 1377. To set upper- and lower-band estimates around population totals generated from the recorded taxpayer numbers, certain assumptions have to be made. It is possible to establish a minimum estimate by assuming a relatively low level of underassessment at 5 per cent (once termed derisory by Hatcher 1977: 14), as well as treating the prevailing mortality regime as severe. By assuming a low, indeed negative, demographic growth rate it is also, by resort to model life tables, possible to obtain an age structure thereby enabling estimation of the proportion of the population under the age of 14. Such a procedure creates a minimal proportion of the population under the age of 14 of 32 per cent. In the space available for the present discussion the precise details of this exercise cannot be set out fully, although they are available elsewhere.[2] A maximal estimate of population size assumes at 10 per cent, a higher, although not excessively high level of evasion in 1377. This estimate also assumes a demographic regime with relatively modest mortality levels,

[1] The poll tax returns for Cambridgeshire are deposited in the Public Record Office (PRO E179/81/32–40; E179/149/141; E179/192/4a; E179/237/7a; E179/240/256, 259), for Essex (PRO E179/107/46–58; E179/240/256–259), for Leicestershire (E179/133/17–25; E179/134/325; E179/240/256–259), and for Yorkshire West Riding (PRO E179/206/31–44). The returns for Cambridgeshire, Essex, and Leicestershire have now been conveniently edited and published in Fenwick (1998).

[2] For fuller details see Ramos-Pinto (forthcoming).

TABLE 6.1. *Population estimates for a sample of English manors, c.1310 and c.1370*

Manor	*c.*1310 Estimate A	*c.*1370 Estimate B	A:B
Coltishall	119 (1314)	33 (1370)	3.6
Halesowen	485 (1311–15)	289 (1371–75)	1.7
Great Waltham	320 (1306)	162 (1377)	2.0
High Easter	306 (1306)	135 (1377)	2.3
Margaret Roding	55 (1318)	25 (1365)	2.2
Chatham Hall	63 (1308)	29 (1378)	2.2

Source: Smith 1991: 49.

greater demographic buoyancy, and hence a resulting population age structure in which 45 per cent of the population is under 14 years of age.[3]

In addition to these somewhat speculative manipulations of the tax-payer totals of 1377 we may employ evidence that survives in the manorial sources of certain locations which make it possible to secure serial counts of persons resident in the same community for various dates from the late thirteenth to the early sixteenth centuries. For instance, counts of males aged 12 years and over, resident within tithing in a modest sample of Essex and Leicestershire communities, suggest that their populations in 1300 were two to two and a half times higher than those of 1377 (Poos 1991: 96–103; Postles 1992: 45). Such data imply a rate of decline over the first eight decades of the fourteenth century that is consistent with evidence from other sources. For instance, such data as those summarized in Table 6.1 suggest that the ratio between population totals *c.*1310 and *c.*1377 varied between 1.7 in Halesowen in Worcestershire and 3.6 in Coltishall in Norfolk, with a mode in excess of 2.0.

In proceeding to generate population totals for vills in the four-sample counties in 1300, by working backwards from estimates of population totals in 1377, the relatively conservative inflator of 2 has been adopted, although an inflator of 2.5 seems equally valid. The 1377 poll tax returns for individual Essex vills are not complete. Many of the returns for the south-west of the county, which today would fall within metropolitan

[3] Ranges of derived age structures have been calculated from Princeton Model West life tables (Coale and Demeny 1983: 130–7), proportions of males and females aged 14 and over to total population, assuming population decline at 0.5 per cent per annum and extreme limits of mortality levels 1 and 8 (female e25 = 20.0 and 37.5 years).

Essex, have failed to survive. However, population sizes can be secured for most of the settlements in the remaining parts of the county. In using our maximal and minimal estimates we discover that average population densities fell between 95 and 108 persons per square mile in 1300. If account is taken of the fact that the average population density for Essex in 1801 was 136 persons per square mile—a level secured after a preceding half-century of rapid population growth and significant urban growth in those parts of the county close by London—we discover that over central and north Essex the population totals of individual settlements derived from our estimate for 1300 fall within 10 per cent of those recorded for those same places in the 1801 census.

The 1377 poll tax returns for Leicestershire reveal that county to have been more thickly populated than Essex, with population densities falling on average between 108 and 122 persons per square mile in 1300. In fact, the eastern half of the county supported densities that were closer to 150 per square mile, which strongly suggests population densities in the early fourteenth century that exceeded those to be found in 1801. In Cambridgeshire where 80 per cent of the vills of 1377 can be compared directly with population totals for the same settlements in 1801, estimates of average densities in 1300 fall between 116 and 131 per square mile. In many respects these densities resemble those from nearby eastern Leicestershire. This resemblance with Leicestershire is reflected in the striking fact that this county in 1801 had a total population of 43,926 persons living at an average density of 96.4 persons per square mile. It is clear that for much of the county in the early fourteenth century population totals were significantly greater than those of the early nineteenth century.

An extension of this statistical exercise to West Yorkshire is in certain respects highly problematic, given the significant industrialization in that region in the late eighteenth century. In fact, the area as a whole had a population density in 1801 that was almost three times the level in 1300. However, when the rapid demographic growth that had occurred in the industrializing areas of the Riding is taken into account, and the specifically non-industrialized areas of Tickhill, Claro, Barkston, Osgoldcross, and the Ainsty are considered alone, population estimates for 1300 are remarkably similar to those recorded in the 1801 census.

While a much larger study is needed, applying to all surviving poll tax returns the procedures employed on the four sample counties, it would appear that English population totals in 1300 are hardly likely to have fallen below 5.5 million. This conclusion is reached having applied a conservative inflator to the vill population totals of 1377. Indeed a strong case exists for using an inflator of 2.5 which would point towards a national population total significantly in excess of 6 million in 1300. The latter conclusion seems particularly compelling when it is recalled that the national population in 1801 was 8.7 million. Allowance, of course, has to be made for London which by that date had reached 900,000, as well as the substantial urban growth in the industrializing counties of the north and midlands (Wrigley 1986*a*: 133). If all the urban settlements exceeding 5,000 were subtracted from the English population in 1801 a population of 6.3 million would remain and on the basis of the evidence we have presented from our four-county sample, it is unlikely that the total English population in 1300 would have fallen far below the non-urban total of the later date.

That this early fourteenth-century population of *c*.5.5 to *c*.6.5 million had fallen by at least 50 per cent by the last quarter of the fourteenth century is ample testimony to the changing demographic regime that had emerged as that century had progressed. If recourse is made to the counts of males over the age of 12 as a framework for charting the course of population change in Essex from the late thirteenth until the early sixteenth centuries, some striking features are detectable. From 1538 the tithing penny totals can be compared with early parish registers for certain of these communities and both source categories would seem to be in agreement over population sizes and trends (Poos 1991: 109). These series confirm that by the beginning of the sixteenth century population levels were well under one-half, perhaps barely more than one-third, of those found in these localities two centuries earlier. Indeed little net recovery, if any, could be detected from a late medieval demographic low point in the 1520s. An English national demographic estimate, using the lay subsidy returns points to a population total of *c*.2.2 million in 1524–5 (Wrigley and Schofield 1981: 566–8) which in relation to an English population total of 1300 in excess of 6 million suggests long-term national change of very much the same order of magnitude as the Essex tithing penny totals. It is noteworthy, too, that a sizeable share of the demographic decline in the Essex samples had taken place before the crisis associated with bubonic plague's arrival in 1348 (see Figure 6.1). Of course, Essex was in no sense England, although it is noteworthy that evidence of a similar type for the Leicestershire manor of Kibworth Harcourt, where a variable tithing penny was also collected, shows a remarkably similar trend over the course of the fourteenth century (see Figure 6.2).

English demographic recovery appears to have coincided with the arrival of systematic parochial registration of baptisms, marriages, and burials after 1537. The trend after 1520 in the Essex tithing penny counts follows a course that is compatible with the national picture reconstructed from the post-1537 sample of parish registers and a national estimate reconstructed from the Chantry Certificates of the 1540s (Wrigley and Schofield 1981: 207–10, 564–5). Indeed all three sets of evidence point

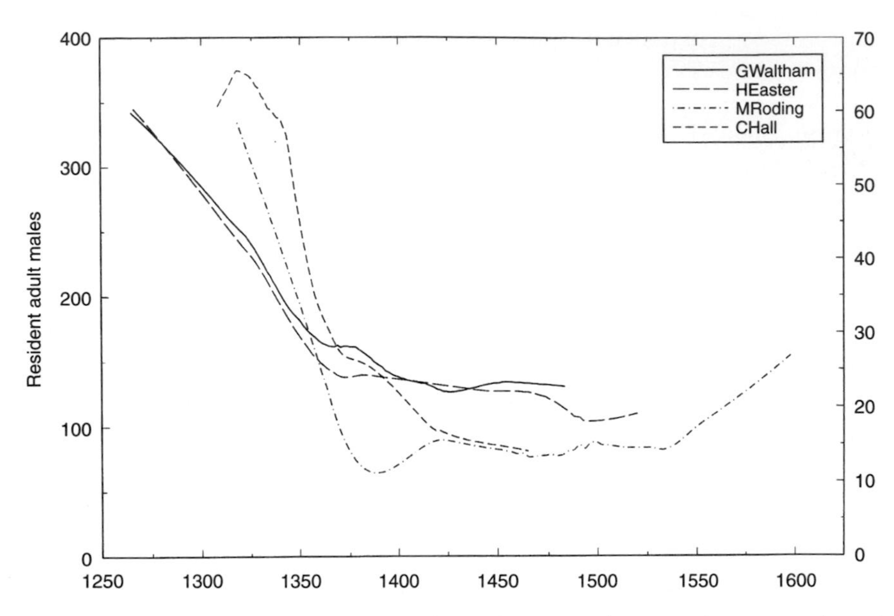

FIG. 6.1 Smoothed population trends (males over the age of 12) on selected English manors, 1270–1600.

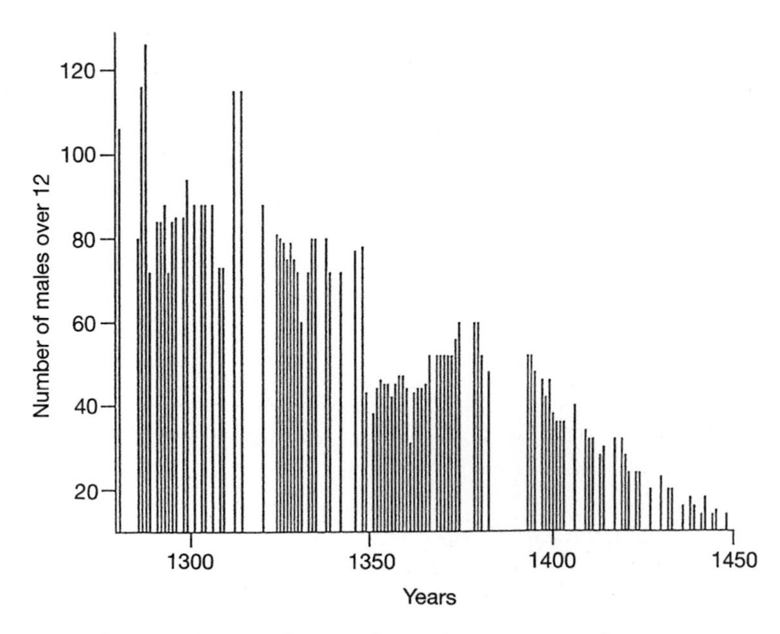

FIG. 6.2 Males over the age of 12 at Kibworth Harcourt, 1280–1450.

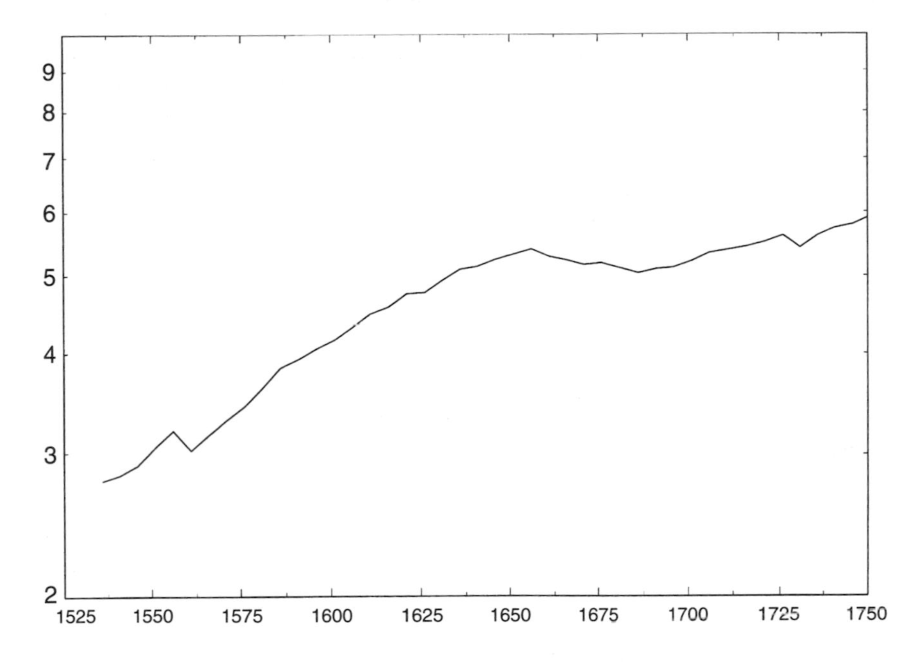

FIG. 6.3 English population totals, 1541–1871.

towards demographic growth between the 1520s and 1540s at the relatively swift rate of 0.8 per cent per annum. Growth at this pace was not sustained through the 1550s when at the conclusion of that decade very heavy mortality caused the momentum that had certainly characterized the second quarter of the sixteenth century to be temporarily lost. By the 1570s there are signs that population had at last reached, and was beginning to move above, the level of 3 million, at which it most likely stood some two centuries earlier. The third quarter of the sixteenth century exhibits some of the fastest and most sustained demographic growth rates of any phase of the parish register era before the late eighteenth century. By 1600 national population totals had risen to 4 million and the following half-century saw a further million added to the total number of persons living within the national borders. None the less, in the early seventeenth century growth rates were on the wane and by the 1650s population was stationary (see Figure 6.3). Indeed negative growth rates appear to have characterized the 1660s, 1670s, and 1680s, ensuring that the long population cycle had run its course by settling down at a population total that was smaller by at least 1 million than it had been in the early fourteenth century. In fact, it was not until 1760, almost three centuries after plague had registered such a devastating short-term blow to the English population in 1348–9, that a national population total once again reached 6 million. It did so in a context that was very different both in terms of the domestic economic structure and the country's position within a wider international setting.

SOME ECONOMIC CORRELATES AND CONSEQUENCES OF THE DEMOGRAPHIC CYCLE

Falling population obviously shifted the balance between the supply of, and demand for, land on the downward phase of the cycle. Land was withdrawn from agricultural use, although this was a process that was subject to considerable geographical variation that depended on a complex mixture of environmental and political factors. Water encroached on cultivated lands in many locations from the early fourteenth century onwards. Notable losses occurred in the fenlands of eastern England, the land surrounding the Thames estuary, the Kentish and Sussex marshes abutting the English Channel (Bailey 1991: 190). While some of this flooding arose from a marked deterioration in weather conditions and rising sea levels this abandonment of land to agricultural use was fundamentally the product of a reduced incentive to invest in drainage systems and sea defences, given the declining land values, rising labour costs, and falling prices for agricultural products. The long-term decline in high-altitude townships of Northumberland and Durham was another consequence of falling populations, although an effect exacerbated by falling mean summer temperatures and the ever-present reality and threat of Scottish invasions, particularly in the contested borderland areas (Tuck 1991: 36–9). Other environmentally marginal areas such as moor-edge communities in Devon and Cornwall (Fox 1991: 158–9) and the 'hungry' sandy soils of the Norfolk and Suffolk Brecklands reveal some signs of a withdrawal from cultivation (Bailey 1989: 9–25, 309–23). However, in neither of the aforementioned cases should the changes be overstressed since both regions displayed highly commercialized economies that remained strikingly vibrant in the later Middle Ages. A relatively buoyant tin industry on the margins of Dartmoor (Hatcher 1970: 29–32) and large-scale rabbit farming in the Brecklands (Bailey 1988) are just two instances of economic activities that were not necessarily adversely affected by the falling population levels in regions where grain-growing had never been very well developed. However, in general the plough was in retreat and pasture, woodland, and regenerating scrub were the land uses that were accounting for rising acreages, certainly after 1370. Botanically these processes reveal themselves in the findings from pollen analysis in the form of a rising share of grassland and woodland species relative to grain species prior to 1500 (Bartley 1979: 133–42; Beckett 1981: 246–66).

As population recovery became more marked and, in particular, as the national total moved towards 4 million by the turn of the sixteenth century, evidence is relatively abundant indicating expansion of agricultural pursuits. Active colonization of royal forest regions is one noteworthy development (Hoyle 1992: 353–88). For instance, in the reigns of James I and Charles I the crown embarked on the disafforestation of Glatres and Knaresborough forests in Yorkshire in response to its apparent inability effectively to stop the growing numbers of individuals illegally grazing and felling timber (Thirsk 1967: 37–8). Perhaps the most dramatic development was the concerted attack on areas of marsh and fen in the early seventeenth century most spectacularly represented by reclamation in the peatlands of the southern fenlands of Cambridgeshire and Huntingdonshire (Darby 1940). Drainage also occurred in the Somerset Levels, Hatfield Chase, the Isle of Axholme, on the coastlands of the Thames estuary in Essex and Kent, and the marshes of Holderness in East Yorkshire (Thirsk 1967: 78, 38–9, 59–64).

The aforementioned processes of retreat and expansion resulted in profound transformations in local and regional distributions of population. It is hardly surprising that in the early sixteenth century when national population levels only marginally exceeded 2 million that the famous *Dialogue* between Cardinal Pole and Thomas Lupset as composed by Thomas Starkey should reflect on 'the grete lake of pepul and skarseness of men' in the England of the 1530s (Herrtage 1878: 72). None the less, the population over the course of the previous century redistributed itself, with the south-eastern and south-western corners of the country increasing their relative shares with significant areas of the Midlands losing their place among the most densely settled regions (Sheail 1972: 123). Likewise, although population growth after 1550 was basically ubiquitous, not all areas expanded at the same rate. Surplus population which could not be readily absorbed into more densely populated arable, open-field parishes was channelled towards those rural areas which retained some capacity to support greater numbers. Margaret Spufford's (1974: 10–18) classic study of Cambridgeshire communities demonstrates these points with maximum clarity. Over the sixteenth century the fen-edge parishes of the county became the most densely peopled part of the county, since their extensive pastures and opportunities for fishing and wild fowling provided a living for families whose tiny holdings of land would have been inadequate for their support in the corn-growing uplands. Indeed, numbers in southern Cambridgeshire, where as we have seen medieval settlement was particularly dense, actually fell between 1524 and 1563.

While settlement and population totals waned and waxed agricultural land was rarely completely abandoned and, the case of Cambridgeshire notwithstanding, the store of unreclaimed land was by no means large. A more common development was that land use changed from more intensive to extensive modes of exploitation over the course of the cycle. During the era of population decline, especially over the course of the fifteenth-century depression, much arable was converted to pasture. In certain contexts, such as the south Midlands, this conversion may have been a prominent factor in causing village desertion. For example, in the south-east Warwickshire hundred of Kineton almost one in every four villages was deserted in the second half of the fifteenth century, although demise of most settlements was the result of a process of decline extending over a much longer period (Dyer 1989*a*: 55–7). In these cases, it has been shown that a number of determinants came into play. The primary factor was undoubtedly population decline. However, the most vulnerable settlements were those oldest established, open-field arable farming communities whose continued viability depended upon the presence of a labour force which if not forthcoming threatened the system's very existence. Once populations in this type of area fell below a critical threshold the agrarian regime was barely sustainable. It was frequently the case, and no coincidence, that landlords were also particularly powerful, indeed free agents, in such ecological settings, and were therefore possessed of a political authority that made it easier to complete the process of depopulation by putting the land under pasture, often in the form of one large sheep farm. Here, it is important to note, we have an instance of large-scale depopulation that was not the consequence of prior village development on marginal or inferior soils, but a vulnerability that was principally the result of a complex set of institutional factors that were held in place by a subtle balance between agrarian technology and labour inputs.

To some extent when population expanded after 1550 pasture made way for arable farming. Piecemeal colonization of wood, pasture, and waste was more frequently encountered in areas where lordship was a relatively weak force. Large numbers of smallholders and rising immigrant populations, for example, were distinctive characteristics of many forest areas of the east Midlands (Thirsk 1967: 93–9). Similar features were to be found in the decidedly problematic environments, at least for arable farming, in the uplands of the north-west which were increasingly populated; in the diocese of Carlisle the population expanded by 43 per cent in the forty years between 1563 and 1603, a development confirmed by the evidence on the number of tenants in manorial surveys (Appleby 1978: 25). For instance, in the Cumbrian forest of Inglewood numerous encroachments on the waste produced a multiplicity of marginal agricultural holdings carved from the waste (Appleby 1975).

There were also changes in the nature of woodlands as demand for wood grew and the areas available to supply that rising need shrank in geographical extent. One feature that distinguished a growing number of woodland areas was more systematically managed coppicing thereby reducing the acreage of less productive 'natural' woodland (Rackham 1986: 62–118). Rising coal production in the later stages of the population cycle may have reduced some of the pressure on woodlands enabling further conversion of woodland to other agricultural uses (Hatcher 1994: 554–5). Norfolk, for instance, lost three-quarters of its medieval woodland between the late sixteenth century and the beginning of the eighteenth century (Overton 1996: 90).

The intensity with which resources were exploited also varied over the cycle and those factors of production that were available in abundance, and hence relatively less costly, were substituted for those that were scarce and expensive. During the era of high population totals in the late thirteenth and early fourteenth centuries approximately 10.5 million acres was under the plough compared with *c*.6 million acres of arable at the time of Domesday Book (Overton and Campbell 1996: 290–1). However, that greatly expanded acreage was also farmed more intensively, reflected in a general trend towards increased labour inputs per unit area. In many areas there was partial or complete substitution of waged for servile labour as the former became abundant, cheap, and certainly relatively more efficient than the latter (Stone 1997: 640–56). Hired rather than corvée labour was more easily deployed seasonally on a casual basis for weeding, mowing, and harvesting as it became more common to hire and remunerate workers by the task (Farmer 1988: 760–72). More flexible deployment of labour facilitated more complex rotational arrangements, less land under fallow, especially in areas of irregular and flexible field systems such as eastern and south-eastern England (Bishop 1938: 38–44; Campbell 1981: 21–2). Likewise more comprehensive preparation of seedbeds, through repeated ploughings, heavier seeding, and frequent weeding, the growth of legumes, the folding of sheep, the spreading and transport of urban-derived night soil, the digging and application to soils of lime and marl formed a constellation of practices which while dependent upon substantial labour inputs also led to higher yields per acre, if not per capita (Campbell 1983*a*, 1983*b*, 1988, 1997). In fact in the century after 1250 the arable and pastoral components of farming systems became more intimately interconnected. With labour cheap more animals were stall-fed making it easier to employ more systematic recycling of nitrogen via the collection and purposeful spreading of animal waste on to the fields that were primarily devoted to grain production (Campbell 1992, 1995). An older view that supposed there was a conflict between manure supplies for the arable sector and human population numbers and needs has recently been overturned (Stone 1998). It is now known that manuring was facilitated and less costly to undertake when ratios of humans to livestock were high *c.*1300 in contrast to the post-Black Death period when flock and herd sizes held up relative to human population totals. A correlate of this intensification of land and labour-usage was a shift in dietary patterns that were driven by falling per capita incomes. For instance, the processing of grain into ale results in more significant loss of available kilocalories than milling and baking or cooking it in pottage. It is therefore noteworthy that over the late thirteenth century the acreage of land under food grains and under cheaper grain varieties increased relative to that under brewing and more expensive (luxury) grains (Campbell 1998: 29). Hence the acreage under rye, mixtures, oat, and dredge expanded relative to that under barley and wheat. As part of the intensification process acreages under legumes used both as animal feed and for nitrogen fixing also rose (Biddick 1989: 121–5; Campbell and Power 1992: 237). Horses increased in number at the expense of oxen, milch cows too increased in number as dairying became more important relative to beef-eating (Langdon 1986; Campbell 1992: 107–18). These features of the agrarian landscape reflected shifts in mass diets which saw ale and beef consumption declining, and the consumption of coarse bread, pottage, and dairy products increasing (Dyer 1989*b*: 151–60). Hay meadows and coppiced woodland were all managed more intensively as labour inputs rose per unit area.

A reduced intensity of agricultural activities, reflecting diminished labour inputs, was characteristic of the century and a half after 1350. A swing from arable to pastoral pursuits went hand in hand with reduced seeding rates, more fallow land, and less weeding, with the result that output per acre fell quite sharply, especially after 1370 (Campbell 1988, 1997). Wheat and barley production became more characteristic of grain farming as rye and oats lost ground as rising per capita incomes prompted a shift away from the consumption of cheaper grains and marginal soils more suited to their production were abandoned. The spread of the horse as a draught animal was halted which as a consequence of its high cost of maintenance yielded part of the agricultural stage to the oxen whose lower maintenance charges enabled it to recover some of the ground it had relinquished in the period before the Black Death (Langdon 1986: 212). On the demesne farms draught animals fell in importance, contributing to the decline in the demand for oats, and beef cattle became more important relative to milch cows (Campbell 1990: 107–8). Sheep farming is the least labour intensive form of pastoralism and in the labour-starved world of the later Middle Ages, notwithstanding depressed wool prices, it increased in importance. On manorial demesnes the ratio of sheep to sown acres increased threefold and one in three of all manorial livestock were sheep compared with one in five in the thirteenth century (Lloyd 1973; Mate 1987: 523–36). Wheat consumption rose since more bread was baked, and less grain was boiled in pottage as more houses came to possess individual baking ovens. More ale was consumed, as ale houses became more regularly encountered features of village life. Meat, especially beef consumption, grew and the rural butcher and the butcher-grazier became a more prominent occupation or dual occupation in town and country alike (Dyer 1998: 67–71).

As the population showed signs of recovery from the mid-sixteenth century a process of agrarian intensification set in. Labour now began to be substituted for land and the area of tillage expanded. Livestock became increasingly fodder fed and there were moves to integrate more fully arable and pastoral husbandry. In effect, systems of husbandry more reminiscent of those of the early fourteenth century were re-established with a rise of arable yields back to their earlier levels after the falls that had accompanied less labour-intensive practices in the fifteenth century. A unique study of Norfolk farming practices and productivity from 1250 through to the nineteenth century has shown that grain yields, after falling from a high point *c.*1300 by 25 per cent, recovered to their medieval maxima in the early seventeenth century when population had at least doubled from its early sixteenth-century level (Campbell and Overton 1993: 38–105). Once again it is possible through the surviving price data to identify a substitution of wheat, the luxury bread grain, by cheaper grains such as oats and rye (Appleby 1979: 107–10). However, it is noteworthy that the pressure on livestock densities that was detectable when population peaked in the early fourteenth century was not replicated in the early seventeenth century. For instance, stocking densities doubled in Norfolk between the early fifteenth century and the third decade of the seventeenth century. It seems that pasture land had become more productive—a development helped by enclosure in the two previous centuries, as well as the growing tendency to plough and reseed pastures, combined with the increased use of convertible husbandry and ley farming. This may have also served to sustain nitrogen levels within the arable sector marginally more effectively than had been the case *c.*1300 (Overton and Campbell 1992: 377–96). In this development we have an important contrast in agrarian tendencies that differentiated the early seventeenth century from the early fourteenth century.

Throughout the cycle urban growth aided greater regional specialization and intensification of farming systems in city hinterlands. English urban settlements reached their medieval population maxima in the early fourteenth century. For instance, at that time London may have contained 75,000 to 80,000 persons and Norwich 25,000. London exerted a sizeable influence on the farming systems of the regions around it, particularly those regions which were able to deploy water transport as a means of shipping sizeable quantities of grain to the capital. Economic rent was clearly a key factor reflected in the types of products that were supplied at differing distance from the concentrated demand created by Londoners. It has been estimated that by the close of the thirteenth century London's normal grain provisioning hinterland encompassed over 4,000 square miles from which the city took from 10–15 per cent of all the food produced. Within this hinterland the choice of grains produced reflected the cost-distance factor of transporting them to the metropolis. As a result the cheapest fodder and bread grains were produced in greatest quantities close to the city, high quality brewing grain at an intermediate distance, and wheat—the most expensive bread grain—at the greatest distance of all. It was in the immediate hinterlands of London and Norwich that there is the strongest evidence that urban consumers *c.*1300 were trading down to cheaper bread and brewing grains. The concentrated demand of the urban poor gave rise to specialist cultivation of rye, rye mixtures, oats, and barley in such areas (Campbell *et al.* 1993: 37–45).

Certainly by the close of the fourteenth century most urban centres were shrinking in size. Indeed by 1500 London may not have exceeded 50,000 inhabitants and its provisioning hinterland contracted accordingly (Nightingale 1996: 35–8). Important structures of urban demand emerged; Londoners over the course of the fifteenth century consumed per capita more meat, more white bread, and barley-brewed ale than did the inhabitants of its demographically more substantial thirteenth-century predecessor (Carlin 1998; Galloway 1998). River-located entrepôts that had acted as assembly points for grain produced in the hinterland, such as Henley to which grain gravitated from southern Oxfordshire, eastern, and southern Berkshire, lost their importance. However, these trading patterns and transhipment points were rejuvenated again by renewed London growth in the late sixteenth century and especially throughout the seventeenth century (Chartres 1986: 168–96; Fisher 1990: 60–81). Invigorated by political developments and the opening up of the new maritime trade routes, particularly the growth of the North Atlantic economy, and aided by easy availability of energy through the coastal coalfield of Tyneside which could be exploited using little innovation of significance in mining or transportation technology, London broke through its medieval population ceiling in dramatic fashion. By 1600 it had attained a size of *c.*200,000. London was then of a similar size to Paris, although the French city was part of a national population that numbered 20 million in comparison to England's population of 4 million. By 1670 London was approaching 500,000 and between one in seven and one in eight of the English population resided there. The influence of this extremely large market on the demand for food and marketing of agricultural products has attracted the attention of economic historians, particularly as the impact of London on the demand for food was greater than these figures indicate (Wrigley 1967: 44–70). Indeed average per capita food consumption in London was at least double the national average (Chartres 1986: 170). In these developments we encounter another feature relating to a shifting balance of urban and non-agricultural population to rural and agrarian populations that was an entirely novel development, distinguishing the England of the early fourteenth from that of the early seventeenth century.

The terms under which land was held by the bulk of the farming population altered quite fundamentally over the course of the demographic cycle. To comprehend these changes it is necessary to view the manorial system as a composite of seigneurial and tenant rights, since the manor was generally an amalgam of demesne and peasant tenures. The manorial demesne was in the lord's full possession or ownership but the lord was only the final, rather than overall, owner of the tenure. In the period of high late thirteenth- and early fourteenth-century population levels demesne lands were being directly farmed by landlords, using in part resources extracted from the tenantry to fuel the labour needs for the various agricultural tasks that such a mode of exploitation necessitated. The peasantry who held by customary tenure or villeinage were not just tenants since the tenure holder could transfer his tenure to his 'heir' both in the form of *inter-vivos*, as well as *post-mortem* land transactions and was able to sell or lease such land to non-family members, although this had to be done publicly through the lord's court with the incoming tenant paying a fine and doing fealty. The tenure holder would pay his lord a set or 'certain' rent—a rent in theory fixed in perpetuity as a manorial custom and in consequence unresponsive to economic conditions. Such an arrangement implied that the manorial system offered to customary tenants an array of benefits as well as disadvantages, the relative balance between the two being by no means stable over time (Smith 1998: 341–7). The fixity of customary obligations during periods of rising population and demand for land and high inflation might be supposed to be relatively disadvantageous to lords. However, for the peasantry the specific value of these tenure rights depended upon the lord's ability to circumvent or countenance the fixed rents by levying other charges such as entry fines, marriage licences, or tallage. The arbitrary character of these payments did offer to landlords the potential to exploit their tenants. The balance of advantages varied considerably within the peasantry, and the larger landholders (i.e. full virgators) within their ranks were certainly best placed to secure benefits from the potential insulation provided by customary tenure (Hatcher 1981: 14–21; Smith 1983: 104–6). Of course, the peasantry were not just at risk as a potential prey of landlords within the landed aristocracy. The crown as well as the Church were potentially ever-present agents of surplus removal from the peasant sector. Royal taxes and ecclesiastical tithes could and almost certainly did function to siphon off surpluses from what would have been relatively comfortably situated holders of tenant rights (Maddicot 1987: 285–359; Schofield 1997: 1–17). Furthermore, high rates of population growth, particularly if they gave rise to the fragmentation of holdings and occurred in the periods of variable climate associated with recurrent harvest deficiencies, could quickly bring about widespread misery to the holders of tenant rights. On balance, it would seem that the disadvantages for the majority of those holding under tenant rights may have outweighed the advantages for much of the first century of the population cycle (Bailey 1998).

Notwithstanding the probable advantage held by landlords, tenant rights formed an institution that, from a landlord's perspective, was ripe for dismantling or abolition. It was in periods of high inflation that the interests of landlords might be served by expanding the size of their demesne lands upon which landlords' freedom of action was not barred and from which leaseholds could be created and not shackled by the protection of custom. However, it was in the later fourteenth and especially the fifteenth centuries during a phase of demographic decline, deflation, and low rents (falling demand for tenancies) that opportunities available to landlords increased, enabling them to expand the area of land in demesne, by incorporation into it of tenant-right lands or the conversion of such tenancies into leaseholds. It was also a phase when personal servility lapsed and was finally abolished in the second half of the sixteenth century (Smith 1998: 360–1).

By the sixteenth century, in addition to freehold, two more tenurial categories had emerged under which the bulk of the English peasantry held land; tenure could be by copyhold or by beneficial lease (Allen 1992: 60–71). There were two principal categories of copyhold—copyhold of inheritance and copyhold for lives. The former category of copyhold was widespread over East Anglia, south-east England, and the east Midlands, and the latter was more common over regions further to the west and north. The major difference between the two types concerned the right to renewal when the terms expired. With copyholds of inheritance the tenants paid a small annual rent and a more substantial fine when the property was sold or when it passed to an heir. Sometimes the fine was fixed by custom and sometimes it was arbitrary. In theory, just as under villein tenure, a landlord could make the transmission problematic for the incoming tenant by setting an entry fine that was cripplingly high and in practice unpayable. Copyholds for lives were not heritable over the longer term. They were usually grants for three lives—often the peasant husband, his wife, and a son. Usually when the son initiated his family he surrendered his copyhold and was readmitted with a new copy specifying himself, his wife, and son as the three tenants. He paid a fine which was, in theory, arbitrarily determined for the extension of the agreement. Unlike copyhold of inheritance, such an agreement need not have been automatically renewed.

It is sometimes supposed that in the land-abundant conditions of the fifteenth century there had been no pressures to test whether copyhold of either type offered much protection against arbitrary landlord action, particularly if they sought to enclose or engross holdings. In the eastern counties of England it is clear that copyhold allowed copyholders to treat their land as if it was a fee simple resource through an elaborate array of procedures from which they were relatively free to choose. Furthermore, the size of transfers rose significantly, such that they were six or seven times larger on average than they had been in the thirteenth century. Increasing numbers of wealthy individuals, including townspeople, clerics, and gentlemen, by 1500 also showed themselves willing to acquire copyhold now no longer tainted with the stigma of villeinage. This was a key factor promoting engrossment and larger mean farm sizes (Whittle 1998).

In the areas away from the east of England, where copyhold for lives and leases for specified terms of years predominated, tenures may have been less secure. However, by 1600 copyholders could recover possession of their land if a lord did take action to evict them and some historians now feel that by this date a high point in the history of English peasant proprietorship was reached (Allen 1992: 68; Hoyle 1990: 4–12). Such developments may have enabled the growth of social differentiation within the ranks of copyholders in conditions of rising agricultural product prices and land values, driven by demographic growth, taking population levels back towards, if not completely to, their medieval maxima (Croot and Parker 1985: 85). It is clear that at the moment of the new seventeenth-century demographic peak, land tenurial terms for the English peasantry were far more favourable to wealth accumulation than they had been in 1300. The net effect of these changes was that tenants rendered less of their surpluses to landlords in the form of rent, retained more of the profit of their own labours, and were endowed with a stronger incentive to invest in their own enterprises. Under these conditions the demand for land held in the form of larger farms grew. Larger holdings increased the use made by such enterprises of non-familial, wage-paid labour which represented a significant shift towards a rural social structure in which capitalist farmers were gaining a prominent visibility and endowing England with a characteristic that was beginning to distinguish her from her European neighbours where, with recovery from late medieval decline having taken place, holding fragmentation rather than engrossment of landholdings was the dominant trend (Smith 1998: 370–1).

EXPLAINING THE DEMOGRAPHIC CYCLE

At the heart of the problem of explaining the 400-year cycle around which the current discussion is focused is the provision of an answer to what the distinguished economic and mathematical demographer Ronald Lee (1986: 76) has termed the 'most basic in economic-demographic history'. That is, 'did long-run trends and swings in population and living standards primarily reflect variations in the demand for labour or did they largely reflect disturbance in the relative natural powers of increase independent of economic progress'.

An orthodox Malthusian would of course favour a positive response to the former rather than latter question. Malthus accepted the classical economic concept of diminishing returns to labour and supplemented it with an explanation of how death rates and birth rates were affected by per capita living standards or wages. These components of Malthus's arguments have suggested to later scholars a way of constructing an account of the pre-industrial economy which portrays it as a long-run equilibrium system, or what is often termed a homeostatic model of individual behaviour and aggregative market relationships that determine population size and per capita well-being (Wrigley 1986*b*: 49–50). The basic elements of Malthusian equilibrium can be identified in Figure 6.4*a*. They are contained in three functional relationships. Figure 6.4*a* gives an aggregate production function (AB) showing the standard of living (income per capita) of a population of given sizes. It is distinguished by diminishing returns to labour. Figure 6.4*b* sets out the rudiments of demographic behaviour. The crude death rate (DR) rises as the standard of living falls and represents the Malthusian 'positive check'. The crude birth rate (BR) falls as the standard of living falls and represents the Malthusian 'preventive check'. Population grows when births exceed deaths and falls when deaths exceed births (on the assumption of no net migration). If population rises this leads via the production function (AB) to a lowering of the standard of living which in turn leads to an enhancement of the death rate (DR) or a depression of fertility (BR) which eventually curtails population growth. Equilibrium is achieved at zero population growth (BR = DR). At such a point the living standard is steady as well as the birth and death rates. The equilibrium is

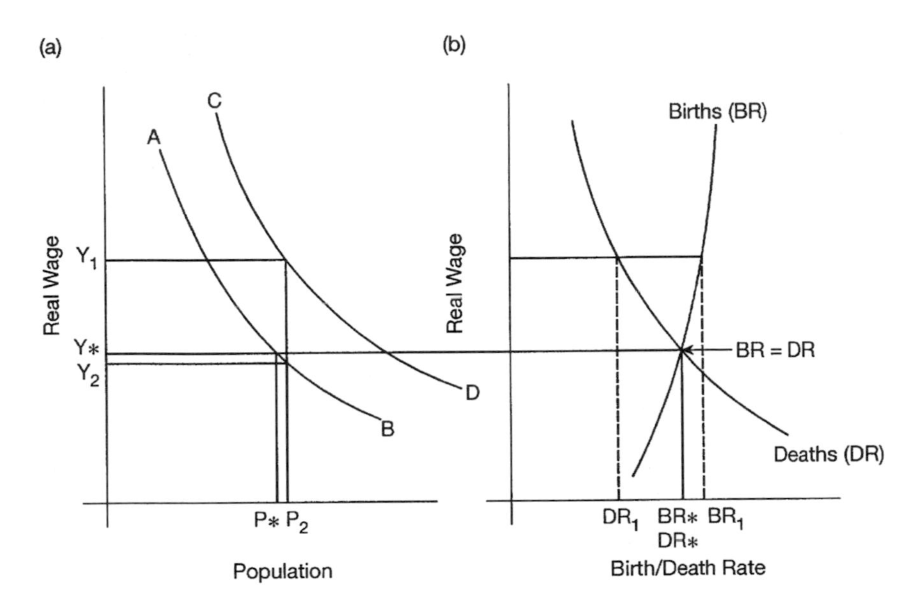

FIG. 6.4 Malthusian population dynamics.

over the medium term stable since any disturbance sets in motion compensatory changes in the form of negative feedback processes. For instance, an exogenous expansion of the opportunities for labour might lead to a rise in real incomes to Y_1, in the short term through an increase in the supply of capital brought about by the colonization of new land, introduction of new agrarian technology, or greater agrarian output associated with climatic amelioration (i.e. equivalent to a movement to the right of the production function from AB to CD). As a result of the amelioration of conditions, mortality would decline to DR_1 and fertility rise to BR_1 leading to demographic growth. As population rises above its initial size $P*$, it is assumed that more persons seek land and/or employment and with a larger number subsisting on each parcel of land some persons now cultivate land that had previously been idle, and possibly, but not necessarily, less productive. Consequently, the addition to agricultural output brought about by an extra day's work falls. The remuneration of labour declines from $Y*$ to Y_2 as the labour force increases in size from $P*$ to P_2. As a result of these shifts in real incomes demographic adjustments occur, serving to depress fertility from BR_1 to $BR*$ and increase mortality from DR_1 to $DR*$.

The in-built tendency to reinstate an equilibrium living standard (i.e. $Y*$) is the basis of the pessimism regarding long-run improvements in well-being which Malthus is traditionally seen as championing. Of course, this way of thinking has influenced many who have viewed the state of the English rural economy *c.*1280 to 1325 when population levels were undoubtedly high, harvest failures were relatively frequent, grain prices highly volatile, and short-term death rates particularly responsive to food price changes. The surge in death rates in bad harvests and the evidence from manors across southern and eastern England of population losses of the order of 10 to 15 per cent in the Great Famine of 1315–17 would seem to indicate that a move to a new equilibrium population was being secured by a rise in mortality (Smith 1991: 52–8). Evidence on fertility changes, in particular nuptiality, is more difficult to identify and measure. The downward trend in population in the first half of the fourteenth century might be appropriately interpreted in terms of the conventional Malthusian framework. What weight might be given to fertility falls depends in large measure on whether it is supposed there existed at that time a marriage regime in which females entered matrimony in their mid-twenties rather than their teens and a substantial minority never married at all (Smith 1991: 63–73). Such a regime was clearly present after 1537 when for the first time we can measure key nuptiality parameters with some certainty using parish registers (Wrigley and Schofield 1981: 417–30). There is far less certainty on this issue for the early fourteenth century and an early resolution of this problem is unlikely to be forthcoming, given evidential lacunae.

While the debate about the determinants of population trends from the turn of the thirteenth century to the arrival of the Black Death is ridden with uncertainties there would seem to be a broader measure of agreement about the principal causes of demographic decline and sustained demographic malaise for the subsequent 150 years. The failure of population levels to recover, having fallen by at least a half over the course of the first seventy-five years of the fourteenth century, has suggested to many scholars the irrelevance of a Malthusian framework within which to understand these trends (Hatcher 1977: 55–6). A new equilibrium, so it is argued, should have been achieved relatively swiftly as population decline stimulated rising living standards in the form of a massive infusion of what one scholar termed 'demographic Marshall aid' perversely administered through rising frequencies of particularly virulent outbreaks of epidemic disease, thereby improving ratios of land to labour in highly dramatic terms (Bridbury 1962: 91). That a growth in numbers was not forthcoming suggests the superiority of exogenously determined mortality over any endogenous response from fertility as the key determinant of population growth rates. Evidence on mortality, by no means abundant, is patently more readily available than that concerning fertility and marriage. Apart from the evidence from manorial court rolls indicating the scale of the death tolls among rural landholders in the first and second plagues of 1348–9 and 1361–2 (Bolton 1996: 22–9), there are increasingly abundant testamentary sources from *c.* 1400 which reveal a highly volatile pattern of deaths registered annually by will-makers in will registers. In fact many of the years with high will counts also correlate with years which chroniclers identified as particularly unhealthy (Goldberg 1988: 38–55; Gottfried 1978: 35–57). In addition, efforts to measure generational replacement potential through frequency counts of the occasions when deceased males were succeeded by adult sons, paint a very depressing demographic scene for most of the period; replacement rates never rose above unity before the sixteenth century (Thrupp 1965: 113–28; Dyer 1980: 237–8). The tendency for the seasonality of deaths among will-makers to display a late summer and early autumn peak has inclined many commentators to see a leading role for plague in this demographic drama (Gottfried 1978: 84–125).

Two exceptionally carefully expedited studies of Benedictine monastic communities in Canterbury and Westminster undertaken respectively by John Hatcher (1986: 19–38) and Barbara Harvey (1993: 129–42) point to a sharp fall in life expectancy among the resident monks at the end of the fifteenth century. The existence of such unfavourable mortality among well fed and housed individuals cannot fail to strengthen the views of those who would see disease, no respecter of fitness or wealth, as trampling indifferently over both high and low status persons as it depressed demographic growth possibilities. Of course, in assessing this evidence, sight should not be lost of the fact that Benedictines were in no sense a closed order, but interacted intensively with the communities of which they were part. Canterbury and Westminster were both urban centres and it is firmly established that urban centres of that size had particularly severe mortality (Rosser 1989), indeed exhibiting levels of mortality in the early modern period that quite closely resembled those encountered in the worst years of both of these monastic communities (Landers 1993; Galley 1994).

There has been frequent speculation that plague had for some decades after 1348 been a regular visitor to large areas of England in the form of epidemics that hit town and country with equal fury. Karl Helleiner (1967: 74) in a classic essay notes that the pioneering nineteenth-century historian of disease, Charles Creighton, wrote that 'plague henceforth [after mid-fifteenth century] is seldom universal; it becomes more and more a disease of the towns, and when it does occur in the country, it is for the most part at some few limited spots'. Paul Slack (1985: 79–110) emerges to date as the only scholar to confront this issue systematically in research which makes use of wills in the period from 1485 through to 1538 and parish registers thereafter. He would appear to accept Creighton's proposition that in the late fifteenth century the geographical incidence of plague epidemics was narrowing, notwithstanding the case he makes for plague being more widely and evenly distributed across rural areas before *c.*1550 than thereafter. In a fascinating case study of Devon, Slack shows that a plague epidemic in 1546–7 was widespread in its incidence within the community, affecting 26 of the 33 parishes with extant registers, in which 20 of the 26 communities experienced at least a doubling of burial totals. He even ventures the suggestion that the plague of Devon in 1546–7 may be regarded as a late example of the generalized outbreaks of plague which had previously been more common. In addition to making the case for a greater incidence of rural plague in the early sixteenth century, Slack also presents more compelling evidence to suggest that prior to 1560 plague and dearth were more frequently associated and that later in the century the two causes of crisis mortality were far less likely to conjoin, thereby making it easier to distinguish one from the other. It is, of course, possible to read such an account as suggesting that the narrowing of the plague's geographical range was not a development occurring in the fifteenth century, but was a transformation that occurred later in the sixteenth century when a minority, possibly none whatsoever, of villagers were likely to encounter it during a lifetime.

It is therefore not without significance that Wrigley and Schofield (1981: 650) noted that the 1540s and 1550s—the first decades for which parish register analysis can be undertaken—experienced crisis rates respectively of 15 per 1,000 and 28 per 1,000 months observed, compared with only 5 and 8 per 1,000 respectively for the 1560s and 1570s. In fact Wrigley and Schofield might be interpreted as concurring with Slack when, in commenting on the first twenty years of their 330-year series (1541–61), they noted that 'the violent and frequent upsurges of the numbers of deaths recorded before 1565 look as if they may have been the last throes of a late-medieval regime of widespread epidemic mortality' (1981: 178–9). They are, however, more equivocal about the spatial incidence of epidemic mortality and underlying movements away from trend on the part of the national crude death rate. Six of the forty-five national mortality crises over the years 1541–1871 (defined as a year in which the crude death rate moved more than 10 per cent above trend) occurred in the 1540s and 1550s. The most striking crises of 1558–9 and 1557–8 when the crude death rate was 124.7 and 60.5 per cent above trend were also distinguished as years when 39 and 33 per cent of all parishes in observation experience at least one month of crisis. However, the other years in the two decades when the crude death rate was between 12 and 25 per cent above trend showed no systematic relationship between severity of national crisis and proportion of parishes experiencing at least one crisis month. For instance, 1546–7 is perhaps an example of a year when mortality appears to have risen sharply in a number of places, but the net impact on national death rates was somewhat muffled because the crisis was of short duration and few places were affected. That year reveals a characteristic combination of statistical patterning that we might associate with regionalized rural plague (Wrigley and Schofield 1981: 652–3). We have already noted that Slack has identified 1546–7 in Devon as a year of plague throughout the county. In fact, locally it was the most widespread crisis of the whole century after *c.*1540. None the less, the national death rate was that year placed only modestly in thirty-third place in the league table of the forty-five severest crises (Wrigley and Schofield 1981: 653). Notwithstanding the difficulties confronting the historian of the century between 1450 and 1550, at the end of which demographic growth is most certainly achieved, it would be unwise to underplay the extent to which England's demographic fabric was undermined by disease outbreaks which were part of a wider pan-European phenomenon.

Yet we should recall that a sizeable body of evidence suggests that considerable demographic decline predates the arrival of plague in 1348. Furthermore, it is also important to note that the rates of demographic recovery were far from closely synchronized over the different regions of Europe. It has been proposed above that the English population in the early sixteenth century was still less than half, possibly only a third of its size in 1300—a level relatively much lower than that displayed by significant tracts of continental Europe, especially in the southern or Mediterranean regions. For instance, being better endowed than England with cross-sectional taxation sources that survive to offer snapshots at fairly frequent intervals, Tuscany provides us with evidence to chart the course of population change from 1427 to 1551. For example, in the countryside or *contado* of Prato, population had fallen to one-third of its early fourteenth-century size in 1427, but by 1551 the rural population had grown a further 80 per cent. Over the whole of Tuscany population growth rates averaged between 0.6 and 0.8 per cent per annum from *c.*1420 to 1550. Furthermore fifteenth-century Tuscan growth rates, very rapid by English standards, should be regarded as relatively modest when compared with those for Sicily where the population expanded at a rate closer to 1 per cent per annum over the same period. Calculations of Provençal population trends suggest annual growth closer to 1 per cent per annum from 1417 to 1540—trends that this areas seems to have shared with the Rhone valley and other areas of south-central France, Rousillon, and Catalonia (Epstein 1991: 17–18; Lorcin 1981). In fact there seems a solid body of demographic evidence which indicates that much of southern France and large tracts of the western Mediterranean region more broadly had returned to pre-Black Death population levels by the middle of the sixteenth century. This suggests a demographic cycle of far narrower amplitude than that which took place in England, since such a recovery was barely achieved by 1650 at the earliest, and probably was delayed for considerably longer than that.

Some efforts have been made by historians to suggest why in the immediate aftermath of the Black Death, and during the years of demographic decline in the later fourteenth century, certain forces may have been unleashed which held back population growth or a fertility rise. Many towns, especially those in the eastern regions of England which were implicated in the great growth of export-oriented textile manufactures, fared rather well up until the second or third decades of the fifteenth century. They clearly attracted large numbers of women as immigrants which led to their populations exhibiting female surpluses and low proportions of those females currently married. Women were undoubtedly drawn into urban labour markets in a society where sex segmentation was surprisingly muted. In the countryside the poll tax returns of 1377 and 1381 reveal relatively large numbers of unmarried males and females living as servants in the households of their employers—at levels that seem surprisingly similar to those of the late seventeenth century in an agrarian economy that was increasingly pastoral and in need of resident labour hired by the year rather than the day. Such a feature of the social structure appears to be incompatible with early and universal female marriage, notwithstanding the protestations of some historians who regard such behaviour as irrational in the context of conditions in which land had become relatively abundant. Some historians have suggested that labour shortages may have drawn unmarried females into the workforce in such quantities that their actions served to depress marriage rates at a time when recourse to simple Malthusian reasoning would have suggested quite the opposite response. There may well be some support for this argument, particularly when comparisons are made with southern European societies, where such substitution of females for males did not occur and where unmarried females above the age of 18 and certainly above the age of 20 were demographic rarities. The absence of sex substitution in southern European labour markets may have been a factor securing a more swiftly operating population recovery in these areas (Smith 1992*a*: 16–59; Goldberg 1992: 203–79). However, our best evidence for these behavioural contrasts comes from the period *c.*1370–1430. We might therefore have to entertain the possibility that either mortality levels remained more severe or that a combination of low fertility and moderately high mortality held back English demographic recovery far longer than in many parts of continental Europe (Bailey 1996; Smith forthcoming). These, of course, are no more than possibilities since no hard evidence really exists allowing the key fertility and mortality measurements to be made. It might be argued that the surviving evidence, especially that to do with life expectancy, increases inversely in relation to the social significance or representativeness of the groups concerned. The experience of celibate monks whose mortality was undoubtedly very severe is exemplary of this feature of our evidence. Yet it is clear that, in the second half of the sixteenth century, when it is first possible to estimate background mortality for the bulk of the English population using parish registers, there seems little reason to indicate that English mortality was severer than that to be found in Europe. In fact English mortality of the late Tudor period seems to be very moderate by wider European standards (Wrigley *et al.* 1997: 206–7).

What is striking about the period after 1550 is that as population growth rates climbed, and the pressure on living standards which they induced began to take hold, nuptiality rates embarked upon a steady falling course. In fact Wrigley and Schofield (1981: 460–71) see the progressive closing of what has been termed the 'nuptiality valve', as the principal brake slowing down demographic growth to zero per cent by *c.*1650. Their analysis of short-term grain price movements in relation to vital rates suggests that marriage rates were far more responsive than were burial rates to price stimuli, notwithstanding the presence of significant harvest failures and dearth conditions in the 1580s, 1590s, 1620s, and 1640s (Wrigley and Schofield 1981: 320–6). The northern and north-western regions seem to have been more prone to mortality rises associated with grain shortages, to a degree that historians feel confident in the existence of a major regional divide in the relative importance of the 'positive' and 'preventive' checks in late Tudor and early Stuart England. A number of explanations have been used to account for this spatial patterning. In particular emphasis has been placed on the notion of weak regional market integration with a sharp deterioration in the terms of trade between pastoral products, the principal sources of income in the north, and bread grains, the production of which was the primary agrarian activity of the south and east; northern pastoralists were confronted with declining incomes at a time when bread prices were especially high. Furthermore, as has been shown above, these areas suffered most from fragmentation of holdings as marginal environments were colonized in association with the renewed population growth. In certain respects these areas manifest responses to population growth that may have been particularly reminiscent of larger parts of early fourteenth-century England. Furthermore, institutional innovations associated with the Books of Orders, setting out precise procedures for handling dearth conditions and the implementation of rate-based poor relief in the late sixteenth century, were less effectively implemented, or of limited significance, in the north and north-western areas which were also handicapped in their capacity to import bread grains using a transportation system that was still far from being integrated regionally (Appleby 1979: 182–93; Walter and Schofield 1989: 21–5; Fogel 1992: 262–6; Slack 1999: 62–6). To use a term now so inextricably associated with the Nobel laureate Amartya Sen (1981: 45–51), the inhabitants of these vulnerable north-western areas were unable to protect their 'entitlements' when nationally there may well have been sufficient food physically available to secure their dietary needs.

Some of these features suggest possible answers to why the early seventeenth-century demographic equilibrium was secured at a national level a million or more lower than that of the early fourteenth century. We have already noted that widespread mortality crises, and large-scale dearth-associated mortality surges, were a relatively common characteristic of the more productive areas of grain-based farming in southern Britain in the period *c.*1280–1340. Such vulnerability was indubitably not characteristic of these same areas in the early seventeenth century when demographic losses of the kinds associated with the 1290s and especially 1315–17 were noteworthy for their complete absence (Wrigley and Schofield 1981: 671–6). Of course, such a view would not necessarily be applicable to many other areas of early modern northern Europe or other parts of the British Isles where mortality showed far greater susceptibility to a clear-cut positive relationship with grain prices (Galloway 1988). We may speculate that certain institutional developments, and especially agrarian changes that have been described above as occurring in the fifteenth and sixteenth centuries, enabled the most densely populated parts of England south and east of the Tees–Exe line to avoid a classic Malthusian catastrophe as the population edged towards 5 million. However, this apparent avoidance is a subject of vital importance for understanding a fundamental shift in pre-industrial English economy and society and is crying out for a comparative analysis by the combined forces of medieval and early modern historians.

At present we can only speculate on reasons for the probable higher equilibrium population in 1300 compared with that of 1600 or 1650 which may have had much to do with the greater susceptibility of the medieval period to harvest failure-induced mortality rises than the late Tudor and Stuart decades. One highly plausible contributory demographic factor may have been lower levels of urbanization in the earlier period. Estimating town populations at any period before 1801 is especially difficult, but, even allowing for the inaccuracy that is bound to occur, there would appear to be striking contrasts between the two eras. Recent estimates show that the proportion of the population resident in towns containing at least 10,000 persons more than tripled between *c.*1500 and *c.*1650 while the national population approximately doubled. Much of the relative decline in the non-urban share of the population was a product of London's remarkable growth, so that by 1650 it was close to 400,000 when the national population was *c.*5.2 million. Such a relationship suggests that the London of 1650 was five times larger than it had been in 1300. Growth elsewhere in the urban hierarchy was less impressive, but most likely managed to keep pace proportionally with the upward march of national population totals. Such developments point unambiguously to a rise in agrarian output and more effective means of delivering that food to urban markets (Wrigley 1986*a*: 123–68).

Recently there have been distinct signs that students of English medieval towns in the early fourteenth century have begun to push their estimates of the populations of major urban centres upwards. For instance estimates of London (*c.*75,000) and Norwich (*c.*25,000) are almost twice those offered by an earlier generation of scholars. Notwithstanding this more positive portrayal of urban growth potential in England by the late thirteenth century, it is unlikely that in 1300 more than 250,000 persons lived in settlements larger than 10,000 which would mean that they contained at most about 0.5 per cent of the total population. Such a proportion should be compared with Wrigley's estimate of 11 per cent of the total population being resident in such settlements in 1650 (Smith 1991: 50–1). The redistribution of persons into densely settled urban communities increased the proportion of the population resident in 'unhealthy' environments and was an important development helping to bring down national life expectancies after 1600, notwithstanding the diminishing incidence of plague (Wrigley and Schofield 1981: 471–2). Infants and young persons, in particular, paid the lion share of this rising urban penalty. The downward impact on national life expectancy caused by urbanization and the associated national and international circulation of diseases was intensified in their demographic impact because of the preceding and unusually low levels of mortality in the Tudor and early Stuart countryside (Schofield and Wrigley 1979: 75–7). Such urban growth, fuelled principally by immigration, also significantly reduced pressure on the land in rural areas which were also distinctive in a wider European setting in releasing emigrants in very large numbers.

This latter feature points to another important contrast between the first halves of the fourteenth and seventeenth centuries which concerns the levels of national net migration. England in the late sixteenth and the first two-thirds of the seventeenth centuries witnessed sizeable flows of emigrants to Ireland, the Caribbean, and North America, which in addition to simultaneous falls in life expectancy contributed to a further slowing down of demographic growth rates that were already being depressed by nuptiality declines (Wrigley and Schofield 1981: 227–8). We know very little about English net migration trends in the first half of the fourteenth century, but there is no reason to suppose that rates were noteworthy—certainly not as high as 1.5 to 2.5 per 1,000 which were the rates *c*.1650. Indeed these mid-seventeenth-century rates of net migration were as high as any that held in the nineteenth century. England in the first half of the seventeenth century was an extremely 'open' society and economy in so far as it was greatly affected by imported diseases, whose circulation domestically was greatly intensified by the burgeoning urban population and by the willingness or ability of the population to move geographically, thereby relieving the accumulation of people on the land (Smith 1992*b*: 175–91).

Such an interpretation is not intended to devalue the importance of the declining marriage rates that at the end of the cycle were to show few signs of recovery, notwithstanding improving living standards and falling life expectancies after the early seventeenth century. However, there does not seem to be sufficient evidence to feel fully content with the view associated with Ronald Lee that throughout the full duration of the cycle it was 'inescapable that exogenous change in mortality drove the long-run changes in fertility and wages' (1986: 100). Nor could it be argued that demographic growth assumed a course that was largely determined by demand for labour in the manner of orthodox Malthusianism. There were sufficient changes in the constitution of English society, both economically and culturally, over the course of the cycle, and in England's place within an international economy and consequent metropolitan growth, to suggest that substantial endogenous influences were working their course, although they were not necessarily of the kind that classical Malthusianism would predict. None the less, it has to be accepted that Malthus sensed such possibilities himself when he wrote of 'the sort of oscillation [which] will not probably be obvious to common view; and may be difficult even for the most attentive observer to calculate its periods'. Furthermore, Malthus thought the 'times of their vibration must necessarily be rendered irregular from the operation of many interrupting causes' (Malthus 1803: 26–7). It would seem that the 'interrupting causes' are those which are of interest to the social and economic historian since they require in their elucidation that more attention be given to the 'peoples' than the 'plagues' that have been the subject of this discussion. To subvert a notion associated with the distinguished French historian, Emmanuel Le Roy Ladurie (1981: 1–27), in following the course of a great population cycle with its very different equilibrium points for per capita well-being, we are most definitely not observing a case of 'histoire immobile' any more than we are seeing an outcome compatible with what classical economists would have regarded as submissive adherence to the 'iron law of wages'.

REFERENCES

Allen, R. C. (1992). *Enclosure and the Yeoman: The Agricultural Development of the South Midlands 1450–1850*. Oxford: Oxford University Press.

Appleby, A. B. (1975). 'Agrarian capitalism or seigneurial reaction: the northwest of England 1500–1700', *American Historical Review*, 80: 574–94.

Appleby, A. B. (1978). *Famine in Tudor and Stuart England*. Liverpool: Liverpool University Press.

Appleby, A. B. (1979). 'Diet in sixteenth century England: sources, problems, possibilities', in C. Webster (ed.), *Health, Medicine and Mortality in the Sixteenth Century*. Cambridge: Cambridge University Press, 94–116.

Bailey, M. (1988). 'The rabbit and the Medieval East Anglian economy', *Agricultural History Review*, 36: 1–20.

Bailey, M. (1989). *A Marginal Economy? East Anglian Breckland in the Later Middle Ages*. Cambridge: Cambridge University Press.

Bailey, M. (1991). '*Per impetum maris:* natural disaster and economic decline in Eastern England, 1275–1350', in B. M. S. Campbell (ed.), *Before the Black Death: Studies in the 'Crisis' of the Early Fourteenth Century*. Manchester: Manchester University Press, 184–208.

Bailey, M. (1996). 'Demographic decline in late medieval England: some thoughts on recent research', *Economic History Review*, 49: 1–19.

Bailey, M. (1998). 'Peasant welfare in England, 1290–1348', *Economic History Review*, 51: 223–51.

Bartley, D. D. (1979). 'Paleaobotanical evidence', in P. H. Sawyer (ed.), *English Medieval Settlement*. London: Edward Arnold, 133–40.

Beckett, S. C. (1981). 'Pollen analysis of the peat deposits', *Proceedings of the Prehistoric Society*, 47: 245–66.

Biddick, K. (1989). *The Other Economy: Pastoral Husbandry on a Medieval Estate*. Berkeley and Los Angeles: University of California Press.

Bishop, T. A. M. (1938). 'The rotation of crops at Westerham, 1297–1350', *Economic History Review*, 9: 38–44.

Bolton, J. (1996). '"The World Upside Down": plague as an agent of economic and social change', in W. M. Ormrod and P. G. Lindley (eds.), *The Black Death in England*. Stamford: Paul Watkins, 17–78.

Bridbury, A. R. (1962). *Economic Growth: England in the Later Middle Ages.* London: Allen and Unwin.

Campbell, B. M. S. (1981). 'The regional uniqueness of English field systems? Some evidence from eastern Norfolk', *Agricultural History Review*, 29: 1–23.

Campbell, B. M. S. (1983*a*). 'Agricultural progress in medieval England: some evidence from eastern Norfolk', *Economic History Review*, 36: 26–46.

Campbell, B. M. S. (1983*b*). 'Arable productivity in medieval England: some evidence from Norfolk', *Journal of Economic History*, 43: 379–404.

Campbell, B. M. S. (1988). 'The diffusion of vetches in medieval England', *Economic History Review*, 41: 193–208.

Campbell, B. M. S. (1990), 'People and land in the Middle Ages, 1066–1500', in

R. A. Dodgshon and R. A. Butlin (eds.), *An Historical Geography of England and Wales*. 2nd edn., London: Academic Press, 69–122.

Campbell, B. M. S. (1992). 'Commercial dairy production on medieval English demesnes: the case of Norfolk', *Anthropozoologica*, 16: 107–18.

Campbell, B. M. S. (1995). 'The livestock of Chaucer's Reeve: fact or fiction?', in E. B. Dewindt (ed.), *The Salt of Common Life: Individuality and Choice in the Medieval Town, Countryside and Church, Essays Presented to J. Ambrose Raftis on the Occasion of his 70th Birthday*. Kalamazoo, Mich.: State University of Michigan Press, 271–306.

Campbell, B. M. S. (1997). 'Matching supply to demand: crop production and disposal by English demesnes in the century of the Black Death', *Journal of Economic History*, 57: 827–58.

Campbell, B. M. S. (1998). 'Constraint or constrained? Changing perspectives on medieval English agriculture', Inhoud NEHA-JAARBOEK, 61: 15–35.

Campbell, B. M. S., and Power, J. P. (1992). 'Cluster analysis and the classification of medieval demesne-farming systems', *Transactions of the Institute of British Geographers*, NS 17, 3: 227–45.

Campbell, B. M. S., and Overton, M. (1993). 'A new perspective on medieval and early modern agriculture: six centuries of Norfolk farming, *c*.1250–*c*.1850', *Past and Present*, 141: 38–105.

Campbell, B. M. S., Galloway, J. A., Keene, D., and Murphy, M. (1993). *A Medieval Capital and its Grain Supply: Agrarian Production and Distribution in the London Region c.1300*. Norwich: Historical Geography Research Series No. 30.

Carlin, M. (1998). 'Fast food and urban living standards in medieval England', in M. Carlin and J. T. Rosenthal (eds.), *Food and Eating in Medieval Europe*. London: Hambledon Press, 27–54.

Chartres, J. (1986). 'Food consumption and internal trade', in A. L. Beier and R. Findlay (eds.), *London 1600–1700: The Making of the Metropolis*. London: Longman, 168–96.

Coale, A. J., and Demeny, P. (1983). *Regional Model Life Tables and Stable Populations*. 2nd edn., London: Academic Press.

Croot, P., and Parker, D. (1985). 'Agrarian class structure and the development of capitalism: France and England compared', in T. H. Aston and C. H. E. Philpin (eds.), *The Brenner Debate: Agrarian Class Structure and Economic Development in Pre-Industrial Europe*. Cambridge: Cambridge University Press, 79–90.

Darby, H. C. D. (1940). *The Draining of the Fens*. Cambridge: Cambridge University Press.

Dyer, C. (1980). *Lords and Peasants in a Changing Society: The Estates of the Bishopric of Worcester, 680–1640*. Cambridge: Cambridge University Press.

Dyer, C. (1989*a*). '"The retreat from marginal land": the growth and decline of medieval rural settlements', in M. Aston, D. Austin, and C. Dyer (eds.), *The Rural Settlements of Medieval England*. Oxford: Blackwell, 45–59.

Dyer, C. (1989*b*). *Standards of Living in the Later Middle Ages: Social Change in England c.1200–1520*. Cambridge: Cambridge University Press.

Dyer, C. (1998). 'Did the peasants really starve in medieval England?', in M. Carlin and J. T. Rosenthal (eds.), *Food and Eating in Medieval Europe*. London: Hambledon Press, 53–72.

Epstein, S. R. (1991). 'Cities, regions and the late medieval crisis: Sicily and Tuscany compared', *Past and Present*, 130: 3–50.

Farmer, D. L. (1991). 'Marketing the produce of the countryside, 1200–1500', in E. Miller (ed.), *The Agrarian History of England and Wales, iii. 1348–1500*. Cambridge: Cambridge University Press, 324–430.

Fenwick, C. C. (1988) (ed.). *The Poll Taxes of 1377, 1379, and 1381. Part 1 Bedfordshire–Leicestershire*. Oxford: The British Academy.

Fisher, F. J. (1990). 'The development of the London food market, 1540–1640', in P. J. Corfield and N. B. Harte (eds.), *London and the English Economy 1600–1700: F. J. Fisher*. London: Hambledon Press, 61–80.

Fogel, R. W. (1992). 'Second thoughts on the European escape from hunger: famines, chronic malnutrition and mortality rates', in S. R. Osmani (ed.), *Nutrition and Poverty*. Oxford: Oxford University Press, 219–42.

Fox, H. S. A. (1991). 'The occupation of the land: Devon and Cornwall', in E. Miller (ed.), *The Agrarian History of England and Wales. iii. 1348–1500*. Cambridge: Cambridge University Press, 152–74.

Galley, C. (1994). 'A never-ending succession of epidemics? Mortality in early modern York', *Social History of Medicine*, 7: 29–58.

Galloway, J. A. (1998). 'Driven by drink? Ale consumption and the agrarian economy of the London region, *c.*1300–1400', in M. Carlin and J. T. Rosenthal (eds.), *Food and Eating in Medieval Europe*. London: Hambledon Press, 87–100.

Galloway, P. R. (1988). 'Basic patterns in annual variations in fertility, nuptiality, mortality and prices in pre-industrial Europe', *Population Studies*, 42: 275–304.

Goldberg, P. J. P. (1988). 'Mortality and economic change in the diocese of York, 1390–1514', *Northern History*, 24: 38–55.

Goldberg, P. J. P. (1992). *Women, Work and Life Cycle in a Medieval Economy: Women in York and Yorkshire c.1300–1520*. Oxford: Oxford University Press.

Gottfried, R. A. (1978). *Epidemic Disease in Fifteenth Century England: The Medical Response and the Demographic Consequences*. Leicester: Leicester University Press.

Harvey, B. (1993). *Living and Dying in England 1100–1540: The Monastic Experience*. Oxford: Oxford University Press.

Hatcher, J. (1970). *Rural Economy and Society in the Duchy of Cornwall, 1300–1500*. Cambridge: Cambridge University Press.

Hatcher, J. (1977). *Plague, Population and the English Economy 1348–1530*. London: Macmillan.

Hatcher, J. (1981). 'English serfdom and villeinage: towards a reassessmernt', *Past and Present*, 90: 3–39.

Hatcher, J. (1986). 'Mortality in the fifteenth century: some new evidence', *Economic History Review*, 39: 19–38.

Hatcher, J. (1994). *The History of the British Coal Industry. i. Before 1700*. Oxford: Oxford University Press.

Helleiner, K. F. (1967). 'The population of Europe from the Black Death to the eve of the vital revolution', in E. E. Rich and C. H. Wilson (eds.), *The Cambridge Economic History of Europe, iv. The Economy of Expanding Europe in the Sixteenth and Seventeenth Centuries.* Cambridge: Cambridge University Press, 1–95.

Herrtage, S. J. (1878) (ed.). *England in the Reign of King Henry the Eighth.* Oxford: Early English Text Society.

Hoyle, R. W. (1990). 'Tenure and the land market in early-modern England: or a late contribution to the Brenner debate', *Economic History Review*, 43: 1–20.

Hoyle, R. W. (1992). 'Disafforestation and drainage: the crown as entrepreneur', in R. W. Hoyle (ed.), *The Estates of the English Crown, 1558–1640.* Cambridge: Cambridge University Press, 353–88.

Landers, J. (1993). *Death and the Metropolis: Studies in the Demographic History of London 1670–1830.* Cambridge: Cambridge University Press.

Langdon, J. (1986). *Horses, Oxen and Technological Innovation: The Use of Draught Animals in English Farming from 1066–1500.* Cambridge: Cambridge University Press.

Le Roy Ladurie, E. (1981). *The Mind and Method of the Historian.* Brighton: Harvester Press.

Lee, R. (1986). 'Population homeostasis and English demographic history', in R. I. Rotberg and T. K. Rabb (eds.), *Population and Economy: Population and History from the Traditional to the Modern World.* Cambridge: Cambridge University Press, 75–100.

Lloyd, T. H. (1973). *The Movement of Wool Prices in Medieval England.* Cambridge: Economic History Society Review Supplement 6.

Lorcin, M. T. (1981). *Vivre et mourir en autrefois en Lyonais à la fin du Moyen Age.* Paris: Presses Universitaires de France.

Maddicott, J. R. (1987). 'The English peasantry and the demands of the crown, 1294–1341', in T. H. Aston (ed.), *Landlords, Peasants and Politics in Medieval England.* Cambridge: Cambridge University Press, 285–359.

Mate, M. (1987). 'Pastoral farming in south-east England in the fifteenth century', *Economic History Review*, 40: 523–36.

Malthus, T. R. (1803). *An Essay on the Principle of Population* (selected and introduced by D. Winch). Cambridge: Cambridge University Press.

Nightingale, P. (1996). 'The growth of London in the medieval English economy', in R. H. Britnell and J. Hatcher (eds.), *Progress and Problems in Medieval England: Essays in Honour of Edward Miller.* Cambridge: Cambridge University Press, 89–106.

Overton, M. (1996). *Agricultural Revolution in England: The Transformation of the Agrarian Economy 1500–1850.* Cambridge: Cambridge University Press.

Overton, M., and Campbell, B. M. S. (1992). 'Norfolk livestock farming 1250–1740: a comparative study of manorial accounts and probate inventories', *Journal of Historical Geography*, 18: 377–96.

Overton, M., and Campbell, B. M. S. (1996). 'Production et productivité dans l'agriculture anglais, 1086–1871', *Histoire et Mesure*, 11: 255–97.

Poos, L. (1991). *A Rural Society after the Black Death: Essex 1350–1525*. Cambridge: Cambridge University Press.

Postan, M. M. (1966). 'Medieval agrarian society in its prime: England', in M. M. Postan (ed.), *The Cambridge Economic History of Europe, i. The Agrarian History of the Middle Ages*. Cambridge: Cambridge University Press, 549–632.

Postles, D. (1992). 'Demographic change in Kibworth Harcourt, Leicestershire, in the later Middle Ages', *Local Population Studies*, 48: 41–8.

Power, J. P., and Campbell, B. M. S. (1992). 'Cluster analysis and the classification of medieval demesne-farming systems', *Transactions of the Institute of British Geographers*, NS 17: 227–45.

Rackham, O. (1986). *The History of the Countryside*. London: Dent.

Ramos-Pinto, P. (forthcoming). 'Spatial variations in English settlement sizes and population densities: county case studies from the 1377 poll tax returns'.

Rosser, A. G. (1989). *Medieval Westminster 1200–1540*. Oxford: Oxford University Press.

Schofield, P. R. (1997). 'Dearth, debt and the local land market in a late thirteenth-century village community', *Agricultural History Review*, 45: 1–17.

Schofield, R. S., and Wrigley, E. A. (1979). 'Infant and child mortality in the late Tudor and early Stuart period', in C. Webster (ed.), *Health, Medicine and Mortality in the Sixteenth Century*. Cambridge: Cambridge University Press, 61–96.

Sen, A. (1981). *Poverty and Famines: An Essay on Entitlement and Deprivation*. Oxford: Oxford University Press.

Sheail, J. (1972). 'The distribution of taxable population and wealth in England during the early sixteenth century', *Transactions of the Institute of British Geographers*, 55: 111–26.

Slack, P. (1985). *The Impact of Plague in Tudor and Stuart England*. London: Routledge and Kegan Paul.

Slack, P. (1999). *From Reformation to Improvement: Public Welfare in Early Modern England*. Oxford: Oxford University Press.

Smith, R. M. (1983). 'Some thoughts on "hereditary" and "proprietary" rights in land under customary law in thirteenth and fourteenth century England', *Law and History Review*, 1: 95–128.

Smith, R. M. (1991). 'Demographic developments in rural England, 1300–1348: a survey', in B. M. S. Campbell (ed.), *Before the Black Death: Studies in the 'Crisis' of the early Fourteenth Century*. Manchester: Manchester University Press, 25–78.

Smith, R. M. (1992*a*). 'Geographical diversity in the resort to marriage in late medieval Europe: work, reputation, and unmarried females in the household formation systems of northern and southern Europe', in P. J. P. Goldberg (ed.), *Woman is a Worthy Wight: Women in English Society c.1200–1500*. Stroud: Alan Sutton.

Smith, R. M. (1992*b*). 'Influences exogènes et endogènes sur le "frein préventitif" en Angleterre, 1600–1750', in A. Blum, N. Bonneuil, and D. Blanchet (eds.), *Modèles de la démographie historique*. Paris: Presses Universitaires de France, 149–74.

Smith, R. M. (1998). 'The English peasantry, 1250–1650', in T. Scott (ed.), *The Peasantries of Europe from the Fourteenth to the Eighteenth Centuries*. London: Longman, 339–71.

Smith, R. M. (forthcoming). 'The Population of England in the Fifteenth Century'.

Spufford, M. (1974). *Contrasting Communities: English Villages in the Sixteenth and Seventeenth Centuries.* Cambridge: Cambridge University Press.

Stone, D. (1997). 'The productivity of hired and customary labour: evidence from Wisbech Barton in the fourteenth century', *Economic History Review*, 50: 640–56.

Stone, D. (1998). 'The management of resources on the demesne farm of Wisbech Barton, 1314–1430', Ph.D. diss., University of Cambridge.

Thirsk, J. (1967). 'The farming regions of England', in J. Thirsk (ed.), *The Agrarian History of England and Wales. iv. 1500–1640*. Cambridge: Cambridge University Press, 1–112.

Thrupp, S. L. (1965). 'The problem of replacement rates in late medieval England', *Economic History Review*, 18: 101–19.

Tuck, J. A. (1991). 'The occupation of the land: the northern borders', in E. Miller (ed.), *The Agrarian History of England and Wales. iii. 1348–1500*. Cambridge: Cambridge University Press, 34–42.

Walter, J., and Schofield, R. S. (1989). 'Famine, disease and crisis mortality in early modern England', in J. Walter and R. S. Schofield (eds.), *Famine, Disease and the Social Order in Early Modern Society*. Cambridge: Cambridge University Press, 1–74.

Whittle, J. (1998). 'Individualism and the family–land bond: a reassessment of the land transfer patterns among the English peasantry', *Past and Present*, 160: 25–64.

Wrigley, E. A. (1967). 'A simple model of London's importance in changing English society and economy, 1650–1750', *Past and Present*, 37: 44–70.

Wrigley, E. A. (1986*a*). 'Urban growth and agricultural change: England and the Continent in the early modern period', in R. I. Rotberg and T. K. Rabb (eds.), *Population and Economy: Population and History from the Traditional to the Modern World*. Cambridge: Cambridge University Press, 123–68.

Wrigley, E. A. (1986*b*). 'Elegance and experience: Malthus at the bar of history', in D. Coleman and R. S. Schofield (eds.), *The State of Population Theory: Forward from Malthus.* Oxford: Blackwell, 46–64.

Wrigley, E. A., and Schofield, R. S. (1981). *The Population History of England 1541–1871: A Reconstruction.* London: Edward Arnold.

Wrigley, E. A., Davies, R. S., Oeppen, J. E., and Schofield, R. S. (1997). *English Population History from Family Reconstitution 1580–1837.* Cambridge: Cambridge University Press.

COMMENT

Perceptions and People

Paul Slack

AT an earlier point in this book Andrew Sherratt remarked that with the arrival of *Homo sapiens* the genetic part of our story was largely over; the rest was essentially 'culture'. In commenting on Dr Smith's expert analysis of the long demographic cycle between 1250 and 1670, I want to point to some of the cultural changes which accompanied the later stages of the cycle, in the sixteenth and seventeenth centuries. They interacted with demographic change, either as consequences or as what Smith terms 'interrupting causes'. They did much to determine the nature of the environment and perceptions of it, and thus influenced senses of 'identity'—a term which has been as prominent as 'culture' in earlier contributions. And because they helped to shape a recognizably 'modern' Britain, they also serve as an introduction to the chapters which follow.

The first issue of interest concerns social and economic expectations and the contribution which they made to the demographic equilibrium which was reached in the middle of the seventeenth century, at a total population level much lower than that of the early fourteenth century. As Dr Smith indicates, there were several demographic regulators involved in the process. Heavy emigration overseas in the mid-seventeenth century was one. An increase in mortality was another: the result, not of bubonic plague, which disappeared for good after 1665, but of other diseases, especially among infants and children, aggravated by urbanization. There was also a decline in fertility because of some unusual marriage patterns: despite improvements in living standards, people continued to marry late (at 27 or 28 in the case of men, 25 or 26 in that of women), and an increasing proportion of them never married at all (as many as 20 per cent in the mid-seventeenth century). Emigration and urbanization played a part here too, through their effect on the balance of the sexes in particular localities. It might seem that there is little more to be said.

Yet it is worth raising the question of whether expectations about adequate living standards—and therefore human deliberation—may not also have been at work in what seems to have been a remarkable shift towards celibacy. Some contemporaries at the end of the seventeenth century naturally noticed and disapproved of what one of them called 'a spirit of madness running abroad, and possessing men against marrying' (Thirsk and Cooper 1972: 742). Another observer, William Petty, thought the reason was that 'the prolific people are afraid they shall not be able to maintain the children they shall beget' (Lansdowne 1927: i. 267). It is conceivable, to put it no higher, that population growth was restrained in the later seventeenth century—and restrained at a much lower level of pressure against resources than in the later thirteenth century—partly because people were trying to defend as much as they could of the improved real incomes which they had enjoyed in the fifteenth century. If so, the Black Death and the prolonged demographic stagnation which followed had a profound and lasting effect on perceptions of what an adequate standard of living was.

Whatever one thinks of that speculation, it is undoubtedly the case that in the later seventeenth century, when population stopped growing, living standards in England were higher than in many other parts of Europe; and English men and women were conscious of the fact. Scotland was an obvious point of comparison. There too population stopped rising in the middle of the seventeenth century, but it did so at a point where living standards were very much lower. When harvests failed in the 1690s, the result was famine, and the population may have fallen by 13 per cent (Gibson and Smout 1995: 170). Peasants were starving at the same time in France, and William Petty had no doubt that 'the poor of France' had much lower incomes and faced much higher prices for staple commodities than those of England (Hull 1899: i. 294). In south Britain, by contrast, there was no repetition of the great famine of 1315: by 1670 a new and favourable balance between agricultural productivity and population had been achieved, and that facilitated economic growth and the economic diversification described in the next chapter.

Political developments provide a second quasi-cultural factor which needs to be taken into account in explaining the achievement. The growth of the English state under the Tudors and Stuarts impinges on our subject at various points, since it influenced the social structure, provision for social welfare, and—not least—the growth of London.

Dr Smith shows the importance for agricultural practices, agrarian productivity, and rural social structures, of the gradual emergence of a class of capitalist farmers, with large holdings, employing wage labour. The richest of them were the gentry and yeomen of England, both much larger, wealthier status groups in 1650 than they had been in 1500. Their good fortune depended in part upon a shift in the distribution of land, which was powerfully assisted by the Protestant Reformation and the dissolution of the monasteries in the 1530s. It has been estimated that the middling landed classes were able to gain something like an extra fifth of all the land of England between the fifteenth and the seventeenth centuries, largely at the expense of the Church (Clay 1984: i. 156–8). Gentlemen and yeomen were the people who permanently marked the landscape, with new houses in the 'great rebuilding of rural England' after 1570 (Hoskins 1963: 131–48), and with boundaries around newly enclosed fields. By 1700 more than two-thirds of England was enclosed by hedges and walls, and a quarter of the country had been enclosed in the course of the seventeenth century (Overton 1996: 148).

By 1700 England also had an administrative machine for relief of the poor which was more uniform and effective than that in any other country. Its origins lay in the sixteenth-century poor laws which were a response to demographic growth and to the need to fill the vacuum left by the Reformation's dismantling of the welfare apparatus provided by the medieval Church. In the hundred years after the Poor Law of 1601 virtually every parish became accustomed to raising poor rates and to defining those entitled to the dole because they were legally 'settled' there. As Dr Smith suggests, this welfare system offered some protection for the 'entitlements' of the poor in crisis years, at least in southern England. It may also have functioned as a brake on marriage among the labouring population, since in several parishes churchwardens and overseers used the threat of withholding relief to deter pauper marriages and hence limit future burdens on the rates (Hindle 1998). Although its practical effects are uncertain and were probably very uneven, the machinery of poor relief was potentially a demographic and economic regulator of some power. It was certainly a prominent symptom of the growth of the early modern state.

Still more prominent was the growth of London, and the roots of that lie partly in the growth of the state and partly (paradoxically) in the growing wealth of the landed classes. As a political capital, the city attracted the gentry and nobility to its courts and parliament, and to temporary residence in the West End; and it became a centre of consumption where the élite spent their rental incomes, and a single market dominating much of the rest of the country. It was also increasingly important as a centre of international trade, catering first for aristocratic demand for foreign luxuries and then profiting from exports and re-exports as London became a major European entrepôt. Dr Smith points to the demographic consequences as urbanization intensified the national and international circulation of disease. In the next chapter Professor Wrigley shows that urbanization was the vital partner to agricultural improvement in shaping England's peculiar and precocious occupational structure in the eighteenth century.

None of these changes went unrecognized by contemporaries, and their reflections upon them provide the final cultural shift which requires emphasis. Partly because of the rapidity of change, partly because of the educational expansion and cultural exchange encouraged by metropolitan growth, people became more self-conscious about their environment and about their place and identity within it. In the later seventeenth century there was an interest in new diseases and their association with particular localities and changes in climate, for example. It produced the work of Thomas Sydenham, John Locke, and others, and those precise climatic records which in England go back further than in any other country. London's expansion naturally attracted attention, and there was much debate about whether the metropolis was a stimulus to economic growth or increasingly parasitic, draining population and wealth from the provinces. Judgements were increasingly favourable, especially when the centre of the city was rebuilt after the Great Fire of 1666, and the whole built-up area could be acclaimed as the largest town in Europe (Slack 1999: 99, 146; 2000).

The growing dominance of London seems also to have prompted a discovery of the provinces, and an interest in their peculiarities. Local histories multiplied after 1600, and by 1700 surveys of fourteen English counties had been published or largely completed, praising the gentry, farmers, and manufacturers who were responsible for provincial prosperity (Butlin 1990: 228–34). Road books and lists of towns and villages and gentlemen's seats were published to assist travellers, and their printed and manuscript 'tours' showed how 'the face of the kingdom' had been transformed in the past century—'improved', to use the contemporary word, which was much in vogue. Looking back from 1699, Charles Davenant noted that a hundred years before the cultivated land was 'very much . . . capable of melioration', and 'there was a great deal more' barren and waste ground 'which our wealth did enable us from time to time to enclose, cultivate and improve' (Thirsk and Cooper 1972: 813). By 1700 improvement was a cultural force of major importance for the environment.

There was even an interest in how environments might in turn shape culture. In his *Natural History of Wiltshire*, written in the 1660s, John Aubrey commented on the different characters of people bred in the cheese country and the chalk. In the cheese country, on the heavy clay soils of north Wiltshire, he wrote, people 'feed chiefly on milk meats, which cools their brains too much': they were inhospitable and spiteful, 'melancholy, contemplative and malicious', inclined to Puritanism and all kinds of deviance and rebellion. By contrast, in the more open air on the chalk of the Wiltshire downs, people worked hard at tillage and keeping sheep: they were 'strong' and 'hard', satisfied with their lot, having 'not leisure to read or contemplate of religion' (Underdown 1985: 72).

Aubrey's environmental determinism should not be dismissed out of hand. Some modern historians have indeed followed in his footsteps, in investigating local allegiances in the Civil War, for example (Underdown 1985). On close examination, of course, crude environmental determinism proves to be wholly unconvincing. As earlier chapters have shown, the environment had been shaped by man, and economic activities had become specialized, suited to the soil, in relatively recent times; they were not an eternal given. The Puritanism which Aubrey worried about came into the Wiltshire cheese country from outside. His conservative industrious shepherds on the Wiltshire chalk were producing wool which was made up into cloth in the cheese country and exported via London to the Mediterranean. Men emigrated as indentured servants from the cheese country through Bristol to Virginia and Barbados. The effective environment of Wiltshire farmers, whether strong or melancholy, conformist or disaffected, was much wider than Aubrey supposed.

Yet Aubrey and other contemporary antiquaries, who were as interested in the monuments and peoples of ancient Britain as in those of their own day, deserve a mention in this collection. The seventeenth-century English pioneers of anthropology and archaeology testify to the arrival of new perceptions—more inquisitive, comparative, and historical—of a changing environment (Hunter 1975: 148–208; Piggott 1956). Their consciousness of different countrysides, identities, and cultures in England emerged—and probably could only emerge—in a country which was increasingly focused on one metropolitan centre, and hence part of a European-wide and even world-wide economy

REFERENCES

Butlin, R. A. (1990). 'Regions in England and Wales *c*.1600–1914', in R. A. Dodgshon and R. A. Butlin (eds.), *An Historical Geography of England and Wales*. 2nd edn., London: Academic Press, 223–54.

Clay, C. G. A. (1984). *Economic Expansion and Social Change: England 1500–1700*. 2 vols. Cambridge: Cambridge University Press.

Gibson, A. J. S., and Smout, T. C. (1995). *Prices, Food and Wages in Scotland 1550–1780*. Cambridge: Cambridge University Press.

Hindle, S (1998). 'The problem of pauper marriage in seventeenth-century England', *Transactions of the Royal Historical Society*, 6th series, 8: 71–89.

Hoskins, W. G. (1963). *Provincial England: Essays in Social and Economic History*. London: Macmillan.
Hull, C. H. (1899) (ed.). *The Economic Writings of Sir William Petty*. 2 vols. Cambridge: Cambridge University Press.
Hunter, M. (1975). *John Aubrey and the Realm of Learning*. London: Duckworth.
Lansdowne, Marquis of (1927) (ed.). *The Petty Papers*. 2 vols. London: Constable.
Overton, M. (1996). *Agricultural Revolution in England: The Transformation of the Agrarian Economy 1500–1850*. Cambridge: Cambridge University Press.
Piggott, S. (1956). 'Antiquarian thought in the sixteenth and seventeenth centuries', in L. Fox (ed.), *English Historical Scholarship in the Sixteenth and Seventeenth Centuries*. London: Dugdale Society and Oxford University Press, 93–114.
Slack, P. (1999). *From Reformation to Improvement: Public Welfare in Early Modern England*. Oxford: Oxford University Press.
Slack, P. (2000). 'Perceptions of the metropolis in seventeenth-century England', in P. Burke, B. Harrison, and P. Slack (eds.), *Civil Histories: Essays presented to Sir Keith Thomas*. Oxford: Oxford University Press, 161–80.
Thirsk, J., and Cooper, J. P. (1972) (eds.). *Seventeenth-Century Economic Documents*. Oxford: Oxford University Press.
Underdown, D. (1985). *Revel, Riot and Rebellion: Popular Politics and Culture in England 1603–1660*. Oxford: Oxford University Press.

7

Country and Town

The Primary, Secondary, and Tertiary Peopling of England in the Early Modern Period

E. A. Wrigley

THERE are many ways of depicting the constitution of a given society and of defining and measuring the changes within it. They reflect the interests and purposes of the scholars concerned, tempered by the source materials available to them. This chapter reflects the conviction that the occupational structure of a society and the changes therein offer the opportunity to gain an insight into much else about that society and its development. The way in which men and women earned a living reveals much about them and their communities. Though true of all societies, this was perhaps especially true of societies before the industrial revolution.

It is instructive to consider why this should be so. At bottom it follows from the fact that occupational structure in pre-industrial societies reflected the hierarchical nature of human needs, which produced some notable and readily observable regularities. The thinking and terminology of the classical economists reflected their appreciation of this point. They frequently referred to what they termed the necessities of life, of which there were four: food, shelter, clothing, and fuel.[1] These they distinguished both from what they characterized as comforts, other material products which were less central to life than the necessities but eagerly sought after when circumstances permitted; and from luxuries, goods or services to which only the affluent could aspire. If circumstances are sufficiently bleak people will favour spending on necessities above all other forms of expenditure, so that a very high proportion of the total spending of the poor will

[1] The term used by the classical economists was normally 'necessaries' but it avoids confusion to use the modern equivalent.

be devoted solely to necessities and above all to food. It was not uncommon for an impoverished household in early modern England to spend as much as three-quarters of its income on food alone and a still higher proportion, of course, on the four necessities taken together. But when income rises the proportion spent on necessities declines. If a poor man's income suddenly doubles, he and his family will spend more thereafter on food but their expenditure on food will not double. Or, to express the matter more formally, the income elasticity of demand for the necessities of life is less than unity. Conversely, of course, spending on comforts and, if resources permit, on luxuries, will more than double in the same circumstances. In an era of rising real incomes expenditure on comforts and luxuries will increase disproportionately rapidly. In an era of contracting real incomes, in contrast, the percentage share of spending on necessities will rise.

The Oxford economist, Colin Clark, interested himself in these and cognate issues. He distinguished between primary, secondary, and tertiary forms of employment.[2] These were not, of course, the same categories as necessities, comforts, and luxuries, but his three categories can be used for broadly comparable analytic purposes. Primary employment comprises agriculture, forestry, fishing, and mining, those forms of production which supply the raw materials from which finished products are made. Secondary employment refers to productive activities which convert raw materials into forms which can be consumed or otherwise made use of by their final purchasers. Tertiary employment relates to the production of services rather than material products: the professions; government service; the arts and entertainment; the provision of food, drink, and lodging; and transport, for example.[3]

Because of the way in which the marginal unit of income is spent as personal income rises, in the transition from a traditional society where income levels are low to a modern economy with high average incomes, such as contemporary Western Europe or North America, the structure of aggregate demand will change steadily. The absolute level of demand will rise for the products of all the three main employment categories, but the rate of growth will be least in the primary sector and greatest in the tertiary sector. Occupational structure must change in sympathy, since one man's expenditure is another man's source of employment. As a result, the percentage of the labour force engaged in primary production will fall slowly

[2] Clark (1951). Ch. 8 of this work provides much empirical information about income elasticities of demand for a wide variety of products principally drawn from the first half of the twentieth century.

[3] There is room for argument about the placing of certain economic activities within the three chief categories of employment, but this is not an issue that requires exhaustive treatment in this context.

but inexorably from, say, 75 per cent to 5 per cent or less, while the percentage in the tertiary sector will rise from a very modest level initially to 75 per cent or more in wealthy countries. In the interim period, reflecting the differing income elasticities of demand for the products of the three categories of employment, the percentage employed in secondary industry will rise rapidly at first, attaining at its peak perhaps 35 to 50 per cent of the labour force, but will subsequently fall back substantially as the tertiary sector comes to dominate the economy. Expressed in the language of the classical economists, if real incomes rise there will be a fall in the proportion of the labour force engaged in the production of necessities and a matching rise in the proportion engaged in the making of comforts and the provision of luxuries.

Since the form which economic growth has taken in the past two centuries, the form brought about by the industrial revolution, was first apparent in England, there is a special interest in any source of information or technique of analysis which can throw light on what was distinctive about England in the centuries preceding the industrial revolution. One should perhaps pause to note that making use of the term industrial revolution has become a possible source of confusion. What was largely unproblematic thirty years ago has ceased to be so. Neither the dating of the event to the last decades of the eighteenth and the early decades of the nineteenth centuries, nor the view that the rate of growth increased abruptly when the industrial revolution began, nor the conviction that England served as a paradigm for other countries has survived unscathed.[4] Despite this, it remains instructive to identify the respects in which England had become demonstrably different from continental Europe by the early nineteenth century. Among the more striking of these were the distinctive changes in its occupational structure, and the growing urbanization taking place during the seventeenth and eighteenth centuries. These two developments were closely interrelated phenomena. They jointly constitute the core of this chapter because they afford an opportunity to explore, for the quarter millennium preceding the industrial revolution, the unifying theme of this volume, the peopling of England.[5]

[4] On these issues see Crafts (1984, 1985). The very validity of the concept of the industrial revolution has been contested by Cameron (1981). There is a stimulating review of the historiography of the industrial revolution in Cannadine (1984). A critical survey of studies of the industrial revolution may be found in Hoppit and Wrigley (1994). See also Hoppit (1990) and Berg and Hudson (1992).

[5] The general title of this volume refers to Britain rather than England, but, however desirable it may be to treat the island as a whole, it is not easy to do so in the context of this discussion for lack of comparable source materials and analyses for the three countries concerned.

This theme can be explored by extending the distinction between primary, secondary, and tertiary employment to serve an unfamiliar purpose. I shall use the term primary population to refer to those engaged in primary production; and define secondary and tertiary population using the same principle. The primary peopling of England therefore, for example, does not refer to that which occurred first chronologically, but to that part of the population at a given point in time which earned its living from farming, forestry, and fishing.[6] The primary population includes, of course, not only those who were actually labouring on the land or putting to sea in fishing boats but all those directly dependent upon them. *Mutatis mutandis* the same applies to secondary and tertiary population so that every individual in a given area must always fall into one of the three categories. The three types of peopling may be thought of as successive layers superimposed upon the surface of the country. The population distribution as a whole is the joint product of these layers.

The distributional characteristics of the three population categories differed markedly. Before considering the particular circumstances of early modern England, the general nature of the three distributions requires brief discussion. The primary population characteristically formed a shallow covering over the whole country. Its depth was closely proportional to the fertility of the soil, shallowest where the land was high, or steeply sloping, or where the soil was thin, acidic, or waterlogged; deepest where the soil was a productive loam. The covering was very shallow on, say, high moorland, but even on fertile soils it was nowhere very thick. Even in early fourteenth-century East Anglia, for example, the most densely peopled part of the country in the period when the medieval population of England was at its peak, the primary peopling was probably no greater than 150 persons per square mile, or 4 acres per person, over the region as a whole, though locally densities might be two or three times greater.[7] This is a high density for primary population, but very sparse when compared with the densities which were supported by some types of secondary and tertiary employment.

[6] Primary employment is normally taken to include mining. I have excluded it in this case because the distributional characteristics of mining employment are more akin to certain types of industrial employment than to farming, forestry, and fishing.

[7] The 1377 poll tax data reveal taxpayer densities of 20 per square kilometre, or 50 per square mile, over East Anglia as a whole. On the assumption that taxpayers were roughly one-half of the total population and that population had halved between its early century peak and 1377, this suggests the figure of 200 per square mile for the total population in 1300. However, since East Anglia had many towns and an important woollen industry, it is unlikely that the primary population density was higher than 150 per square mile (Smith 1988: 190, 196–202).

Because the primary population was invariably widely and fairly thinly spread, if its density were plotted using contour lines, the resulting map would reflect a landscape without prominent relief. The highest ground, the areas with the densest primary population, did not rise dramatically. Secondary and tertiary populations, in contrast, were often highly localized and sometimes large in number. To extend the contouring analogy, these populations might at times produce Himalayan heights in sharp contrast with the Ganges plain-like pattern of primary population. The tendency to cluster was not by any means universal in secondary and tertiary peopling. The use of such inclusive general categories obliterates the different characteristics of their constituent occupations. Some secondary and tertiary occupations, bakers or barbers, for example, were necessarily found distributed about the country in broad sympathy with the overall distribution of the population. The perishability of bread and the unwillingness of the purchasers of a cheap service to move far to obtain it left those employed in such occupations no option but to mirror the geographical distribution of the purchasers of their products.

But there were also elements within the secondary and tertiary peopling of the country which were subject to very different economic imperatives. Consider, to take an example which illustrates the opposite extreme, Adam Smith's pinmakers. The product of the pin manufacture is almost weightless, so that, as with spices, the cost of transporting the finished product to market can only be a tiny fraction of the cost of manufacture. If, therefore, the division of labour were capable of being carried even further than Adam Smith suggested, so that unit costs of production would continue to fall appreciably in consequence of achieving higher and higher levels of output through increased specialization, then production would become concentrated on fewer and fewer sites, and, ultimately, in the paradigm case, on a single site. If employment in a given industry is highly concentrated, those who make their living from it will be equally concentrated.

In both secondary and tertiary industries a pattern that lies partway between these two extremes is more commonly found. In tertiary industry the professions illustrate the point well. An increasingly prosperous country, for example, can afford more lawyers and demand for their services will rise. Those lawyers who are least specialized in their skills will be found relatively widespread throughout the country, though more commonly in the larger than in the smaller towns and rarely in mere villages. In contrast, barristers will be found disproportionately in the largest centres. To illustrate the point, in 1841, 69.2 per cent of all men aged 20 and over in the occupational category 'barrister, advocate, and conveyancer' in England were in the metropolis. In the category 'attorney, solicitor, writer and law student', in contrast, only 31.5 per cent were in London. Similarly, the

TABLE 7.1. *Contrasting levels of agricultural employment and of urbanization in Britain and the Continent (percentages)*

	Great Britain 1840	Germany 1870	France 1870	Italy 1910
Urbanization	48.3	36.1	31.1	n.a.
Labour force in primary sector	25.0	50.0	49.3	55.4
Income generated in primary sector	24.9	39.9	33.5	38.2
Male labour force in industry	47.3	n.a.	28.7	26.5
Income generated in industry	31.5	29.7	36.0	23.9

Note: The dates shown at the head of each column indicate the approximate date at which each country reached an average income level equal to $550 (1970 US dollars).
Source: Crafts 1985, table 3.4, 57–8.

country's carpenters and joiners were widely scattered. Only 15.0 per cent were in London, but 32.9 per cent of the more specialist occupational category of cabinet makers and uphosterers were in the capital (in 1841 Greater London contained 2,239,000 people or 14.9 per cent of the total English population of 15,929,000: Mitchell 1981: tables 1.3, 1.6, 1.8).[8]

Most pre-industrial societies were poor and in consequence primary population dominated. A three-dimensional map of a typical pre-industrial society, displaying primary, secondary, and tertiary population as successive layers upon the land surface, would show that the bulk of the total population portrayed was contributed by the primary layer even though there might be prominent local peaks of secondary and tertiary peopling. What set England apart from the major countries of continental Europe in the seventeenth and eighteenth centuries was that the primary layer gradually ceased to dominate the scene during these two centuries, whereas on the Continent the early modern period saw only relatively slight changes in this regard. Early modern England experienced a remarkable surge in its secondary and tertiary peopling.

The scale of England's exceptionalism is reflected in Table 7.1 which reproduces some data collected by Crafts for a somewhat different pur-

[8] The relevant totals of barristers, solicitors, carpenters, and cabinet makers were respectively (total for London in brackets): 2,076 (1,437); 10,919 (3,437); 112,872 (16,965); and 19,752 (6,497) (Census, 1841 *Occupation Abstract*, Preface). Occupations of persons enumerated in Great Britain, distinguishing England and Wales, Scotland, and isles in the British seas in the year 1841, 31–44. Occupations of persons enumerated in the metropolis in the year 1841, 48–51.

TABLE 7.2. *Sectoral structure of the male labour force (percentages)*

	Italy (1871)	Ireland (1841)	Sweden (1860)	Finland[a] (1805)
Agriculture, forestry, and fishing	61.2	68.5	64.6	82.1
Manufacturing	13.2[b]	12.2	20.8	3.6
Other	25.6	19.3	14.6	14.3
	100.0	100.0	100.0	100.0

Notes: a. Male and female combined. b. Assumes manufacturing and construction split in 1871 in the same ratio as in 1881.

Source: Mitchell 1981, table C1, 161–73.

pose. He wished to illustrate how different Britain was from continental countries at the *same point of general economic advance* (when average real incomes had reached $550 (1970 US dollars)). A far smaller proportion of the British workforce was to be found in agriculture at this 'standard' stage of development than was the case in Germany, France, or Italy and, most unusually, output per head in agriculture was little different from output per head in the rest of the economy, as may be seen from a comparison of the percentages of the labour force in the primary sector and the percentages of national income generated in that sector. Elsewhere agriculture dominated the employment scene to a far greater extent, but output per head in agriculture was modest compared with that in secondary industry. The dates at which each country reached the 'standard' stage varied substantially, of course, with England well before the others. If it were feasible to make a similar comparison at the *same date* for each country and at a relatively early point in time, the contrasts in occupational structure between a 'peasant' Europe and a relatively non-agricultural England would be even more pronounced.

Such a comparison is not readily possible because national occupational census data are rarely available before the middle of the nineteenth century. By then countries such as Belgium, France, or Germany were already in the course of rapid economic change and urbanization. Extensive tracts of Europe, however, were still at a much earlier stage of development in the mid-century. The data in Table 7.2 refer to male occupational patterns. The information for Italy, Ireland, and Sweden is taken from the earliest readily available source, which was in each case in the middle decades of the century. Exceptionally, there is information for a much earlier date for Finland. Broadly speaking, in Italy, Ireland, and Sweden about two-thirds of the male labour force were working on the land. In Finland at the beginning of the century the comparable proportion was four-fifths. If returns existed for the other three countries for *c.*1800, it is highly probable that about three men in four would have been engaged in primary occupations. Yet in England in 1811 only 39 per cent of adult males aged 20–64 were employed in agriculture (Wrigley 1986: table 11.12, 332). Although the different ways in which occupational data were collected and tabulated in different countries should discourage the belief that precise comparisons can be made, the scale of the contrast is inescapable. Nor can the much lower English figure be attributed to dependence on imported food. At that time, England, though a net food importer, was still very largely self-supporting.[9]

It appears to be a fair inference from Tables 7.1 and 7.2 that during the quarter millennium before the nineteenth century the course of economic change in England must have been very different from that in her near neighbours. On the assumption that her occupational structure in the early sixteenth century did not set England apart from, say, France, much must have changed in the interim to have produced such wide differences by the beginning of the nineteenth century. This assumption is difficult to substantiate by direct quantitative evidence about occupational structure, but it is much strengthened by considering the course of urban growth in England and elsewhere over this period. Here the empirical evidence, while not without its problems, is much more abundant and tolerably reliable. In the early sixteenth century England was less urbanized than most continental countries. In 1800 it was the most highly urbanized country in Europe with the exception of the Netherlands. The difference between England and the larger continental states was marked. About 28 per cent of the population of England lived in towns and cities of 5,000 or more inhabitants in 1800, for example, compared with a figure of 11 per cent for France at the same date.[10] What was true of France was also true of countries such as Germany or Spain, and even of Italy despite the vivid and vigorous his-

[9] Jones has suggested that 90 per cent of the population of Great Britain were fed from domestic agricultural production in 1800, while Thomas estimated that in 1814–16 the value of imports of grain, meat, and butter was equal to 6.4 per cent of the total income of British agriculture (Jones 1981: 68; Thomas 1985: table 2: 743).

[10] Wrigley 1987: table 7.2, 162; table 7.9, 184–5; the comparable figure for the Netherlands was 33 per cent: table 7.8, 182. Choosing 5,000 inhabitants as the criterion for inclusion in the category 'urban' is arbitrary. Many market centres with 'urban' characteristics had fewer than 5,000 inhabitants but, equally, there were many small towns in which a substantial proportion of the workforce was engaged in agriculture. Using 5,000 inhabitants as a lower bound for urban population ensures that only a tiny fraction of the urban workforce was agriculturally employed.

tory of urban achievement there.[11] In contrast, in the early sixteenth century, the proportion of the population of England living in towns of 5,000 or more inhabitants was only 5 per cent: the comparable figure for France at that date was 9 per cent (Wrigley 1987: table 7.2, 162; table 7.9, 184–5). The striking contrast in the extent of urban growth between England and her neighbours, especially in the course of the eighteenth century, is reflected in the fact that during the second half of the eighteenth century approximately 70 per cent of all the urban growth taking place in Europe as a whole was occurring in England alone, even though the English population constituted less than 8 per cent of the European total (Wrigley 1987: table 7.7, 179).[12]

Rapid urban growth connotes rapid change in occupational structure. A major increase in the urban percentage necessarily means a substantial fall in the proportion of the population engaged in agriculture. It also implies a proliferation of occupational categories since the greater the size of the settlement, the wider the range of specialized individual occupations.

In parallel with any relative decline in the primary population, there must be, of course, a commensurate relative rise in secondary and tertiary employment. Although direct evidence of occupational change is limited, there is further support for the belief that rapid change was taking place in the seventeenth and eighteenth centuries from the investigations carried out by Gregory King at the end of the seventeenth century and by Joseph Massie in the middle of the eighteenth. Both men produced tables from which national occupational structure can be approximately estimated.[13] King's work is particularly interesting in this context. He was in a position to make use of such information as was at the disposal of the government of the day, and he found a compulsive fascination in the assemblage and interpretation of these data and other sources of economic, social, and demographic information.[14] King was not attempting to produce an

[11] In Italy 18 per cent of the populaton was living in towns with 5,000 or more inhabitants in 1800. This estimate of Italian urban population was obtained by inflating the total population of individual towns with 10,000 or more inhabitants in 1800 by a factor which represents the ratio of the population of towns of between 5,000 and 10,000 inhabitants to towns of 10,000 and above derived from a table showing the relative size of towns in different size groups in Mediterranean Europe as a whole at that date, and then relating the resulting total to the national population total to obtain a percentage figure. The data were taken from de Vries (1984: table 3.7, 39; table 4.13, 72, and app. 1, 269–78).

[12] Europe in this calculation comprised the British Isles, Scandinavia, Spain, Portugal, the Low Countries, Germany, France, Switzerland, and Italy.

[13] Mathias (1979) provides an interesting discussion of the work of Massie and its relation to that of King.

[14] Stone (1997) provides a penetrating review of King's aims and methods, and of the validity of his findings.

occupational census as the term is understood today.[15] The descriptors he used sometimes represented status rather than occupation. Nevertheless, his estimates can be recast in such a way as to allow the extent of the reduction in the dominance of primary employment during the eighteenth century to be gauged, and the same is possible with Massie's estimates. King's investigations suggest that about 60 per cent of families made a living from agriculture in 1688. Massie's work suggests a figure of about 50 per cent *c.*1760.[16] Their estimates, therefore, support the common-sense view that England had once been similar in occupational structure to the Continent, just as it had once been in the extent of its urbanization. The change in the share of agriculture in total employment implied by the estimates of Massie and King, if extrapolated backwards, would suggest a 'continental' occupational structure in Tudor times.[17] If this assumption is justified, the distinctive character of this aspect of the population history of England in the early modern period is plain.

[15] He was probably moved chiefly by a wish to improve his knowledge of data bearing on the relative strengths of England and her rivals, and especially to arrive at a better assessment of the tax potential of the country at a time of expensive war.

[16] The assumptions made in deriving these percentage estimates from the original tables are set out in Wrigley (1987: 171–2 n. 19).

[17] There is scope for much further work on this point. One of the few tolerably confident comparisons which can be made between the early seventeenth and the early nineteenth centuries, and which covers a significant area, is possible because of the work of the Tawneys on a Gloucestershire muster roll of 1608. This affords occupational data relating to men aged between 20 and 60 years of age for the whole county excluding Bristol. The Tawneys discuss at length the possible defects and sources of bias in the source but conclude that it will yield trustworthy estimates of such matters as the proportion of the male population engaged in each named occupation. Their tabulations show that 46.2 per cent of the men for whom occupational information is given were engaged in agriculture (Tawney and Tawney 1934: table 1, 36). The 1831 census provides the data necessary to calculate the comparable percentage for the same area. In 1831 there were 25,866 men aged 20 and over engaged in agriculture in Gloucestershire excluding Bristol out of a total population of 69,502 in the same age range: 37.2 per cent of adult males were therefore farmers or agricultural labourers (Census 1831, *Enumeration Abstract*, i. 226–7). The fall in the percentage engaged in agriculture is modest, and, if this pattern were typical of the country as a whole, it would suggest that the key issue is to account for an exceptionally high percentage of the workforce outside agriculture in the sixteenth century rather than to explain the rise in secondary and tertiary employment subsequently. However, it is improbable that Gloucestershire was typical of England as a whole. It was early a centre of the wool textile industry which subsequently declined substantially in importance. Textiles employed 15.5 per cent of the male labour force in 1608, but only about 6.5 per cent in 1831 (the 1831 census provides sufficient information to make a calculation possible but not sufficient to remove some doubt as to its accuracy). If textile employment is excluded at both dates the decline in the agricultural percentage is more pronounced: from 54.7 to 39.8. The presence of a large textile industry in 1608 also created related employment in dealing and retailing, so that the true impact of its presence on the agricultural percentage is probably understated by removing textile employment alone from the calculation. Nevertheless, Gloucestershire data suggest caution in attempting to estimate the scale of the decline in primary employment and underline the urgency of making fuller use of all available evidence on this point.

An earlier exercise suggested that in England the absolute number of men directly employed on the land at the end of the sixteenth century did not differ materially from the number similarly engaged at the beginning of the nineteenth century. The fall in the percentage of the labour force employed in agriculture offset the rise in total population. On the Continent, in contrast, even though there was probably a modest decline in the *percentage* of the primary population, the rise in overall numbers was sufficient to ensure a considerable growth in its *absolute size*. The rural agricultural proportion of the total population of France may have fallen from about 76 per cent to about 66 per cent between 1600 and 1800, but this would still imply an increase in the absolute size of the rural agricultural population of about 30 per cent (Wrigley 1987: table 7.9, 184–5).

To underline the exceptional character of the history of the primary peopling of England, it is illuminating to glance still further back in time. It is virtually certain that the primary population of the country reached a level early in the fourteenth century which was never again to be matched. It is now widely supposed that at its medieval peak, which was reached about that time, the total population of the country exceeded 6 million.[18] The comparable total in 1600 was only about two-thirds as great, at 4.2 million (Wrigley *et al.* 1997: table A9.1, 614–15). Since the proportion of the total population engaged in agriculture was probably as high in 1300 as in 1600, if not higher, and on the assumption that there was little growth in the agricultural population in the two and a half centuries after 1600, it follows that there were more, and probably substantially more, men and women working in English fields and meadows in the early fourteenth century than at any subsequent time. Agricultural employment rose somewhat in the early decades of the nineteenth century before declining after the mid-century, but even in 1851 was probably less than *c.*1300. It is extremely improbable that such a statement would hold true for any other substantial tract of Europe.

By 1800 about 64 per cent of the population of England was making a living outside agriculture, and therefore formed part of the secondary or tertiary population of the country (Wrigley 1987: table 7.4, 170).[19] The number of people dependent on non-agricultural income may be estimated to have increased from about 1.24 million in 1600 to about 5.52 million

[18] In a recent review of many aspects of the demography of medieval England, Smith suggests that in 1348 the national total probably lay in the range between 5 and 6 millions but also that it was probably significantly higher at the beginning of the fourteenth century (Smith 1988: 191).

[19] An estimate made on a different basis and relating only to male adults suggests that non-agricultural employment formed between 60 and 62 per cent of the total (Wrigley 1986: table 11.12, 332).

in 1800, a rise of 345 per cent (Wrigley 1987: table 7.4, 170). The contour map of overall population, produced by the superimposition of secondary and tertiary peopling on top of the primary surface, was beginning to acquire the vertiginous peaks which are the distinguishing mark of a modern society. London became the largest city in Europe, and one of the largest in the world, before the end of the seventeenth century and at the end of the eighteenth century was nearing the million mark. During the eighteenth century, several English towns approached a total of 100,000 inhabitants, at a time when such a size was still most unusual.[20] Moreover, several of the largest cities at the end of the eighteenth century had only arrived very recently in the upper echelons of city size. Before the mid-nineteenth century there were no parallels on the Continent to Liverpool, Birmingham, and Manchester in their combination of large size and rapid growth without the stimulus of being a seat of government. Such urban growth as there was elsewhere in Europe usually failed to disturb the existing city rank order. In France, for example, the eight cities which were largest in 1600 were still the eight largest in 1800 with only minor changes in their rank ordering. In England, London was always by far the largest city, but only two other of the eight largest towns in 1600 were still in the top eight in 1800. After London, in 1800 five of the next six were newcomers (Manchester, Liverpool, Birmingham, Leeds, and Sheffield) (Wrigley 1987: table 7.1, 160–1: de Vries 1984: app. 1, 269–78). Plainly, exceptional changes were afoot in England which were transforming its economy and its peopling at a time when on the Continent such change was, by comparison, in a very minor key.

It should not be supposed, however, that a move away from agriculture as a means of livelihood necessarily meant a move away from the land. Much of the growth in secondary and tertiary peopling took place in the countryside rather than in the town.[21] To clarify this development, a brief digression into the complex issues to do with occupational descriptors may not be out of place.

In an advanced economy in the late twentieth century, if a man describes himself as a solicitor's clerk or as a garage mechanic, it is likely that his income is derived exclusively, or at least predominantly, from the occupation which he has named. His contribution to the total output of goods and services in the community may well comprise things not produced in the

[20] In the whole of Europe in 1800 there were seventeen towns with a population of 100,000 or more. Only eight at most were not capital cities: Hamburg (100,000); Lyons (100,000); Milan (135,000); Venice (138,000); Palermo (139,000); Barcelona (115,000); Naples (427,000); and Dublin (168,000) (de Vries 1984: app. 1, 269–78). Several of these might reasonably be treated as capitals or quasi-capitals.

[21] For a convincing demonstration of the nature of this process, see Patten (1979).

solicitor's office or on the floor of the garage. The clerk may make violins in his spare time; the mechanic may be an amateur carpenter. But normally a single occupational descriptor will capture most of the contribution made by the individual in question to the total output of goods and services in the community. This was much less true in the past, and this has sometimes been seen as presenting a serious obstacle to the use of occupational data for historical purposes.

The implicit assumption which justifies using occupational information for the analysis of economic activity in the past is that if, say, 5 per cent of the labour force described themselves as framework knitters, then in round terms about 5 per cent of the hours worked by the labour force were devoted to framework knitting. There are several persuasive reasons for doubting that this is a legitimate inference. One of the most important stems from the nature of the seasonal pattern of activity in most agrarian societies. In general, the cereal harvest was the centrepiece of the agricultural year. In the great majority of communities it was vital to the well-being of the population that the harvest should be brought in as rapidly as possible in order to limit the loss to pests, sprouting, and foul weather. But the scale of the labour force needed to minimize harvest-time loss was much larger than that needed during the rest of the year. The 'normal' agricultural labour force was insufficient, yet to have retained in agriculture a workforce large enough to cope with the peak demand of harvest would have involved many men and women being idle for much of the year. Equally, to have failed to provide enough hands to bring in the harvest would have meant communal disaster. It was therefore frequently beneficial that there should develop other types of local employment, such as framework knitting, to provide profitable occupations during the bulk of the year for the additional hands needed at harvest. Occupational symbiosis as well as specialization was essential.

The same basic point can be expressed slightly differently. If it were possible, it would be preferable to measure hours worked on primary, secondary, and tertiary tasks, or in particular occupations in each category, rather than counting occupational designations. This would serve not only to overcome the problems associated with the harvest peak problem but also many comparable difficulties. The more prominent include the following. Some men changed their jobs seasonally. A seventeenth-century London coal heaver who could find employment in the summer when colliers brought coal south from Tyneside to the Thames would need to find other employment in the winter since the ships were then laid up. Or again, many men habitually and routinely had two jobs simultaneously, or, more accurately, found that two different forms of employment dovetailed neatly. Occasionally this may be stated explicitly. For example, under the provisions of Rose's Act,[22] the occupation of fathers was set down in Anglican baptism registers. A man might there be described as, say, 'grazier and butcher', but when in this or any other source a man is described only as a 'butcher', this should not necessarily be taken to mean that he pursued no other trade. A comparable problem arises because specialization of function was much less far advanced in the past than in the present. As a result, for example, many farmers carried their produce to market and therefore in effect spent several hours a month as transport workers. Or again, a large fraction of all those engaged in domestic manufacture or in mining covered a variable, but often significant, part of their food needs by what they grew in their closes, gardens, or allotments.

Another important difference between the past and the present was the very extensive amount of work which would today appear as a form of economic activity giving rise to a marketable product but which was then performed at home, chiefly by women, and largely consumed by the household in question. The conversion of milk into butter, the baking of bread, the repair and often the making of clothes, the nursing of the sick, even such mundane tasks as the washing of potatoes or the shelling of peas, which are now done outside the home by a paid labour force, were in the past performed unpaid within the home. All such tasks were part of the production process and involved a substantial opportunity cost, and it is a defect of occupational data, which, with rare exceptions, relate principally to men, that information about a substantial part of work which turned raw materials into finished products escapes the net when using occupational data. They almost always refer to work performed in the market sector of the economy but, in the past, a much larger fraction of productive activity was performed outside the market economy than is the case today.

It follows from the above that occupational data must be interpreted with discretion. If there were detailed information about the hours of work devoted to productive tasks by individuals in particular occupational groups, it would be clear, for example, how much of the time spent by those who described themselves as framework knitters was spent in work on the land. The crude data about occupational structure could then be weighted to reflect the realities of economic life in the past. Such information, however, except in the rarest instances, is not attainable. Yet it does not therefore follow that occupational data are such a fallible guide to the structure of the economy in the past as to be of little value. Notwithstanding their limitations as a surrogate measure of the relative amounts of time spent on different productive activities, there is much to be learnt from them.

[22] 52 Geo. III, cap. 146.

First, a distinction should be drawn between the absolute and the relative. It may be impossible to discover with precision from occupational data what proportion of total labour time was devoted to agricultural tasks in 1600 or 1800. But if at one point in time 60 per cent of the labour force in a given area were agriculturally employed and at a later date only 35 per cent, this may be taken as clear evidence that agriculture had declined substantially in *relative* importance, even though it may be unsafe to assume that at the earlier date 60 per cent of hours worked were spent on agricultural pursuits and only 35 per cent at the later date. And what is true of change over time is true *a fortiori* of assessing regional or local differences at the same point in time. Occupational data may be a less than perfect guide to *absolute* quantities and yet a safe indication of *relative* differences.

Second, the complexity of the occupational mix present in a particular community is instructive. A community which has reached a relatively high level of economic development will have a more diverse occupational structure than a community of the same size but more impoverished. Some sources which do not permit even a primitive quantification of occupational structure but which do provide an insight into its occupational complexity may therefore prove instructive, just as data on nominal or ordinal scales can have great value even in the absence of interval data. Local trade directories are a case in point. They do not provide a full coverage of local occupations since their principal purpose was to put buyers in touch with sellers. Nevertheless to be able to enumerate the range of specialist occupations locally present gives a valuable insight into the degree of development of the local economy and provides clear evidence of the existence of a market for the products in question. At one extreme, the metropolis supported a bewildering range of specialized occupations. In the parish of St Margaret's Westminster, for example, occupations which appear in the baptism register in the period 1813–20 include the following: optician, mathematical instrument maker, fiddle string maker, livery lace weaver, paper stainer, and even a comedian.[23] But lesser urban centres and even many rural parishes also provide evidence of a notable degree of specialization of function.

One further comment may be made about the use of occupational data, a point which leads us back to the issue of the distinctiveness of early modern England. Occupational terminology itself sometimes changed as time

[23] The list could be extended enormously. In all a total of well over 400 different occupations appear in the baptism register of St Margaret's in this period. The exact number is a matter of definition. In arriving at a total in excess of 400, subdivisions within certain common occupational categories were ignored: there were, for example, scores of different types of clerk, labourer, messenger, porter, soldier, and servant, but these were largely ignored in counting up the total of occupations in the years 1813–20.

went by. This is both instructive in itself and a reason to be cautious in interpreting change. For example, the descriptors used for those working in agriculture changed radically between the sixteenth and nineteenth centuries. Husbandman and yeoman were largely displaced as occupational terms by labourer and farmer. That there should have been a wholesale change of this kind in the most important single industry in the country is itself highly suggestive about the fundamental nature of change in English agriculture, but it would be an error to suppose that agricultural tasks had necessarily changed radically or that the changes which did occur kept step with the changes in terminology.[24]

Having described the uncertainties attaching to the use of occupational data, we may revert to a discussion of the great expansion in the secondary and tertiary peopling of the country which took place during the early modern period. This did not consist, for the most part, of employment in 'new' industries making use of major advances in productive technique. Even as late as the 1831 census, the first which allows analysis of the point, only one man in ten in the adult male labour force was engaged in 'manufacture', which comprised both factory-based production and those types of domestic manufacture which were tied to distant markets, the range of employments, that is, which is sometimes termed proto-industrial.[25] Well over half of the men engaged in 'manufacture' were living either in Lancashire or the West Riding of Yorkshire. Out of a national English total of 314,106, Lancashire and the West Riding accounted for 172,186 (Census 1831, *Enumeration Abstract*, ii. *Summary of England*, 832–3). Elsewhere manufacture afforded little employment. 'Retail trade and

[24] One man's husbandman was another man's labourer, as is very clear from some parish registers in the early nineteenth century. The same man might appear as a husbandman in one year and a couple of years later when his next child was baptised be described as a labourer. The parish of Blackawton in Devon provides a striking example of the waywardness of usage, since, having earlier adopted the 'modern' term 'labourer', 'husbandman' returned to favour in 1814, only to be superseded once more by 'labourer' in 1819. The occupation which was variously designated in this fashion did not alter, however.

[25] The collection of the occupational information for the 1831 census was carried out by the parish overseers. The definitions of the occupational categories in their instructions which were intended to determine the allocations which they made were quite brief. In the case of manufacture those to be included were 'males upwards of twenty years old—employed in manufacture or in making manufacturing machinery; but not including labourers, porters, messengers, etc.' while the comparable definition for retail trade and handicraft referred to those employed in 'retail trade or in handicrafts as masters, shopmen, journeymen, apprentices, or in any capacity requiring skill in the business' with the same exclusion of labourers, etc. (Census 1831, *Enumeration Abstract*, i, Preface, p. vi). However, what was intended to be included in retail trade and handicraft was made much clearer by appending a list of the 100 individual occupations which were supposed to occur most commonly, while the main manufacturing occupations in each county were listed at the end of the county statement. This further information sustains the interpretation of the difference between the two categories given in the main text.

handicraft' was a much larger category than 'manufacture', by a factor of three.[26] The occupations under this head were all or almost all long established forms of employment using traditional techniques of production in the main. The great bulk of the rapidly growing secondary and tertiary population, in other words, drew its livelihood from occupations which were already familiar in Tudor England, though their relative importance was much increased. The ten largest sources of adult male employment in retail trade or handicraft in descending order of size in 1831 were shoemakers, carpenters, tailors, publicans, shopkeepers, blacksmiths, masons, butchers, bricklayers, and bakers. These ten occupations jointly employed just over half a million men aged 20 and over (516,979) and between them they alone supported five men and their families for every three supported by industrial or proto-industrial activities. The total male labour force employed outside agriculture was 2,219,234 (Census 1831, *Enumeration Abstract*, ii. 832–3, 1044–51): therefore almost a quarter of male non-agricultural employment was in the ten occupations listed. Of these occupations, all except that of shopkeeper and possibly bricklayer would have been widely found two centuries earlier.

The dominance of trades such as the ten quoted in providing employment outside agriculture; the fact that they represented forms of economic activity tied exclusively or dominantly to local demand; and their ubiquity all suggest that increased purchasing power was a pervasive phenomenon. It is a pattern which, when combined with the knowledge that a roughly stationary agricultural labour force coped effectively with the food needs of a rapidly growing population, sits easily with the supposition that the striking divergence of England from the continental norm during the seventeenth and eighteenth centuries was largely a function of a distinctive surge in agricultural productivity. It is instructive in this regard that the ten occupations formed almost exactly the same fraction of total male employment in the rural counties as in the rest of the country, suggesting that the rise in the demand for the goods and services provided by retail trade and handicraft was very evenly spread (Wrigley 1986: table 11.2, 300–1).

The altered balance between the primary population and those in secondary and tertiary employment was to be found throughout the length and breadth of the country. The effect was to raise the population totals of settlements of all sizes, but rates of growth were not uniform in the several size categories. In small rural parishes growth was relatively modest and was largely confined to the trades which figured so prominently in the 1831 census returns. Even very small villages commonly had a resident

[26] There were 964,177 men engaged in retail trade and handicraft compared with 314,106 in manufacture (Census 1831, *Enumeration Abstract*, i, p. vi).

carpenter, shoemaker, and tailor, and many had a variety of other basic trades and services, able to secure sufficient custom from the farming community, from one another, from the local parson, and, in some instances, from the households of any resident gentry, to make an adequate living. Occupations frequently found in predominantly rural parishes in addition to the ten listed above included miller, sawyer, gardener, coachman, gamekeeper, painter, plumber and glazier, barber or hairdresser, and wheelwright.[27]

Moving further up the settlement hierarchy, rates of growth increase, though some long established centres did not outpace the general rise in numbers in the early modern period.[28] But urban England as a whole was, of course, expanding very rapidly indeed. Port cities, such as Liverpool, Bristol, or Sunderland; new industrial centres of which the two most outstanding examples were Manchester and Birmingham, but which included a large clutch of other towns, such as Leeds, Sheffield, Bolton, Stockport, Stoke, and Wolverhampton; and leisure centres, notably Bath and Brighton: these towns enjoyed strikingly high rates of increase. The combined population of Manchester, Birmingham, Leeds, and Sheffield, for example, was 70,000 in 1750 and 262,000 in 1801, a rate of growth of 2.6 per cent per annum (Wrigley 1987: table 7.1, 160–1). London, however, which in the seventeenth century had grown far more quickly than other urban centres, settled back to a more sedate growth rate in the eighteenth century. It remained by far the largest city in the country, enjoying the full range of stimuli to further growth experienced elsewhere and in addition those of an imperial capital, but it ceased to display the disproportionately high growth rates of the previous century, expanding in step with national growth rather than well ahead of it. At all levels of the urban hierarchy the same rule normally held true: the bigger the settlement, the greater the variety of occupations to be found.

The basic assumption underlying much of the description and analysis embodied in this chapter was set out in its opening paragraphs. Given that people will always ensure that they have an adequate supply of the neces-

[27] This information is drawn from a study which is in progress based on the occupational information, routinely recorded in Anglican baptism registers over the eight-year period 1813–20. Rose's Act of 1812 required this information to be recorded in the new printed registers which came into use under the provisions of the Act from the beginning of 1813. The data are drawn from a random sample of 300 registers used for this purpose. The county details in the 1831 census are also informative in this regard.

[28] For example, Exeter, King's Lynn, Chester, Cambridge, Worcester, Oxford, Colchester, and Ipswich, all in the upper echelons of urban England in the sixteenth century, grew collectively by 115 per cent between 1600 and 1800. At the former date their combined total population was 46,000; at the latter date 99,000. This increase was almost exactly in step with the national population total which rose from 4.16 to 8.67 million, or by 108 per cent (Wrigley 1986: table 7.1, 160–1; Mitchell 1988: ch. 1, table 7, 26–9).

sities of life before indulging in other expenditures, it seems safe to argue that a major proportional shift in the structure of the labour force, favouring secondary and tertiary employment at the expense of primary employment, must reflect a large improvement in the lot of the average consumer. This in turn can only be secured if the consumer, wearing a different hat as a producer, increases his productivity commensurately. In some industries the strength of the evidence of major gains in productivity per head during the quarter millennium before about 1800 is plain. In agriculture, for example, the fact that a largely static workforce coped with the food needs of a greatly increased population leaves no room for doubt on this score.

The balance of evidence favours the view that access to the comforts of life and to some of its luxuries was widespread in the population as a whole, but this view is not shared universally, and there are a number of grounds on which it can be challenged. Since the direct evidence is not conclusive, it may be of interest to close by reviewing some of the difficulties which attend the argument advanced.

The first difficulty is well known and has attracted much attention. Almost half a century ago Phelps Brown and Hopkins, in a remarkable pioneering study, produced a real wage series which, while displaying striking secular fluctuations between the mid-sixteenth and early nineteenth centuries, showed no decided upward trend (Phelps Brown and Hopkins 1955, 1956). Their work does not suggest that there was a large enough rise in purchasing power to have underwritten the sweeping changes in occupational structure which occurred. Having been at a very high level in the later fifteenth century, the index declined in the early decades of the sixteenth century and plunged thereafter. Using decadal averages, if the 1530s are taken as 100, the index falls to a nadir of 57 in the 1610s before rising to a high point in the 1730s at 107, but thereafter falling back again to no more than an average of 72 in the 1800s, largely because the impact of poor harvests could not readily be offset by increased imports during wartime. Only in the 1840s did the series exceed its 1730s level, reaching 108 in that decade (Wrigley and Schofield 1981: table A9.2, 642–4).[29]

The violence of the secular fluctuations in the series is partly spurious so far as the experience of individual families was concerned. The price series used consisted of wholesale prices and Rappaport's work shows convincingly how strongly the swings in the series are damped if retail prices are used. The purchasing power of individual consumers did not fall by one-half between the early sixteenth and the early seventeenth centuries, as the

[29] The accompanying text makes clear the assumptions which were used in deriving estimates of values in the PBH series for years which were missing in the original.

PBH series suggests. The fall was probably closer to a quarter than to a half.[30] The issue of long-term trend is more complex and has been the focus of much discussion. Those who find difficulty in accepting an absence of significant gain in household purchasing power during the early modern period can advance the following arguments. First, the PBH series, as its authors well knew, probably understates the rise in wages during the eighteenth century because its data are drawn from the agricultural south of England and therefore both the effect of rising wages in the northern industrial areas and the impact of their rapidly rising share in the national population are ignored.[31] Second, the index assumes, in effect, that adult male daily wages are a dependable guide to average earnings. If, however, the average number of days worked each year changed, or if the balance of earning power between men, women, and children altered, or if what was given in kind rather than in cash rose or fell, the match between the PBH series and the 'real' world would be affected.[32] The exploration in recent literature of the idea of an 'industrious' revolution as a prelude to the industrial revolution shows how it is possible to reconcile an absence of secular increase in male daily wages with a substantial rise in household purchasing power (de Vries 1994; Voth 1996).

The PBH series is therefore a fallible guide to trends in adult male annual earnings, and a still more fallible guide to the purchasing power of families. Moreover, if the focus of attention is switched from trends within England to a comparison between England and other countries, it is difficult to resist the conclusion that English consumers were unusually favourably placed to acquire necessities and to purchase comforts by the end of the early modern period.

No other scholar has done more than Maddison to assemble and assess comparative national economic data over long periods of time. He has taken a particular interest in deriving estimates of output per head for this purpose. Output per head and income per head are necessarily closely correlated. At first sight his work does not suggest large differences between

[30] See the discussion and evidence presented in Rappaport (1989: 144–53).

[31] The effect of taking into account the very different wage trends in the north of England in the eighteenth century is illustrated by the discussion in Wrigley and Schofield (1989: pp. xx–xxii).

[32] There are also a number of further grounds for disputing the authority of the PBH series as a guide to secular real wage trends. In addition to the problems created by the advent from time to time of new and ultimately important elements into the consumer price index, such as the potato, some major items of consumer expenditure which must be important at all times were not included for lack of an available data series. The most notable example under this head is the absence of a measure of the cost of accommodation. In addition, many of the price series which were employed were subject to lengthy gaps. All these problems were, of course, well known to Phelps Brown and Hopkins who were admirably candid about the deficiencies of their index.

England and advanced continental countries at the beginning of the nineteenth century. For example, his estimates of gross domestic product per head in 1820 for France, the Netherlands, and the United Kingdom fall within quite a narrow range: that for France (expressed in 1970 US dollars) is $377, for the Netherlands $400, and for the United Kingdom $454. But the UK figure includes Ireland and Maddison estimated Irish output per head at only half the British figure. Since Irish population was 32.6 per cent of the UK total in 1821, this implies that the British figure for GDP per head would be $542 rather than $454, or 36 per cent higher than the Dutch and 44 per cent higher than the French, rather than 14 and 20 per cent as suggested by a comparison using UK GDP estimates. Since Scottish output per head was lower than the English, a figure for England only would be still higher and the advantage over France and the Netherlands therefore still more pronounced (Maddison 1982: table 1.4, 8 and 167; Mitchell 1988: table 1.2, 9–10). Unless Maddison's work can be shown to be deeply flawed, therefore, the scale of the contrast between England and other European countries at the end of the early modern period suggests a substantially different structure of aggregate demand in England, and reinforces the likelihood of a distinctive prior history. If data for other European countries were available, the contrast would, in general, be still more pronounced.[33]

There are other grounds on which the argument of this essay can be challenged. For example, one might concede that there must have been a major increase in purchasing power to have provoked such a massive shift in occupational structure as took place in England, but put a different gloss on the change by arguing that the bulk of the population was no better provided for in Georgian than in Tudor times. Such a pattern was not unknown. In the countryside of southern England, for example, agricultural labourers derived little benefit from rising agricultural productivity, though it should not be overlooked that agriculture employed a declining share of the total population even in rural areas. Economic growth might have benefited only a relatively small minority. If this had been the case,

[33] It should be noted that Maddison has produced a number of revised estimates since the early 1980s. In a more extended study these should be considered. In the main they imply a more marked difference between England and other countries in 1820 than that described in the main text since Maddison has accepted the arguments of Crafts that growth in England was slower in the later eighteenth and early nineteenth centuries than had earlier been supposed, which implies a higher level of output in, say, 1820 than in earlier estimates, since the mid-nineteenth-century estimates are little changed. To balance this point it should also be noted, however, that it is probable that a higher proportion of the total output of goods and services in England went through the market and was therefore more readily measurable than was the case in France or much of the rest of continental Europe in the early nineteenth century.

there might conceivably have been a sufficient increase in the demand for the products of secondary and tertiary industry to have caused a surge of employment in these industries even though the bulk of the population contributed little to this increase. Put so starkly the argument is hardly persuasive but a less extreme version, focusing on the greatly increased prosperity of the middling groups in the population, has a respectable ancestry.[34]

Or again, England might have been experiencing at a later date a reorientation of her economy comparable to that which occurred in the Netherlands in the sixteenth and early seventeenth centuries. In this period the Netherlands became a major importer of basic foodstuffs, grew heavily dependent upon international trade, and became the most urbanized country in Europe. Although developments in England did not in all respects parallel those in Holland since, for example, England remained largely self-sufficient in basic foodstuffs, and indeed was for a time a major exporter of food,[35] nevertheless the rapid expansion in her trading links with the rest of the world might be held to account for a substantial part of the growth in employment outside agriculture. In principle, it might have been international rather than local demand which occasioned the rise in secondary and tertiary employment, though attempts to quantify the relative importance of home and foreign demand lend little support to this possibility.[36] And, of course, both of these reasons for doubting the thesis advanced earlier might have been operative simultaneously, reinforcing one another. A reorientation of the economy towards international markets and a marked shift in the distribution of income towards élite groups, for example, might easily have run in parallel.

There are, therefore, grounds for hesitation about accepting the argument for a significant rise in the purchasing power of the average household in the early modern period. None should be dismissed out of hand. They may prove to require some shading of an explanation of the changing occupational structure of the country which depends principally on a substantial rise in real incomes spread widely through the population. But the evidence of the divergence of England from the Continent in the seventeenth and eighteenth centuries seems incontrovertible and is most easily explained by the occurrence of major changes in the pattern of aggregate demand for goods and services arising from a widely based increase in purchasing power to match the occupational diversification and the local and

[34] Eversley (1967).

[35] See n. 9 above on the first point; on the second Deane and Cole (1962: table 17, 65), also Ormrod (1975).

[36] See Cole (1981) and McCloskey (1994: 253–8); also O'Brien (1982) who reviews a wider but related issue.

regional occupational characteristics which took place. There is much support for this interpretation from the evidence of developments other than those described in this chapter, though space prevents their recounting here. The penetration of new products into more and more households; the increased sophistication of articles of attire and fabrics of all kinds; the proliferation of retail outlets for a widening range of products; evidence of a burgeoning network of credit; as well as that of extensive new domestic construction to much higher standards, all offer support in this connection.[37]

New and better empirical evidence would nevertheless be of great help in resolving some of the remaining paradoxes. It is important to make progress in this regard since the transition from an agrarian world of limited productive potential to a world of exponential economic growth at a relatively high annual rate has revolutionized so many aspects of individual and social life in the last two hundred years. There is therefore a compelling interest in achieving a better understanding of how this came about. The striking changes in the peopling of England which took place in this period were, of course, a reflection of the contemporary economic changes which were in train. Effecting a complete account of the history of the primary, secondary, and tertiary peopling of England in the seventeenth and eighteenth centuries would therefore be the equivalent of achieving a definitive economic and social history of the period. This is not an ambition likely to be fulfilled even over an extended timescale, but making fuller use of the substantial, if scattered, evidence about occupational structure and change, and further reflection on its best use, bids fair to inform and improve future discussion of the divergence of England, of that period in English history which was not only the herald of radical change in this country, but also a portent of the changes which have transformed the face of the globe as they fanned out from their point of origin.

REFERENCES

Berg, M., and Hudson, P. (1992). 'Rehabilitating the industrial revolution', *Economic History Review*, 45: 24–50.

Cameron, R. (1981). 'The industrial revolution, a misnomer', in J. Schneider (ed.), *Wirtschaftskräfte und Wirtschaftswege*. v. Stuttgart: Klett-Cotta, 367–76.

Cannadine, D. (1984). 'The present and the past in the English industrial revolution', *Past and Present*, 103: 131–72.

[37] There is a large and varied literature to support these claims as, for example, Hoskins (1953); Machin (1977); Weatherill (1988); Shammas (1990); Muldrew (1998); Falkus and Jones (1979); Spufford (1984); Harte (1991); Thirsk (1978); McKendrick, Brewer, and Plumb (1982).

Census (1831). *Enumeration Abstract. PP* 1833, xxxvi and xxxvii.
Census (1841). *Occupation Abstract*, pt. I. *England and Wales. PP* 1844, xxvii.
Clark, C. (1951). *The Conditions of Economic Progress*. 2nd edn., London: Macmillan.
Cole, W. A. (1981). 'Factors in demand 1700–80', in R. Floud and D. McCloskey (eds.), *The Economic History of Britain since 1700*, i. *1700–1860*. Cambridge: Cambridge University Press, 36–65.
Crafts, N. F. R. (1984). 'Patterns of development in nineteenth century Europe', *Oxford Economic Papers*, 36: 438–58.
Crafts, N. F. R. (1985). *British Economic Growth during the Industrial Revolution*. Oxford: Clarendon Press.
Deane, P., and Cole, W. A. (1962). *British Economic Growth, 1688–1959: Trends and Structure*. Cambridge: Cambridge University Press.
Eversley, D. E. C. (1967). 'The home market and economic growth in England 1750–80', in E. L. Jones and G. E. Mingay (eds.), *Land, Labour and Population in the Industrial Revolution*. London: Edward Arnold, 206–59.
de Vries, J. (1984). *European Urbanization 1500–1800*. Cambridge, Mass.: Harvard University Press.
de Vries, J. (1994). 'The industrial revolution and the industrious revolution', *Journal of Economic History*, 54: 249–70.
Falkus, M. E., and Jones, E. L. (1979). 'Urban improvement and the English economy in the seventeenth and eighteenth centuries', *Research in Economic History*, 4: 193–233.
Harte, N. B. (1991). 'The economics of clothing in the late seventeenth century', *Textile History*, 22: 277–96.
Hoppit, J. (1987). *Risk and Failure in English Business 1700–1800*. Cambridge: Cambridge University Press.
Hoppit, J. (1990). 'Counting the industrial revolution', *Economic History Review*, 2nd series, 43: 173–93.
Hoppit, J., and Wrigley, E. A. (1994). 'Introduction', in J. Hoppit and E. A. Wrigley (eds.), *The Industrial Revolution in Britain*. Vol. ii in R. A. Church and E. A. Wrigley (eds.), *The Industrial Revolutions*. Oxford: Blackwell, pp. ix–xl.
Hoskins, W. G. (1953). 'The rebuilding of rural England, 1570–1640', *Past and Present*, 4: 44–59.
Jones, E. L. (1981). 'Agriculture, 1700–1780', in R. Floud and D. N. McCloskey (eds.), *The Economic History of Britain since 1700*. Cambridge: Cambridge University Press, i. 66–86.
McCloskey, D. (1994). '1780–1860: a survey', in R. Floud and D. McCloskey (eds.), *The Economic History of Britain since 1700*, i. *1700–1860*. 2nd edn., Cambridge: Cambridge University Press, 242–70.
Machin, R. (1977). 'The great rebuilding: a reassessment', *Past and Present*, 77: 33–56.
McKendrick, N., Brewer, J., and Plumb, J. H. (1982) (eds.). *The Birth of a Consumer Society: The Commercialization of Eighteenth-Century England*. London: Europa.

Maddison, A. (1982). *Phases of Capitalist Development*. Oxford: Oxford University Press.

Mathias, P. (1979). 'The social structure in the eighteenth century: a calculation by Joseph Massie', in P. Mathias, *The Transformation of England: Essays in the Economic and Social History of England in the Eighteenth Century*. London: Methuen, 171–89.

Mitchell, B. R. (1981). *European Historical Statistics 1750–1975*. 2nd rev. edn., London and Basingstoke: Macmillan.

Mitchell, B. R. (1988). *British Historical Statistics*. Cambridge: Cambridge University Press.

Muldrew, C. (1998). *The Economy of Obligation: The Culture of Credit and Social Relations in Early Modern England*. London and Basingstoke: Macmillan.

O'Brien, P. (1982). 'European economic development: the contribution of the periphery', *Economic History Review*, 2nd series, 35: 1–18.

Ormrod, D. (1975). 'Dutch commercial and industrial decline and British growth in the late seventeenth and early eighteenth centuries', in F. Krantz and P. M. Hohenberg (eds.), *Failed Transitions to Modern Industrial Society: Renaissance Italy and Seventeenth-Century Holland*. Montreal: Interuniversity Centre for European Studies, 36–43.

Patten, J. (1979). 'Changing occupational structures in the East Anglian countryside, 1500–1700', in H. S. A. Fox and R. A. Butlin (eds.), *Change in the Countryside*. London: Institute of British Geographers, 103–21.

Phelps Brown, H., and Hopkins, S. V. (1955). 'Seven centuries of building wages', *Economica*, 23: 195–206.

Phelps Brown, H., and Hopkins, S. V. (1956). 'Seven centuries of the prices of consumables', *Economica*, 24: 296–314.

Rappaport, S. (1989). *Worlds Within Worlds: Structures of Life in Sixteenth-Century London*. Cambridge: Cambridge University Press.

Shammas, C. (1990). *The Pre-Industrial Consumer in Britain and America*. Oxford. Clarendon Press.

Smith, R. M. (1988). 'Human resources', in G. Astill and A. Grant (eds.), *The Countryside of Medieval England*. Oxford: Blackwell, 188–212.

Spufford, M. (1984). *The Great Reclothing of Rural England: Petty Chapmen and their Wares in the Seventeenth Century*. London: Hambledon Press.

Stone, R. (1997). 'Gregory King and the development of economic statistics', in R. Stone, *Some British Empiricists in the Social Sciences 1650–1900*. Cambridge: Cambridge University Press, 71–115.

Tawney A. J., and Tawney R. H. (1934). 'An occupational census of the seventeenth century', *Economic History Review*, 5: 25–64.

Thirsk, J. (1978). *Economic Policy and Projects: The Development of a Consumer Society in Early Modern England*. Oxford: Clarendon Press.

Thomas, B. (1985). 'Escaping from constraints: the industrial revolution in a Malthusian context', *Journal of Interdisciplinary History*, 15: 729–53.

Voth, J. (1996). 'Time-Use in eighteenth-century London: Some evidence from the Old Bailey, D.Phil. diss., University of Oxford.

Weatherill, L. (1988). *Consumer Behaviour and Material Culture in England, 1660–1750*. London: Routledge.

Wrigley, E. A. (1986). 'Men on the land and men in the countryside: employment in agriculture in early nineteenth-century England', in L. Bonfield, R. M. Smith, and K. Wrightson (eds.), *The World We Have Gained: Histories of Population and Social Structure*. Oxford: Blackwell, 295–336.

Wrigley, E. A. (1987). 'Urban growth and agricultural change: England and the Continent in the early modern period', in E. A. Wrigley, *People, Cities and Wealth: The Transformation of Traditional Society*. Oxford: Blackwell, 157–93.

Wrigley, E. A., and Schofield, R. S. (1989). *The Population History of England 1541–1871: A Reconstruction*. Paperback edn. with new introd., Cambridge: Cambridge University Press.

Wrigley, E. A., Davies, R. S., Oeppen, J. E. O., and Schofield, R. S. (1997). *English Population History from Family Reconstitution 1580–1837*. Cambridge: Cambridge University Press.

COMMENT

Promethius Prostrated?

John Langton

PROFESSOR Wrigley's neo-Smithian argument that economic growth depends on the subdivision of labour is characteristically rigorous, elegant, and eloquent, and the reinterpretation of the industrial revolution to which he alludes provides a wide and dense mesh of contextual support for it. A model of cumulative consumption-led economic growth through the eighteenth and early nineteenth centuries is superseding the notion of sudden supply-driven technological change based on increased use of mineral fuel and power at the end of the eighteenth century. Adam Smith was even cleverer than we thought: he did not notice an industrial revolution of the latter kind (Wrigley 1987: 38) because no such thing happened. This shift of attention away from Britain's technological dynamism towards consumption and the subdivision of labour has facilitated comparisons with other parts of Europe, which Wrigley (1985) and others (Crafts 1985; Maddison 1982) have used to great interpretative effect. It also corresponds with the neo-Liberal orthodoxy of current economics, and therefore, if only by implication, it carries with it some very strong prescriptions of the kind to which Wrigley alludes in his conclusion.

Some authorities continue to believe that a supply-side driven industrial revolution occurred in England in the late eighteenth and early nineteenth centuries (Mokyr 1990; Landes 1998), and it is always worth pausing for *anamnensis*: to tell ourselves what we already know—not least from the work of Wrigley (1962, 1967, and 1988)—but need continually to be reminded of (Bambrough 1974: 277). I will do this by examining some of the categories used by Wrigley, and more generally in quantitative economic history of this kind. 'Entitation is more important than quantification: only when the right things have been found to be measured are measurements worthwhile' (Gerard 1964: 120–1). To throw economic categories across time and space in order to measure historical changes and geographical differences assumes that constant or congruent economic systems existed to contain them. If this were not so, then the numbers registered must mean different things at different times and in different places, and their explanatory significance is dubious. I will deal in turn with some of the analytical entities whose historical constancy or geographical congruence in early modern times seems to me to be questionable.

THE AGRICULTURAL SECTOR

Peasantry is not the same as commercial farming. Wrigley shows great ingenuity in dealing with the consequences of this disjunction for his argument. However, in fact, it completely vitiates all measures that purport to chart the progress of agricultural efficiency through time, or its differences across Europe in the early modern period. Peasants were jacks-of-all-trades who produced for themselves, in domestic and communal groups, most of what they consumed (Hoppe and Langton 1994; Langton 1996 and 1998). They sold little except for the products of bi-employments on which their subsistence did not depend, and bought even less. The surplus produced beyond their own requirements rarely amounted to 30 per cent of total output. It was taken through command as rents, taxes, tithes, tolls, and so on. Markets only operated to redistribute the surplus amongst the small sector of society who abstracted and circulated it. Amongst themselves peasants operated a 'moral' economy in which exchanges of commodities and factors of production followed social obligations. More than 70 per cent of their outputs moved, therefore, in a 'hidden economy', impenetrable by the measuring instruments normally used to quantify economic activity (Boqvist 1978).

The number of occupationally specialized farm labourers cannot be compared with the number of peasants per unit of area or of marketed output to measure agricultural productivity. On the one hand, farm labourers often depended on supplements to their wages from poor relief, which increased by 1 per cent per annum between 1782 and 1834, partially levied from the non-farming sector (Boyer 1990). And surely their pitiful wages—which bought in 1830 only half as much bread and one-quarter as much beer as in 1732 (Dyck 1992: 135)—long periods of idleness, and dependence on welfare hardly suggest economic efficiency (to say nothing of distributional equity) in the system that produced this degree of labour specialization? On the other hand, peasants produced many other things than food crops: their number cannot be used to measure the labour expended in the 'agricultural sector' of an economy. The pastor of Mora in northern Sweden told a visitor in 1857 that his peasant parishioners 'wander all over Europe to sell their little wares—hair chains, bracelets and watches. There are about 2,000 now absent from my parish. They go to Russia and Italy, even to England' (Brace 1857: 179–80). They produced craft goods, transported, and marketed them—plus some of the iron on which Swedish national income depended, and the ore, charcoal, and haulage required in its production—as well as crops for their own consumption and sale. Given that all this is hidden in 'agriculture' in the labour force statistics of econometric historians, it is not surprising that peasant economies seem completely dominated by that activity. Given that the other enterprises took labour away from crop production, it is hardly surprising that peasants' agricultural output per head was less than that of specialized English farm labourers. Or that (with the usual sleight of hand: the comparison is never with farm labourers) English commercial farmers lived at a higher standard on large holdings worked by abject hirelings than European peasants on much smaller holdings worked entirely by themselves (Allen and O Grada 1988). The specialization (that is, the proletarianization) of farm labour tells us more about changes in the distribution of the wealth created by English agriculture than about changes in its amount (Allen 1992).

Peasants operated in 'ecosystem economies' (Klee 1980) where nearly everyone was dependent upon the vegetable outputs of their localities for food and raw materials because transportation systems were generally of low capacity, expensive, and unreliable. The labour of nearly everybody was *necessarily*, therefore, applied to both agriculture *and* industry (Postel-Vinay 1994). As Wrigley says, the harvest was paramount. In addition, before the use of mineral fuel and power in production, transportation, and communication, societies were subject to the iron limits of what elsewhere Wrigley (1994: 33) felicitously called 'the photosynthetic constraint'. There was insufficient energy for production and transportation to allow continuous large-scale manufacturing, and therefore for labour to specialize in discrete roles within it. Coal removed that constraint: only one four-hundredth of the energy released is consumed in the process of its production, a further sixth in moving it to where it is consumed (Odum and Odum 1976: 52). The amount of energy available per head trebled as population more than doubled in Europe in the nineteenth century (Cook 1971). Only then did the choice between working in agriculture *or* industry become available (Postel-Vinay 1994). There could not be an 'agricultural sector' before then. The categorical insistence that there was ignores most of the output of peasant economies, and simply assumes what needs to be explained.

PRIMARY, SECONDARY, AND TERTIARY SECTORS, AND THEIR RELATIONSHIP TO URBANIZATION

Wrigley's image of the peopling of land as a series of successively more clumped layers, with primary production giving a thin veneer that was interspersed with dense patches of people in towns dependent on secondary and tertiary economic activities, is elegant and evocative. Like all striking metaphors, it is also misleading. This is not because most secondary and tertiary activities could not be separated from primary production in order to become spatially clustered in peasant economies: that is his argument. It is because primary production itself became spatially concentrated when coal came into use. Large relatively specialized settlements could be sustained by mining, especially after locomotives and marine steam engines allowed coal to be used in its own transportation. In 1851 the census registration district of Auckland contained 30,083 people, with 39 per cent of the occupied males of 20 years old or more employed in coal mining. In Durham the total population was 55,951, with 35 per cent in mining; Tynemouth had 64,248 and 28 per cent; Wigan 77,539 and 26 per cent; Abergavenny 59,229 and 25 per cent; Merthyr Tydfil 76,805 and 23 per cent. Wigan and Merthyr Tydfil each housed more than 5,000 coal miners and their (generally very large) families, whilst in much less populous registration districts like Easington (5,604), Chester-le-Street (5,437), and Houghton-le-Spring (5,037) coal miners accounted for well over half of the employed adult males. As Wrigley says, mining shares some characteristics with secondary production, notably the clustering of population directly supported by it. This meant that 'urbanization' did not necessarily reflect increased secondary and tertiary economic activity. The neat link between economic sectors and population distribution patterns and densities was shattered by the use of mineral fuel.

On the other hand, secondary activities using abundant energy became clustered at the points where that energy was most cheaply available. Hence the much lower percentages employed in coal mining itself in industrializing districts like Wigan and Merthyr Tydfil than in Durham pit villages that exported coal. Food and fuel derived from organic sources are sparsely produced per unit of land area and bulky in relation to their value. City populations dependent on manufacturing and services could not grow much beyond 100,000 (Bairoch 1988: 14), nor could cities be grouped in geographical space, except where waterways made food and vegetable fuel cheaply accessible over long distances. The use of coal changed this, and Adam Smith recognized that already by the 1760s 'all over Great Britain manufactures have confined themselves principally to the coal countries', even though he misinterpreted the reason for it (Wrigley 1987: 38). The urge to benefit from the internal economies of scale allowed by the availability of effectively limitless fuel and power in particular places was the most potent stimulus to technological innovation in manufacturing industry (Marshall 1966: 219–20). Factory production and the proletarianization it precipitated impelled further spatial clustering of population. So did the development of external economies of scale by related secondary and tertiary processes that were no longer kept apart by competition for scarce supplies of fuel and power. 'The locomotive . . . virtually reduced England to a sixth of its size' (Smiles 1904: p. vii). 'Probably more than three-fourths of the whole benefit [Britain] has derived from the progress of manufactures during the nineteenth century has been through its indirect influences in lowering the cost of transport of men and goods, of water and light, of electricity and news' (Marshall 1966: 561). Access to wider markets and sources of raw material supplies and services allowed large-scale industries to cluster together where fuel was cheap alongside complementary economic activities. Technological change was driven ever faster by the cumulative growth of these industrial districts and by reciprocation between them (Pred 1973; Scott 1985 and 1988).

It seems most likely that British urban growth in the eighteenth and nineteenth centuries was uniquely quick and extensive because the British economy of the time was uniquely well equipped to harness mineral fuel and power in manufacturing and communication (Langton 2000*b*, 2000*d*). Coal output increased tenfold between 1700 and 1830, from half a ton to 2 tons per head of population (Daunton 1995: 219, 391; Wrigley 1962: 78). In 1850 Britain produced 80 per cent of Europe's coal (Pounds 1979: 335). Just as mineral-based towns had a different economic *raison d'être* from those of earlier times, so their proletarian majorities and dominant but aetiolated middle classes had different social, institutional, and cultural characteristics (Langton 2000*d*). At the same time, industrial settlements based on water power, coal, and other point-based resources were emerging thick and fast in many parts of the countryside, as in the Durham census registration districts mentioned earlier. To classify population into the binary groups of 'urban' and 'rural' is the same kind of categorical conflation as lumping peasants and farm labourers into 'agriculture' (Langton and Hoppe 1983).

What Wrigley (1988) diagnosed as the transition from organic to energy rich economy utterly changed the nature of the primary sector, altered its relationships with secondary and tertiary sectors, and created in consequence completely new economic bases for, and topographical expressions of, both towns and countrysides. Because what these categories comprised changed so radically historically and varied so fundamentally geographically, differences in their measured sizes are chimerical.

STATES AS SPATIAL ENTITIES

The processes set in motion by the increased use of mineral fuel did not simply shrink geographical space. They also made it much more variegated. In peasant economies geographical differences in energy consumption per head could not exceed the 20:1 difference between the natural productivity of the Earth's biomes (Odum and Odum 1976): in 1980, with mineral energy surging through the biosphere, the difference was 1,162:1 (*Times Atlas of the World* 1980: pp. xx–xxi). The geographical patterning of the increasing variety of economic and demographic growth precipitated by this shift was determined by location relative to coalfields, cheap transportation routes, and dynamic industrial complexes, and with linkages to particular overseas markets and sources of supply. There are compelling theoretical reasons to believe that these increasing geographical differences would be expressed at the interregional, rather than international, scale: that regions trade with each other, not states, and that once a mesh of trading connections has been established regions are 'locked into' trajectories with powerful historical continuities (Krugman 1991, 1995; David 1993; Leibowitz and Margolis 1995).

That is what happened in Britain through the eighteenth and nineteenth centuries. Maps showing increased regional concentration and specialization in the British economy through the nineteenth century are commonplace. They show the rapidly ramifying and differentiating growth of manufacturing and related service activities in the energy rich economy of the coalfields, London, and some other ports, and comparatively little change in the organic economy of what had been Britain's agrarian heartland (Langton and Morris 1986). Between 1806 and 1860/1 the percentage of the national total of business income taxes paid by residents of Lancashire and Yorkshire increased from 11 per cent to 23 per cent as London's share fell from 40 per cent to 27 per cent (Rubinstein 1993: 26). The geography of population growth reflected this convulsion of economic geography. In 1701 three groups of counties each 'accounted for about a third of the population of England and Wales, but by 1831 the share of the industrial and commercial group had risen to 45 per cent, while that of the agricultural counties had fallen to 26 per cent' (Deane and Cole 1962: 104). In Kent, Surrey, Warwickshire, Monmouthshire, Cheshire, Lancashire, and the West Riding of Yorkshire population more than trebled, whilst in half of the counties, all of them except for Westmorland south of a line between the Tees and the Severn, it did not double (Deane and Cole 1962: 103). Estimated country rates of annual natural increase between 1701 and 1750 ranged from −10.8 to 9.7 around a national average of 1.1, and between 1801 and 1830 from 4.4 to 20.5 around a national average of 14.3 (Deane and Cole 1962: 115). These contrasting rates of growth were echoed by distribution patterns. Nineteen of the twenty fastest growing towns in Britain between the 1660s and 1801 were located on or near to coalfields, fifteen between 1801 and 1841; twenty of Britain's fifty biggest towns were on and near coalfields in 1801, thirty-five by 1841. The population increase of Manchester alone was greater than the aggregate increase of all the resorts spawned by increased consumerism in southern and coastal England between 1801 and 1841 (Langton 2000*b*: 479–80).

When these massive variations in economic and demographic changes between one part of the country and another are recognized, statistical trends that are deeply puzzling when plotted as national aggregates or averages begin to make sense. Mushrooming statutory poor relief payments did not accompany industrialization, but were confined to the organic economy of the south and east (Levitt 1986; King 2000). Perhaps the great ingenuity deployed to reconcile rising rates of population growth with falling estimates of national average real income per head (Wrigley and Schofield 1981) is misplaced. Regional statistics show real wages increasing by 20 per cent between 1750 and 1800 in north-western England, where industry and population were growing fastest, as the national average fell by 60 per cent (von Tunzelmann 1979). When price statistics are also adjusted for regional differences in consumption patterns, they yield a doubling of the real wages of colliers and potters in north Staffordshire between 1775 and 1790 (Botham and Hunt 1987). Industrialization did not bring falling standards of living for the workers supported by it, whatever nationally aggregated averages might suggest.

Massive regional disparities were not produced by spatial sorting in a unitary economic system: to a significant extent each region had its own, different, path-dependent dynamic, operating semi-independently from those of other regions and from nationwide influences (Langton 1984). This was important for the way that Britain was peopled during the industrial revolution. Liverpool grew faster than any other British city in the eighteenth and early nineteenth centuries. Its population increased from about 1,210 at the end of the seventeenth century, when it was the 257th biggest town in Britain, to 92,295 in 1801 and 286,487 in 1841, when at both dates it was Britain's third ranking city (Langton 2000*b*: 474). Its growth seems to have been unconnected with the organic economies of southern and eastern England, or London, or Europe. In 1753 it was linked to north-western England by 9 carriers per week and 80 sloops, to the Irish Sea basin by 125 vessels, to North America and the West Indies by 106 vessels, and to Africa by 88 vessels. Not a single stagecoach left the town for London, Manchester, or any other place; only 4 carriers a week left for London, and only 28 vessels plied between Liverpool and the whole of continental Europe (Baines 1852: 418). In 1764, 66 per cent of its shipping contacts were with Ireland, Bristol, and the Isle of Man, 19 per cent with North America, Greenland, and the Northern Fishery, and only 15 per cent with all other destinations (Bristol was the only English port to be recorded) (Liverpool Record Office, H Q942 721 ENF). At the end of the eighteenth century only 6 per cent of Liverpool's inland waterway connections extended outside Lancashire and Cheshire, mostly to the Potteries (Langton 1983). The origins of its immigrants reflected this pattern of economic contacts. Only 55 of the 635 apprentices registered from 1707 to 1757 originated in counties which were not adjacent to the Irish Sea, the north coast of Ireland, or the western Scottish coast as far as the Orkneys. Thirty-eight of the 55 came from inland counties neighbouring Lancashire and Cheshire. Of the remaining 17, 4 came from London—no more than were supplied by Lisbon, the Gambia, Jamaica, and Virginia (Liverpool Record Office, 352 CLE/REG/4/1). In 1801 'the number of Welch . . . is estimated at 6,000, who occupy entire neighbourhoods, where scarce a word of English is spoken' (Moss 1801: 153). Already by 1767 there was a significant proportion of Irish names among its Catholic population (Worrall 1980), which was greatly increased after the Irish uprising of 1798.

Liverpool's exceptionally rapid growth, the preponderance of casual humping and hauling jobs in its labour market, and its Irish Sea connections, gave its population a unique ethnic and cultural complexion. Most industrial regions, even that immediately inland on the south-west Lancashire coalfield, depended far less on long-distance migration. Control over the recruitment of fresh employees by workers meant that immigrants were generally both unwelcome and marginalized as jobs were protected for neighbours and kinsfolk (King 1997; Langton 2000*a*, 2000*c*). Of 4,471 moves recorded in a sample of longitudinal migration records for Lancashire 1750–1879, 77.0 were within the county, and only 14.6 and 8.4 per cent, respectively, into and out of it (Pooley and Turnbull 1998: 80). There was far less genetic mixing of population or relief of overpopulated farming areas in the south and east than geographically differentiated growth rates might lead us to expect. Almost the whole stimulus of economic growth in particular regions was projected narrowly on to the populations of those regions, bringing far bigger falls in age at marriage and increases in birth rates than would have been produced if it had been more widely disseminated (Langton 2000*a*, 2000*c*). There was not a national economy or population, nor singular (or even coherent) national economic or demographic trends, but numerous regional economies and populations, each with their own peculiar and more or less independent dynamics (Hudson and King 2000).

CONCLUSION

All economic measurements 'identify the *components* of a system, and the *interactions* operating on these . . . Such a model . . . can only be correct for as *long as the structure of the system remains unchanged* . . . until . . . there is an adaptation or innovation, and new behaviour emerges' to change the nature of the categories within the system (Allen 1997: 4–5). This is what happened in the industrial revolution as a result of the increasing use of mineral fuel and power. The content of some of the entities defined for the purpose of measurement changed fundamentally, and so did the ways in which they interacted. Worse than that: the economic categories appropriate to the pre-industrial economy disappeared to be replaced by completely new ones. To call them by the same names is an analytical convenience that disguises some things in order to reveal others. Of course, this would be true of any set of categories imposed on the past in order to understand how change occurs. All lights cast shadows and the brighter the light the blacker the shadow. Projecting measurements across the industrial revolution in order to apply current neo-Liberal economic theories hides completely some other important contemporary concerns. A fundamental transformation in the relationship between human beings and the natural world; the end of peasantry, the *emergence* of the current socio-economic structures (and problems) of specialized cities and countrysides, and the *birth* of interaction between regional economies in a global system are not negligible omissions. Their projection into the future through policies derived from looking at the past through these categories has already helped to destroy peasantry, natural environment, food security, and local democracy across great swaths of the globe (Polanyi 1957; Davis 2001). Perhaps, as has often been said, the only lesson of history should be that it has no lesson—simply because it is a procession of continually changing and always contestable categories (Perlin 1994).

REFERENCES

Allen, P. M. (1997). *Cities and Regions as Self-organizing Systems: Models of Complexity*. Amsterdam: OPA.

Allen, R. C. (1992). *Enclosure and the Yeoman: The Agricultural Development of the South Midlands 1450–1850*. Oxford: Clarendon Press.

Allen, R. C., and O Grada, C. (1988). 'On the road again with Arthur Young: English, Irish and French agriculture during the industrial revolution', *Journal of Economic History*, 38: 93–116.

Baines, T. (1852). *History of the Commerce and Town of Liverpool and of the Rise of Manufacturing Industry in the Adjoining Counties*. London and Liverpool: Longman, Green, Brown and Longman.

Bairoch, P. (1988). *Cities and Economic Development from the Dawn of History to the Present*. London: Mansell Publishing.

Bambrough, R. (1974). *Wisdom: Twelve Essays*. Oxford: Blackwell.

Boqvist, A. (1978). *Den Dolda Ekonomin: en Etnologisk Studie av Näringsstrukturen i Bollebygd 1850–1950*. Lund: Lund University Press.

Botham, F. W., and Hunt, E. H. (1987). 'Wages in Britain during the industrial revolution', *Economic History Review*, 2nd series, 40: 380–99.

Boyer, G. R. (1990). *An Economic History of the English Poor Law, 1750–1850*. Cambridge: Cambridge University Press.

Brace, C. L. (1857). *The Norse Folk: Or Visits to the Homes of Norway and Sweden*. London: Richard Bentley.

Cook, E. (1971). 'The flow of energy in an industrial society', *Scientific American*, 225: 135–45.

Crafts, N. F. R. (1985). *British Economic Growth during the Industrial Revolution*. Oxford: Clarendon Press.

Daunton, M. J. (1995). *Progress and Poverty: An Economic and Social History of Britain 1700–1850*. Oxford: Oxford University Press.

David, P. (1993). 'Historical economics in the long run: some implications of path-dependence', in G. D. Snooks (ed.), *Historical Analysis in Economics*. London: Routledge, 29–40.

Davis, M. (2001). *Late Victorian Holocausts: El Niño Famines and the Making of the Third World*. London: Verso Books.

Deane, P., and Cole, W. A. (1962). *British Economic Growth 1688–1959: Trends and Structure*. Cambridge: Cambridge University Press.

Dyck, I. (1992). *William Cobbett and Rural Popular Culture*. Cambridge: Cambridge University Press.

Gerard, R. W. (1964). 'Entitation, animorgs and other systems', in M. D. Mesarovic (ed.), *Views on General Systems Theory*. New York: Wiley, 119–24.

Hoppe, G., and Langton, J. (1994). *Peasantry to Capitalism: Western Östergötland in the Nineteenth Century*. Cambridge: Cambridge University Press.

Hudson, P., and King, S. (2000). 'Two textile townships, *c.*1660–1820: a comparative demographic analysis', *Economic History Review*, 53: 706–41.

King, S. (1997). 'Migrants on the margin? Mobility, integration and occupations in the West Riding, 1650–1820', *Journal of Historical Geography*, 23: 284–303.

King, S. (2000). *Poverty and Welfare in England, 1700–1850: A Regional Perspective*. Manchester: Manchester University Press.

Klee, G. A. (1980). *World Systems of Traditional Resource Management*. London: Edward Arnold.

Krugman, P. R. (1991). *Geography and Trade*. Cambridge, Mass.: MIT Press.

Krugman, P. R. (1995). *Development, Geography and Economic Theory*. Cambridge, Mass.: MIT Press.

Landes, D. S. (1998). *The Wealth and Poverty of Nations: Why Some Are So Rich and Some So Poor*. London: Little, Brown and Company.

Langton, J. (1983). 'Liverpool and its hinterland in the late eighteenth century', in B. L. Anderson and P. J. M. Stoney (eds.), *Commerce, Industry and Transport: Studies in Economic Change on Merseyside*. Liverpool: Liverpool University Press.

Langton, J. (1984). 'The industrial revolution and the regional geography of England', *Transactions of the Institute of British Geographers*, NS 9: 146–67.

Langton, J. (1996). 'The origins of the capitalist world economy', in I. Douglas, R. Huggett, and M. Robinson (eds.), *Companion Encyclopedia of Geography: The Environment and Humankind*. London: Routledge, 206–27.

Langton, J. (1998). 'Conclusion: the historical geography of European peasantries, 1400–1800', in T. Scott (ed.), *The Peasantries of Europe from the Fourteenth to the Eighteenth Centuries*. London: Longman, 372–400.

Langton, J. (2000*a*). 'People from the pits: the origins of colliers in eighteenth-century southwest Lancashire', in D. R. Siddle (ed.), *Migration and Mobility in Early Modern Europe*. Liverpool: Liverpool University Press, 70–89.

Langton, J. (2000*b*). 'Urban growth and economic change from the seventeenth century to 1841', in P. Clark (ed.), *Cambridge Urban History of Britain*, ii. Cambridge: Cambridge University Press, 253–90.

Langton, J. (2000*c*). 'The geography of proletarianization in the industrial revolution: regionalism and kinship in the labour markets of the British coal industry from the seventeenth to the nineteenth centuries', *Transactions of the Institute of British Geographers*, NS 25: 31–49.

Langton, J. (2000*d*). 'Town growth and urbanization in the Midlands from the 1660s to 1841', in J. Stobart and P. Lane (eds.), *Urban and Industrial Change in the Midlands 1700–1840*. Leicester: Centre for Urban History, 7–47.

Langton, J., and Hoppe, G. (1983). *Town and Country in the Development of Early Modern Western Europe*. Norwich: Historical Geography Research Series, 11.

Langton, J., and Morris, R. J. (1986) (eds.). *Atlas of Industrializing Britain 1780–1914*. London: Methuen.

Leibowitz, S. J., and Margolis, S. E. (1995). 'Path-dependence, lock-in and history', *Journal of Law, Economics and Organisations*, 11: 205–26.

Levitt, I. (1986). 'Poor law and pauperism', in J. Langton and R. J. Morris (eds.), *Atlas of Industrializing Britain 1780–1914*. London: Methuen, 160–3.

Maddison, A. (1982). *Phases of Capitalist Development*. Oxford: Oxford University Press.

Marshall, A. (1890; 1966). *Principles of Economics*. 6th edn., London: Macmillan.

Mokyr, J. (1990). *The Lever of Riches: Technological Creativity and Economic Progress*. Oxford: Oxford University Press.

Moss, W. (1801). *The Liverpool Guide*. 4th edn., Liverpool: W. Jones.

Odum, H. T., and Odum, E. L. (1976). *Energy Basis for Man and Nature*. New York: McGraw-Hill.

Perlin, F. (1994). *Unbroken Landscape: Commodity, Category, Sign and Identity: Their Production as Myth and Knowledge from 1550*. Aldershot: Variorum.

Polanyi, K. (1957). *The Great Transformation: The Political and Economic Origins of our Time*. Boston: Beacon Press.

Pooley, C., and Turnbull, J. (1998). *Migration and Mobility in Britain since the Eighteenth Century*. London: UCL Press.
Postel-Vinay, G. (1994). 'The dis-integration of traditional labour markets in France: from agriculture *and* industry to agriculture *or* industry', in G. Grantham and M. MacKinnon (eds.), *Labour Market Evolution: The Economic History of Market Integration, Wage Flexibility and the Employment Relation*. London: Routledge, 64–83.
Pounds, N. J. G. (1979). *An Historical Geography of Europe 1500–1840*. Cambridge: Cambridge University Press.
Pred, A. (1973). *Urban Growth and the Circulation of Information: The United States System of Cities 1790–1840*. Cambridge, Mass.: Harvard University Press.
Rubinstein, W. D. (1993). *Capitalism, Culture and Decline in Britain 1750–1990*. London: Routledge.
Scott, A. J. (1985). 'Location processes, urbanization and territorial development: an exploratory essay', *Environment and Planning*, series A, 17: 479–501.
Scott, A. J. (1988). *Metropolis: From the Division of Labour to Urban Form*. Berkeley: University of California Press.
Smiles, S. (1857; 1904). *The Life of George Stephenson, Railway Engineer*. 4th edn., London: Murray.
The Times Atlas of the World (1980). London: Times Publishing Company.
von Tunzelmann, G. N. (1979). 'Trends in real wages, 1750–1850: revisited', *Economic History Review*, 2nd series, 32: 33–49.
Worrall, E. S. (1980). *Returns of Papists in 1767: Diocese of Chester*. London: Catholic Record Society Occasional Papers 1.
Wrigley, E. A. (1962). 'The supply of raw materials in the industrial revolution', *Economic History Review*, 2nd series, 15: 1–16.
Wrigley, E. A. (1967). 'A simple model of London's importance in changing English society and economy, 1650–1750', *Past and Present*, 37: 44–70.
Wrigley, E. A. (1985). 'Urban growth and agricultural change: England and the Continent in the early modern period', *Journal of Interdisciplinary History*, 15: 683–728.
Wrigley, E. A. (1987). *People, Cities and Wealth: The Transformation of Traditional Society*. Oxford: Blackwell.
Wrigley, E. A. (1988). *Continuity, Chance and Change: The Character of the Industrial Revolution in England*. Cambridge: Cambridge University Press.
Wrigley, E. A. (1994). 'The classical economists, the stationary state, and the industrial revolution', in G. D. Snooks (ed.), *Was the Industrial Revolution Necessary?* London: Routledge, 27–42.
Wrigley, E. A., and Schofield, R. S. (1981). *The Population History of England 1541–1871: A Reconstruction*. London: Edward Arnold.

8

Empire, the Economy, and Immigration

Britain 1850–2000

Ceri Peach

To survey the changes in British population between 1850 and 2000 requires some large-scale generalizations. At the beginning of my period, Britain had an empire that held a quarter of the world's population, but by the end of the period Britain had become part of the European Union and contained one-sixth of the Union's population. For the first hundred years of the period, Britain was exporting its population to the empire; for the last fifty years, the empire had struck back.

The last 150 years have seen huge transformations of the British economy. There has been a shift from agriculture to industry and from industry to services. Coal production rose from 50 million tons in the middle of the nineteenth century to 300 million tons in 1913. By 1999 it had returned to below its 1851 level. Mining scarred the landscape of all the coalfields. Oil production rose from none in 1970 to about 128 million tonnes in 1997, but left hardly a mark on settlement. The steel industry rose and fell. In 1860 there was no crude steel produced (Mitchell 1975: 399). By 1960 25 million tons were produced and now it is down to about half that level.

The United Kingdom has undergone the demographic transition. The population rose from 10 million in 1801 to 38 million in 1901 to 59 million now. Six million more people have left the United Kingdom than have entered it since 1851. A tide, from the beginning of the twentieth century, has swept the rural population into the biggest cities until the post-1950 backwash has scattered it out to suburbia, exurbia, and market towns. Urbanization has been followed by suburbanization; suburbanization by counter-urbanization. The Fordist system of mass production produced the Fordist city of mass-produced housing design, the Victorian, terraced inner city. The post-Fordist era hollowed out the inner cities and produced the green belts, the new towns, and the scatter of light industry. The new international division of labour squeezed the manufacturing employment of the country out to the third world. At the same time, third world population has been drawn into the country to fill the jobs which became unattractive to the native population. Into the gaps in our largest cities came the new waves of immigrants from the former empire. Britain changed from an exclusive imperial power to a multicultural society. The landscape carries the marks of all these changes. The uplands have lost much of their population. The old industrial regions are the unburied dead of the industrial revolutions.

The period falls into two. The first is from 1850 to 1950 (or to the end of the Second World War). The second comprises the second half of the twentieth century. The first period is one of rapid natural increase, rural to urban movement, and massive emigration. The second is one of relatively gentle population increase, counter-urbanization, and immigration.

POPULATION INCREASE

Between 1851 and 1996, the population of the United Kingdom grew from 22 to 59 million (Table 8.1). Of the 59 million, 57 million lived in Great

TABLE 8.1. *Population of the United Kingdom, 1851–1996 (000s)*

Year	England	Wales	Scotland	Northern Ireland	Great Britain	United Kingdom
1851	16,765	1,163	2,889	1,442	20,817	22,259
1901	30,515	2,013	4,472	1,237	37,000	38,237
1911	33,649	2,421	4,761	1,251	40,831	42,082
1921	35,231	2,656	4,862	1,258	42,749	44,007
1931	37,359	2,593	4,843	1,243	44,795	46,038
1951	41,159	2,599	5,096	1,371	48,854	50,225
1961	43,461	2,644	5,179	1,425	51,284	52,709
1971	46,412	2,740	5,236	1,540	54,388	55,928
1981	46,821	2,813	5,180	1,538	54,814	56,352
1991	48,209	2,891	5,107	1,601	56,207	57,808
1996	49,089	2,921	5,128	1,663	57,138	58,801

Note: Enumerated population 1851–1996; resident mid-year population estimate, 1971–1996.

Source: *Annual Abstract of Statistics 1997*. See Mitchell 1975.

Britain; 49 million lived in England, 5 million in Scotland, 3 million in Wales, and 1.6 million in Northern Ireland (Table 8.1). England's share of the UK population grew from 75 per cent in 1851 to 83 per cent in 1996. While the population of England tripled over this period and the population of Wales increased 2.5 times and Scotland's nearly doubled, the population of Northern Ireland hardly changed.

At the beginning of the period, the United Kingdom included the whole of Ireland. The partition of Ireland into the Irish Free State and Northern Ireland took place in 1922. The figures presented for the United Kingdom before this event have been adjusted, as far as possible, to refer to only that part of Ireland that remained in the United Kingdom.

However, although the Southern Irish figures are excluded, the tragedy of the Irish potato famine of 1846 and the collapse of the Irish population, from a peak of 8.2 million in 1841 to 4.5 million, or almost half its 1841 figure, by 1901, must be recognized. Ireland's population has remained near that figure for most of the twentieth century. Part of this staggering decrease was due to the famine, which killed 1 million people. Part was due to the massive emigration. Between 1851 and 1911, 4,191,552 people emigrated from Ireland (Thomas 1954: 74; Census of Ireland 1913: lix).

Most of the growth of the UK population in the nineteenth century came from natural increase. Britain was one of the first countries to experience the demographic transition. Yet the British transition looks rather puny in relation to the transitions since experienced in the developing world. In some third world countries, crude birth rates of 40 per 1,000 were experienced and crude death rates of 10 per 1,000 giving a rate of natural increase of 30 per 1,000 or 3 per cent per annum which would produce a doubling of the population in twenty-three years. Kenya, for example, has a growth rate of 4 per cent per annum, giving a doubling time of seventeen years. The gap in England and Wales between CBR and CDR never exceeded 1.6 per cent per annum (Coleman and Salt 1992: 75).

GEOGRAPHICAL CHANGES

Not only did the total population of the United Kingdom increase, but it was marked by a series of remarkable geographic transformations. Between 1801 and 1911, the country changed from rural to urban (Table 8.2). In 1801 the population was one-third urban; by 1851 it was over half urban and by 1911 it had reached an urban saturation point of nearly 80 per cent. It has continued at this level ever since. At the same time, the urban population became progressively concentrated into the largest conurbations. In 1801, just over a tenth of the population of England and Wales

TABLE 8.2. *Urban populations in England and Wales, 1801–1911*

Census year	Total population (millions)	Percentage change	Percentage of total	Percentage of total population in towns of			
				<10,000	10–50,000	50–100,000	>100,000
1801	8.9		33.8	9.9	9.5	3.5	11.0
1811	10.2	14.0	36.6	10.8	8.4	3.7	13.7
1821	12.0	18.1	40.0	11.0	9.2	4.3	15.6
1831	13.9	15.8	44.3	10.6	11.1	4.0	18.6
1841	15.9	14.3	48.3	10.0	12.1	5.5	20.7
1851	17.9	12.6	54.0	9.9	13.4	5.8	24.8
1861	20.1	11.9	58.7	9.8	14.1	6.1	28.8
1871	22.7	13.2	65.2	10.8	16.2	5.6	32.6
1881	25.9	14.7	70.0	10.5	16.0	7.3	36.2
1891	29.0	11.6	74.5	10.2	16.2	8.6	39.4
1901	32.5	12.2	78.0	8.9	18.0	7.4	43.6
1911	36.1	10.9	78.9	8.8	18.3	8.0	43.8

Source: Lawton 1983: table 1, 182.

lived in towns that were over 100,000. By 1911, nearly half of the population of England and Wales lived in such cities.

The motor of these changes was the developing industrial revolution in Britain. But there was not one revolution but several. They were marked by changes in the source of power from water to coal, to grid-generated electricity. They were marked by successive shifts from resource-based locations on the coalfields to market-based locations for manufacturing in the Midlands and service-based locations in the south. Over the course of the period 1850 to the present, the country's population centre of gravity moved from the south and east of the Tees–Exe line to the north and west of the country and then back again.

KONDRATIEFF CYCLES

All these processes have been powered by economic change. Even if we do not subscribe wholeheartedly to the theory, Kondratieff's cycles are a neat heuristic way in which we can envisage and model the processes (Table 8.3). To summarize, the Russian economist Kondratieff envisaged that development since the beginning of the industrial revolution, placed at about 1790, took place in a series of 55-year cycles, each powered by a particular technological innovation (Hall and Preston 1988).

Each of the Kondratieff cycles had specific geographical requirements. That of Kondratieff I (1787–1845) was water power, shifting to coal power. Kondratieff II (1846–95) was coal powered and approached the peak of coalfield development (although 1913 was its true apogee). Kondratieff III (1896–1947) was electricity powered and saw a shift from the peripheral coalfields to more central market locations in the Midlands and the south-east. Kondratieff IV was market and environmentally dominated. It saw a shift to the south-east, the M4 corridor, away from the major conurbations towards smaller free-standing market towns and rural areas, but still within the ambit of large cities. Places such as Witney, Thame, or Abingdon in the Oxford region, for example, would fit into this category.

These changes in the industrial base are mirrored in the changing occupational structure of the workforce (see Wrigley's chapter in this volume). In 1851, agriculture and fishing still provided work for about 30 per cent of the male labour force, but at the end of our period for only about 2 per cent. Extractive industries (largely coal mining) employed nearly a million men in 1901, but a tenth of that number by the 1990s (Mitchell 1975: 163; *Annual Abstract of Statistics 1998*). Manufacturing reached its peak of male employment in 1951 when it occupied over 6 million men and about 40 per cent of the labour force. But after the inflation of the 1970s and the ravages

TABLE 8.3. *Kondratieff long cycles in Britain*

Dates	Motive power	Key innovation	Key industries	British geography	Overseas geography
Kondratieff I 1787–1845	Water	Power loom, iron puddling	Cotton and woollen textiles, iron	Lancashire, West Riding, Yorkshire, Peak District	British dominance
Kondratieff II 1846–95	Coal	Bessemer steel steamships	Steel, machine tools, ships, railways	South Wales, Scotland, Durham, Northumberland	British dominance giving way to German and US challenge
Kondratieff III 1896–1947	Grid electricity, coal powered	Alternating current, electric light, automobile	Cars, electrical engineering, chemicals	Midlands	US, British, and German leadership
Kondratieff IV 1948–2000	Grid electricity, coal, gas, petroleum, and nuclear fuelled	Transistor, computer, IT	Electronics, computers, communications, aerospace, producer services	South-east, M4 corridor	American hegemony, Japanese challenge

Source: Hall and Preston 1988: 21.

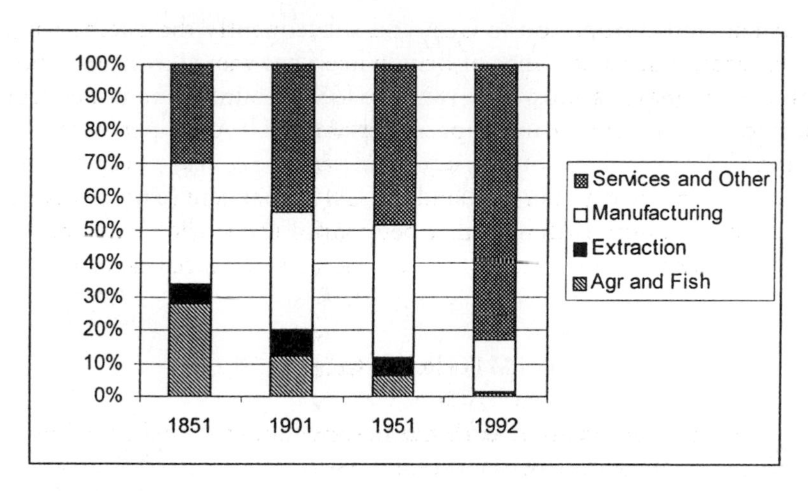

FIG. 8.1 Male occupational change in Great Britain, 1851–1992.

Source: Mitchell 1975: 163; *Annual Abstract of Statistics 1998*.

of globalization of competition in the 1980s and 1990s its share fell to less than 20 per cent by 1992 (Figure 8.1). Finally, we see the inexorable rise of the service industries, now accounting for over 80 per cent of the male labour force.

IMPACT ON LANDSCAPE: SLASH AND BURN INDUSTRIALIZATION

The impact of each of these Kondratieff cycles was to alter radically the population geography of Great Britain. The march of the Kondratieffs is visible on the map of England and Wales (Lawton 1983: 183) showing the date at which regions of England and Wales achieved their peak population increases between 1801 and 1911. We can see the first three waves as a kind of industrial slash and burn economy, each despoiling its environment then moving on, leaving a burnt-out industrial wasteland in its wake (see for example Hoskins's (1955: 171) comments on St Helen's). We may regard each of the Kondratieff cycles as the successive stages of rockets which propelled the British economy into orbit, but, having achieved lift-off, they remain as so much decaying space detritus around the country.

While the first two Kondratieffs had a British epicentre albeit in different parts of Britain, the subsequent Kondratieffs have marched westwards from Britain and Europe to the USA and subsequently the Pacific Rim. Thus, the economic importance of Britain itself has waned over this time. As Brinley Thomas has shown, in 1870 the UK accounted for 32 per cent of the world's manufacturing capacity and the USA 23 per cent. By 1896–1900, the positions of the UK and the USA had reversed. By 1906–10, the USA had 35 per cent and the UK 15 per cent (Thomas 1954: 120). As time goes on, Britain with 1 per cent of the world's population, will move towards having 1 per cent of the world's industrial capacity.

IMMIGRATION

During the whole of the nineteenth century, Britain was a net exporter of population. There was nevertheless immigration into the country. Of course, immigration from Ireland was internal migration at the time, but viewed from today's perspective we can regard it as external immigration. We have already seen how the population of Ireland nearly halved during the second half of the nineteenth century. As well as the death from starvation of a million people, the largest part of the decrease was due to the massive emigration to the United States. Between 1849 and 1856, nearly one and a half million people emigrated from Ireland to the USA (Thomas 1954: 95). In the sixty years (1851–1911) from 1851 when the collection of Irish emigration figures were first collected on a systematic basis, 4,191,552 people emigrated (Census of Ireland 1913: lix). Most of this emigration was destined for the USA. In the decade 1901 to 1910, when the flow was of course a lot lower, nearly 80 per cent was destined for the USA and only 10 per cent to Great Britain (Census of Ireland 1913: lx).

The number of Irish in Britain doubled from 420,000 in 1841 to 800,000 in 1861 (Walter 1980: 298). Thereafter, numbers declined. In 1911, there were only 550,000 Irish-born persons in Britain (Peach *et al.* 1988) and by 1931 their numbers reached their nadir of 505,000. However, this was the beginning of the second wave of Irish immigration (Walter 1980) reaching a new peak of just under 1 million in 1971 (Peach *et al.* 1988).

By 1990 those claiming Irish ancestry in the USA amounted to 38.7 million (Geolytics national data from US 1990 census). This figure is the equivalent of 15.6 per cent of the total US population of 248.7 million in 1990. It is a larger figure than the Black population of the USA. It is also a larger number than the 32.7 million in the USA claiming English ancestry, the 5.4 million of Scottish ancestry, and the 2 million of Welsh ancestry, which together make a total of 40 million or 16.1 per cent of the US total and put the British combined total ahead of the Irish. It is notable, however, that while the English, Scottish, and Welsh ancestry groups in the USA are roughly comparable with the numbers currently living respectively in England, Scotland, and Wales, the Irish numbers are nearly ten times larger than the contemporary population of Ireland.

Irish immigration

Irish migration to Britain has not been on the scale of the efflux to the USA. The Irish-born population living in Great Britain in the 1991 census was only 837,000 (Table 8.4). However, those living in households headed by a person born in Ireland (a surrogate for the first and second generations) amounted to over 1 million and most of the 5 million Roman Catholics in Britain are thought to be descended from Irish immigrants in the nineteenth and twentieth centuries (Coleman and Salt 1992: 480). The degree of Irish intermarriage with the British is substantial. Caulfield and Bhat (1981) suggest that about 30 per cent of Irish men and 30 per cent of Irish

TABLE 8.4. *Numbers of Irish born (32 counties) in Great Britain, 1851–1991*

Date	Number
1851	727,000
1861	806,000
1871	775,000
1881	781,000
1891	653,000
1901	631,629
1911	550,040
1921	523,767
1931	505,385
1951	716,028
1961	950,978
1971	952,760
1981	850,387
1991	836,934

Sources: 1851–91: Thomas 1954: 73; 1901–91: Chance 1996.

women are out married in Britain. The Irish, broadly defined, constitute the largest ethnic minority group living in Britain.

Jewish immigration

The other significant immigrant population arriving at the end of the nineteenth and beginning of the twentieth centuries was the Jewish population. There was already a small Sephardi Jewish population dating back to the time of Cromwell's readmission of the Jews, but today only 3 per cent of British Jews belong to Sephardi synagogues (Coleman and Salt 1992: 494). Pogroms and persecution of the Jewish population of Russia and what had been Poland drove out large numbers of refugees, the large majority of whom made their way to North America. Between 100,000 and 150,000, however, settled in Britain between 1880 and the turn of the century (Census of England and Wales 1913: xvi; Coleman and Salt 1992: 494). Their numbers were increased by Jewish refugees from Nazi persecution in the 1930s, although much smaller numbers were allowed to settle. By 1918, the Jewish population of the United Kingdom was estimated to have been about 300,000 (Waterman and Kosmin 1986) and to have reached a peak of about 430,000 in the 1950s. Since then it has declined to about 290,000 (see Halsey 2000: 134). Together the Eastern and West European Jewish population, together with a few from Sephardic sources, have produced an extraordinarily creative impact on the country.

Settlement patterns

The nineteenth- and early twentieth-century immigrant Irish population settled in the expanding industrial centres of the country, with a strong northern distribution. Their settlement was particularly concentrated in Scotland and the north-west: Glasgow, Liverpool, and Manchester were the main centres. In Scotland and the north-west, the Irish formed over 5 per cent of the regional population between 1851 and 1891 (Walter 1980: 299).

The second wave of Irish migration, from 1931 to 1991, showed a concentration in the Midlands and south-east. By 1991, over half of those born in Southern Ireland living in Great Britain lived in the south-east region and over a third of the total lived in London (Chance 1996: 235).

The Jewish settlement, from its early days, was much more concentrated on London. Of the 95,541 foreigners born in Russia and Russian Poland living in England and Wales in 1911, 63,105 were living in London. Within London, the early settlement was highly concentrated on the East End. Of the London Russian population, 44,000 were living in Stepney and a further 6,000 in Bethnal Green (Census of England and Wales 1913: xiv). There were, however, significant Jewish communities in Manchester (6,868), Leeds (5,444), Liverpool (4,644), Salford (1,285), and Hull (1,226) (Census of England and Wales 1913: xix).

Non-European presence in Britain at the turn of the century seems to have been negligible. The 1911 census of England and Wales specifically tabulated the non-Europeans born in India and Ceylon present in the country. This showed 3,891 males and 171 females. The great majority of the males (2,531 out of 3,891) were Lascar seamen and a further 931 were returned as students and scholars (Census of England and Wales 1913: xv). No similar disaggregation on racialized lines was carried out for other parts of the empire. The 1911 census, however, seems to be the first census attempt at ethnic counting.

EMIGRATION

The tide of emigration, however, was much stronger during the nineteenth and twentieth centuries than was the flow of immigrants. Over the course of the twentieth century, 1.2 million more people emigrated from Britain than immigrated to it (Table 8.5).The debates over immigration, although

TABLE 8.5. *United Kingdom net migration balance, 1901–1996*

Years	Net decadal migration balance
1901–11	−820,000
1911–21	−920,000
1921–31	−670,000
1931–51	220,000
1951–61	120,000
1961–71	−140,000
1971–81	−270,000
1981–91	430,000
1991–96	830,000
Net migration balance 1901–96	−1,220,000

Source: *Annual Abstract of Statistics 1998.*

often framed in terms of 'this tight little island' have more often been to do with racial or religious antipathy rather than purely numbers.

COUNTER-URBANIZATION

However, by 1951, growth of population in the largest cities had come to an end. Wartime bombing, post-war green belts, leapfrogging suburbanization, and the development of new towns ended the process. Counter-urbanization had set in and the regional swing towards the Midlands and the south had re-established itself. If the urbanization process resembled the rise of a giant volcano, like Vesuvius, the counter-urbanization process represents the explosive Caldera-type volcano that blows out its centre leaving a hollow cauldron. Counter-urbanization is a process of blowing out the population of the central city into the surrounding rural areas or to small free-standing towns and villages. The population of the large conurbations began to decline through a process of redistribution of their populations beyond their administrative boundaries. These processes are extremely important in understanding the immigration process in the second half of the twentieth century. Unlike the USA, where counter-urbanization is often represented as 'white flight', that is, white population fleeing from cities in which black ethnic minorities are growing, in Britain the flight came first and immigration afterwards. Immigration was a consequence of upward and outward mobility, not vice versa.

By the 1950s the growth of the megacities had also peaked. The cores of the metropolitan cities began to empty as the population first suburbanized and then spread beyond the physical bounds of the cities themselves. The process was actively assisted, in some cases by government policy, which confined the physical spread of cities through green belt planning and also through the creation of new towns. But the process of counter-urbanization had its own dynamic, whether it was assisted by government policy or not. Post-1960 the new urban growth came through the expansion of market towns.

The result of these post-war processes was to produce both an upward mobility of the British occupational structure (abandoning jobs in the less attractive sectors: dirty working conditions, long hours, anti-social shifts) and an outward movement from the largest conurbations into more attractive smaller towns, within range, nevertheless, of the large conurbations. Thus the post-war years were marked by a severe shortage of jobs in the major industrial conurbations. These shortages were most marked in London and the Midlands.

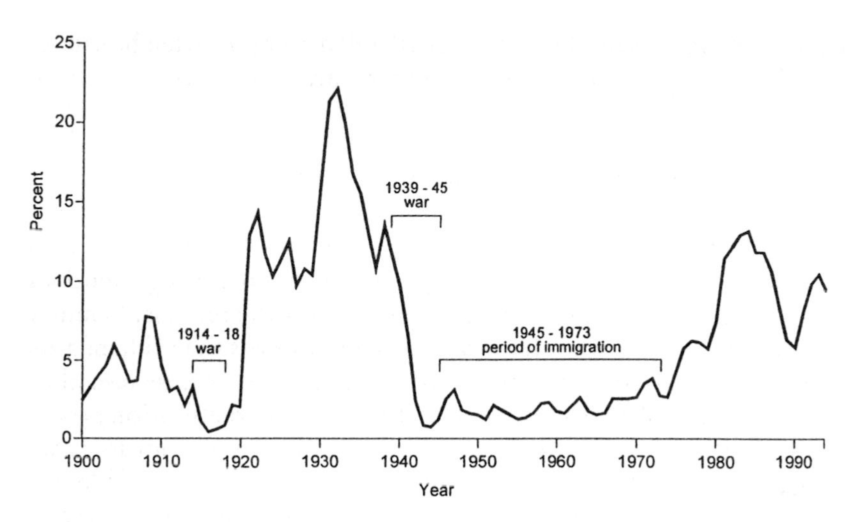

FIG. 8.2 Percentage rate of unemployment, United Kingdom, 1900–1994.

Source: Data from Price and Bain 1988: table 4.17, 170.

The cause of this demand for labour can be seen from Figure 8.2 which tracks the changes in the rate of unemployment from the beginning of the twentieth century to the present. It can be seen that the post-1945 levels of unemployment were at their historically lowest point since the First World War. The post-1945 boom lasted until 1973, when the oil shock following the Yom Kippur War produced a massive increase in inflation in the West and a major industrial slump.

The post-1945 industrial expansion and demand for labour was not limited to Britain. It is sometimes thought that immigration from the New Commonwealth was the result of failure of legislation to keep immigrants out. (In fact, although there were no legislative controls, administrative devices were just as effective; see Spencer 1997) The truth of the matter seems to be that all western Europe experienced the same demand for labour and differed only in the source from which they sought it. Britain was first in the cycle and sought it in Ireland, in European displaced persons and Italy, then in the Caribbean, and finally in South Asia. France sought it in Italy, Spain, Portugal, and particularly in its North African possessions. The Germans sought it in East Germany, in Greece, and overwhelmingly in Turkey. France had a foreign population of 3.6 million in 1990, of which 1.4 million were North African (Peach 1997). Germany had a foreign population of 7.1 million in 1995, of which 2 million were Turks (SOPEMI 1997: 226–7).

The first sources of labour were sought in the West Indies. Britain had started to recruit wartime labour for the munition factories in the Caribbean during the war. There had also been volunteers for the armed forces, particularly the RAF. From this nucleus came the first labour migrants in the post-war period. Ironically, the first migrant ship, generally taken to be the *Empire Windrush* in 1948, was on its return trip from taking British emigrants to Australia. Direct recruitment of labour for London Transport and for the National Health Service started later in the 1950s and there were also schemes by the Barbadian government to promote emigration. Labour migration from India and Pakistan started a few years later than that from the Caribbean, in the late 1950s (Figure 8.3).

The movement from the Caribbean showed a remarkable sensitivity to the British labour situation. Caribbean net migration showed a high inverse correlation with British unemployment ($r = -0.65$ for the period 1955–74; Peach 1991). It was also lagged by about three months on British trends, so that it was prior changes in the British economy that formed the dynamic of the movement from the Caribbean. Movement from the Indian subcontinent showed similar but weaker correlations with British conditions (Robinson 1986: 28).

The ethnic minority populations of Britain grew from about 80,000 in 1951 to 3 million in 1991 (Peach 1996*a*: 9). The 1991 census was the first in Britain to include a question on ethnicity, and the population appeared extremely homogeneous. The ethnic minority population as defined by

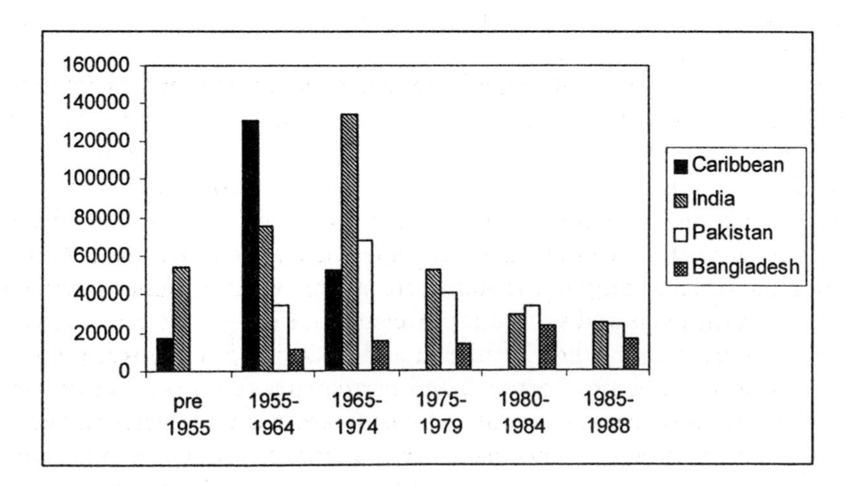

FIG. 8.3 Year of arrival in Great Britain of the Caribbean, Indian, Pakistani, and Bangladeshi population present in 1988.

Source: Labour Force Survey 1992: table 6.39, 38, and Peach 1996a: 9.

the census accounted for 5.5 per cent of the British total while over 94 per cent were White.

There is, nevertheless, a significant degree of diversity among the White population. Apart from the Irish and Jewish populations there are also the 'invisible' survivors and descendants of European refugee populations from the Second World War, returning administrators and settlers from the colonies with their white but colonial-born families (340,000 Whites born in the New Commonwealth), and settlers, students, and transients from Australia (72,000), Canada (62,000), New Zealand (40,000), and South Africa (61,000). There are also the Italians and the Cypriots (Greek and Turkish) for whom we lack space for discussion. Other groups brought by the increasing flow of multinational employees and the free circulation of European Union citizens are also excluded; just under half a million people (494,000) in Britain in 1991 had been born in the European Union, excluding the United Kingdom and the Irish Republic, though this number includes a significant number of children born to British forces stationed in Germany.

The ethnic minority population, as defined by the 1991 census, is dominated by the South Asian population (Table 8.6) which makes up half (49 per cent) of the 3 million total. Indians number 840,000, Pakistanis 477,000, and Bangladeshis 163,000. The Caribbean, African, and 'Black Other' population makes up 30 per cent of the minority. The Chinese number 157,000, and the mysteriously named 'Other Other' (largely an Arab group) number 290,000.

About a third of the Indian ethnic population group originate from East African Asian expulsions at the end of the 1960s and the beginning of the 1970s. These population groups are not only very recent, but very young compared with the White population. Nearly half of the ethnic minority population is British born.

For the most part, however, the majority of the primary immigrants came as worker migrants and have acted as a replacement population for the upward and outward movement of the White population. They have thus gone to fill the gaps at the bottom end of the employment structure, particularly in the hospitals, railway, undergound, and transport services and in some of the metal bashing industries of the West Midlands, the textile industries of West Yorkshire and Lancashire, the knitwear industry of the East Midlands, the rag trade in the East End of London, and in the catering and restaurant trade. Geographically they settled in precisely that class of urban area that was losing population, the large conurbations (see Table 8.7).

The ethnic minority immigrant population was a replacement population, drawn into those jobs that the white population was abandoning,

TABLE 8.6. *Great Britain, ethnic population for selected groups, 1991, total persons*

Ethnic group	England	Wales	Scotland	Great Britain	Percentage of Great Britain
Total persons	47,055,204	2,853,073	4,998,567	54,888,844	100.00
White	44,144,339	2,793,522	4,953,933	51,873,794	94.51
Black Caribbean	495,682	3,348	934	499,964	0.91
Black African	206,918	2,671	2,773	212,362	0.39
Black Other	172,282	3,473	2,646	178,401	0.33
Indian	823,821	6,384	10,050	840,255	1.53
Pakistani	449,646	5,717	21,192	476,555	0.87
Bangladeshi	157,881	3,820	1,134	162,835	0.3
Chinese	141,661	4,801	10,476	156,938	0.29
Other Asian	189,253	3,677	4,604	197,534	0.36
Other Other	273,721	7,660	8,825	290,206	0.53
Total Minorities	2,910,865	41,551	62,634	3,015,050	5.49
Persons born in Ireland	767,439	20,841	49,184	837,464	1.53

Source: Ethnic groups and total population from table 6 of 1991 census of Great Britain, *Ethnic Groups and Country of Birth*, ii (OPCS 1993).

settling in areas which found it difficult to attract white settlers. The distribution of the ethnic minority populations acts like a barium meal for an X-ray photograph. They pick out the areas of unsatisfied demand for labour in the British space economy. They avoided the areas of high unemployment; they are blocked from entering the areas of high and successful demand for labour. They settled in largest numbers in areas where there is a demand for labour but where conditions are not good enough to attract the local population.

All of the minorities were two or three times more concentrated in the five major conurbations than was the population as a whole.

Although the main ethnic groups started from broadly similar positions on arrival in Britain in the post-war period, significant differences have opened up in their current socio-economic positions. The major economic contrasts are between, on the one hand, the Chinese, Indian, African, and Other Asian populations and, on the other hand, the Caribbean,

TABLE 8.7. *Relative concentration of ethnic groups in large metropolitan areas, Great Britain, 1991*

	Total	White	Black Caribbean	Black African	Black Other	Indian	Pakistani	Bangladeshi	Chinese
Great Britain	54,888,844	51,873,794	499,964	212,362	178,401	840,255	476,555	162,835	156,938
Greater London	6,679,699	5,333,580	290,968	163,635	80,613	347,091	87,816	85,738	56,579
West Midlands Metropolitan County	2,551,671	2,178,149	72,183	4,116	15,716	141,359	88,268	18,074	6,107
Greater Manchester Metropolitan County	2,499,441	2,351,239	17,095	5,240	9,202	29,741	49,370	11,445	8,323
West Yorkshire Metropolitan County	2,013,693	1,849,562	14,795	2,554	6,552	34,837	80,540	5,978	3,852
Percentage ethnic group in named areas	25.04	22.58	79.01	82.66	62.83	65.82	64.21	74.45	47.70

Source: OPCS 1993, table 6.

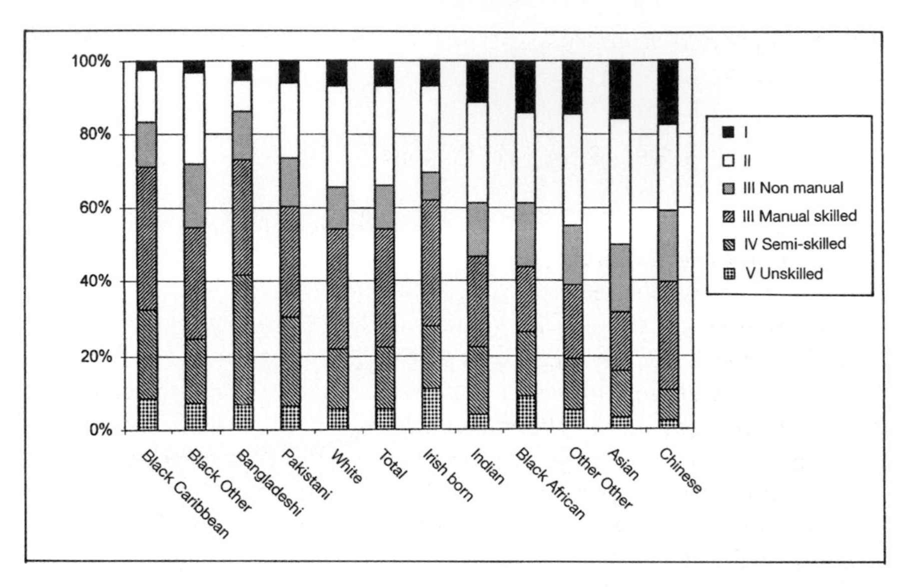

FIG. 8.4 Socio-economic class of men aged 16+ by ethnicity, Great Britain, 1991.

Source: Peach 1996: 35.

Pakistani, and Bangladeshi populations. The first group is predominantly white collar and professional (Figure 8.4). The second group (the Pakistanis, Bangladeshis, and Caribbean) are predominantly blue collar. The Chinese have the highest proportion of men in the top socio-economic class of professionals. The Indians also have a higher percentage in class 1 than the White population. They also have a much higher rate of owner occupation than the White population.

These economic differences are broadly reflected in housing. The Caribbean and Bangladeshi populations have a higher reliance on council and social housing, while the Indians have an overwhelming concentration in owner occupation. However, the Pakistani population, although low on the economic scale, has, like the Indians, a massive presence (80 per cent) in owner occupied property. This housing is predominantly inner city, Victorian, and Edwardian terraced housing, however. Caribbean housing, as a result of the substantial presence in the council sector, is predominantly in flats, often inner city high rise.

FAMILY STRUCTURE

Despite the predominantly economic working-class profile of the Caribbean population, there is a high degree of social integration. There is a high proportion of mixed Caribbean and White households (Table 8.8, Panels 1, 2, and 3).

SEGREGATION PATTERNS

The British pattern is very different from the American model as far as segregation of black minority groups is concerned. While there are ethnic enclaves and areas of concentration (Table 8.9) there are no ghettos on the American model. Many African Americans live in areas which are almost exclusively black. In New York, for example, in 1990 28 per cent of African Americans were living in tracts which were over 90 per cent black and 50 per cent were living in tracts which were over 75 per cent black. If one took the same cut-off point of 30 per cent that we took for London, then it would account for 84 per cent of the black population. Not only is this the case but the level of segregation of the Caribbean population is decreasing, while that of African Americans maintains high levels amounting to hypersegregation. If we look at change in the distribution of the Caribbean-born population in London between 1981 and 1991, the outward movement of suburbanization is clearly apparent (Peach 1996*b*).

The Indian, Pakistani, and Bangladeshi groups have a much more closed and traditional social profile. Nuclear or extended families are the modal pattern and the degree of out-marriage is much less than is the case for the Caribbeans. Cohabitation is a lot less frequent too.

The Indian settlement pattern in London is the reverse of that of the Caribbeans and Bangladeshis. Eighty per cent of the London Indian population lives in Outer rather than Inner London. However, although levels of segregation are not high, changes 1981–91 have served to reinforce existing distributions rather than disperse them.

The Bangladeshis show the highest degree of segregation of all the new ethnic groups in Britain. They are the newest, youngest, and poorest. A quarter of the whole Bangladeshi population living in Britain resides in Tower Hamlets Borough in London. Their level of segregation is generally the highest of all groups in any of the cities in which they live and they are the group which most closely approximates to the African American model. Their population change 1981–91 also has reinforced the existing pattern, with the highest growth taking place in the areas of already densest settlement.

RELIGION AND CULTURAL LANDSCAPE

One of the consequences of the growth of population from Islamic, Hindu, and Sikh societies has been significant additions of

TABLE 8.8. *Inter ethnic unions. All married and cohabiting men and women. Resident population, Great Britain, 1991*

Panel 1. *Total number of unions in sample*

Ethnic group of male partner	Ethnic group of female partner										
	White	Black Caribbean	Black African	Black Other	Indian	Pakistani	Bangladeshi	Chinese	Other Asian	Other Other	Total
White	**126,150**	120	41	63	71	10	0	79	148	139	126,803
Black Caribbean	225	**559**	8	10	4	2	0	2	3	12	825
Black African	48	16	**208**	4	2	1	0	0	0	2	281
Black Other	76	3	2	**62**	1	0	0	0	2	1	147
Indian	134	2	4	1	**1,762**	18	0	5	4	5	1,935
Pakistani	42	0	0	1	6	**775**	0	0	4	3	831
Bangladeshi	7	0	2	0	4	1	**217**	0	0	2	233
Chinese	34	0	0	0	2	0	0	**234**	0	0	270
Other Asian	55	4	1	1	4	4	1	2	**296**	6	374
Other Other	218	2	1	2	7	4	0	2	5	**191**	432
Total	126,989	688	267	144	1,863	815	218	324	462	361	132,131

Note: Original figures for total Caribbean are 40 too high in both row and column.

Source: Ann Berrington in Berrington 1996: table 7.9.

Panel 2. *Unions expressed as percentage of male's ethnic group*

Ethnic group of male partner	Ethnic group of female partner										
	White	Black Caribbean	Black African	Black Other	Indian	Pakistani	Bangladeshi	Chinese	Other Asian	Other Other	Total
White	**99.49**	0.08	0.03	0.05	0.06	0.01	0.00	0.06	0.12	0.11	100
Black Caribbean	**27.27**	**67.76**	0.97	1.21	0.48	0.24	0.00	0.24	0.36	1.45	100
Black African	**17.08**	**5.69**	**74.02**	1.42	0.71	0.36	0.00	0.00	0.00	0.71	100
Black Other	**51.70**	2.04	1.36	**42.18**	0.68	0.00	0.00	0.00	1.36	0.68	100
Indian	**6.93**	0.10	0.21	0.05	**91.06**	0.93	0.00	0.26	0.21	0.26	100
Pakistani	**5.05**	0.00	0.00	0.12	0.72	**93.26**	0.00	0.00	0.48	0.36	100
Bangladeshi	**3.00**	0.00	0.86	0.00	1.72	0.43	**93.13**	0.00	0.00	0.86	100
Chinese	**12.59**	0.00	0.00	0.00	0.74	0.00	0.00	**86.67**	0.00	0.00	100
Other Asian	**14.71**	1.07	0.27	0.27	1.07	1.07	0.27	0.53	**79.14**	1.60	100
Other Other	**50.46**	0.46	0.23	0.46	1.62	0.93	0.00	0.46	1.16	**44.21**	100

Panel 3. *Unions expressed as percentage of female's ethnic group*

Ethnic group of male partner	Ethnic group of female partner									
	White	Black Caribbean	Black African	Black Other	Indian	Pakistani	Bangladeshi	Chinese	Other Asian	Other Other
White	**99.40**	**14.83**	**15.36**	**43.75**	**3.81**	1.23	0.00	**24.38**	**32.03**	**38.50**
Black Caribbean	0.18	**81.25**	**3.00**	**6.94**	0.21	0.25	0.00	0.62	0.65	**3.32**
Black African	0.04	**2.33**	**77.90**	**2.78**	0.11	0.12	0.00	0.00	0.00	0.55
Black Other	0.06	0.44	0.75	**43.06**	0.05	0.00	0.00	0.00	0.43	0.28
Indian	0.11	0.29	1.50	0.69	**94.58**	2.21	0.00	1.54	0.87	1.39
Pakistani	0.03	0.00	0.00	0.69	0.32	**95.09**	0.00	0.00	0.87	0.83
Bangladeshi	0.01	0.00	0.75	0.00	0.21	0.12	**99.54**	0.00	0.00	0.55
Chinese	0.03	0.00	0.00	0.00	0.11	0.00	0.00	**72.22**	0.00	0.00
Other Asian	0.04	0.58	0.37	0.69	0.21	0.49	0.46	0.62	**64.07**	1.66
Other Other	0.17	0.29	0.37	1.39	0.38	0.49	0.00	0.62	1.08	**52.91**

TABLE 8.9. *Ghettoization of ethnic groups at ED level, in Greater London with 30 per cent cut-off*

1 GROUP	2 Group's city population	3 Group's 'ghetto' population	4 Total 'ghetto' population	5 Percentage of group 'ghettoized' (Column 3 as a percentage of column 2)	6 Group's percentage of 'ghetto' population (Column 3 as a percentage of column 4)
Non-white	1,346,119	721,873	1,589,476	53.6	45.4
Black Caribbean	290,968	7,755	22,545	2.6	34.4
Black African	163,635	3,176	8,899	2.0	35.6
Black Other	80,613	nil	nil	nil	nil
Indian	347,091	88,887	202,135	25.6	44.0
Pakistani	87,816	1,182	3,359	1.4	35.2
Bangladeshi	85,738	28,280	55,500	33.0	51.0
Chinese	56,579	38	111	0.0	34.2
Other Asian	112,807	176	572	0.2	30.8
Other Other	120,872	209	530	0.2	39.4
Irish born	256,470	1,023	2,574	0.4	39.8

Source: Peach 1996*b*.

non-Judaeo-Christian architecture to our townscapes. In 1991 there were probably about a million Muslims living in Britain and about 400,000 Hindus. From 1951 to 1996 the number of Mosques officially registered in England and Wales rose from 6 to 600. The number of Sikh Gurdwaras rose from 0 to 300 and the number Hindu Mandirs from 0 to 200. The largest of these buildings are cathedral like in scale and add a new dimension to the cultural landscape of British cities.

SUMMARY

How is this story of the United Kingdom from 1850 to the present to be summarized? The theme that suggests itself is that of transitions. First is the demographic transition: Britain changed from a small, rapidly growing population into a large, stable population. Secondly, in the course of the nineteenth century it changed from a rural to an urban society. The pattern of population growth changed from massive concentration in the largest conurbations from 1850 to 1950, to counter-urbanization during the last half of the twentieth century. Thirdly, employment structure changed from the prominence of the primary sector in the early nineteenth century to the dominance of the secondary sector from 1850 until 1950. From 1950 to the present the balance of employment has altered from secondary to tertiary. Over the period of one and a half centuries, the mode of production has changed from pre-industrial to industrial to post-industrial and from Fordist production to post-Fordist. Fourthly, the population of the United Kingdom has not only undergone the demographic transition, but has experienced the cataclysm of the Irish famine and massive net emigration. While the period 1851–1951 was dominated by massive rates of emigration, the period 1951 to the present has seen, in common with the rest of Europe, a significant growth of minority populations. The landscape has been utterly transformed: rural depopulation, larger farms, bigger fields, less hedgerows; industrialization, deindustrialization, urbanization, urban blight in the physical lanscape, but hopeful signs at least of a multicultural future.

REFERENCES

Annual Abstract of Statistics 1998 (1998). London: HMSO, Office for National Statistics.

Berrington, Ann (1996). 'Marriage patterns and inter-ethnic unions', in D.

Coleman and J. Salt, *Ethnicity in the 1991 Census*, i. *Demographic Characteristics of the Ethnic Minority Populations.* Oxford: Oxford University Press, 178–212.

Caulfield, B., and Bhat, A. (1981). 'The Irish in Britain: intermarriage and fertility levels 1971–1976', *New Community*, 9: 73–83.

Census of Ireland (1913). *Census of Ireland for the Year 1911, General Report.* London: HMSO.

Census of England and Wales (1913). *Census of England and Wales 1911*, ix. *Birthplaces.* London: HMSO.

Chance, J. (1996). 'The Irish: invisible settlers', in C. Peach (ed.), *The Ethnic Minority Population of Great Britain*, ii. *Ethnicity in the 1991 Census.* London: HMSO, Office for National Statistics.

Coleman, David, and Salt, John (1992). *The British Population: Patterns, Trends, and Processes.* Oxford: Oxford University Press.

Geolytics (1998). *Census CD + Maps*, CD ROM of the US 1990 Census, version 2.1. East Brunswick, NJ: Geolytics Inc.

Hall, Peter, and Preston, Paschal (1988). *The Carrier Wave: New Information Technology and the Geography of Innovation.* London: Unwin Hyman.

Halsey, A. H., with Webb, Josephine (2000). *Twentieth-Century British Social Trends.* Basingstoke: Macmillan.

Hoskins, W. G. (1955). *The Making of the English Landscape.* London: Hodder and Stoughton.

Labour Force Survey (1992). *Labour Force Survey 1990 and 1991.* London: HMSO.

Lawton, R. (1983). 'Urbanization and Population Change in Nineteenth-Century England', in J. Patten (ed.), *The Expanding City: Essays in honour of Professor Jean Gottman.* London: Academic Press.

Lieberson, Stanley, and Waters, Mary (1988). *From Many Strands: Ethnic and Racial Groups in Contemporary America.* New York: Russell Sage Foundation.

Mitchell, B. R. (1975). *European Historical Statistics.* London: Macmillan.

OPCS (1993). 1991 Census of Great Britain, *Ethnic Groups and Country of Birth.* 2 vols. London: HMSO.

Peach, C. (1991). 'The Caribbean in Europe: contrasting patterns of migration and settlement in Britain, France and the Netherlands'. Coventry: University of Warwick, Centre for Research in Ethnic Relations Research Paper 15.

Peach, C. (1996*a*). *The Ethnic Minority Population of Great Britain*, ii. *Ethnicity in the 1991 Census.* London: HMSO, Office for National Statistics.

Peach, C. (1996*b*). 'Does Britain have Ghettos?' *Transactions, Institute of British Geographers*, NS, 21: 216–35.

Peach, C. (1997). 'Postwar migration to Europe: reflux, influx, refuge', *Social Science Quarterly*, 78, 2: 269–83.

Peach, C., Robinson, R., Maxted, J., and Chance, J. (1988). 'Immigration and ethnicity', in A. H. Halsey (ed.), *British Social Trends Since 1900.* Basingstoke: Macmillan.

Price, R., and Bain, G. S. (1988). 'The labour force', in A. H. Halsey (ed.), *British Social Trends Since 1900.* Basingstoke: Macmillan.

Robinson, V. (1986). *Transients, Settlers and Refugees: Asians in Britain.* Oxford: Clarendon Press.

SOPEMI (1997). *Trends in International Migration: Annual Report 1996.* Paris: OECD.

Spencer, Ian R. G. (1997). *British Immigration Policy Since 1939: The Making of Multi-Racial Britain.* London: Routledge.

Thomas, Brinley (1954). *Migration and Economic Growth: A Study of Great Britain and the Atlantic Economy.* Cambridge: Cambridge University Press.

Walter, Bronwen (1980). 'Time-space patterns of second-wave Irish immigration into British towns', *Transactions, Institute of British Geographers,* NS, 5, 3: 297–317.

Waterman, Stanley, and Kosmin, Barry (1986). *British Jewry in the Eighties: A Statistical and Geographical Study.* London: Board of Deputies of British Jews.

INDEX